The Work Ethic in Industrial America 1850-1920

The Work Ethic in Industrial America 1850-1920

Daniel T. Rodgers

The University of
Chicago Press
*Chicago
and London*

The University of Chicago Press, Chicago 60637
The University of Chicago Press, Ltd., London

© *1974, 1978 by The University of Chicago*
All rights reserved. Published 1978
Phoenix Edition 1979
Printed in the United States of America

83 82 81 80 79   9 8 7 6 5 4 3

Title page illustration by Thomas Nast originally published
26 March 1881

LIBRARY OF CONGRESS CATALOGING IN PUBLICATION DATA

Rodgers, Daniel T
  The work ethic in industrial America, 1850-1920.

  Includes index.
  1. Labor and laboring classes—United States—History.
2. Work.   3. Middle classes—United States—History.
I. Title.
HD8072.R76   301.5′5   77-81737
ISBN 0-226-72351-8 (cloth) 0-226-72352-6 (paper)

For Rene

Contents

Acknowledgments

Nineteenth-century moralists distrusted the debtor. The man living beyond his own earned resources skated at the edge of moral respectability, a misstep away from bankruptcy. By these lights, mine has been a shaky enterprise, for it has been freighted with obligations and I have lived off many an unearned increment since its inception. This study had its beginnings as a doctoral dissertation at Yale University, and I owe a large fraction of my debts to my readers there: David Brion Davis, Edmund S. Morgan, and, in particular, C. Vann Woodward. Freedom to take one's own chances amid the example of exceptionally skilled and humane practitioners of one's craft is the sum total of good graduate education, and I was granted it beyond my deserts. I have been equally fortunate in finding discerning readers since. Donald Worster listened to the germs of these ideas over many years and innumerable cups of coffee and gave the finished product the benefit of his perceptive eye and his considerable talents as an intellectual historian. At a later stage, John King lent criticism and encouragement when both were needed, as did Dorothy Alice Bell, with her poet's care for language and a sister's exacting rigor. To others who read the manuscript or portions of it—John M. Cooper, Jr., Elizabeth R. Harvey, Kent Lesandrini, David Peeler, and Richard H. Sewell—I am no less thankful. If I have been a stubborn and obtuse student at times, the fault has not been theirs.

Back of these scholarly obligations, I owe an older debt to a group of fervent moralizers about work and temperamental rebels against it whom I came to know long ago as a private in the ranks of the antipoverty campaign. These were men whom nineteenth-century writers would have termed the "unworthy poor," able-bodied resisters of the discipline of regular, day-to-day labor, and it was my lot to try to teach them more economically advantageous habits. I failed at my end of the bargain, but in their turn—in their stubbornly inappropriate hold on the conventional phrases of the work ethic and their ability to compartmentalize values and behavior—they gave me one of the seeds out of which this study has ultimately grown. In leaving them nameless I do not mean to minimize either the obligation or the old friendship.

Yet large as these obligations are, the last debt dwarfs them all. To my most unstinting and indispensable creditor I can only give this book, though it cannot begin to pay her back and she has heard it all many times already.

Introduction

All work, even cotton spinning, is noble.
    Thomas Carlyle, *Past and Present* (1843)

This is at bottom a study not of work but of ideas about work. In particular it is a study of those threads of ideas that came together to affirm work as the core of the moral life. By now reiteration of that claim has dulled its audacity. But in the long run of ideas it was a revolutionary notion. In and of itself work involves only an element of burden and, for most people, the goad of necessity. Few cultures have presumed to call it anything more than a poor bargain in an imperfect world. It was the office of ideas to turn the inescapable into an act of virtue, the burdensome into the vital center of living. That presumption—the work ethic—begins in a momentous act of transvaluation.

But it is change of another sort that is the focus here. The transvaluation of work so central to Western history ran its course in a society whose everyday labors were vastly different from those of any nation on the other side of the industrial revolution. Whether in Calvin's Geneva, Puritan England, or Jacksonian America, the work ethic belonged to a setting of artisans' shops, farms, and countinghouses. It was the ideology of that simple but dynamic world that intervened between the manors and the factories, the distinctive credo of preindustrial capitalism. To ask which came first—the economic structure so vastly in contrast with the older, peasant life or the new conceptions of work—is, it seems to me, to bustle down a profitless alley. The work ethic and its economic context were not related as cause and effect, phenomenon and epiphenomenon, but took shape together as values and practice fused and collided, quarreled with and reinforced one another, in an inextricably tangled relationship. By the middle of the nineteenth century, the process had created in the American North an expansive, though still largely pre-industrial, economy and an unequaled commitment to the moral primacy of work. In all the talk that came later, when Americans wrote of work, this setting of farmers, craftsmen, and merchants remained the moral norm.

In the second half of the nineteenth century, however, that world began to give way to a new one of mills and massed wage earners, machinery and subdivided labor. The factory system represented in one sense the triumph of the work ethic. Harnessing a restless faith in change to an immense capacity for work, Northern entrepreneurs turned the land into a stupendous manufacturing workshop, which by 1920 was the wonder of the world. But it was an ironic triumph. For in the process, Northerners so radically transformed work that the old moral expectations would no longer hold. Born as much in faith as in self-interest, the industrial revolution in the end left in tatters the network of economics and values that had given it birth.

I have fixed upon the irony far more than the triumph in the pages that follow. That will seem, no doubt, as obtuse to many readers as it will seem self-evident to others. But the question I have tried to pursue is a simple one. What happened to work values when work itself was radically remade? As a world Max Weber's Puritans would have found disturbing but recognizable whirled on to produce an industrial setting far more alien and potentially far more unnerving, what was the fate of their equation of work and godly virtue? This is, in short, an essay on ideas focused where it seems to me intellectual history becomes most vital—on the meeting of fact and value.

To anticipate the argument, one of the results of the encounter between the old work ideals and the new work forms was a series of intense and anxious reckonings with the factories and the economy of which they were a part. That quarrel, which ran from workingmen to professors, was more serious than has generally been recognized. If America spawned relatively few thorough-going machine wreckers, and if its one potential move in that direction, the handicraft crusade, was an abject failure, the factories generated a host of half-doubts and nervous intimations. In a string of efforts, the best of the doubters cast about for ways to bring industrial work and the work values of an exploded farm and workshop economy back into accord. Most of their efforts ended in compromise and failure. Yet the result was not to shatter the presumptive tie between work and morality but to reinforce it, pitched at a new level of abstraction. Harder and harder pressed to find a satisfactory defense for industrial society's characteristic work, Northerners responded by slipping off the ideal from the increasingly unnerving reality and holding to their shattered faith all the more firmly. As rhetorical commonplace, as political invective, or as moral shibboleth, the equation of work and virtue continued to pervade the nation's thinking long after the context in which it had taken root had been all but obliterated. Perhaps this is the way of most ideas in the face of change. The record of the work ethic, at any rate, was at once one of failure and persistence.

Work is not the whole of life, nor did the work ethic even in its heyday embrace the whole of American thinking. Work values impinged on American life and thought in myriad ways—far more, certainly, than it has been possible to trace here. But it would be wrong to conclude that they formed the only moral ideology afoot in industrializing America, or the strongest faith in an age of intense moral commitments. Cultures are woven out of a host of distinctive strands, and to follow a single thread is necessarily to miss a vast amount of the larger pattern. And yet the fact remains that the work ethic played an immense part in the nation's moral life. Industrializing America would not have been remotely the same without it.

This is only one of the stories that need to be told about work in America, and its limits should be confessed at the outset. Its focus is exclusively on the North and within that region primarily on the middle class. The choice needs acknowledgment but not, I think, apology, for it was among the middling classes of the North—the Yankee bourgeoisie—that the work ethic was most firmly rooted, and it was in the North that the encounter with the factories came first and most eventfully. As late as 1919, the region bounded east and west by the Atlantic Ocean and the Mississippi River and on the south by the Ohio River and the Mason-Dixon line contained almost three-quarters of the nation's manufacturing wage earners, while its factories spewed out by value fully 70 percent of the nation's manufactured goods. To a great extent the citadels of middle-class opinion were concentrated there as well. Virtually all the nation's major publishing houses and national magazines—though transplanted Southerners such as Walter Hines Page might at times control them and Westerners like Twain write for them—were to be found somewhere in the triangle between Chicago, Philadelphia, and Boston. Outside that region, in the West and South, industrialization came more tardily and impinged on different moral traditions. The codes of the plantation, mining camp, or hacienda diverged in important ways from the Puritan-descended work ethic of the North, and the story of their distinctive encounters with the transformation of work deserves its own careful telling. But in the end it was the North that set the pattern of economic life that has since rolled inexorably out from its first, Yankee stronghold.

This study is narrow in a second way in drawing its bounds at the Atlantic Ocean. Like most of Northern middle-class culture, the work ethic was an Anglo-American possession, and from Samuel Smiles to Thomas Hughes many of its most influential prophets were Britishers. Most powerful of them all was Thomas Carlyle. His messages thundered through the regional consciousness. "Whatsoever of morality and of intelligence; what of patience, perseverance, faithfulness, of method, insight, ingenuity, energy; in a word, whatsoever of Strength the man had in him will lie written in the Work he does.... Produce! Produce! Were it but the pitifullest infinitesimal fraction of a Product, produce it, in God's name!" Through this "earthquaky style," as Louisa May Alcott called it, rumbled the intense faith in activity, the contempt for the idler, and the horror of idleness itself (a chaos of "perpetual despair," Carlyle called it) that were central to the work ethic. And through it also rumbled the doubts that, long before the Americans were propelled into imitation, escalated the stakes from works to *Work*—all of it, even cotton spinning, noble.[1] If in the American North Carlyle's dicta echoed with particular force, if they flowed copiously from the pens of scores of home-grown moralists, the work ethic was no more unique to the Americans than the factories which it created and which ultimately undermined it. In that sense too this is, like most finite history, a truncated tale.

Carlyle was a moralist in the best meaning of the word, a man propelled to fame as a lay preacher, tussling with the ethical nub of things. We moderns tend to be squeamish about such terms as "morals" and "moralists." The latter, in fact, as the nineteenth and early twentieth centuries knew them, have largely disappeared. Moralists commanding partial audiences remain with us, as do the temptations of elected officials to make moral pronouncements. But the giant lay preachers of another day and the presidents who, like Theodore Roosevelt, could claim their whole interest was "plain morality" are gone. Even a half-century ago, however, it was different, and I have used the word "moralist" freely and without apology. They were a fact of the day and one of the most prominent features of the cultural landscape.

Work is, as it has always been, an emotionally charged word. This essay rides no single hobbyhorse, but I have not refrained from judgment, and it is only fair to state as much at the outset. I have been far more drawn to the factory critics, with all their defects, than to the factory builders, despite the virtues they admittedly possessed. The nervous, ascetic side of the work ethic, so prominent in Carlyle or in a Frederick W. Taylor, strikes me as an unlovely creation. Joined with the driving, often ruthless ambitions of a Carnegie or a Henry Ford, its results were often unlovely indeed. Amid the preoccupation with discipline and callous strenuosity, I have been all the more ready for the lonely voices raised against "this incessant business." Yet surely the picture Josephine Shaw Lowell sketched of "the normal, the ideal commonwealth, where all its members are useful, supporting themselves and adding to the common stock," is a worthy utopia.[2] So too was Charles W. Eliot's ideal of a society of loved and joyful labor. My quarrel with the work ethic is that in claiming all work as noble, it helped to push discussions of labor toward the barrenly abstract. No task was degrading, Carlyle insisted, if approached in the proper spirit. The conviction possessed an immense potency in Puritan-descended America, and most of us would still find it hard to dismiss it completely. And yet Ruskin's plea that all forms of toil are not equally good for man seems to me the far wiser starting place. In thinking not more strenuously but more critically about work lies our best chance of recovering the hopes so long invested in it.

Work Ideals and the Industrial Invasion

Works and days were offered us, and we chose work.

> Ralph Waldo Emerson,
> "Works and Days" (1857)

"Work, work, work," Henry David Thoreau lectured an audience in the budding factory town of New Bedford in 1854. "It would be glorious to see mankind at leisure for once."[1] Like so many of Thoreau's public activities, his "Getting a Living" was a quixotic gesture, a tilt at one of the most formidable windmills of mid-nineteenth-century opinion. It was the kind of irreverence to be expected of a man who could seriously describe his occupation as inspector of snowstorms and anticipator of sunrises. In a land reared on Franklin's Poor Richard aphorisms and the busy bee of Isaac Watts's poem—a land of railroads and heady ambitions, poised on the edge of a thoroughgoing experiment with industrialization—to doubt the moral preeminence of work was the act of a conscious heretic. But in the longer sweep of time, it was Thoreau who spoke as a conservative and a traditionalist. For the first American dream, before the others shoved it rudely aside, had been one not of work but of leisure. In the Western tradition, in fact, Thoreau's vision was the oldest dream of all.

One could begin with Aristotle's claim that leisure was the only fit life for man—the commonplace of a slave society that passed from there into one of the axioms of Western philosophy. Or one might begin with the fact of slavery itself and the social hierarchies that all through the West had set a man's worth and freedom by his exemption from toil and had made gentility synonymous with leisure. Still closer to the common life was speech, where the ache of toil was fashioned into a tangled etymological relationship between the words "labor" and "pain" that remains deeply embedded in the languages of Western Europe.[2] But it was myth that most clearly gathered up and broadcast the painful indignity of work. Classical and Christian alike, the central fables of the West were shot through with longing for a leisured paradise.

The Greek and Roman poets mined the theme through the legend of a lost, workless past, a golden age at the beginnings of human history when the rivers had flowed with wine and honey and men had lived the effortless life of the gods. "All goods were theirs," Hesiod wrote at the head of the tradition, and "the fruitful grainland yielded its harvest to them of its own accord." And yet somehow, whether through punishment or confusion, man had lost that first innocent state. The age of gold had given way to a poverty-saddled age of want, pain, and endless work. Vergil's lament summed up the centuries of mythmaking: "Toil conquered the world, unrelenting toil, and want that pinches when life is hard."[3]

Where the classical poets had clung to the past, Christian mythology captured the same compound of protest and desire in a more complex design—first in the vision of a garden "eastward in Eden" in which all man's wants had been satisfied, and still more hopefully in what Augustine called the "eternal leisure" of heaven. The biblical tradition was more ambiguous than the classical, and from the beginning it contained seeds of more positive attitudes toward labor. Adam was no idler in Eden, after all, but was placed in the garden to watch and to "till" it, while the Judeo-Christian God himself "worked" and "rested." But Christianity heightened the vision of paradise by pushing it into the reachable future, and the pattern of the Christian myth—in which men fell out of a bounteous harmony into a vale of toil and sorrow, to endure until redeemed to permanent, heavenly rest— reverberated no less strongly than the classical fables with the aching pain of labor. By the end of the Middle Ages, popular versions of the two myths were close enough to coalesce, Christian optimism merging with the sensuousness of the classical golden age as the paradises fused and fused once more with the palpable milk-and-honey Edens that, according to European folk legends, lay hidden somewhere at the ends of the earth for an adventurous explorer to regain. It was a compelling vision, the more so because its roots sank so deeply into the potent stuff of experience. To work was to do something wearisome and painful, scrabbling in the stubborn soil. It was the mark of men entrapped by necessity and thus of men who were not wholly free. At best work was an inescapable necessity, a penance for old sins. Surely not this but leisure was man's first estate, the telltale mark of paradise, the proper focus of men's longings.

The myths waited only for a land to claim them, and with the discovery of America Europeans eagerly turned the hints the new continent offered into visions of a world untouched by the age-old curse of work. Columbus was the first to see the outlines of the ancient fables in the new world, finally giving up his hopes for a passage to the Indies only to conclude that he had all but reached the gates of Eden itself, perched like the stem end of a pear somewhere in present-day Venezuela. His report was but the first of the images of a land of all but workless plenty, soon inextricably intertwined with stories of the fabulous wealth of Mexico and Peru, which long hovered over the American continents. Exploring the Carolina coast a century after Columbus, Captain Arthur Barlowe found himself in the midst of such "incredible" fruitfulness that, seen through the mists of classical learning and desire, he was certain it was the "golden age" intact—a land where "the earth bringeth forth all things in abundance, as in the first creation, without toil or labor." Even farther to the north the shaping force of desire produced visions only slightly dimmer. Captain John Smith was a veteran of Virginia's first, starvation years by 1614 when he undertook a careful mapping of the New England coast. But he came away convinced that three days' work a week would satisfy any settler in that fruitful land, much of that spent in the "pretty sport" of fishing.[4]

Soberer, disillusioned adventurers often brought back far less flattering reports of America, bearing tales of native savagery and cannibalism and of a coast that turned to barrens and ice as one penetrated northward. But the European imagination fed on stories such as Barlowe's, on the image of an American paradise where the fruitful earth and innocent men lived in the original leisured harmony. As astute a reader of the explorers' reports as Montaigne concluded that the American natives whiled away their days in dancing in an ease far more perfect than the ancient poets had ever imagined. No cares troubled them, he wrote, no poverty, and "no occupations but leisure ones." "All men idle, all," Shakespeare caught the same hopes in *The Tempest*, his "American fable" in Leo Marx's phrase; but

> . . . Nature should bring forth,
> Of its own kind, all foison, all abundance,
> To feed my innocent people.

Not only for those Europeans who stayed at home but for the Englishmen who came to Virginia and the colonies to the south, that dream of a leisured America was to have a long and stubborn history. Here was a new Eden, they claimed of Virginia, "the paradise of the world," "a land even as God made it."[5]

Yet among those Englishmen who settled the country north of the Chesapeake, nothing was more common than to describe their American paradise as a "wilderness"—as a "howling wilderness" during moments of stress. Disappointment figured in the wilderness cry, most clearly in William Bradford's poignant description of Cape Cod in autumn that stands at the head of the tradition. Theology likewise buttressed the idea, for every Puritan minister knew the Book of the Revelation's promise that when troubles were thickest God would send his church into the "wilderness" for safekeeping. Still, the wilderness image had deeper roots than these, and throughout the seventeenth century, long after the Northern colonists had learned to love their land and prosper in it, it echoed and reechoed in their writings.

In the end the word "wilderness" served as a shorthand for a sense of self and of mission. Unlike the first new world adventurers, the settlers of Puritan New England and Quaker Pennsylvania came with no hopes for prelapsarian ease. They were laborers for their Lord, straighteners of crooked places, engaged in a task filled with hardship, deprivation, and toil. They did not expect to pluck treasures from the land but planned to civilize and tame it, even as they expected to struggle to civilize and tame the wild places in themselves. At times this amounted to a thirst for affliction, a distrust of idly gotten fortune as a snare and a temptation. God's people "must come into, and go through a vast and roaring Wilderness, where they must be bruised with many pressures, [and] humbled under many overbearing difficulties," Thomas Hooker told his Connecticut flock with the same trust in adversity with which other Puritans warned prospective settlers away from the "overflowing riches" of the West Indies. Such men came ready, if not eager, to work in the sweat of their faces and to see, as William Penn wrote, "what sobriety and industry can do in a wilderness against heat, cold, wants, and dangers."[6] They chose to call America a wilderness because it fit the countervision in their minds' eye that the moral life was a matter of hard work and hard-bitten determination. Out of the American Eden they fashioned a land preoccupied with toil.

During the first half of the nineteenth century, when Europeans began to come in numbers to inspect the new American nation, they marveled at the extent of the transformation. Almost without exception, visitors to the Northern states commented on the drawn faces and frantic busyness of Jacksonian Americans and complained of bolted meals, meager opportunities for amusement, and the universal preoccupation with what Charles Dickens damned as the "almighty dollar." The visitors' assessments of the pace of American life are not to be fully trusted. Moving in the company of business and professional men, few of the Europeans actually entered an American workshop or followed a farmer across his fields. There was, moreover, something of a litany to the repeated complaint about the Northerners' compulsive activity; it became a ritual as much a part of the American tour as the Patent Office or Niagara Falls. Yet the Europeans were genuinely perplexed at the absence of an extensive class devoted to the pursuits of leisure. "In the United States," Tocqueville wrote, "a wealthy man thinks that he owes it to public opinion to devote his leisure to some kind of industrial or commercial pursuit or to public business. He would think himself in bad repute if he employed his life solely in living." After ten years as a resident of Boston, the Viennese immigrant Francis Grund came to the same puzzled conclusion:

> There is, probably, no people on earth with whom business constitutes pleasure, and industry amusement, in an equal degree with the inhabitants of the United States of America. Active occupation is not only the principal source of their happiness, and the foundation of their national greatness, but they are absolutely wretched without it, and instead of the "*dolce far niente*," know but the *horrors* of idleness. Business is the very soul of an American: he pursues it, not

as a means of procuring for himself and his family the
necessary comforts of life, but as the fountain of all human
felicity ... it is as if all America were but one gigantic
workshop, over the entrance of which there is the blazing
inscription, *"No admission here, except on business."*[7]

It was not the pace of work in America that inspired responses
like this so much as its universality, its bewilderingly exalted
status, the force of the idea itself.

Yet, on the whole, the objects of these complaints were not
disturbed at their ignorance of what another visitor, in a distinctly
European phrase, called "the difficult art of being gracefully
idle." Mid-nineteenth-century politicians and poets alike in the
North dwelled expansively on the dignity of labor and the moral
worth of those who worked. "Labor, gentlemen, we of the free
States acknowledge to be the source of all our wealth, of all our
progress, of all our dignity and value," William Evarts told a
campaign audience in 1856, in a conviction that, with slightly
altered nuances, could be heard at virtually any lyceum series or
political rally—Whig, Democrat, or Republican.[8] Amid the
paeans to industry and the disrepute of leisure, it was little
wonder the Europeans concluded that the Americans had mort-
gaged the pleasures of life to the wilderness virtues: business,
speculation, work, and action.

Ultimately Penn and Hooker and their heirs assaulted the
paradise myths themselves, redrawing their moral to suit their
revaluation of toil. Like the Puritans before them, nineteenth-
century moralists agreed that Adam had worked in Eden or, if
not, that his idleness had been all the worse for him. Over and
over again, to anyone who would listen, they insisted that work
was not a curse, whatever the hints in the Genesis story. Nor was
it merely a painful means to moral health and redeeming grace.
Labor was a blessing: not "a burden or a bare necessity ... [but]
a privilege, a glory, and a delight."[9] Among academic moralists,
the economists held out against the idea that work was natural to
man, clinging, by and large, to the older idea that labor was a
fragile, irksome habit grafted onto a human nature as lazy as it
dared to be. But the weight of moral thinking was against them.
Man was "made to labor," the century's orators asserted. "It is
his destiny, the law of his nature," placed there by a creator who
was himself, as Henry Ward Beecher—mid-nineteenth-century

America's most famous preacher—insisted, the most tireless laborer of all.[10]

In the end, even heaven itself—Augustine's "perpetual sabbath"—fell before the onslaught. The idea of an eternity of rest vexed and troubled many nineteenth-century American Protestants, and their most widely read spokesmen answered that uneasiness with promises of more "palpable" and "useful" tasks than mere praise and singing. "Surely there must be work to do in heaven, / Since work is the best thing on earth we know," the mill girl turned poet, Lucy Larcom, wrote toward the end of the century. New York's flamboyant evangelist DeWitt Talmage claimed more confidently that heaven was "the busiest place in the universe."[11] Shunting aside generations of mythmaking, the moralists succeeded in writing the gospel of work not only on the land but on paradise itself. "God sent you not into this world as into a Play-house, but a Work-house," ran a Puritan reminder.[12] It was, in fact, a choice Northerners made for themselves.

In our day we know that perplexing decision as the "work ethic." It is a simplified label, as inviting to abuse as it is convenient, but it points to an important truth: for the elevation of work over leisure involved not an isolated choice but an ethos that permeated life and manners. It reared its head in the nineteenth and early twentieth centuries in countless warnings against the wiles of idleness and the protean disguises of the idler. It gave a special reverberation to the word "duty" and set an infectious model of active, conscientious doing. Theodore Roosevelt caught its tenor in his thundering insistence that only the strenuous life was worth living, that "nothing in this world is worth having or worth doing unless it means effort, pain, difficulty."[13] That conviction was by no means Roosevelt's alone. The doctrine of the industrious life pervaded churches and children's storybooks, editorial columns and the stump rhetoric of politics. Not least, it transformed the processes of work themselves, energizing, mechanizing, and systematizing them in ways that made those who cared most about the worth of toil at once immensely proud and profoundly uneasy. But in another sense the phrase is misleading, for the work ethic as it stood in the middle of the nineteenth century, at the threshold of industrialization, was not a single conviction but a complex of ideas with roots and branches.

The taproot, as Max Weber suggested long ago, was the Protestant Reformation. Universalizing the obligation to work and methodizing time, the Reformers set in motion convictions that were to reverberate with enormous consequences through American history. At the heart of Protestantism's revaluation of work was the doctrine of the calling, the faith that God had called everyone to some productive vocation, to toil there for the common good and His greater glory. Paul had said as much centuries before, but the Reformers stripped down the list of admissible callings, lopping off not only the beggars and rascals whose idleness cumbered the land but the courtiers and monks who were no better. The medieval *summum bonum*, a life of contemplation and prayer, suddenly was no vocation at all. "True Godliness don't turn men out of the world" into "a *lazy, rusty, unprofitable self-denial*," William Penn insisted, joining the attack on the monasteries; faith set men to work in the occupations of the secular, commonplace world. Nor was their labor there to be seen as an act of penance and mortification, as Christian tradition so long had had it. *Laborare est orare*: work itself was prayer, from the governing duties of kings to the meanest peasant's task. In the end faith, not labor, saved, of course; the Reformers never confused the secular vocation with a believer's primary, spiritual calling. But Protestantism extended and spiritualized toil and turned usefulness into a sacrament. Zwingli's benediction put the point succinctly: "In the things of this life, the laborer is most like to God."[14]

Protestantism tried to turn religion out of the cloisters into the world of work, but it emptied the monasteries only to give everyone the ascetic responsibilities of a monk. This was the side of the Protestant ethic that most interested Weber: the obligation to survey and order the moral life that the Reformation, and English Puritanism in particular, imposed on its adherents. Striking down the Catholic rhythm of sin and confession, folly and remorse, Puritanism required that the believer ceaselessly analyze, rationalize, and forge his life into a systematic service to the Lord. Weber's argument exaggerated the somber, pleasure-destroying side of the Puritans, for they were not nearly the beetle-browed enemies of the spontaneous enjoyment of life he took them for. Even the strictest Calvinist did not object to the "seasonable recreations" that sharpened the wits or exercised the body. But Weber was certainly right in his claim that Puritanism tried to "penetrate ... [the] daily routine of life with its methodicalness." Puritans methodized the English calendar, throwing out the irregular carnival of saints' days and replacing it with the clocklike rhythm of the weekly Sabbath, when men were to be as tireless and unbending in their rest as they had been during the week at their labors. In the same manner, Puritanism saturated its believers with an acute sense of the dangers of idleness, enjoining them to guard against the misspence of time and to improve the passing moments, each of which, in the end, had to be accounted for in heaven. This was an asceticism of a novel sort, worldly and systematic, looking forward to the time-and-profit calculus of industrial life rather than backward to the flesh-denying torments of the desert hermits. Joined with the doctrine of the calling, it demanded not only that all men work but that they work in a profoundly new way: regularly, conscientiously, and diligently.[15]

Puritans and Quakers carried these injunctions to the new world as articles of faith. Long before Isaac Watts solidified the idea in rhyme, New Englanders spoke of time as "precious" and censured those who used it idly and unprofitably. "Abhor ... one hour of idleness as you would be ashamed of one hour of drunkenness," Thomas Shepard wrote to his son at Harvard. And from every corner ministers like Shepard broadcast the necessity of a calling. "Away to your business," Cotton Mather charged; "lay out your strength in it, put forth your skill in it."[16] Part of the persistent strength of the work ethic was due to the skill with which the preachers joined the ideal of diligent, productive labor to the demands of faith and gave it the form in which it was to be handed down the generations in homilies and countless Sunday school tracts and carried west on the efforts of revivalists and home mission societies.

Yet the nineteenth-century work ethic was not simply the Protestant ethic in modern dress. In the first place, by the middle of the nineteenth century a good deal of secularization had taken place. The old ideas never completely died out, but gradually the term "calling" faded from common speech and with it the idea that in work one labored in the first instance for the glory of God. Increasingly the moralists talked instead of usefulness. Benjamin Franklin helped set the new tone in his tireless string of maxims

and projects for the public good, and by the era of the American
Revolution political writing was saturated with the ideal of public
usefulness, the common weal filling the place the Reformers had
given to God. The legacy persisted well into the nineteenth
century. In one of her short stories of the 1830s, Sarah Hale had
her Yankee hero try the elegant leisure of a Saratoga resort and
come away to conclude that "this trifling away of time when there
is so much to be done, so many improvements necessary in our
country, is inconsistent with that principle of being useful, which
every republican ought to cherish."[17]

So much to be done. Hale's concerns pointed forward as well as
backward, for intruding amid the eighteenth-century phrases she
placed the idea that increasingly preoccupied nineteenth-century
moralists. Not only did immense projects seem to wait at every
hand, but with rising conviction, economists, editors, and preachers insisted that a failure to meet them, a slackening of the pace,
would send the nation skidding into poverty and decay. The
Victorian concern with scarcity, with the economic necessity of
constant doing, was evident well before Darwin's *Origin of
Species* made its full impact in America. In phrases foreign to the
eighteenth century, mid-nineteenth-century writers castigated
businessmen who thought to retire and slip out of harness while
there was labor left in them. Economics imposed stricter necessities than this. The moralists were loath to call economic life
cruel, but they did insist that it demanded constant effort.
William Ellery Channing told a Boston mechanics' group in 1840:

> The material world does much for the mind by its beauty
> and order; but it does more for our minds by the pains it
> inflicts; by its obstinate resistance, which nothing but pa-
> tient toil can overcome; by its vast forces, which nothing
> but unremitting skill and effort can turn to our use; by its
> perils, which demand continual vigilance; and by its ten-
> dencies to decay.

"Life is a stern, hard service," a contributor to the *Atlantic
Monthly* wrote a generation later; "it takes a great deal of hard
work to keep this world going on."[18] In sentiments like these,
scarcity gradually nudged out the common good, just as the ideal
of public usefulness had all but nudged out God. Where Puritans
had been called to their vocations, nineteenth-century Americans

were told that in a world of pressing material demands it was one's social duty to produce.

Working also held one back from the sink of idleness. Despite the gradual dropping away of the theological superstructure of Puritanism, the ascetic injunctions of the Protestant ethic retained and multiplied their force in the mid-nineteenth century. Looking back on her New England childhood years in the 1830s, Lucy Larcom remembered growing up "penetrated through every fibre of thought with the idea that idleness is a disgrace. It was taught with the alphabet and the spelling-book; it was enforced by precept and example, at home and abroad; and it is to be confessed that it did sometimes haunt the childish imagination almost mercilessly."[19] This harrowing of the imagination was often quite deliberate. In his immensely popular *Seven Lectures to Young Men* of 1844, Henry Ward Beecher described the idle mind as an eerie, abandoned castle:

> Its gates sag down and fall; its towers gradually topple over; its windows, beaten in by the tempest, give entrance to birds and reptiles; and its stately halls and capacious chambers are covered with the spider's tapestry, and feebly echo with mimic shrieks of the bat, blinking hither and thither in twilight sports. The indolent mind is not empty, but full of vermin.

There was nothing in this that Thomas Shepard would not have agreed with; idleness was the parent of all sin, the devil's workshop, the Puritans had insisted. But in Beecher's choice of images—the shrieking bats and slithering reptiles—there is more than a hint of the gathering nervousnesses that were particular to the nineteenth century. Sexuality was one of these, as the metaphors made clear. The imagination of the idler was rank with weeds, Beecher and his contemporaries warned; it was the haunt of unlawful visitors, a hothouse of "salacious day-dreams ... rosy at first and distant, [which] deepen every day, darker and darker, to the color of actual evil." In what Carlyle called the "purifying fire" of regular labor, mid-nineteenth-century moralists hoped to consume the sexual passions that seemed increasingly to threaten them. But they hoped for more as well. Work cleared away doubts and vanquished despair; it curbed the animal instincts to violence; it distracted the laborer from the

siren call of radicalism; it redeemed the convict prisoner. It did
all this in part by character-building, by ingraining habits of
fortitude, self-control, and perseverance, and in part by systematic exhaustion. The truly moral man was at once a person of
strength and a *perpetuum mobile* of repressing energy, the man
"whose days are so crowded full of honest and healthy tasks that
he has no room for dreaming."[20] Victorians were somewhat more
apt than Puritans to reserve their asceticism for others. But for
those who saw their world as beset with temptations and dangers,
the sanitizing effects of constant labor offered at once a social
panacea and a personal refuge.

The doctrine of usefulness and an intense, nervous fear of
idleness were both indirect legacies of the Reformation. The
other two ingredients of the mid-nineteenth-century work ethic—
the dream of success and a faith in work as a creative act—had
other roots and implications. By diligence a man could improve
his lot; as the proverbs had it, he could stand before kings. The
hope had seeped early into Puritanism, overturning the initially
static implications of the "calling." Benjamin Franklin had
condensed it into the kind of aphorisms that stuck in one's head
and helped shape the axioms of a culture. But none of this was a
match for the massive outflow of literature that the nineteenth
century produced on behalf of the argument that work was the
highroad to independence, wealth, and status. This is a country
of "self-made men," where from the humblest beginnings a man
with "merit and industry" could rise to the top, Calvin Colton
announced in 1844 at the beginning of the flood.[21] Endless
repetition—in conduct guides, boys' storybooks, handbooks of
business advice, and magazine fillers—ingrained the idea as one
of the century's most firmly held commonplaces. In the fluid
American economy, hard work, self-control, and dogged persistence were the certain escalators of success. Despite the
speculative booms that so conspicuously dotted economic life—
despite the financial adventurism and ardent pursuit of the main
chance that Twain totted up in *The Gilded Age*—businessmen
and moralists stuck to the canon. Even on Wall Street, the "law"
of success was "unbending and regular," Matthew Hale Smith
wrote in 1873, the year Twain's book appeared: "Industry,
honesty, perseverance, sticking to one thing, invariably lead to
success." Henry Ward Beecher, who served as the conduit for so

many of the presuppositions of mid-nineteenth-century Americans, insisted that the one thing necessary for wealth was "Industry—plain, rugged, brown-faced, homely clad, old-fashioned Industry."[22] By his labor a man worked out the position he deserved on the economic ladder; it was the key to success in the business of living.

Finally, it was urged, through work men impressed something of themselves on the material world. "A small Poet every Worker is," Carlyle wrote. Emerson seconded the idea: "Labor: a man coins himself into his labor; turns his day, his strength, his thoughts, his affection into some product which remains a visible sign of his power." Craft traditions, the legacy of the Renaissance artist-craftsmen, and romanticism all converged on the theme, often with extravagant results. In a poem picked up from the transcendentalist *Harbinger* and passed through the labor papers of the 1840s, Augustine Duganne apotheosized the artisan as "God's high priest," standing "midway / Between the earth and heaven, all things sway / To thy high-working mind!"[23] Perorations of this sort were most common among writers who, like Duganne, stood at the boundary between artisan and literary culture. The more frequent acknowledgment of the creative role of labor was a simpler conviction that "work" was not "drudgery," and that it was room for employment of the mind that told them apart. One stumbles over the distinction again and again. Drudgery was the word the writers recurred to when faced with blind, thoughtless toil—the labor of slaves or the bent, haunting peasant of Millet's famous painting "The Man with the Hoe." In work, they insisted, mind and spirit had a part, transforming "dead" muscle labor into acts of skill. Work was creation. "To become an artist in dealing with tools and materials is not a matter of choice ... [but] a moral necessity," Hamilton Wright Mabie told the readers of the *Outlook* at the end of the century. "Work is sacred ... not only because it is the fruit of self-denial, patience, and toil, but because it uncovers the soul of the worker."[24]

Obviously there were tensions within this set of ideas. Work was a creative act and a means of self-repression, a social obligation that paid off in private rewards. The ingredients of the work ethic were not held together by the logical consistency of their premises. The clearest of the tensions lay between the idea

of work as ascetic exercise and work as art. The one looked
toward system, discipline, and the emerging factory order; the
other toward spontaneity, self-expression, and a narrowing of the
gulf between work and play. The latter, creative ideal was clearly
the weaker of the two in the nineteenth century. For a moment in
the 1880s a large number of Americans discarded it altogether
and devoured an enormously popular tract entitled "Blessed Be
Drudgery,"[25] and it was long a half-suspect intruder amid the
calls to effort, self-discipline, and ambition.

There was a second, nagging contradiction between the ideals
of duty and of success—between the appeal to the dignity of all
labor, even the humblest, and the equally universal counsel to
work one's way as quickly as possible out of manual toil. Manual
workers felt the full force of the contradiction and complained
repeatedly of the disjuncture between the grandiloquent rhetoric
and the practical disrepute of their occupations. William Dean
Howells, who agonized over the point in the 1880s and 1890s, was
finally driven to conclude that Americans liked their inconsis-
tencies on a large scale.[26] And yet a man like Beecher, and scores
of other writers as well, demonstrably held all these ideas at once:
the creative and the ascetic ideals, the rhetoric of an expansive
economy and of early Protestantism, a sincere, fervent belief in
toil and elitist reservations. The disparate strands all came
together to reaffirm the central premise of the work ethic: that
work was the core of the moral life. Work made men useful in a
world of economic scarcity; it staved off the doubts and temptations that preyed on idleness; it opened the way to deserved
wealth and status; it allowed one to put the impress of mind and
skill on the material world. At the advent of the factory system,
few of the keepers of the Northern moral conscience did not, in
some measure, believe in them all.

The Henry Ward Beechers no more spoke for all Northerners, of
course, than they spoke for all Americans. There was a sociology
to the work ethic as well as an amalgam of ideas. Praise of work
in the mid-nineteenth century was strongest among the middling,
largely Protestant, property-owning classes: farmers, merchants,
ministers and professional men, independent craftsmen, and
nascent industrialists. Such groups had formed the backbone of
English Puritanism, flinging their gospel of labor at the idle

aristocracy and the dissolute mass of laborers that seemed to beset them on either side. The work ethic, too, was largely their creation. The Europeans who marveled at the untiring energy of the Americans were describing not ordinary laborers but their own social counterparts, particularly merchants of moderate means, who in America seemed as hard at work as their junior clerks.

On both ends of the social scale one can readily find other ethics and other styles of life. The ascetic injunctions of Puritanism never penetrated very far into the urban working classes. When Arthur Young wrote that "everyone but an idiot knows that the lower classes must be kept poor or they will never be industrious,"[27] he voiced the virtually unanimous conviction of seventeenth- and eighteenth-century English employers. A mass of prejudice obviously entered into statements of this sort, but they were not manufactured wholly out of class bias. In early nineteenth-century America, it is clear that many urban laborers did their best to punctuate work and play in the irregular, clock-defying pattern that is far older than the Protestant ethic. Gambling, rioting, generous drinking habits, and a good deal of boisterous, elbow-shoving, Sabbath-defying amusement played an important part in urban working-class life. If by no means every laborer, journeyman, and apprentice escaped the inner compulsions of the work ethic, enough of them did to make their presence felt in Jacksonian America.[28] Among the very rich, too, the ideal of industriousness met with resistance. Compared with Europe or the American South, in the North the thoroughly idle gentleman was a rarity. The leisured aristocracy there was small, and its resources were relatively limited. But wealthy businessmen like New York City's Philip Hone showed no inclination to chain themselves to their counting tables or to consume their pleasures moderately.[29] Conspicuous leisure was everywhere the identifying mark of the aristocrat, his bastion against the moralistic assaults of the middle classes; and in this regard the North was no exception.

Work was the gospel of the bourgeoisie, above all of the Protestant bourgeoisie, but it was not for that reason simply a subcultural peculiarity. In the American North, as nowhere else in the Western European orbit, the middle classes set the tone and standards for society as a whole. They did so through their hold over the strategic institutions of economics and culture. Business enterprise was theirs. So were the Protestant churches and the myriad agencies of moral reformation they spawned in the nineteenth century to care for the poor, educate the ignorant, and hold the wayward to the path of virtue. So were the institutions of learning: the schools and the colleges, the nation's publishing houses, and the major journals of opinion. It was in the last, in particular, that the ideals of middle-class Protestant respectability were debated, codified, and—with the conservative power of print—preserved. Editors like E. L. Godkin of the *Nation*, J. G. Holland of *Scribner's Monthly*, Howells and Beecher of the *Atlantic* and the *Christian Union*, and Mary Mapes Dodge of the children's *St. Nicholas*—or, after the turn of the century, George H. Lorimer of the *Saturday Evening Post* and Edward Bok of the *Ladies' Home Journal*—oversaw the process with an acute sense of responsibility and self-importance. They opened the pages of the middle-class magazines in a careful and considered way to the organizers of economic and cultural life and to the nation's most prominent writers as well as to a dedicated corps of anonymously conventional scribblers. I have called this interlocking set of persons the "moralists," keepers of their countrymen's moral conscience. They were not the only Northerners who felt keenly about ethics, but, given the institutional structure of their society, their opinions carried uncommon weight and influence. [30]

The work ethic radiated not only from the secular pulpits of journalism but from all the institutional fortresses of the middle class. Campaigns to inculcate the values of industriousness in schoolchildren, and to impose it upon employees and social dependents, gathered and spent their force over and over again in nineteenth-century America, leaving behind a crust of middle-class morality of uncertain but perceptible depth. Still more important, probably, was the subtle contagion of example, aided by the moralists' near-monopoly on the definitions of respectability. In the years after the Civil War, praise of work noisily invaded the South, as its spokesmen turned upon their old "bondage to leisure" to announce their love affair with toil. It officially overrode whatever reservations the bishops of the American Catholic church may have felt about the repressive sobriety of Protestantism and led them, in the midst of the

Americanist campaign of the 1880s, to put the weight of their influence behind thrift, industry, temperance, and Protestant Sabbatarianism.[31] Elsewhere, too, potential resistance crumbled. Political aspirants, who presumably knew what they were about, regularly curried the favor of workingmen with orations on the dignity of toil. Frederick W. Taylor's father, a genteel Phila-delphia lawyer, retired while still a young man to devote himself to study, public affairs, and the broadening influence of travel; yet the younger Taylor absorbed the work ethic, somehow, into the very marrow of his bones. Over and over again the opposite could be heard, that the old respect for labor was faltering in its paces. But the sense of decay was as indispensable to the moralists' temper as it was to the work ethic itself, a reassurance that there were still urgent tasks to be done and moral wilder-nesses still to be tamed.

None of the ingredients of the work ethic were unique to America. It was John Locke who announced that all property took its title from labor, Adam Smith who claimed that labor was the ultimate source of wealth, and Henri Bergson who in the phrase *homo faber* made work synonymous with man himself. Samuel Smiles's *Self-Help* dominated nineteenth-century success writing, just as Thomas Carlyle's example loomed over virtually all those in America who wrote in praise of work. But nowhere else than in the American North, with its truncated social structure, was resistance to these claims so limited. The result was an odd creation: a class and sectarian dogma that was at the same time as close to an article of popular faith as the region afforded.

Exactly how busy is a diligent man? It was only after the factories had overrun economic life that Northern industrialists set out to answer that question with any precision and to graft onto their countrymen the time obsession characteristic of modern indus-trial societies. The work ethic in its mid-nineteenth-century form did not entail a particular pace of activity so much as a manner of thinking, a moral preoccupation with labor. Moreover, the ideas that came together in praise of work took shape and flourished in an era when, by modern standards, time moved at a haphazard gait. First-generation New England ministers might urge their congregations that each moment was precious and that "one

grain of time's inestimable sand [was] worth a golden moun-
tain."[32] But in a society in which household clocks were extraordinarily rare and the best of them possessed only a single,
marginally accurate hand, such words hardly carried their modern
meaning. By the end of the seventeenth century affluent families
could purchase pendulum clocks of two and three hands; but
large-scale production of brass household clocks did not begin in
America until the end of the 1830s, and it was not until the Civil
War that the characteristic arbiters of industrial time—cheap,
mass-produced pocket watches—began to pour out of the American Watch Company plant at Waltham.[33] "Time is money,"
Franklin had said, but when so much of time passed by unreck-
oned it is doubtful that he intended the meanings Frederick W.
Taylor was to find in the words two centuries later. There is,
in short, a misleading modernity to the phrases of the work ethic.
They were rooted in, and creatures of, an economy older than and
quite different from that of the factories.

Not only time but work moved in irregular, often leisurely
rhythms in preindustrial America. Colonial workers who hired
out their labor were generally expected to work the "whole day"
six days a week, or from dawn to dusk in winter and from ten to
twelve hours a day of actual labor in summer. But work itself was
scarcely this even. Farming, the dominant colonial occupation,
oscillated between bouts of intense labor and the short, much
slower days of winter and was punctuated by country recreations—fishing, horse racing, visiting, and tavern-going—that
even in Puritan New England were as much a part of rural life as
the aching toil of planting and harvesting. In the same manner,
the typical colonial workshop, with its three or four journeymen
and apprentices, went through cycles of activity and probably was
rarely busy day in and day out. By the early nineteenth century
the tempo of economic life had increased perceptibly. In the
East, many rural families now filled in the slack periods of
farming by turning materials put out to them by nearby wholesale
merchants into boot and shoe uppers, woven cloth goods, straw
hats, and a variety of other products. The stores and workshops
of Jacksonian America were bigger and considerably more bustling than their colonial counterparts. But weather, changes in
demand and availability of materials, and poor communication
and transportation facilities still conspired to interrupt the

steadiness of work. "Incessant toil ... was not the bane of Philadelphia's antebellum artisans," their most recent historian has concluded, but "the fitful pace of work, the syncopated rhythm of the economy."[34] This context, too, qualified the calls to diligence. For all their intense fears of the idle life, mid-nineteenth-century moralists did not demand that men work with the ceaseless regularity of machines, but merely asked that they keep soberly and steadily to what tasks lay before them. In a world remote from the time clock and the efficiency expert, the work ethic was not a certain rate of busyness but a way of thinking.

Yet the strength of mid-nineteenth-century work ideals was exactly in their mesh with the bustling, irregular economy of the antebellum North. In this regard two characteristics of the antebellum economy were acutely important: its expansive energy and its limited industrial technology. The first is difficult to exaggerate. In the early nineteenth century the North underwent a startling transformation from an essentially agricultural to a commercial economy. Within the generation between 1815 and 1850, Northerners dug a regional transportation system of canals and waterways and started on a railroad network to replace it, dotted the Middle West with new settlements and at the same time burst the institutions of the seaboard cities at the seams, flooded the Patent Office with inventions, and raised the value of manufactures produced severalfold. "Go ahead" was the motto of the age, the European travelers reported, and with good reason.[35]

But, for all the aggressive innovation of the age, as late as 1850 the centers of manufacturing remained the home and the workshop. Home production was not simply a rural phenomenon. The putting-out system flourished in every manufacturing town, employing shoemakers, weavers, tailors, and seamstresses in the traditional hand processes. Moreover, the workshops that threatened the livelihood of the home workers were on the whole far from the factory stage. In Boston, according to a careful enumeration of its factories and workshops in 1832, almost half the workmen were employed in shops of ten or fewer employees, and 80 percent worked in shops of no more than twenty. Philadelphia in the mid-1850s was much further into the industrial revolution, and its two sprawling locomotive works alone employed about 1,600 hands. But even in the nation's preeminent manufacturing center 100 employees was enough to rank an establishment as a major enterprise, and the dozens that reached this size were still surrounded by literally hundreds of tiny one- to five-man workshops.[36]

The cotton textile industry was the great exception. Barn-sized, water-powered spinning mills had begun to appear in southern New England as early as the 1790s. It was the founding of Lowell, Massachusetts, in the early 1820s, however, that marked the real beginning of the new industrial order in America. Lowell was the first of the large-scale mill towns, an unprecedented assemblage of machines, bosses, and operatives. Within a decade there were nineteen textile mills in operation in the city, employing an army of 5,000 factory hands. With its paternalistic regulations and its boarding houses full of Yankee farm girls turned short-term mill hands, Lowell was the marvel of the nation and an obligatory part of the American tour. By the middle of the century, however, rivals had sprung up at Chicopee, Manchester, Manayunk, and a dozen other textile centers. The cotton mills were the first and archetypal factories, set off by their size, discipline, and thorough mechanization. Dwarfing most other enterprises, the largest mid-nineteenth-century textile mills employed a thousand or more workers, operatives for the most part, tied to the power looms and spinning machinery they tended and hemmed in by rigid sets of factory rules. Less dramatically, a few other industries moved in the direction of the cotton mills. Arms manufacturers began extensive use of machinery and subdivision of labor early in the century, ingeniously enough to warrant inspection by an official English delegation in the mid-1850s, which found the same techniques in use in the manufacture of clocks, furniture, and a variety of wood and metal products. In the 1840s iron rolling mills, too, moved swiftly toward factory dimensions.[37] "Stave-machines, planing-machines, reaping-machines, ploughing-machines, thrashing-machines, steam wagons," Walt Whitman chanted in his "Song for Occupations." But this was in 1855, when the shift in manufacturing processes had begun to accelerate rapidly. Outside the textile centers, the home, farm, and workshop still ruled the early nineteenth-century economy. In 1841, in a judgment that comes closer to the truth of the period, a Cincinnati observer claimed: "Our manufacturing establishments, with the exception of a few, ... are, in the literal sense, manufactures,—*works of the hand.*"[38]

This was an economy in the earliest stages of industrialization—expansive yet simple—and it went hand in hand with the intellectual legacies to fashion the mid-nineteenth-century work ethic. The economic matrix reinforced old assumptions about work, stirred up new ones, and held them all together in a way logic could not. Expansion fueled the command to be up and doing and helped turn the ideal of usefulness out of the religious and political spheres and make it an economic obligation. "The busy world angrily shoves aside / The man who stands with arms akimbo set." James Russell Lowell put the phrase in Oliver Cromwell's mouth, but its accents were those of Lowell's own mid-nineteenth-century generation, impressed by the immensity of the enterprises to be undertaken, the goods to be made, the projects to be done.[39]

Expansion likewise took the hope of upward mobility and screwed it to a new pitch. In a world that seemed to have jumped the old restraining ruts—where a Cornelius Vanderbilt could ride the new transportation systems to a fortune and a skillful Yankee carpenter such as Thomas Rogers could become one of the nation's leading locomotive manufacturers—the dream of success was hardly to be escaped. It rose in close correlation with economic growth, gathering strength in the 1830s and 1840s and turning into a flood after the middle of the century. But if the promise of mobility was virtually inevitable, it was no less inevitable that the moralists should try to control the unleashed promises and turn them, by insistent praise of work and self-control, into safe, familiar channels. Exhilaration and nervousness were both part of mid-nineteenth-century life. Enterprises that boomed hopefully also collapsed spectacularly, and the economy itself fell apart disastrously in 1819, again in 1837, and every twenty years thereafter throughout the nineteenth century. If growth fueled dreams of success, the sudden collapses and paralyses ingrained the lessons of scarcity, heightened anxieties over the disorders of commercial and urban life, and added to the Victorian nervousness. In all, it was a paradoxical society—booming yet fragile, engaged in the march of progress yet adrift in flux, inspiring expansive hope even as it reinforced the fears that encouraged the ascetic, nerve-numbing discipline of dili-

gence. On all counts, even in its contradictions, it helped
reinforce the primacy of work.

Finally, the economy of the antebellum North was one in which
a certain measure of independence and creativity could be taken
for granted. No one directly supervised home workers or farmers,
and in the shops and small mills supervision was rarely exacting.
The heated political arguments that accompanied the making of
shoes or cigars were more than a figment of later, nostalgic
imaginations. Pick and shovel labor was a matter of another sort,
but in general the hand processes of manufacture, the flexible
rhythms of labor, and the absence of strict discipline made it
possible for most workers to impress some of their idiosyncrasies
on their toil, if not always to love it. Intellectuals have long
romanticized the state of things before the coming of the
factories. Preindustrial America had ample share of hardships,
poverty, and pain. In hindsight, in fact, the degradation of the
urban craftsman was well under way by 1850, as artisans found
themselves increasingly caught in dependency to merchants whose
capital enabled them to control the supply of raw materials and
the marketing of the finished products. In the 1840s, New
Englanders likewise peered under the Lowell mills' attractive
facade and debated the merits of the factories. But, in the face of
an enormous enthusiasm for technology, little of this penetrated
far into the consciousness of middle-class Northerners.[40] They
thought their society what it seemed to be: a land of bustling
farms and workshops where work told; where indeed it was the
core of living.

In the second half of the nineteenth century the factory system
invaded the antebellum farm and shop economy, overturning not
only the familiar patterns of work but the ways Northerners had
been accustomed to think of their labor. The speed of the
transition to the factory economy varied widely from industry to
industry and from place to place. It was an uneven movement—
felt not as a shock, as it has often been described, but as a series
of shivers, greatest in years of major labor unrest when the nation
suddenly reckoned up the extent of change. But in the end the
factory system challenged each of the certainties upon which the
work ethic had rested and unsettled the easy equation of work
and morality in the minds of many perceptive Americans.

Well after 1850 the economy still presented a patchwork array of contrasts. In Philadelphia, handloom weavers worked in their own homes virtually in the shadow of the mechanized textile mills. In New York City, tiny tenement cigar shops competed with factory establishments of several hundred employees. Rural and urban industrial workers differed, the country factory hands often retaining a degree of community power their urban counterparts had lost. The detailed disciplinary codes of the textile mills contrasted with the haphazard management typical of many other mechanized industries. As late as 1889, David A. Wells, one of the nation's leading economists, could depreciate the importance of the factory system altogether and insist that no more than one-tenth of the gainfully employed were properly described as factory hands.[41] Yet for all the variety and confusion, the drift of change was evident. As the century progressed, the mills grew larger, labor discipline more exacting, and the work processes more minutely subdivided and dependent on machinery.

At times and in places, moreover, the transition to the factory economy took place with wrenching, unsettling speed. The shoe industry was for most nineteenth-century Americans the pre-eminent example of the rate at which the new could obliterate the old. As late as the 1840s the typical New England shoe shop was a 10' x 10' cottage housing a handful of skilled workers who made shoes by time-honored hand methods according to their personal, often eccentric, notions of size and fit. Some subdivision of tasks set in during that decade under the pressures of the merchants who controlled the trade, but the real revolution in shoemaking came in the 1860s with a rash of inventions, beginning with a sewing machine capable of stitching soles to uppers. Aggressive subdivision of labor, mechanization, and factory building quickly followed. By the 1870s, the shoemaking cottages were empty, and the men who had once been shoemakers now found themselves factory machine operators: beaters, binders, bottomers, buffers, burnishers, channellers, crimpers, cutters, dressers, edge setters, and so on through some thirty or forty subdivided occupations.[42] Glassmaking was another example of the rapid destruction of a craft. In 1896 the entire output of bottles, jars, and window glass was made by gangs of skilled men and boy helpers, who gathered, blew, and shaped the glass by hand. Twenty years later half the jar and bottle blowers were gone, and the window glass workers were rapidly being replaced with automatic or semiautomatic machines.[43] More commonly than this, the foundations shifted under an entire town. In 1850 Paterson, New Jersey, was a small city with a number of modest manufacturing establishments. Twenty-five years later the city boasted three huge locomotive works, fourteen silk mills, and the largest jute, linen, and mosquito netting factories in the country. The number of inhabitants had trebled; the number of saloons had increased almost sixfold.[44]

Size, discipline, and displacement of skill characterized the factories. The physical growth of the workplace was evident at every hand. The Baldwin locomotive works had been a giant among factories in the mid-1850s with 600 employees. Twenty years later there were 3,000 factory hands at Baldwin, and by 1900 there were more than 8,000. The McCormick reaper plant in Chicago followed the same course, growing from about 150 employees in 1850 to 4,000 in 1900. But the manufacturing colossi of the early twentieth century dwarfed even these. By 1916 the McCormick plant had grown to 15,000 workers; and in that year the payroll at the Ford Motor Company works at Highland Park reached 33,000.[45] Workshops of the size that had characterized the antebellum economy, employing a handful or a score of workers, persisted amid these immense establishments. But they employed a smaller and smaller fraction of the workers. By 1919, in the Northern states between the Mississippi River and the Atlantic Ocean, three-fourths of all wage earners in manufacturing worked in factories of more than 100 employees, and 30 percent in the giants of more than 1,000.[46]

In plants of this size, the informality of the small workshop was an inevitable casualty. From the beginning the great textile mills had laid down extensive regulatory codes and enforced them with heavy fines and the threat of discharge. Other industries adopted such measures more slowly. The Winchester Repeating Arms plant in New Haven, for example, did not begin to insist that employees arrive on time until the 1890s, and in the piecework trades workers clung for a long time to their traditional right to set their own hours of labor. By the 1890s, however, gates were common around factories, supplemented by the exacting eye of the first factory time clocks. Inside the plants the baronial foremen, who had commonly hired, fired, and cajoled the necessary labor out of their workers on their own whim and responsibility, slowly disappeared. In their place the larger factories evolved tighter, more systematic, and more centralized schemes of management. By 1920 personnel departments, rational and precise cost accounting, central planning offices, and production and efficiency engineers had become fixtures of the new factory bureaucracies.[47] Defenders of the new management techniques argued that they were fairer than the old. Certainly by the end of the century there was little to be envied in the lot of the workers left behind in the sweatshops and tenement rooms. But neither qualification lessened the growing distance between a factory hand and his employer or the subordination of the rhythms of work to the increasingly exacting demands of efficiency.

By the same token, skills disappeared in the new factories. Whether owing to such a simple device as the cigar mold—a wooden frame that enabled an untrained worker to bunch cigar tobacco—or the complex, automatic tools of the machine shop, the factories made obsolete a host of carefully preserved hand trades. Tailoring, cabinetmaking, barrel making, felt-hat making, and pottery making all gave way before new inventions and the specialization of labor. The clothing and slaughtering industries were particularly conspicuous examples of the relentless subdivision of tasks. In 1859, less than a decade after the introduction of the sewing machine, a Cincinnati clothing factory had succeeded in dividing the making of a pair of men's pants, formerly the job of a single tailor, into seventeen different occupations. At Smith's packing plant in Chicago at the turn of the century, 150 men, each with his specific mite of butchering to perform, handled each hog on its way from the pen to the cooling room. Dressing the tail of a beef carcass alone occupied the labor of five men: two skinned it, another two cut it off, and a fifth threw the skinned and severed appendage into a box. Nowhere did the pursuit of efficiency go on more aggressively than in the automobile industry, where the jobs were relentlessly morseled before being chained to the assembly line. One of the tasks at Ford's Highland Park plant consisted in joining pistons and rods by driving out, oiling, and replacing a pin, inserting and tightening a screw, and installing a cotter pin. All together the operation took three minutes. The Ford engineers divided the job into four pieces and doubled the output. The automobile had been a triumph of the mechanic's art, but by the second decade of the twentieth century fewer than one job in twelve in the auto plants took more than half a year to learn.[48]

The factories made skills as well as destroyed them. Mule spinners in the textile factories and heaters and rollers in the steel mills worked at highly skilled, factory-created jobs. But the drive toward ever-greater efficiency made every skilled job precarious. A New York City machinist, complaining of the subdivision of labor in his trade in the 1880s, insisted that ten years earlier the machinist had "considered himself a little above the average workingman; he thought himself a mechanic, and felt he belonged to the middle class; but to-day he recognizes the fact that he is simply the same as any other ordinary laborer, no more and no less." Employers did not hesitate to enforce the point. When in 1885 the managers at the McCormick plant found themselves in a dispute with their unionized iron molders, they dismissed the entire force and installed molding machines and unskilled recruits in their places.[49] Despite occasional compensations, all factory jobs increasingly converged toward the semiskilled; the typical factory hand became a machine operator or fractionated workman, toiling at a single bit of the manufacturing process.

How extensive the new modes of work actually were was a matter of some debate. In 1860, one-fifth of the gainfully occupied population of the Northern states worked in what the census defined as a manufacturing establishment; by 1919, when the correlation between factory and "manufacturing establishment" was considerably closer, the proportion had grown to about a third.[50] But the new forms of toil affected not only manufacturing workers but spread out from the factories as well. In the late 1870s, large-scale production methods invaded agriculture in the wake of the rapid mechanization of farm tools. The most famous of the early "food factories," as their critic William G. Moody called them in the 1880s, sprawled over 30,000 acres of Dakota Territory wheat land, and at its peak employed two hundred reapers, thirty steam-powered threshers, and a thousand hands to bring in the crop. Individual bonanza farms like this came and went, and their number grew fairly slowly after the initial spurt of the 1870s.[51] The transformation of coal mining in the early twentieth century was more complete. Between about 1900 and 1910, coal-cutting machinery and subdivision of labor began to enter the bituminous coal mines of the Middle West, remaking the operations and shoving out the hand miners who had once worked at the pit faces virtually as autonomous subcontractors. About the same time the efficiency experts began to turn their attention to the huge new clerical forces employed by firms like Sears and Roebuck. Arrayed behind banks of desks, strictly supervised, paid at times like industrial workers on piecework, many of the new clerical workers differed from factory hands only in status and neatness—just as the big, turn-of-the-century department stores employing several thousand saleswomen and cash girls differed little from fair-sized industrial establishments.[52] In 1850 the job of a clerk or a farmer had been worlds away from that of a mill hand, but slowly, perceptibly, all work grew more and more like factory work.

What industrialization offered in return was a fantastic increase in output. The constantly growing flood of goods impressed and bewildered Northerners. In 1894 Congress instructed the Bureau of Labor to try to compute the savings in time and costs the new methods of manufacture had brought. The two volumes that resulted added nothing to the science of statistics. But the report that the factories were now making ten times as many fine-grade women's shoes and overalls a week as had been possible with the old, hand methods, fourteen times as many hardwood bedsteads, and twenty-two times as many stem-winding watches gave a striking, if impressionistic, suggestion of the economic dividends of the factory system. Modern indexes of production, though they must find approximate ways to equate cotton textile bolts and automobiles, provide a more reliable measure of the change. Between 1860 and 1920, the nation's population a little more than tripled, but the volume of manufactured goods produced increased somewhere between twelve- and fourteenfold. In international terms, the growth of manufactures was just as striking. In 1850 the factory economy was just emerging in America. By the turn of the century the United States had pushed past all other nations in industrial production. By 1910 it had outstripped its nearest rival, Germany, by nearly two to one.[53]

This avalanche of factory-produced goods might have been expected to flow neatly into greater general well-being, but it did not. By the 1880s many businessmen had begun to worry that there were too many factories for the economy to absorb. Excess productive capacity in such diverse industries as steel, stoves, textile machinery, and sewing machines, in fact, troubled the economic waters, driving down prices, encouraging industrial consolidations to jack them up again, and in the process widening still further the gap between the old, workshop economy and the new.[54] Intellectually, too, the phenomenon of more goods than the market could absorb was deeply troubling. Production had long been the chief of the economic virtues, impossible to take to excess. But if the industrial cornucopia could easily spew out far more goods than the nation was able to buy, what then was the place of work?

This was only one of the questions the invasion of the factories posed to those who cared deeply about work. The whole issue was a maze of paradoxes. The industrial economy was in large part a creature of the intense regional faith in the worth of labor. The work ethic helped impell the restless personal energies of the Northern manufacturers, blessed their enterprises with a sense of mission, .and gave them a transcendent sanction. It helped anesthetize employers to the eleven- and twelve-hour days they imposed on their workers and the pace at which the factories drove them. The work ethic provided the language of calculation, system, and diligence into which the efficiency engineers poured their new and stricter meanings, turning the new plants into matchless hives of industriousness. But if the factories were creatures of middle-class work ideals, they devoured those ideals as well. In disturbing ways, the transformation of labor undercut virtually all the mid-nineteenth-century assumptions about the moral preeminence of work.

Industrialization upset the certainty that hard work would bring economic success. Whatever the life chances of a farmer or shop hand had been in the early years of the century, it became troublingly clear that the semiskilled laborer, caught in the anonymity of a late-nineteenth-century textile factory or steel mill, was trapped in his circumstances—that no amount of sheer hard work would open the way to self-employment or wealth. Still more rudely, the factory system overturned the equation of work and art. Amid the subdivided and monotonous tasks, the speed, and the discipline of a box factory or an automobile plant, where was the room for mind or for the impress of individual creativity?

Even the successes of the industrial transformation unsettled ideas and values. As the factories poured forth an ever-larger volume of goods into the homes of the middle class, the ascetic legacies of the Protestant ethic slowly and steadily eroded, giving way to a noisy gospel of play and, at the fringes of middle-class thought, to a cultivation of a life free of effort itself. As industrialization shook the idea of the permanence of scarcity, as the measure of economic health turned from how much a society produced to how equitably and conscientiously it consumed, it became harder and harder to insist that compulsive activity, work, and usefulness were the highest goals of life.

The moralists did not perceive these troubling questions all at once. When they did there were always the ancient maxims to fall back on. Work, they continued to insist, was what man was made to do—the foundation of happiness, the condition of existence since the days of Adam's husbandry in the garden. But industrialization could not be stopped from wedging into the preserve of ethics. And as the economy was transformed a deeply rooted set of presumptions cracked and shifted.

Hireling Laborers

There is really very little in the present industrial *régime* to stimulate the intelligence, excite
the ambition, and sweeten the toil of ordinary
mortals. The work is, after all, another man's
work; the gain is to be his, and the honor of
success is to be his too.

> E. L. Godkin, "The Labor Crisis" (1867)

As they watched the new forms of work slowly push aside the old,
the first issue to trouble the moralists was the matter of wage
working. Nothing more clearly distinguishes the years in which
the factory system was built from the modern age, inured to its
ranks of wage and salary earners, than that the simple fact of
employment should have deeply disturbed so many Americans.
But labor at the beck and call of another was not among the
ideals even of work-obsessed, mid-nineteenth-century Northerners. Part of what gave labor its immense value to the keepers
of the mid-nineteenth-century work ethic was the assumption that
the worker owned his own toil—that a man's efforts were his to
exert and the successes his to be reaped. Puritans could still talk
of a hierarchy of servants leading up to God, but when mid-
nineteenth-century moralists urged the dignity of work their
minds habitually ran first to those who were their own masters:
farmers, self-employed craftsmen, shopkeepers, and small businessmen. It was hard, in fact, to find a positive label for all the
others. In the expansive, insistently democratic antebellum North,
the word "servant" slid into a term of reproach. "Employee,"
the term that eventually filled the gap, was still a foreign import,
hesitantly spelled and its implications resisted. Antebellum manufacturers preferred to talk of "operatives" and "factory hands,"
just as Yankee farmers invented the term "help" for their
servants and hired men, as if the evasive labels would rectify the

anomaly of dependence in a society in which self-employment was the moral norm. They had good reason for their evasions; behind all the other terms for the worker who labored at the will and for the profit of another was the oldest, bluntest, and most troubling word of all: "slave."

A parallel between slavery and wage employment was far more than a simple play on words for mid-nineteenth-century Americans. Sooner or later the expansion of the factories would in itself have jarred up against the moralists' vision of a society of economically independent workers. But what forced the issue of wage working, long before the factories overran the Northern economy, was the struggle over slavery. Both Northern and Southern partisans in the slavery debates played a part in joining the issues. The proslavery forces were first, turning back the abolitionists' critique of slavery with an equally searing attack on the cruelties of the "hireling" wage system of the North. But the more important step was the shift of the focus of the Northern argument against slavery from the fate of the slaves to the fate of labor itself. Conviction joined with opportunism in this welding of the antislavery cause to the immense moral reserves of Northern work ideals. By the 1850s, when the process was well under way, it had become a commonplace of Republican rhetoric to describe the contest between North and South as essentially a contest between two radically different forms of labor. In the South, shiftlessness and exploitation were the rule. As the Republicans depicted the slave economy, it was a nightmarish inversion of Northern work values, where idlers ruled and laborers stood in chains. Still worse, the inefficiencies of the slave labor system had forced it for its very survival into a policy of aggressive expansion, which threatened to reduce virtually to slave status first the settlers of the territories and ultimately free laborers everywhere. "There is but one issue in this prolonged and bitter contest," the Chicago *Press and Tribune* could maintain by 1858; "it is this, *shall labor be degraded?*"[1]

Skirting the deep Northern reserves of anti-Negro prejudice, the free labor argument gave the antislavery men an immensely appealing case. Yet to pose the question in this way it was necessary to insist all the more adamantly that the North was different, that it was a land where labor was not only respected but genuinely free. If exploitation dominated the Republicans'

picture of the South, masterlessness was at the center of their
vision of the North. They saw themselves as a society of hard-
working and economically independent farmers, mechanics, and
tradesmen, defending the cause of a worker's freedom against the
inroads of the Southern master-servant economy. They went to
war that way, or thought they did, and when it was over many of
them were eager to plant their free labor standard in the heart of
the beaten South. Three months after Appomattox, the *Nation*
claimed that the real contest had just begun. The task ahead was
economic—to colonize and Yankeeize the South, "to renew [its]
soil, to raise unheard-of crops, to clear the forest and drain the
swamp, to impress the water-power into service, to set up the
cotton-mill alongside of the corn-field, to build highways, to
explore mines, and in short to turn the slothful, shiftless Southern
world upside down."[2] The work ethic and war zeal joined in this
Reconstruction vision. Yet if the North should produce its own
class of permanent hirelings—if there should turn out to be a
grain of truth to the argument advanced by both Southerners and
a generation of labor spokesmen that there was not a great deal of
difference between bond slavery and slavery at wages—where
then would be the victory?

These became immediate and pressing questions in the aftermath of the war. "It is inconsistent with Christian freemanship
for any man to work for wages for any body," the antislavery
partisan and Christian socialist Jesse H. Jones declared in 1875,
and if the phrasing was eccentric the substance of Jones's concern
was not. The abolitionist Wendell Phillips, who before the war
had dismissed the phrase "wages slavery" as "utterly unintel-
ligible," by 1871 had joined a Massachusetts labor-reform convention in declaring "war" on the system of wages that cheated,
demoralized, and "enslaved" the workingman. From close to the
opposite end of the political spectrum, the *Nation*'s E. L. Godkin
urged the agitation on "until the *régime* of wages, or, as we might
perhaps better call it, the servile *régime*, has passed away as
completely as slavery or serfdom."[3] It was not the factories alone
that triggered the rush of concern over wage working. To a writer
in the *New York Times* in 1869, the news that the typical
manufacturing establishment employed five men at wages confirmed a "slavery as absolute if not as degrading as that which
lately prevailed at the South."[4] Yet if the five-man workshop

threatened the free labor ideal, the armies of employees the factories had already begun to assemble were occasion for real alarm. The rhetoric of the slavery contest had promised independence; mid-nineteenth-century work ideals had assumed it. As the drift of the economy set in in the opposite direction, tugging against ideals, the result was a nagging, anxious sense of betrayal.

In the tangled debates that ensued, wage earning as a temporary stage in one's career was not at issue. It was the thought of a man who spent his whole life working for others that troubled Northerners and seemed so little different from slavery. In the first instance, wage working of this sort jarred, like slavery, against the principle of democracy. The Jeffersonian conviction that political liberty was safe only where no man was economically beholden to any other died hard in America, and in the nineteenth century it still had considerable force. In the minds of most Northerners of the Civil War generation, democracy demanded independence, not only political but economic; it demanded the maximum diffusion of self-reliant habits; and it demanded that the distance between the status of a rich man and a poor man not be so immense as to corrupt the one or provoke the other to a desperate rebellion. Measured against these standards, the new economic order seemed degrading and profoundly subversive. "To put a man upon wages, is to put him in the position of a dependent," Samuel Eliot wrote in the *Journal of Social Science* for 1871; the longer he holds the position, the more his capacities for independent judgment atrophy, and "the less of a man, in fine, he becomes." To Godkin, by the same token, the mass of factory hands seemed simply helpless conscripts in the economic battle, subject to every whim of their commanding chiefs. No lasting democracy could be made out of conscripts and servants, he worried. A system in which a few great capitalists held the fortunes of a small army of operatives in their hands seemed to him fundamentally "hostile to free government."[5]

The convictions of many an erstwhile Jeffersonian collapsed in the war, but Northerners skeptical about democracy had other, equally impelling grounds for fearing the regime of wages. Shiftlessness was one of these. Frederick Law Olmsted, traveling through the South in the 1850s, wrote for many of his fellow Northerners in describing his revulsion at what seemed to him the leering, deceitful laziness of the slave work gangs. By stripping the slaves of any monetary interest in their work, Olmsted was convinced, the Southern masters had molded a labor force of systematic shirkers. But if that were the case, would hired laborers behave differently, particularly those working for a straight, unbending daily wage? The economists' answer was discouraging. It was "in the constitution of things," Francis A. Walker wrote in the late nineteenth century's leading treatise on wages, that the wage worker "not only will not, he can not, being a man, labor as he would for himself."[6] Here, then, was a second dilemma. The farm and workshop economy had been able by and large to ignore the question of incentives. But when the profits were another man's, what was there to keep employees conscientiously at their work?

Last and most alarming of all was the threat of conflict. Slaves not only shirked, or so it seemed, but occasionally in the dead of night they burned the barns and slit their master's throat. Again the parallel with wage working seemed to many Northerners uncomfortably close. Industrialization was a turbulent process that littered the years after the Civil War with strikes and conflict. From the railroad upheavals of 1877 to the massive steel strike of 1919, through Homestead, Pullman, Lawrence, and a host of less famous but equally bitter contests, wage earners and employers collided with a violence that deeply disturbed middle-class Northerners. "Is it peace or war?" Washington Gladden asked in the wake of the eight-hour strikes of 1886, and he concluded it was industrial war, "all along the line."[7] In their concern, many Northerners laid the blame on the system of employment that arrayed class against class and set masters and men in perpetual contest over the division of the wealth they jointly produced. In anxious nostalgia they looked back to an earlier, partly mythical age when all men seemed to have been in business for themselves and their interests made a simple harmony.

For all these reasons, the transition from a society that had spread self-employment remarkably widely to a society of massed wage earners was a troubled and, in many quarters, a reluctant one. Wage working violated the canons of a free society; it was inefficient; it was divisive and potentially disastrous. In the North of 1850, work was still, on the whole, something one did for oneself, a test of one's initiative that gave its direct economic reward. What masters a man had—the weather, prices, the web of commerce—were impersonal and distant. This was the moral norm, the bedrock meaning of free labor. Even as they built an economic structure that undercut it, Northerners found it hard to let go of that ideal upon which so much of their belief in work rested.

The classic answer to the dilemmas posed by wage working was the promise of upward mobility. Abraham Lincoln, whose own career was a compelling vindication of the success theme, gave the conviction its most enduring expression. "There is no permanent class of hired laborers among us," Lincoln told audiences in the late 1850s. "The prudent, penniless beginner in the world labors for wages awhile, saves a surplus with which to buy tools or land for himself, then labors on his own account another while, and at length hires another new beginner to help him.... If any continue through life in the condition of the hired laborer; it is not the fault of the system, but because of either a dependent nature which prefers it, or improvidence, folly, or singular misfortune."[8]

It would be difficult to exaggerate the ubiquity of this hireling-to-capitalist formula in the popular literature of the North. "In this free country no man endowed with average abilities need remain all his life poor," a writer in the *Atlantic Monthly* argued in 1886. "If he has thrift, self-restraint, and perseverance, he will pass from the ranks of labor to the ranks of capital." Twenty years later, John D. Rockefeller told an interviewer that the movement from laborer to captain of industry was still a "constant procession." "No boy, howsoever lowly—the barefoot country boy, the humble newsboy, the child of the tenement—need despair.... They have but to master the knack of economy, thrift, honesty, and perseverance, and success is theirs."[9] Much of what was published as guides to self-advancement was more cautious in its promises than this. In the end, most success writers advised that the true measure of wealth was to be found not in money or position but in character. Yet the titles the success writers chose for their often prosaic messages, like their mercilessly repetitive examples of poor boys who had risen to the top, radiated the hope of upward mobility. "Rising in the World," "Pushing to the Front," "The Secret of Success": the outward message of the success genre was that everyone with health and morals was an incipient capitalist.

Before the turn of the century, only a small minority of writers outside the working class were ready to conclude that that hope was fraudulent. One of them, the economist David A. Wells, warned as early as 1877 that the exhaustion of Western lands and the increasingly large amounts of capital required to enter business had made it far harder than before for the wage earner to rise into the ranks of employers and had rapidly accelerated that day when a man "born a laborer, working for hire, [will] never be anything but a laborer." Ten years later, Wells's fellow economist Richard T. Ely insisted that the day had come: "Every railroad president necessitates the existence of several thousand wage-receivers; every bank president presupposes clerks, book-keepers, and others in subordinate position; every merchant of wealth requires numerous salaried employés. By no human possibility can this be otherwise."[10]

Though their voices fell largely unheard amid the paeans to success, the skeptics, as it turns out, were more accurate social observers than the optimists who so grossly outnumbered them. Editors and interviewers never tired of the stories of the Andrew Carnegies and Henry Fords who worked their way out of the factories and farms to the pinnacles of economic power. Their very presence seemed to ratify the dream of the spectacular mobility possible in America. But business historians showed long ago that for all their conspicuousness there were never as many such men among the captains of the nation's leading industries as there were sons of business and professional men, born several rungs up the occupational ladder.[11]

The essential test of the hireling-to-capitalist formula, however, was not a wage earner's chance of rising to the very top but his chances of working his way into the ranks of the self-employed, and these are much more difficult to ascertain. The crudest measure is simply to count the proportion of wage earners in the working population. Even that is not a task that affords precision, for the census takers did not ask a worker if he were self-employed, and there are large and important occupational cate-gories in which wage earners, self-employed home workers, and small proprietors were indifferently counted alike. But if it is a crude measure, it is nonetheless a revealing one. In 1870, when the first complete occupational census was made, between 60 and 70 percent of the Northern labor force worked in occupations where a master was the rule. In an essentially agricultural state like Indiana, probably half the labor force was self-employed. But where industrialization had begun to take hold, the odds against self-employment were significantly worse. In Pennsylvania in 1870, between 65 and 75 percent of the population worked for someone else; in Massachusetts the proportion was between 75 and 85 percent. For all the brave talk of Northern free labor, to Yankeeize the South in the Reconstruction years—to make Southern ideas of industry conform to those of Massachusetts, as Governor Horatio Seymour urged in 1866—was to make four out of five workers employees. These were not insurmountable odds, of course, but they were formidable enough to suggest that the insistent repetition of the mobility formulas involved a good deal of wishful thinking.[12]

A generation after 1870, in fact, it took a dull reader of the rags-to-riches literature to miss the accumulating signs of strain. One of these was a kind of nervous tic that set in around the turn of the century, a need to rebut the suspicion that the immensely increased scale of business had closed off opportunities. "Are Young Men's Chances Less?" the articles began to ask. And though the answer was still no, the publicists of mobility increasingly put their argument in terms of the room available at the top while saying less and less about the chances of the manual laborer at the bottom.

A second, more portentous sign of strain between the mobility ideal and the reality of widespread wage earning was the displacement in the success formulas of work—"homely clad, old-fashioned Industry," as Henry Ward Beecher had called it. Businessmen, by and large, kept up the old chant. The key to making one's way in life, Horace G. Burt, head of the Union Pacific railroad, insisted in 1902, was simply "Application. Work, work, work, work, work, work."[13] But after the turn of the century, professional success writers were not so sure. As early as 1872, William Mathews's *Getting on in the World* had hinted that "mere industry and economy" were no longer enough. What success under modern conditions demanded was decision, self-advertisement, energy, and aggressiveness.[14] Others came more slowly to much the same conclusions. Orison Swett Marden was

the preeminent self-advancement publicist of the progressive
years, author of some thirty books on the theme and editor of a
magazine, *Success*, which at its peak in 1906 rivaled the muck-
raking *McClure's* in sales. In the 1890s Marden's advice consisted
of the familiar virtues of punctuality, honesty, character, and
hard work. But by the end of the first decade of the twentieth
century, Marden had turned from industry to what contemporaries called "New Thought," the faith that mental power
ruled the world. "Change the Thought, Change the Man," he
urged. "Thousands of people in this country have *thought*
themselves away from a life of poverty." Success depended on
confidence, on banishing the poverty idea; it came to the man
who could energize himself into the prosperity state of mind.[15]
Marden's apostasy was not the only straw in the wind. At the
same time and to still more readers than Marden ever acquired,
the *Saturday Evening Post* began to push the rewards of grit,
brashness, willpower, and what John G. Cawelti has called that
inner "SOMETHING." Finally, to round out the novel advice,
Marden and others all but retreated from the counsel of self-
employment in favor of a salaried foothold in the new business
bureaucracies. When in 1916 the success writer B. C. Forbes
asked New York's leading banker, Frank A. Vanderlip, what he
looked for in a twenty-five-thousand-dollar-a-year man, Vanderlip's answer was not self-reliance but "personality; or shall I say
charm?"[16]

Self-confidence, willpower, salaries, and charm: these were
messages not for factory hands thinking about a business of their
own but for clerks and salesmen struggling to make their mark in
a personality-dominated world of buyers, managers, and bureau-
crats. This new white-collar audience was the one *Success* and the
Saturday Evening Post chose as their own, terrifically eager for
the reassurance and advice Marden and George H. Lorimer gave
it, ready for lessons in everything from the secret of mental
efficiency to pointers on gaining a raise. Well before the First
World War, most of that counsel could be summed up in the
word "pep," the ubiquitous slogan of the 1920s that set the seal
on the transition of middle-class America from an economy of
things to an economy of competing personalities.

But the concentration of the success literature on the middle
classes was, in fact, virtually as old as the genre itself. Nineteenth-

century success writers talked of many avenues to the top, but the one they were most familiar with was the mercantile path that led from clerk to junior partner to merchant capitalist. This was conspicuously true of the success fiction written for boys. Horatio Alger's heroes were farm lads and street urchins pushing their papers under the noses of potential merchant patrons, but he almost never started a boy in a factory, and on the rare occasions when he did so he could only think to have the lad fired or laid off at the outset, as if desperate for some contrivance to expel him as quickly as possible into the world where a man could make his mark.[17] Outside the realm of boys' stories, the advice offered a factory hand was rarely more helpful or more specific than this. Success writing was many things, but it was not a literature aimed at the industrial wage earner. It was a way of preaching lessons in character, an inspiration for bank clerks and schoolboys, and a reassurance to middle-class parents that, despite the expansion of business enterprise, opportunities for their children had not disappeared. It was part of its antebellum legacy, often at odds with the elitist tendencies of the post–Civil War years, that it did all this through a democratic logic that disguised the narrowness of the genre—not by clarifying the advantages of parentage and income but by insisting than any man, even the lowliest, could get ahead.

It would be hard to discount that faith, despite the pressures that by the early twentieth century had forced it into novel and ambiguous forms. For every Vanderlip concerned with personality there were a dozen businessmen ready to testify that it was work that really counted in life. For every critic who puzzled over the census returns there were a dozen writers ready to reaffirm Lincoln's faith that there was no permanent class of hired laborers in America. When in 1903 United Mine Workers president John Mitchell announced that "the average wage earner has made up his mind that he must remain a wage earner" and had "given up the hope of the kingdom to come, when he himself will be a capitalist," he evoked a storm of middle-class protest.[18]

Yet a number of Americans found the natural workings of the economy too slow, too uncertain, or too narrowly gauged to answer their anxieties about wage working. Braver than the success publicists, they turned upon economic life, and the factories in particular, to try to retrieve the antebellum ideal of the independent workman. Though divided on an immense number of issues, all of them hoped, in the face of industrial change, to find a formula that would make the industrial worker in fact a petty capitalist. Their story leads down divergent and somewhat tangled paths, marked with defeats and crippling compromises. The industrial reformers themselves were never very numerous. But their cures repeatedly touched a popular nerve, setting off anxieties hidden below the outward confidences of their age. In their wrestling with the question of wage employment, one catches what the success writers tried so hard to paper over: the unsettling presence of the factories in a society committed to the free labor ideal.

In the immediate aftermath of the Civil War, the idea of reversing the economic forces that pushed toward wage working seemed to many Northerners neither complicated nor remote. If a single worker could no longer realistically aspire to a business of his own, what prevented workers collectively from pooling their resources and banding together in cooperative workshops where they could jointly determine the policies and share as partners in the joint profits? In hindsight the idea seems a futile gesture, flung in the teeth of the trend toward a tighter, more hierarchical industrial order. But hindsight, rarely just to history's failed causes, can be a misleading guide. In the 1860s and 1870s the workshop economy seemed still strong enough, the idea of a life spent at wage working still sufficiently new and threatening, to give the cooperative idea an appeal that cut across conventional lines of class and ideology.

The chief proponents of the cooperative idea were skilled workers—men who harbored hopes of self-employment and watched the chances slip away before them under the pressures of economic and technological change. In the 1830s and 1840s groups of tailors, shoemakers, hatters, and other journeymen had turned to the idea of producers' cooperatives in hopes of forestalling the inroads of merchant capitalists into the urban workshop economy. After the Civil War the hope spread and intensified through the proselytizing first of the National Labor Union in the 1860s and then of the Knights of Labor, the leading labor organization of the 1880s. The Federation of Organized Trades and Labor Unions, the predecessor of the American

Federation of Labor which organized in 1881, held aloof from the cooperative enthusiasm, but it was the first serious claimant to national leadership of the labor movement that did so. Well into the 1890s, Terence Powderly, Grand Master Workman of the Knights, continued to praise cooperation as the first essential step toward banishing "that curse of modern civilization—wage slavery." To William Sylvis, president of the Iron Molders Union and the dominant labor figure of the 1860s, cooperation was simply "the great idea of the age."[19]

Cooperators like Sylvis never held unchallenged sway over the labor movement. Between advocates of political action and of pure and simple trade unions, between the rival socioeconomic formulas of the Greenback-Labor Party, the Eight-Hour Leagues, the single taxers, and a contending set of socialisms, between the cooperators and those who, having given up the hope of self-employment, rested their ultimate faith in shorter hours and decent wages, labor organizations in the generation after the Civil War were divided between an extraordinary number of competing and overlapping counsels. But the cooperators were both prominent and enthusiastic in their faith. Where British workers by the 1860s had concluded that the way to the cooperative commonwealth was first to organize a cooperative store and upon its slowly accumulating profits enter cautiously into the production of goods, American cooperators were eager to move immediately to the cooperative workshop. The time was "not remote when the co-operative principle will carry on the great works and improvements of the age," the National Labor Union's manifesto of 1867 assured the nation's workingmen. "It will build all our cities, dig our ores, fill the land with the noise of loom and spindle."[20] In that day to come, cooperation promised the worker the full value of his toil, returned in a far simpler, more compellingly obvious way than any of the other schemes competing for workers' attentions.

But still more prominently and effectively, cooperation promised independence. Under the regime of the cooperative workshop, the repeated phrase ran, workers would be their own bosses and every man his own employer. There is only one way "by which the toiling millions can protect themselves from the unjust claims and soul-crushing tyranny of capital," a writer in the labor press insisted in the 1860s, and that "is for themselves to become capitalists."[21] Entrepreneurial hopes and anticapitalist despair both mingled in the cooperative vision. But for workers unreconciled to dependency, the idea of jointly buying out their bosses held a compelling logic. Cooperation was a faith for workers caught in the transition to an economy of hired men, far enough down the road to the new economic order to have learned its costs, yet not so far as to make the simplest route back seem impossible.

What is more surprising is that the post–Civil War cooperative movement had the endorsement of far more conservative Northerners as well. One of the most prominent of these was E. L. Godkin. In the terminology of the nineteenth century, Godkin was a "liberal"—filled from his English university years, as he later recalled, "with the teachings of the *laissez-faire* school."[22] As the moving spirit of the *Nation* from 1865 to 1899, he used that small but influential journal to drum home the truisms of classical political economy to his adopted countrymen, and in that cause he found occasion to rail at virtually all the measures embraced by workingmen: the eight-hour-day crusade, the practical ethics of trade unionism, the "twaddle" of labor-reform conventions, and the devious disguises of socialism. In 1867 he told his readers that it was impossible to read the program of the National Labor Union "without pain."[23] But in that same year he embraced the workingmen's cooperative cause as his own.

The convergence was not as odd as it seemed at first glance. Part of what drew Godkin to the cooperative idea was exactly the same kind of shudder at the directions of economic change as ran through the ranks of the labor organizations. In contrast to Adam Smith, who turned laissez-faire into a formula for economic growth, Godkin's creed, like Jefferson's, was defensive and preservative, committed not to progress but to liberty. He watched the farms retreat west with concern, lamenting the passing of their lessons in industry and self-reliance and the eclipse of "the only man, as society is at present constituted, ... who can be said to be really master of himself." Though eventually the Granger and Populist uprisings broke that faith in rural virtue, Godkin never became a friend of what he called the "tumors" of industry, forced under the artificial conditions of a protective tariff. Large-scale industrial capitalism was not compatible with the liberty of yeoman farmers, and if not all Godkin's fellow liberals were consistent enough to see it, he was too clear-sighted in the faith to miss the fact. A society of massed wage earners and a few distant, arbitrary employers could not, by definition, maximize the scope of individual freedom. Even to take the first step, to make a man a hired employee, Godkin argued, was to shackle his freedom, to make him "a servant, in the old sense of the word,—a person who has surrendered a certain portion of his social independence, who has become dependent . . . 'for his bread and butter,' on another person's approval."[24]

It was at this impasse that Godkin seized with relief upon the cooperative idea. Here was a solution to the labor question fitted to his laissez-faire faith, a revolution in the name of freedom that infringed on no property rights and needed no help from the state. But it was characteristic of the Janus faces of the cooperative idea that it served Godkin's anxieties no less well. In the late 1860s and early 1870s, as the labor organizations moved on to agitate for shorter working hours laws and currency inflation, Godkin urged the cooperative cause all the more strongly as an antidote to the threatening socialism he saw in the air. "The working-classes have constructed a political economy of their own," he worried. "You may deliver lectures . . . as much as you please," but "as long as their part in life consists simply in spending a certain number of hours every day in a factory, as a means of drawing a fixed sum of money at the end of every week, . . . they will perhaps listen to you, but they will always either misunderstand you or distrust you." In this light, the primary argument for the cooperative workshop became not liberty but education. It promised to place as many workers as possible in positions where they could "see for themselves where wages come from [and] what the necessities of capital are." It promised an object lesson in self-restraint and industry in the place of the strikes and communistic "blatherskite" Godkin saw gathering darkly around him. Cooperation promised, in short, to diffuse through the proletariat the experiences and sobered mental outlook of the bourgeoisie.[25] From Horace Greeley to Boston's Reverend Joseph Cook, ready to turn the Union army loose upon the ringleaders of socialism, others said the same. But it was Godkin, turning the cooperative idea over and over in his columns for close to a decade, balancing a stubborn Jeffersonian faith in liberty with an aversion to both the new factory magnates and the restless hirelings they ruled, who best caught the middle-class appeal of the cooperative movement.

In the end, the practical results of the cooperative idea never matched the hopes that either the labor organizations or the laissez-faire moralists like Godkin invested in it. The actual number of cooperative workshops established in the generation after the war can only be guessed at, but it was not nearly enough to set the factory system back on its heels. In Massachusetts, a seedbed of cooperative interest, one careful observer counted twenty-five active cooperative workshops in 1875. Sylvis's iron molders managed to start about a dozen cooperative workshops, and the Knights in their day began something over one hundred.[26] For all the enthusiasm surrounding the idea, the typical cooperative venture was a product of duress, organized by workers who had been pressed hard enough by a strike or lockout to gamble what savings they had in an attempt to preserve their jobs and self-respect. Chronically short of capital, only a handful of the workshops and small factories lasted more than a few troubled years, and many of those that did eventually degenerated into hiring wage hands of their own. A phenomenon of skilled, organized workers, practical cooperation scarcely touched the factory hand at all.

Even as an idea in the air, the rationales for cooperation tugged in directions divergent enough to preclude any chance of an alliance among its proponents. Cooperation was a step toward the socialist commonwealth and a means of making a nation of capitalists; it was an expansion of liberty and a synonym for the old-fashioned virtues of thrift and industry. Cooperation had the endorsement of the Lassallean socialists and of the high priest of economic individualism, Herbert Spencer, as well. Yet if the economic obstacles to cooperation were formidable and its adherents splintered, if the upshot of two decades of talk was merely a struggling remnant of cooperative ventures, at the time cooperation seemed a serious possibility. Proposing to emancipate the wage earner by driving wage working out of business, the idea had a protean appeal. In 1872 Charles Francis Adams, Jr., maintained with justice that it was "the one aspect of the labor question which now excites a well-nigh universal interest."[27]

Two decades later, however, there was barely anything left of the cooperative enthusiasm. Godkin continued to insist that it was the only solution to the labor problem with "even a flavor of rationality about it," but he had all but given up any hope of its realization. The Knights of Labor ballooned and then collapsed in the second half of the 1880s, and with the Knights' demise the cooperative idea lost its last major forum in the labor movement. A few stubborn advocates tried to keep the vision alive. The reformer Henry D. Lloyd stumbled across the flourishing co-operative movement in England in the late 1890s and embraced its program as a form of practical socialism, and he was joined in the cause by a small group of eccentric cooperators who used the radical *Arena* as their outlet. But the verdict of the pessimists—that cooperation was "too old-fashioned a subject" to interest the modern social reformer, as one of them lamented in 1889—had the greater measure of truth to it. [28]

Yet the doubts about wage employment remained, and in the collapse of the cooperative movement they spilled over into new formulas with as anxious energies as into the old. None of the schemes that replaced the cooperative ideal in the mid-1880s recaptured either the simplicity of that first counterattack on the wage system or the immense diversity of its adherents. The new crusades were strictly middle-class affairs, and in essential ways the aims of the new formulas were more limited than before. From cooperation to profit sharing and from profit sharing to piecework and its derivatives, one can watch accommodation to the growing presence of the factories, elitism, and allegiance to new ideas of efficiency all stealthily eat away at the reformers' standards of a worker's independence. But if their aims had narrowed, their earnestness had not. Through a new set of formulas a new generation of Northerners tried once more to haul the terms of industrial employment into some sort of rough harmony with the steadily retreating free labor ideal.

Of the schemes that filled the vacuum left by the cooperative movement, profit sharing came closest to a lineal relationship, both in its formula and in the enthusiasms it generated among the middle-class moralists. It was, in fact, cooperation split in half in a Solomon-like judgment; dismissing cooperative manage-ment as unworkable, the plan proposed to transform wage employment by the more limited device of adding to the wage earner's pay a share in the joint profits. This was not a new idea when it burst into prominence in the mid-1880s. John Stuart Mill had endorsed the scheme long before on the basis of several

French examples. Godkin, too, had written of the plan, and in the post–Civil War decade a handful of Northern industrial manufacturers had tried to put it into practice.

What propelled profit sharing into a minor crusade, however, was the combination of a book and what seemed to anxious contemporaries a labor revolt. The book was Sedley Taylor's *Profit-Sharing*, an Englishman's detailed description of European modifications of the wage system, which arrived in America in 1884 at the beginning of a short but severe industrial depression.[29] Even by late nineteenth-century standards, the next two years were particularly turbulent ones, as wage cutting triggered a wave of highly publicized strikes and boycotts, culminating in May 1886 in a massive, nationwide demand for the eight-hour day. All of this had already made middle-class Northerners acutely nervous when, at the height of the eight-hour-day crusade, a bomb thrown into the ranks of a police squad in Chicago's Haymarket Square turned nervousness into the full-blown hysteria of an anarchist scare. In the anxious search for measures of industrial peace that followed, editors, ministers, and economists seized hopefully upon the promises of profit sharing. The plan was taken up in books and in state bureau of labor statistics reports, discussed prominently in the national magazines, and worked into the plots of stories and novels. When in 1892 a handful of manufacturers, several of the nation's leading economists, and the chief of the United States Bureau of Labor organized the American Association for the Promotion of Profit Sharing, there were few well-read middle-class Americans who needed to be told about the idea.[30]

Profit sharing originated as an incentive device. In Sedley Taylor's argument, to share the profits was in the end to multiply them by so stimulating employees that their better, more conscientious work more than paid back the dividends they received. American advocates of profit sharing rarely failed to emphasize the point, but what turned them to profit sharing was not this so much as an intense longing for industrial harmony. Rising out of the turbulence of the 1880s, striking its deepest response in those who felt themselves caught in the nerve-racking crossfires of industrial unrest, the American profit-sharing argument was shot through with the hope that, in giving workers an interest "beyond wages" in their employer's business, profit sharing would forge an effective union between masters and men and rebind the interests that the scale of industry seemed to have torn apart so disastrously. The leading American advocate of the plan, Nicholas P. Gilman, abandoned the term "profit sharing" for "industrial partnership," and in doing so he only reiterated the theme that dominated the profit-sharing tracts and fables. No other device promised so surely to dismantle the present "war footing" in industry, Carroll D. Wright maintained in 1886 as head of the Massachusetts Bureau of Statistics of Labor. Under profit sharing, a worker "thinks of himself always as a proprietor and dignifies himself as such.... It changes the whole current of [his] thought and feeling and economic conduct." Where jostling, discordant interests had been the rule, profit sharing created "a moral organism, ... a community of purpose and endeavor."[31]

Partnership, however, did not imply equality. Just as the profit sharers' nervous concern with social harmony reflected the pressures of their time and class, so too did their rejection of Jefferson's creed for one more compatible with the growing consolidation of industry and the increasing concentration of alien immigrants in the factory ranks. When the profit sharers were pressed for an example of what they meant, their minds repeatedly ran backward to the old-fashioned fishing schooner, where captain and crew had worked together, both taking their pay in shares of the catch, yet where the lines of authority were clear and unbending. A few of the profit-sharing propagandists dissented from this transparent stress on industrial captaincy. One of them, N. O. Nelson, a St. Louis businessman and a patriarch of the movement, maintained that the essential point of profit sharing was to prepare the way for pure workers' cooperatives, and in the 1890s he tried without success to induce his own employees to reorganize their departments as independent cooperative firms. But most advocates of profit sharing had only scorn for the cooperators' efforts to put the bottom rail on top. According to Gilman, the moving spirit of the American Association for the Promotion of Profit Sharing, a dividend on profits meant no diminution of the "aristocratic principle" in industry, no breach in the processes of natural selection that singled out the entrepreneur for his responsibilities. The account books were the employer's alone to keep and the terms of the partnership his to decide. In this "thoroughly conservative" reform, Gilman argued, the employer was "just as much of an autocrat" as before.[32]

In all, profit sharing offered an immensely tantalizing vision.

To workers it promised a bonus and a partner's stake in the business; to society at large, a lasting industrial peace; to employers, profits and autocracy. Elitist and reformative, insistently hard-headed and shot through with nostalgia, the idea cut very close to the awkward compound of dreams and anxieties that middle-class Northerners harbored in the Victorian years.

In practice, however, profit sharing staggered under its heavy burden of hopes. As an incentive device that blurred together the efforts of conscientious and indifferent workers alike, that tried to sustain a worker's interest between remote dividend days, and that, no matter how hard the employees worked, could not pay off in hard times, the profit-sharing formula was badly flawed, and most manufacturers soon concluded that it was a failure. As a nervously introduced strike-forestalling measure profit sharing had more success, but it was too often too blatant in its intentions to overcome the suspicions of the workingmen's organizations. A few prominent labor spokesmen welcomed the idea in the 1880s; twenty years later, organized labor had concluded that in essence profit sharing was a bribe for docility and substandard wages.[33]

Thus the record of practical profit sharing was a bare shadow of the force of the idea. Between 1886 and 1889, when profit-sharing articles could be found everywhere in the middle-class press, some thirty firms installed profit-sharing plans, the Procter and Gamble soap-works outside Cincinnati the most prominent among them. But if this was the bud of a more substantial growth, the depression of the 1890s ruthlessly lopped it off, and by 1896, when Gilman's profit sharing association discouragedly closed down its journal, the number of surviving profit-sharing plans had dwindled to twelve. Experiments continued, a rush of them after 1914, when industrial unrest, the drying up of plentiful immigrant labor by the outbreak of war, and the specter of radicalism, this time in the form of the Industrial Workers of the World, repeated the conditions of the mid-1880s. Still, in the early 1920s there were probably not many more than one hundred profit-sharing firms, the majority of them small, personally managed companies of a few hundred workers.[34] "Profit sharing is in the air," Nelson had maintained bravely in 1911. "It has the approval of nearly everybody except the labor unions and the employers."[35]

Yet Nelson was not simply whistling in the wind. If practical profit sharing, like cooperation, proved ineffectual in the contest with wage working, both the phrase "profit sharing" and the idea of some form of industrial partnership "beyond wages" possessed a stubborn, dogged inertia. In 1902 the U.S. Steel Corporation capitalized on the fact by seizing the name for a plan to make shareholders of its rank-and-file workers by assisting them in installment purchases of U.S. Steel stock. The steel corporation's scheme was not the first to attempt to integrate workers into the corporate structure through a shareholding device. With the growth of business incorporations, many of the profit-sharing firms turned from cash to special labor-stock dividends in their efforts to promote workers' loyalty. But the steel corporation's plan, launched amid overwhelmingly favorable publicity, eventually gathered far more influential imitators than the profit-sharing formula of the 1880s. In the uneasy years during and immediately after the First World War, stock-purchase plans proliferated among the nation's largest manufacturing corporations, until by 1927 almost two and a half million wage earners worked in firms that "shared the profits" on the steel corporation model.[36]

To some of the veterans of the movement, like Nelson, U.S. Steel's plan was not profit sharing at all, and by strict standards it was not. Yet what was remarkable about the stock-purchase plans was the extent to which their publicists returned to the familiar arguments of the profit sharers of the 1880s and even of the cooperators twenty years earlier to mine once more the concerns over wage working. George W. Perkins, the J. P. Morgan partner who devised the U.S. Steel plan, argued that an investment in the business not only made better and more conscientious workmen but made "real partners" of employees. "Gradually, as the employees in the organization become part owners in the business, you broaden and deepen their interest in their work," he maintained. "They begin to think and speak of the business as their business; they work for it as their business." Shareholding workers were no longer mere wage hands arrayed against the forces of capital but men with the feeling and responsibilities of "proprietorship." Others turned to the same language in their enthusiasm for the steel corporation's scheme. The *Review of Reviews* thought it "the best possible substitute for the abolition of small individual ownership." Andrew Carnegie, joining the chorus of praise from his retirement, hailed the move as the first step toward the eventual "reign of working-men proprietors," the "final and enduring solution of the Labor question."[37]

By most standards, the hopeful phrases were badly misplaced. Critics were quick to point out that no access to the seats of power came with stock ownership; no representative of the rank-and-file proprietors sat on the board of U.S. Steel or any of the corporations that imitated it. In several firms, the steel corporation among them, only select, loyal workers were eligible for the full assistance offered, and for the average production worker, in any case, the investment price was often well beyond reach. Samuel Gompers, speaking for the American Federation of Labor, called the new profit sharing still more "chimerical" than the old. Touted as a step toward partnership, in effect stock-purchase arrangements were an attempt to elicit allegiance from a corporation's most essential, skilled blue-collar workers by involving them in a long-term purchase arrangement forfeitable by strike.[38]

This awkward misfit between rhetoric and practice, in fact, plagued the profit-sharing movement throughout its career. Profit sharing was an "industrial partnership" between grossly unequal partners, an incentive device that did not work, a plan to bring about industrial peace that could not, as it turned out, successfully forestall strikes or win over the organizations of labor. Altogether the supposed iron link of the profit-sharing argument—that it was a formula that could alchemize wage working into something close to proprietorship—was never more than a tenuous gossamer thread. But to many of the North's preeminent moralists it did not seem so. While profit sharing contained an ample dose of empty and contrived rhetoric, theirs was a matter of sincere, if misplaced faith. They turned to profit sharing in hopes that it would, as it promised, go beyond wages and restore some of the conditions under which a man could feel he worked for himself. In that vision, thinned and compromised as it was, the free labor ideal kept up a persistent, nagging presence.

In 1887 the manufacturers, engineers, and industrial managers assembled at the annual meeting of the American Society of Mechanical Engineers listened to the case for profit sharing and, almost to a man, dismissed the idea as unworkable. Compared with those of the profit sharers, their concerns were forward-looking and crassly materialistic, and the profit-sharing plea took little root among them. And yet manufacturers and engineers, too, chafed restlessly at contemporary practices of wage employment. What preoccupied them above all was the system of payment for work by the day. Day wages seemed to them an open invitation to malingering, the root of most of their supervision problems, and one of the factories' most troubling diseconomies. But to men who, like Andrew Carnegie, were wont to boast that they had never sought refuge in a salary, the concern ran deeper still, tangled in morals as well as in questions of profit and loss. The daily wage seemed to manufacturers to cut the industrial world in two, sealing off the hired man from the higher, energized, risk-taking world of the entrepreneur. In their mind's eye, they held a vision of factories run not by the sweat and curses of foremen but by the natural laws of mutual self-interest, where initiative, work, and wages were brought into automatic accord by making every hand, in effect, an independent subcontractor. In the generation after 1880, while the profit sharers searched for an elusive partnership for wage workers, employers and engineers turned their own version of the free labor ideal upon the daily wage rate and with effort and painstaking ingenuity splintered it in pieces.

Piecework, of course, was not new to the nineteenth century. In the manufacture of shoes and clothing, piecework entered the trade with the putting-out system and moved with no essential break into the shops and factories. Similarly in the textile mills, where the output of a weaver or spinner was standardized and easily measured, piecework was virtually as old as the industry itself. Yet from common pick-and-shovel labor to the skilled work of the machine shop, most jobs seemed too varied and too hard to measure for anything but a straight daily wage. In the last quarter of the nineteenth century, however, employers began to expand the domain of piecework into areas it had never touched before. The railroad and locomotive repair shops were particularly aggressive innovators. The Pennsylvania Railroad, in a much-heralded move, converted its repair shops from day wages to piecework in the 1880s, and within the next twenty years most of the others followed. The Singer Sewing Machine Company installed a piece-rate system in 1883, Frederick W. Taylor did the same at the Bethlehem Steel works at the turn of the century, and soon afterward metal trades workers everywhere were protesting the incursions of piecework into their trades. The triumph of the incentive wage was never close to complete. Henry Ford, for one, an innovator in so many other ways, had no use for it. In the early 1920s a National Industrial Conference Board survey found a little more than half of production workers in manufacturing still paid on time wages, and the figure has not changed much since. But in the half-century before 1920, particularly in the metal and machinery trades, the shift toward piecework was momentous.[39]

The principal reason for employers' enthusiasm for the device was their conviction that it would elicit faster work. According to an unshakable bit of folk wisdom current among businessmen, piecework resulted in a 25 percent increase in output over day wages, and many manufacturers thought that too low an estimate. They had no doubts as to the cause. What piecework did, they insisted, was akin to emancipation—it turned wage servants into laborers free to set their own pace and their own rewards. This was the moral side to piecework that led one proponent to list it among the "minor forms" of cooperation and the profit sharing association to include it in their roster of causes. But unlike cooperation or profit sharing, piecework did not dilute the rewards for industry in a misty partnership. To each according to his work: piecework promised a realization of the oldest of free labor ideals. If, in industries where work was fitfully irregular, the system proved a convenient way to transfer much of the burden of the market to the workers, that was only just. The argument held that an industrial worker on piece wages was essentially in business for himself, an entrepreneur in overalls.[40]

Several obstacles stood in the way of this vision of a factory turned into a hive of independent businessmen. One of these was the opposition of many of the trade unions, though they were weak enough to make this the least formidable of a manufacturer's difficulties. The second was the sheer complexity of the conversion process. In a large factory, conversion to piecework involved carefully specifying hundreds of tasks, guessing at hundreds of rates, and investing in an unprecedented number of white-collar clerks and timekeepers. It was one of the paradoxical propositions into which the factories forced old ideas that to individualize payment it was necessary to bureaucratize work; to emancipate the industrial workers was to tighten the web of rules and schedules with which a factory ran. Finally, piecework repeatedly succumbed to the profit-maximizing mentality it tried so hard to establish, for when hard-working and ambitious employees succeeded in raising their output and wages significantly above the market norm, few manufacturers could resist the temptation to cut the piece rate and try to glean the same output more cheaply. Yet rate cutting, in turn, sabotaged the incentive to harder work, and it did not take many examples to teach workers the necessity of setting clandestine limits on their output if they were not simply to run faster and faster on a constantly accelerated treadmill. All these dilemmas were fully realized in the engineering profession by the mid-1880s, and they gave rise to a spate of new incentive wage schemes, most of them designed to minimize the temptations of rate cutting. But the man who took piecework's dilemmas by the horns was Frederick W. Taylor.

Taylor was a contradictory and controversial figure from the outset. He was the scion of a well-to-do and cultured Philadelphia family who rejected college for a foreman's job at a local metal-products plant, a man possessed by the idea of work who threw over his exemplarily industrious habits in middle age, an autocrat who played the part of a harmonizer of interests. The genesis of his ideas is buried below layers of self-serving memory. But as Taylor told and retold his own story in the burst of publicity he acquired after 1910, he had been propelled headlong into the incentives question at the very outset of his career through a long and exceptionally bitter contest with his piece-rate paid machinists over their refusal to perform what he considered a proper day's work. The experience left Taylor with an intense preoccupation with the malingering he called "soldiering." There was hardly a worker employed on any wage system "who does not devote a considerable part of his time to studying just how slowly he can work and still convince his employer that he is going at a good pace," Taylor insisted over and again. The fault lay not in piecework, he quickly concluded, but in the crude system of custom, guesswork, and contest by which piece rates were set. His answer was at once simple and audacious: to set incentive wages on a scientific basis by trying to find out as precisely as possible how long a normally efficient worker should take to do each job in a shop.[41]

The time-study experiments Taylor began in the early 1880s have haunted his reputation ever since. From the protests of workingmen to John Dos Passos's caustic description of Taylor winding his stopwatch on his deathbed, the picture of Taylor isolating jobs, severing them into job elements, and timing each of these to the hundredth of a second has long remained the most prominent ingredient in the Taylor legend—and with good reason. For time study was not only the outward symbol of Taylor's solution to the wage problem but the very heart of it, finally settling the question of a fair day's work and a fair piece rate at the impartial hands of science. By establishing standard job times immune from the workman's temptation to cheat and the employer's temptation to pare the rate, time study seemed to Taylor the perfect remedy for the primary defects of the incentive wage.

And yet none of this made sense unless there was a corresponding precision to work itself. Where others recoiled from the web of rules piecework entailed, Taylor plunged deeper and deeper into an attack on the stubborn randomness and variety with which workers habitually went about their jobs and deeper and deeper into measures to standardize work. The drive toward standardization, assuming a life of its own, ultimately turned into a relentless assault on the stubbornness of materials and the autonomy of men. From carrying pig iron to operating a complex machine tool, he was certain that there was "one best way" to do any mechanical task—a matter of science, painstaking experiment, and rigid enforcement. One of Taylor's favorite stories was of the revolution he wrought in the Bethlehem Steel coal yard: first determining the most efficient technique of wielding a shovel, then precisely calculating the optimum shovel load and optimum pattern of rest breaks, redesigning the shovels, carefully training the yard gangs, finally energizing them with a piecework formula, and in the end tripling the yard production. In the machine shop Taylor pushed standardization still further, splitting off the judgmental elements of a machinist's tasks—machine speed setting, tool grinding, even the adjusting of the drive belting—and handing them over to foremen, white-collar clerks, and blue-collar specialists. There was a curious blindness in this consuming search for exactitude, for what Taylor called the "keystone" of his system—time study—was in fact shot through with guesswork, although he disguised this by inventing seemingly precise percentage formulas to account for unexpected circumstances and by equipping his time-study men with carefully constructed record blanks, which were nevertheless of little help in fulfilling the perplexing burden Taylor imposed on them to separate the "necessary" from the useless motions. But Taylor never wavered in his faith that he had found a system of genuinely "scientific" management that substituted the "government of fact and law" for the old rule of "force and opinion."[42]

Taylor, in short, gathered up all the obsessional energies of the work ethic and set them loose in the factories, turning the drive for order and output against the traditions of craft and independence. His own need for systematization, as even his friendly biographers have agreed, verged on the neurotic. One of his followers, Frank. B. Gilbreth, deserted the stopwatch for the higher exactness of micromotion studies and the autostereochronocyclegraph; another, Carl Barth, dreamed of the day when all the world's machine tools would spin in precisely calibrated harmony. Thus when Taylor turned to industrial consulting after 1900 not many employers were willing to swallow his system whole. But Taylor was a master publicist, an influence on industrial management all out of proportion to his actual achievements as a consulting engineer and, for all his exaggerated penchant for system, in step with the essential trend of industrial management. The search for more precise means of payment went hand-in-hand with the creation of more precise jobs, increased economic incentive with narrower responsibilities, and the result everywhere was a steady stripping away of the worker's independence. Taylor himself loathed the word "initiative." "Under our system the workman is told minutely just what he is to do and how he is to do it; and any improvement which he makes upon the orders given him is fatal to success." His converts agreed; when a worker spent time thinking he was wasting his employer's money doing what others should do for him. It was not surprising that Taylor's own preferred wage system included a fine for failure to keep up the prescribed pace as large as the incentives for exceeding it. In a well-run factory, he argued, it was "absolutely necessary" for every man "to become one of a train of gear wheels."[43]

And yet even as Taylor proposed to "take all the important

decisions ... out of the hands of the workmen," he insisted that
no other management system so fully treated the worker as "an
independent personality."[44] This was more than sheer pose, and
to dismiss this side of scientific management is to miss half of
what drew so many of the nation's moralists so eagerly into
Taylor's camp. If they admired the orderliness that set off a
Taylorized plant like the Joseph & Feiss clothing works in
Cleveland from the squalid sweatshops and haphazardly managed
factories that surrounded it, and if they were compelled by
Taylor's vision of painlessly achieved increases in output, they
were equally drawn by scientific management's incorporation of
the old promise of upward mobility. Where most systems of
management dealt with masses of men, the core of Taylor's
message was to the individual, "telling him how, by special
efficiency, he can cut loose from the mass, and rise in wages and
position," one of Taylor's converts maintained. Louis Brandeis,
who more than anyone else was responsible for the burst of
interest in scientific management outside business circles after
1910, and Ida Tarbell, for whom Taylorism stood in spotless
contrast to the muck she had once raked over at Standard Oil,
said essentially the same thing. "Vague averages" and the
"endless repetition" of subdivided jobs ruled the industrial
world, C. B. Going of *Engineering Magazine* protested in 1912,
when the enthusiasm for Taylor's work was at its height. But
managers now had hold of "the germ of the great idea: *separate
consideration of every job, separate observation of every man;
standards and records—the beginnings of the restoration of
individuality.*"[45]

Jostling against the Taylorites' preoccupation with standardization and system, in short, were the old arguments and
economic individualism of the piecework debates. As long as they
took efficiency as their goal, the engineers could hardly escape
the dilemma, for efficiency demanded at once the maximum
release of individual energy and the maximum disposition of
those energies into precisely channeled outlets. Energy and order,
freedom and regimentation—the two elements warred not only
within Taylor's scheme but within virtually all the systematic
management efforts of the early twentieth century. And with
them two ingredients of the work ethic were set against each
other: the free labor ideal, forced into the language of rates and
incentives, and the drive for order and control, propelled no

longer by Protestant faith or Victorian nervousness but by an encompassing belief in efficiency and science. The engineers, Taylor at their head, insisted there was no necessary incompatibility between their double ideals. But in the new world that the Taylorites helped to make the old cluster of work values could no longer hold together, and in scientific management the pieces clattered audibly against each other. Out of the heart of the massed and anonymous workplaces, as they saw them, the engineers insisted that they had drawn a way of individualizing rewards, of unleashing the businessman latent in every worker, minutely calculating his energies, and rewarding them to a fraction of a penny. But it is one of the ironies of the fortunes of the free labor ideal in industrial America that they did all this only by paring down all else that comprised a wage earner's freedom to a ghostly sliver of its former self.

And yet the wage worker's freedom had been the nub of the matter all along. From the initial juncture of the slavery debates with the rapid spread of wage employment at the middle of the nineteenth century, the image of the slave had haunted all the factory reformers. The idea of a worker owned and mastered for all practical purposes by his employer, chained to his task without hope of profit or escape, violated all their convictions of what work should be. In some form or another, it was this fear that led the reformers to turn against the factories with their remedies and panaceas. Even the engineers talked of the "plain and simple slavery" of day labor. With the collapse of the cooperative enthusiasm, however, middle-class antagonists of the new work relations had settled for increasingly limited definitions of freedom. Impressed by the power of the factories and profoundly distrustful of the workers they wished to emancipate, they invested their hopes in a narrowly circumscribed stake in the profits or the limited entrepreneurship of piecework. The last serious reckoning with the issue of wage working—the "industrial democracy" crusade of the World War I years—was different. Buoyed by the tremendous, unspent optimism of the progressive era, it came back in a final burst of anxious recognition to the problem Godkin had posed long before to ask what place the hierarchical order of the factories had in a society committed to popular rule and individual freedom.

The phrase "industrial democracy," which erupted with such

potency at the end of the world war, had had earlier anticipa-
tions. Lyman Abbott, Henry Ward Beecher's successor at the
Christian Union, had seized on the term in the 1880s as the
antithesis of the "wages system," and he carried it through each of
the wage reforms of his day: cooperation, profit sharing, the steel
corporation's stock-purchase plan, and incentive pay formulas.
After the turn of the century, the phrase worked its way with
increasing frequency into the vocabulary of labor unionists and of
progressives like Louis Brandeis.[46]

But it was the world war—a combination of the war production
experience and the extraordinary postwar reconstruction hopes—
that touched off the industrial democracy crusade. The war
production experience itself was novel enough. With the wartime
government directly running the railroads and indirectly running
virtually everything else through its network of production agencies and administrators, labor and management representatives
cooperating on dozens of war labor boards, with Charles Schwab
of Bethlehem Steel heralding the day when labor would rule the
world and Samuel Gompers edging rapidly toward the businessman's creed of maximum production, the war seemed to have
changed the rules of industrial life. On top of this, fueling and
exaggerating the optimism, was the sense that the wartime
changes marked only the beginning of a major restructuring and
democratization of social life. The term "social reconstruction,"
imported from England in 1918, could be heard at virtually every
hand a year later as the National Catholic War Council, the
Protestant Federal Council of Churches, and the American
Federation of Labor joined scores of individual spokesmen in
announcing programs of sweeping postwar change. "The war has
shaken down about our ears an old order of things," the *Century*'s Glenn Frank wrote in 1919 in a conviction shared by many
of his countrymen. "The whole world is yeasty."[47]

The idea of reshaping the basic rules of industry in the name of
democracy blossomed in this fertile soil, as the expansive democratic rhetoric brought to a head the old doubts about wage
employment. Now that the citadels of autocracy and militarism
abroad had fallen, industrial feudalism and the industrial warfare it seemed to have spawned at home seemed all the more
anomalous and all the more dangerous. Woodrow Wilson, writing
from the Paris Peace Conference in May 1919, urged Congress

that the labor question was the most pressing concern before the nation and that it would fall only to "a new form and spirit to industrial organization"—a "genuine democratization of industry" that would give all those who worked the right "to participate in some organic way in every decision which directly affects their welfare or the part they are to play in industry." The churches, from Methodist to Catholic, endorsed the industrial democracy idea; editors opened their columns wide to its discussion; it was talked about in the steel mills and broadcast in the labor press; and it figured in virtually all the reconstruction plans of 1919.[48] The second Reconstruction was still a glimmer in the mind's eye in 1919 when Wilson's message gave shape to it, but its aims and rhetoric were as sweeping as those of the first—to democratize industry by transforming wage hands into industrial citizens, rules and policies into codetermined laws, and the factories themselves, somehow, into full-fledged industrial republics.

If there were hints to be sensed of the limits of the industrial democracy movement, they were not in the seriousness with which these ideas were considered, even by Americans of essentially conservative temper, in that suspended time between the end of the war and the jolting return to the hardpan of "normalcy"; they were in the confusion of programs struggling for the industrial democracy banner. For most businessmen, the democratization of industry meant the establishment of "works committees" where managers and elected employee representatives could meet to consider common problems of production and work standards and to discuss, and sometimes to settle, grievances. Committees of this sort mushroomed in the industrial democracy years, partly under the prodding and order of the National War Labor Board. From some two dozen companies employing works committees of some sort at the outset of the war, by the end of 1921 the number had risen to more than 200 firms employing almost 700,000 workers. In the minds of their government and business proponents, the works committees—or "employee representation plans," as they were eventually called in business circles—were more than simply a wartime efficiency measure; they amounted to a "revolution in industry," "an overthrow [of] absolute autocratic methods."[49] In the patriotic mood of the war the unions had agreed, and they continued through the 1920s to

endorse labor-management cooperation in efficiency and production. But by 1919 the American Federation of Labor had
concluded that the generally toothless and easily intimidated
works committees were a snare and a cooptation and had planted
the standard of industrial democracy over an aggressive organization drive in the steel mills and an equally aggressive series of
hours and wages strikes throughout the unionized industries.

*other
indust.
demo.
plans*

In addition to the company unions and the invigorated labor
unions, moreover, there were a score of other versions of the
industrial democracy ideal. The socialists called for the national-
ization of industry under the phrase; the railroad unions, in a
plan drafted by Glenn Plumb, pressed for joint worker, management, and public control of the nation's utilities and businesses,
together with some form of profit sharing. Others called for
profit sharing pure and simple, for cooperatives, for employee
representation on corporation boards of directors, for worker-
elected foremen, or for the system of joint grievance committees
and arbitration boards that had already gained a foothold in the
clothing industry. The hunger for industrial reconstruction generated its own cast of heroes. John Leitch became a figure of
national importance in 1919 for having thrown out bosses,
foremen, and wage hands at a dozen small factories and installed
cabinets, senates, and houses of representatives in their place.
Skeptical observers maintained that nothing had really changed,
but Leitch claimed fantastic increases in production under the
plan as well as a new spirit to industrial organization. There were
a dozen other firms, too, whose stories were in the air, from the
Filene department store in Boston, where employees set the store
rules, to the Dutchess Bleachery in the Hudson River Valley,
where three elected workers and three company officials sat
together as the Board of Management.[50]

Which of these was truly industrial democracy was no easy
question. From the outset, proponents of the movement worried
that its principal slogan threatened to degenerate into cant.
After the experience of 1919, during which at least a quarter of a
million workers were organized into company unions while four
million workers walked out on strike, both in the name of
"industrial democracy," the journalist Samuel Crowther scoffed
that the term was "easily the most ecumenically satisfying phrase
now at large."[51] Yet something more than sheer opportunism

impelled socialists, trade unionists, progressives, and business-men toward the common slogan. Where the cooperators had urged secession from the factories and the engineers and profit sharers had tinkered with the methods of a worker's rewards, the industrial democracy plans all looked toward reconstruction of the factories on essentially political and constitutional lines. Somewhere between independence and servitude they hoped to create something akin to industrial citizenship. It was this nerve that John Leitch touched so effectively with his senates and houses of representatives, his industrial constitutionalism, and his factory patriotism. How it would come about was unclear, but somehow the industrial democracy advocates hoped to enfranchise the wage earner, to construct a web of rights, responsibilities, and interlocking authorities that would join employers and employees into a common enterprise and, in doing so, finally break down the old troubling divide between them. "No nation can endure as a nation predominantly of hired men," insisted Father John A. Ryan, author of the Catholic bishops' statement on industrial democracy.[52] Splintered as it was, its practice often a bare shadow of its rhetoric, the industrial democracy crusade represented a last gathering up of this old ideal.

Yet the crusade sputtered out almost before it had fairly begun. Late in 1920, a businessman asked Glenn Frank of the *Century* if he would set out short definitions of the new terms that seemed to barrage him everywhere: copartnership, trade parliaments, syndicalism, guild socialism, philosophical anarchism, works councils, industrial democracy. "When these things are mentioned, I look wise, as the rest do, and manage to carry my part of the conversation." But there was hardly one of them he or his acquaintances could carefully describe. "The average talk about these things," he noted, "sticks to glittering generalities."[53] Frank obliged with articles on guild socialism and industrial democracy and then dropped the series, and the earnest beginning and abortive halt made a fitting symbol for the whole crusade. Many forces combined to topple the idea: the strikes of 1919 and the red scare and aggressive antiunion drive that followed hard on their heels, the postwar depression that began late in 1920, and the general deflation of progressive ideals that was visible even earlier. None of the proponents of the industrial democracy idea were strong enough to withstand the pressures.

Aside from the socialist minority, most workingmen were far more interested in steady, well-paid employment than in the control of industrial enterprise, and the primary issues they brought to the works councils were distinctly employee concerns: discipline, grievances, wages and hours, and working conditions. Gompers himself, in step with the trade unions, confessed he had long ago given up thinking about what might eventually supplant the wage system.[54] Businessmen in their turn were eager to see the revolution stop with advisory works committees. As for Congress, it voted down the Plumb plan in 1920, and it left the task Wilson had urged on it of serving as a clearinghouse for new ideas of industrial government to the slender resources of the Russell Sage Foundation. The ideal of the economically independent worker could still vex and trouble Northerners, but it could no longer of itself, outside the extraordinary conditions of the war years, sustain an attack on the industrial system work-eager Northerners had built. In conflict, generalities, and disinterest the crusade fell apart, and by 1921, as his articles ground to a halt, Glenn Frank knew it was over.

From cooperatives to industrial democracy, the remedies for wage working had led to a disparate set of answers. Between the simple mutualism of the joint-stock workshop and the elaborate wartime schemes for industrial representation, between the organic ideal of the profit sharers and scientific management's atomism, there loomed important differences, carrying in them something of the story of industrialization's transformation of a simple, still highly individualistic economy into one of complex, often freedom-crowding interdependence. And yet for all the practical differences in the wage schemes that had caught the public's eye, there was an extraordinary overlap in both language and personnel. Lyman Abbott was not unique in carrying the same hopes through more than one of the causes. Procter and Gamble had gradually expanded its profit sharing plan to include a stock purchase arrangement, employee representation, and the election of employee corporate directors. The Yale and Towne lockworks, another restless innovator, took its measures serially, moving from profit sharing to piecework to scientific management to works councils—each of them, in the language of the day, a step "beyond wages."

What bound the causes together was an unwillingness to let go of the idea that work, if it was to be worthwhile, required the self-direction of the worker. The antislavery men, for all their opportunism, had insisted on the point. But as the factories swallowed the workshops, gathering up wage hands in ever larger numbers, the subsequent assaults on wage working had amounted essentially to a series of anxious moments of recognition. Repeatedly the moralists measured the industrial plants against their ideals of independence, found them wanting, and tilted against them with their reformative hopes. Most of those hopes themselves were severely compromised from Godkin's and Sylvis's day, as the moralists tried to juggle their ideals of freedom with their still-stronger impulses toward progress and efficiency. Even then, for all the popular interest they generated, they could not make work and their ideals of work hold together.

What was left of the free labor vision in 1920 was not very encouraging. The percentage of wage earners in the population was only modestly larger than it had been in 1870, but that disguised the push of increasingly large scale enterprise everywhere, the world of middle-class occupations not excepted. Already by the turn of the century obituaries had been read for the small businessman and the traits of sturdy independence he had represented. Life for the new salariate would be gentler and more secure than for the old-time businessman, the critics acknowledged, but they could not dismiss the concern that it would not forge character as before. Farming held out well past 1920 as a steadily shrinking island of individual enterprise, but even there in 1920 only half the men age twenty-five and over engaged in agriculture owned the farms they worked. As tenants or farm laborers, the rest were—like most of their countrymen—in one way or another hired men. [55]

As for the remedies for wage working, the record was mixed. There was a new class of employee stockholders, though it was a moot point whether their investments had essentially changed their hireling status. There were company unions of uncertain promise and, a decade and a half around the corner, the consolidation of collective bargaining where workers and managers would finally face each other power for power by admitting that they faced each other, fixed and permanently, as employers and employees. Most important were the systematizing legacies of the engineers, harnessing a quest for order, once largely turned inward to the self, to the demands of maximum production. Everywhere wage schedules had grown elaborate and precise, just as work itself had been split and rationalized. Finally, still to be heard above the din of the factories were the trumpetings of a new generation of success writers. Long after 1920 they would continue to play upon the old theme of the independence waiting for any man really willing to grasp it. But in the face of all the rest, their tunes, though brassier, could not reassure as before.

"Mechanicalized" Men 3

But the second way by which competitive commerce destroys our mental wealth is yet worse:
it is by the turning of almost all handicraftsmen
into machines.

William Morris,
"Art, Wealth, and Riches" (1883)

Recognition of industrialization's transforming effects on work
came not as a sudden flash of insight but as a series of
reckonings. Prodded by the slavery debates, the keepers of the
work ethic had been quick to see the issues raised by a system of
hired laborers. With anxious misgivings, nervous denial, and
repeated efforts at reform, they had watched the system of
massed wage employment spread out from the factories and all
but eclipse the man in business for himself. The moralists had
been equally prompt to recognize the economic side effects of the
revolution in work. Since the advent of the cotton mills, they had
engaged in debate over the wages and health of the new industrial
operatives and had pondered the role of the factories in widening
the chasm between rich and poor. The narrowing of the creative
impulse in work as the factories split and routinized the processes
of labor did not begin to trouble most middle-class Northerners
until much later. But when the discovery of industrial monotony
came with a rush shortly after the turn of the century, it was to
drive a second wedge between work ideals and work realities and
to pose a question at least as vexed and unsettling as that of a
worker's economic freedom.

Measured against the changes in work itself, the moralists'
concern with the routinization of industrial labor was a belated
discovery. The cotton mills, with their banks of semiautomatic
looms and spinning frames and their simple machine-tending

tasks, stripped so far of skill and judgment that raw recruits and children could do them, had set a pattern for factory work at the outset of the industrial transformation. When the Committee on the Machinery of the United States, sent from Britain to investigate the state of American arms manufacture, arrived in the mid-1850s they observed self-acting machines at work in the making not only of textiles and firearms but a dozen other products ranging from pianos to hairpins. In a nail factory the British observers watched a machine stamp out nails at the rate of two hundred a minute, attended by a boy whose sole task was to feed it iron bars at a pace set by its own voracious appetite. The committee was equally impressed with the self-acting, pattern-tracing tools they found at work in the larger carpentry and machine shops, automatically turning out gunstocks and chair legs with the aid only of a few semiskilled helpers. Before the end of the century these had given way to still more complex woodworking machines capable of transforming boards into yard upon yard of scrollwork and filigree and to machine tools that required a man only to set the raw material in place and throw the preset cutting tools into action one by one to turn a steel bar into a finished screw or metal fitting.[1]

Machines such as these were potentially liberating, freeing workers from mechanical drudgery for the skilled tasks of repairing, adjusting, and overseeing their mechanical servants. But the economics of machine employment worked in the opposite direction, to make most work increasingly mechanical. Manufacturers quickly learned to concentrate the repair and maintenance skills they needed in the smallest feasible number of highly skilled and highly paid machinists, while giving over the running of the machines themselves to cheaply recruited and quickly trained operatives. By the same token, the economics of manufacturing focused invention not on the dullest or even the most machinelike jobs in a factory but on the most intricate and most expensive. The complex motions of a shoe pegger or a seamstress fell early to mechanization, but there were rarely comparable profits to be made in turning over to machines the far simpler, far more repetitious, but far cheaper tasks that intervened between the mechanized processes.

The result was to create ever-larger numbers of machine tenders, constrained to the pace and machinelike routine of the tools they served. From the children whom Josephine Goldmark observed shortly after the turn of the century dropping metal caps in place one per second on the cannery assembly lines, to the women shoe workers who each day fed upward of three thousand shoes through their stitching or eyeleting machines, to the tired and grimy men who stoked and fed and were maimed in appalling numbers by the iron and steel furnaces, such workers formed the core of the factory labor force.[2] The farm and shop economy had diffused skills widely through the population; virtually all of its occupations had allowed room for variation and idiosyncrasy if not for art itself. But the experience of the first century of mechanization was to narrow and consume skills, to create not only new work relations but a new kind of work: specialized, repetitious, machine-paced, and, often, deadeningly simple.

Nineteenth-century moralists, however, were markedly slow to challenge the new work realities. A number of nineteenth-century writers did indeed raise their voices against the new forms of work emerging in the factories. In 1840, the nation's preeminent Unitarian minister, William Ellery Channing, had criticized the encasement of the modern factory hand in a "monotonous, stupefying round of unthinking toil," confined to "the heading of pins, the pointing of nails, or the tying together of broken strings." Emerson, after the jolt of a trip to England in the late 1840s, had come home to protest the regime of subdivided and mechanized labor; and in "The Tartarus of Maids," with its sexless, life-devouring paper mill, Herman Melville had written a haunting short story on the theme. In 1883, in one of the most penetrating critiques of his generation, the Episcopal clergyman R. Heber Newton told a congressional committee investigating the sources of labor unrest that the roots of spiritless, discontented labor were to be found not in the decaying moral fiber of workingmen but in their being forced into increasingly narrow, unintelligent tasks. "Some few machines require a skill and judgment to guide them proportioned to their astonishing capacities," he admitted, "and for the elect workmen who manage them there is a new sense of the pleasures of power." But the lot of most factory workers was to become a simple "tender upon a steel automaton, which thinks and plans and combines with marvelous power, leaving him only the task of supplying it with the raw material, and of oiling and cleansing it." Working on but a fraction of the product, the factory operative "*makes nothing. He sees no complete product of his skill growing into finished shape in his hands. What zest can there be in the toil of this bit of manhood?*"[3]

Yet most middle-class writers strenuously resisted Newton's indictment. In 1897, after watching another nailer thrust his iron spikes monotonously into the jaws of a trip hammer, Newton's superior, Bishop Henry C. Potter, told a New York City church group that the saloon and the strike were understandable reactions to the "mechanicalization" of the workingman that was turning him "into a simple idiot." But his statement evoked a storm of protest in the press and from the pulpit.[4] William Dean Howells was much closer to the pattern. Looking at the immense steam engine that dominated the centennial celebration at Philadelphia in 1876, he wondered that the machine did not reach down and crush its lounging, newspaper-reading engineer. But "to be honest," his pen ran quickly on, "one never thinks of such things here. One thinks only of the glorious triumphs of skill and invention."[5] In England the transformation of work made its way against formidable protests. But the long and vital English antimachinery tradition that runs from Thomas Carlyle through John Ruskin and Arthur Penty found only feeble echoes in nineteenth-century America.

Some of the moralists' indifference to the erosion of creativity in work stemmed from the social barriers that sealed off the work of the factories from the ken of most middle-class writers and their audiences. The most visible machines in nineteenth-century America, the locomotives and the massive steam engines, radiated not confinement but power. Currier and Ives turned out dozens of prints of onrushing steamboats and locomotives for nineteenth-century halls and parlors, creating icons of restless energy, but not a single print of a factory that modern historians have found. A few late nineteenth-century novelists shouldered their way more boldly into industrial subjects. Yet the center of tales such as Elizabeth Stuart Phelps's *The Silent Partner* (1871) or Martin Foran's *The Other Side* (1886) was not the nature of work but the more melodramatic and visible themes of poverty and exploitation. "The American public does not like to read about the life of toil," a changed William Dean Howells lamented in 1891. "What we like to read about is the life of noblemen or millionaires; ... if our writers were to begin telling us on any extended scale of how mill hands, or miners, or farmers, or iron-puddlers really live, we should very soon let them know that we did not care to meet such vulgar and commonplace people."[6]

Nor did workingmen, on the whole, press the issue of routinized toil. The congressonal committee that heard R. Heber Newton also listened to a delegation of workingmen from the New York City Central Labor Union protest the degradation of the craftsman under the system of subdivided labor. But most skilled workers transmuted their grievances into terms of wages, hours, and the right to unionize, like the sentimental novelists subsuming questions of the content of work under the more pressing issue of economic injustice. As for nineteenth-century American socialists, in their recoil against the economic waste and inefficiency of capitalism most of them, unlike Marx, had made their peace with the subdivision and mechanization of labor. It was a mark both of the limits of labor's protest and the divisions between class experiences that Edward Everett Hale, a minister and story writer of uncommonly broad sympathies, could describe the day of a typical woolen mill operative as spent in "gently releasing a broken thread, [or] quietly soothing a squeaking pivot."[7]

After 1850, as more and more factory places were taken up by immigrants, prejudice joined ignorance in shaping the widespread indifference to industrial monotony. Among the middle-class moralists there was limited sympathy for the Irish or French Canadian cotton mill operative, the Jewish or Italian sweatshop worker, or the East European laborer in the steel mills and packing plants. Many middle-class writers reassured themselves that the simple, routine tasks of the factory only matched the dull faces and sloping brows they thought characterized the immigrant peasant. Under the veneer of nativistic contempt, moreover, lay a reserve of outright terror. Five years after the Haymarket bomb throwing, the English artist Walter Crane marveled at the fortresslike police stations and city armories that had been thrown up after the incident in defense against what had been known since the 1870s as the "dangerous classes."[8] Josiah Strong poured the same sense of terror into *Our Country: Its Possible Future and Its Present Crisis* in the mid-1880s and

created one of the bestselling books of his generation. "When . . .
a commercial crisis has closed factories by the ten thousand, and
wage-workers have been thrown out of employment by the
million," Strong warned:

> when the public lands, which hitherto at such times have
> afforded relief, are all exhausted; when our urban popula-
> tion has been multiplied several fold, and our Cincinnatis
> have become Chicagos, our Chicagos New Yorks, and our
> New Yorks Londons; when class antipathies are deepened;
> when socialistic organizations, armed and drilled, are in
> every city, and the ignorant and vicious power of crowded
> populations has fully found itself; when the corruption of
> city government is grown apace; when crops fail, or some
> gigantic "corner" doubles the price of bread; with starvation
> in the home; with idle workmen gathered, sullen and
> desperate, in the saloons; with unprotected wealth at hand;
> with the tremendous forces of chemistry within easy reach;
> then, with *the opportunity, the means, the fit agents, the
> motive, the temptation to destroy, all brought into evil
> conjunction*, THEN will come the real test of our institutions.[9]

Against this nightmarish vision, an agglomeration of all the
nervousnesses of industrializing America, middle-class writers
often found a small but vital measure of reassurance in the hope
that the simple, repetitive processes of industry were slowly
impressing order and discipline on the factory population. It was
not surprising, then, that in criticizing Bishop Potter's address
the *New York Times* warned that his remarks had been not only
"unsound" but "unsafe."[10]

Finally, and most important of all, was a faith in progress.
"The steam-engine, the spinning-jenny, the power-loom, the
power-press, the sewing-machine," Washington Gladden wrote
in a vein characteristic of the 1870s, "all these mechanical devices
by which labor is saved and production increased, are provided
for in God's design. They are part of his great work of development by which he is carrying the race forward to its perfect
destiny." If occasionally a writer warned that society was at an
awkward sticking place in the course of history, the growing flood
of factory-made products seemed to answer any doubts that the
industrial future promised a higher civilization than the past.
"Machines multiply goods into plenty, and plenty broadcast . . .

brings all millenniums in its hands," one of Potter's critics wrote
in syllogistic rebuttal. The evolutionary figure, virtually inescapable in late nineteenth-century assessments of industrialization, profoundly shaped the American response to mechanized
labor.[11]

No one brought together all these strands—distance, callousness, and an abiding faith in progress—better or more persuasively than Carroll D. Wright, the leading American expert on
the factory in the post–Civil War decades. In many ways Wright
was an unlikely choice for the task of interpreting the industrial
regime to his countrymen. Born into a minister's family in a New
Hampshire village in 1840, Wright was raised in a number of
small New England towns far from contacts with industrial life.
After a short stint of schoolteaching, he enlisted in the Union
army, ultimately rose to the rank of colonel, and after the war's
close settled into a career of law and Republican politics outside
Boston. From there in 1873 he was unexpectedly picked to
become the second chief of the new Massachusetts Bureau of
Statistics of Labor. Politics, not expertise, was responsible for the
appointment. Unlike his predecessor, a former mill manager
whose partisanship toward labor had annoyed the legislature,
Wright knew virtually nothing about the task, but by sticking
carefully to statistical inquiry he not only carved out a personal
career but set a model eventually imitated by other state bureaus
of labor statistics. When the federal Bureau of Labor was
organized in 1885, Wright was appointed its first commissioner.
He publicized his work and opinions widely through lectures and
magazine articles, and when he retired from the Labor Bureau in
1905 to become president of Clark College the honor was an
appropriate symbol of his rise to national prominence.[12]

What Wright lacked in experience he made up for in a firm
conviction of the progressive course of history. He was not blind
to the evils of industrialization. He supported factory laws,
particularly for women and children, and served terms as president both of the American Association for the Promotion of
Profit Sharing and the National Society for the Promotion of
Industrial Education. When in 1881 Wright undertook an investigation of European factory conditions for the Census
Bureau, he sought out model industrial communities and reform
ideas. But the trip was more important in settling Wright's own

view of the past, for Europe gave him a chance to inspect the remnants of the economy the factory had replaced. The cottage handloom weaver and the factory textile worker became the marks by which Wright chose to measure the tendency of history, and his investigation and his reading both worked to confirm the evolutionary figure. "There is something poetic in the idea of the weaver of old England, before the spinning machinery was invented, working at his loom in his cottage, with his family about him," Wright admitted in the argument he reiterated virtually unchanged over the next twenty years; but there had been nothing idyllic in the reality. The domestic worker's cottage, Wright insisted, had been a nest of squalor, ignorance, and drunkenness—a "filthy little shop, occupied by a few foul-talking people." Isolated, steeped in vice and laziness, and desperately poor, the domestic workers and their "sin-breeding shops" represented the dark ages of industrial history.[13]

Into this benighted society, Wright argued, the factories came as a reforming force. By substituting fixed hours and regular habits for the slovenly rhythms of the putting-out system, and by bringing workers for the first time under constant, systematic supervision, the factories had imposed moral order upon a moral chaos. There was a particularly revealing clue to Wright's conception of industrial history in his admiration for the British factory master Robert Owen. In Wright's telling of the tale, Owen had put his textile enterprises down in the midst of "squalor, poverty, intemperance, and crime" and had left a population drilled in orderly, law-abiding habits.[14] The story had an obvious appeal to an ex-military officer, whose Civil War experience had no doubt reinforced, as it did with others, the equation of discipline and morality. And it had a still broader appeal to those who, like Wright, had begun to worry anxiously about the morals of the new industrial proletariat. "Regular employment is conducive to regular living," he wrote in a conviction whose roots stretched back through Henry Ward Beecher's vermin-haunted castles into generations of attack upon idleness.[15] If morality was order, certainly the factories were morality's handmaiden.

With the same certainty with which he insisted upon the ethical force of the factory system, Wright defended its educational influence as well. Here his argument was twofold. By bringing workers into association, the factories created a "mental friction" unknown in the cramped and isolated shops. But the factories did as much by bringing workers into contact with machinery; for machines, in Wright's view, represented not brute matter but the "embodiment" of inventive thought. "There is something peculiarly educational in the presence of the working of mechanical powers," he argued. To watch a complex, automatic machine at work was to absorb intuitively lessons in science, harmony, and beauty. "Brain is king," he proclaimed, "and machinery is the king's prime minister." Granted the actual work of the factories was simple; so too, Wright suggested, was the human material a manufacturer worked with. Reaching down into the "substratum" of society where capacities were often "poor" and intellects "dull," "lifting up" workers into the domain of thought, the factory in Wright's view was an extraordinary mental escalator.[16]

None of these ideas were unique to Wright. He gleaned his convictions from Ure and Cooke-Taylor in England and, above all, from Louis Reybaud in France. Wright's ideas represented Victorian orthodoxy on the mechanization of labor, gathering together with full force the immense outward optimism and nervous fear of chaos, the ability to find the ideal behind the material shell of life, which characterized the mid-nineteenth-century middle class. Broadcast through Wright, the optimistic assessment of the mechanization of work found repeated echoes in America. "The majority of human minds are weak, and slow, and could do little in the world but for simple tasks adapted to small and barren brains," one industrial apologist wrote in the 1890s. "Monotonous toils suit them exactly.... The exact and punctual habit, which the machine engenders, trains careless minds with a discipline most wholesome, ... and the better minds quickly rise out of that class to something better." "The greater the subdivision of labor, the more complex and educative," another argued. Rebutting charges that scientific management reduced the worker to a "mere automaton," Frederick W. Taylor too found his answer in Wright's argument.[17] For the mass of laborers, factory work brought intellectual uplift and the discipline of orderly habits, capped—in the argument that was strongest of all—by an ever-ascending standard of living. "The

divine plan to perfect all creations which make up the universe,"
Wright himself affirmed, "... goes on always polishing, always
purifying, always perfecting."[18]

Time was not kind to the confidence of Wright's generation.
Soon after the turn of the century, a younger corps of social
observers pushed Wright's reassurances aside and turned the
indictment of mechanized labor from a heresy, or at best a
repressed anxiety, into a pervasive commonplace. The moralists'
discovery of industrial monotony was the work of a band of
economists, educators, settlement house residents, and social
workers who came of age in the 1890s. They were far better
educated, on the whole, than Wright's generation of self-trained
men, but they found the classical curriculum of the colleges no
more satisfying than Wright's volume upon volume of dry
statistics. What they were after, they protested, was "experience." Deserting the colleges and the self-contained Victorian
households of their childhoods, they plunged into urban and
industrial life to try to find it. Walter Wyckoff, one of the earliest
of the firsthand social investigators, fled Princeton Theological
Seminary in 1891 to tramp his way across the country for eighteen
months, working at the edge of poverty as a common, unskilled
laborer in what he described as "an experiment in reality." By the
early twentieth century, that gesture had been repeated often
enough to make it one of the symbolic patterns of the progressive
years. Surfeited with books and culture, a new generation of
social investigators moved into one of the new settlement houses,
joined one of the proliferating social surveys, or, more bravely
still, took up work in laundries, department stores, and factories
to try to find out what "real" life was about. Anna Ely moved
from a graduate seminar into a Milwaukee machine shop, Lillian
Pettengill from Mount Holyoke into domestic service as a cook
and chambermaid, Charles R. Walker from Yale and the army
officer corps into the backbreaking common labor of a Pittsburgh steel mill—throwing their old identities temporarily aside
to experience the pulse and pressure of industrial society from the
bottom up.[19]
    Virtually all of those who tried the manual work industrial
America offered, however, emerged from the experience dismayed at what they had found. Wyckoff's first contact with

common labor was with a road-breaking gang, and the mechanical, unthinking rhythm of pick-and-shovel work, the indignity of being bossed by a hard and overbearing foreman, and the wearyingly hard labor all came as a profound shock. "From work like ours there seems to us to have been eliminated every element which constitutes the nobility of labor," he later tried to sum up the experience. "There is for us in our work none of the joy of responsibility, none of the sense of achievement, only the dull monotony of grinding toil, with the longing for the signal to quit work, and for our wages at the end of the week."[20] Most of the others seconded Wyckoff's judgment; what they had found was not work but aching, mind-numbing drudgery.

The reactions of the middle-class sojourners in the industrial world would have been profound in any event, but their impressions of industrial labor were intensified by a shift in attitudes toward work itself. The new social investigators were as certain as the generations that had come before them that work was the indispensable core of the moral life—"the highest good that life offers," as Wyckoff put it.[21] But middle-class children who grew up after the Civil War were heirs to a gradual erosion of the ascetic injunctions of the work ethic, and as a result Carroll Wright's preoccupation with ordered habits and the disciplinary benefits of mechanized labor did not have the same resonance to them as it had had to their parents. Children of an altered religious and economic climate, taught by new kinds of storybooks, instructed by William James and Thorstein Veblen to see the mind as composed not of faculties to be exercised but of instincts to be released, progressive-minded Northerners after the turn of the century gave a new stress to the creative side of labor. They did not doubt work's function as a sanitizing discipline, but at its best they held that it was more than that—a joyful bodying forth of inner energies that was akin to art and, as John Dewey wrote for them, grew "insensibly" out of the vital impulses of play.[22]

Measured against these heightened expectations and their own college work experiences, it was not surprising that the personal encounter with industrialization came as a shock that sent Wright's edifice tumbling to the ground. By broadcasting their experiences through the social survey and the new investigative journalism, the little band who felt it at first hand soon shared that shock vicariously with an entire generation of reform-minded Northerners. There was no beauty of moral force in factory toil, it could be heard at every hand after 1900. It was simply an onerous burden, a "grinding, unvarying, monotonous, joyless" travesty of work. Even the engineering and business press began to echo the pervasive concern with overspecialization and routinized, machine-dominated labor, asking anxiously if the upshot of their systematizing efforts had not been to make virtually extinct the all-round, skilled craftsmen who, in limited numbers at least, were still indispensable in the factories. "All the spouting about the beauty and dignity of factory work is mere moonshine," as the *Saturday Evening Post* announced the new conclusions in 1912.[23]

For Northerners who cared about work, there was realism but little comfort in that statement. Having found out how far most industrial labor was from their intense ideals, they knew it fell to them, somehow, to reform it. But to remedy what Bishop Potter had called the "mechanicalization" of the worker proved a much more tightly knotted puzzle than to discover it.

One solution was to abandon or severely restrict the machine. This was not simply an idle thought but the course urged by two Englishmen—John Ruskin and William Morris—who as interpreters of art had a profound impact on nineteenth-century America. Ruskin, the single most influential arbiter of aesthetics for the Anglo-American middle class, set forth his indictment of mechanized labor in 1853 in a famous essay "The Nature of Gothic," embedded in a study of Venetian architecture. The juxtaposition of medieval art and social economics was no accident. For the glory of the Gothic cathedral front, and the key to its irregular, often grotesque, and compelling beauty, as Ruskin explained it, lay in the fact that each carver on its fantastic statuary had been a genuinely free worker, chipping out the rough imprint of his own thought and artistic sense in his labor. Gothic had been the art of a free society. What had come afterward, under the baleful influence of the machine, had been sheer ugliness. By destroying freedom in work—by dividing men "into mere segments of men, broken into small fragments and crumbs of life"—by making "their fingers measure degrees like cog-wheels and their arms strike curves like compasses"—

morris/
Ruskin

mechanization had destroyed art as well. The task of the nineteenth century, if it was to begin to recover what it had lost, Ruskin insisted, was to extract the "thoughtful" element from its workingmen, "whatever we lose for it"—to find out what kinds of labor were good for men and to retrieve them, whatever sacrifices in convenience or economy stood in the way.[24]

Ruskin's closest approach to a practical formula, announced in a series of letters in the 1870s, was unabashedly reactionary: to take a small piece of English ground on which to revive agriculture and handicrafts and to banish all the steam engines and virtually all the machinery of the nineteenth century. Such a quixotic overthrow of progress was quickly dismissed in America; only here and there did a sympathetic critic perceive in it something more than madness.[25] Ruskin's criticism, however, had made the antimachinery case famous, and the work of his pupil William Morris was still harder to ignore.

Like Ruskin, Morris backed into his social views. He came to fame in the 1860s as a leader in the revival of handicrafts and the decorative arts, a maker of expensively elegant, hand-produced wallpapers, fabrics, and tapestries, and a severe critic of the Victorian taste for machine-made gimcrackery. From his Merton Abbey workshops and, later, his Kelmscott Press came a steady flow of hand-crafted products to counteract the influence of the machine. But ultimately Morris's despair over the ugliness of contemporary England led him, as it had Ruskin, to examine the social conditions responsible for the decay of art. He found his solution early in the 1880s by joining the socialists, and over the next decade, in a remarkable flood of essays and lectures, Morris waged a crusade—a provocative amalgam of Marx and Ruskin—against competitive industrial society.[26]

Morris's criticism went far beyond Ruskin's indictment of subdivided labor and machine regularity. "It is not this or that tangible steel and brass machine which we want to get rid of, but the great intangible machine of commercial tyranny, which oppresses the lives of all of us" and makes labor "a mere weariness to be borne for the greater part of the day." What he was after, he insisted, was a wholesale change in the "system of the production of wares."[27] But in thus embracing Marx, Morris did not abandon Ruskin. The ultimate criterion of his good society was not simply its ability to mete out economic justice but its capacity to insure that every man had work that was free, that was worth doing, and that was in itself an act of pleasure and beauty. To overthrow the system of production for profit and to severely limit the scope of machine manufacture were for Morris means to a common end. It is true that during his most active years as a socialist, when his aestheticism and his Marxism sometimes warred with each other, he set out several sketches of the coming socialist factory as a clean, efficient model of neotechnical engineering. Yet Morris never reconciled himself to factory production. And he never gave up the hope, so seductively broadcast in his utopian *News from Nowhere* in 1890, that the inhabitants of a future socialist England would discard machine after machine for the joys of handicraft work, until finally leaving to power tools only those tasks void of any intrinsic pleasure.[28] Edward Bellamy's goods-flooded, efficient socialism appalled Morris. He aimed for a society filled, like the fourteenth century he loved, with free and creative work, which would "turn all 'operatives' into workmen, into artists, into men." "If the world cannot hope to be happy in its work," he pleaded, "it must relinquish the hope of happiness altogether."[29]

The handicraft movement came to the United States in the second half of the 1890s with William Morris as its prophet. The first arts and crafts societies were organized in Boston and Chicago in 1897, a year after Morris's death, and by the middle of the next decade, at Chautauqua summer assemblies, at settlement houses and church guilds, and in dozens of rural villages, Americans were weaving rugs, throwing pottery, fashioning "honest," nailless furniture, or hand printing books in imitation of the master of Merton Abbey. By 1904 there were twenty-five arts and crafts societies, largely concentrated in the Northeast, and more than a dozen settlements, primarily in the Southern Appalachians, dedicated to the revival of American folk art.[30] And yet it is indicative of the weakness of the antimachinery crusade in America that only a tiny remnant of the American handicrafters preached a gospel that at all resembled what Morris or Ruskin had taught.

For the most influential of the handicraft societies, the patrician-dominated Boston Society of Arts and Crafts, Morris's socialist phase was simply an embarrassment. Inspired by Morris the craftsman, the shaper of beautiful and intricately designed furnishings, they joined in his criticism of machine-fashioned ugliness and took up his mission of elevating aesthetic taste. But their quarrel with industrial society stopped where mechanization impinged upon art, and even there Ruskin's celebration of the rough, democratic grotesquery of Gothic seemed to the Boston craftsmen far less needed than an awakening of "sobriety," "restraint," and "ordered arrangement." As for Morris's economic ideas, the president of the society in his report for 1903 was able to congratuate its members "thus far in keeping those questions entirely out of our midst ... and in attending to our proper concerns." [31]

At the other extreme of the handicraft movement, Elbert Hubbard never acknowledged any subject as outside his proper concerns. If the Boston group served as the aesthetic conscience of the arts and crafts crusade, Hubbard was its Barnum. He was a salesman and writer of advertising copy who quit his soap firm in the early 1890s, discovered Morris, and in imitation built his own handicraft and print shops outside Buffalo. Out of them flowed furniture, bric-a-brac, two magazines, and shelves full of hand-bound Hubbard-written books, while Hubbard himself grew his hair down to his shoulders and became the nation's most prominent Morrisite and one of its most flamboyant eccentrics. "I believe John Ruskin, William Morris, Henry Thoreau, Walt Whitman, and Leo Tolstoy to be Prophets of God," Hubbard claimed, and the credo was more than sheer pose. Janet Ashbee, the wife of one of Morris's talented English disciples, visited Hubbard's Roycroft colony in 1900 and found it "pretty sound ... mostly Ruskin and Morris with a good strong American flavour." The dignity of work ran as one of the few consistent and passionately held threads through Hubbard's willfully inconsistent outpourings, and in sketches such as "The City of Tagaste" and "A Dream and a Prophecy" he took the shoddy toil of the industrial age to task as severely as any of his chosen prophets. But Hubbard remained a shrewd, American-flavored promoter and entrepreneur under his bohemian veneer, and he found richer veins to mine in "A Message to Garcia," a celebration of unquestioning obedience in work that American businessmen catapulted into the most famous essay of its day. By about 1910, in the phrase of his biographer, Hubbard had begun aggressively "fronting for business," trimming his eccentricities and opinions to suit the advertising revenues upon which his expansive enterprises rested. "I believe in Big Business and more of it," the American Morris wrote; "any individual who uses the word 'commercial' as an epithet [is] ... essentially un-American."[32]

Here and there a few of the American handicraft advocates did take an aggressive stand vis-à-vis the machinery of commerce and industry. In Chicago, the Arts and Crafts Society organized at Hull House promised to "insist that the machine be no longer allowed to dominate the workman and reduce his production into a mechanical distortion." From a communal retreat in the Connecticut valley a young printer, Carl Rollins, tweaked the noses of the conservative brahmins of the Society of Arts and Crafts and produced an impassioned, Morris-inspired indictment of wage slavery. From a similar retreat near Philadelphia, Will Price and Walt Whitman's friend, Horace Traubel, promised to question the machine "to the wall" until "all work" was "the sort of work that some man may love."[33] But between the keepers of aesthetic standards and Hubbard's self-advertising bunkum, their voices were all but lost.

The radical attack on the machine stumbled over progress in America and failed to find a footing. Most of those who joined the handicrafts boom looked to Morris essentially as an arbiter of good taste for families whose money had outrun their certainty about propriety and beauty. Hubbard excepted, the handi-crafters were fervently concerned with art. Some of them, like Gustav Stickley, whose *Craftsman* was the most prosperous chronicler of the movement, were willing to lead a revival of rural life and folk crafts. But the idea that the artist must "monkey with production," as one of Morris's American disciples wrote,[34] or that a society's hopes for art hinged upon the contents of the everyday work of the mass of its citizens, was foreign to most of them. Except where it impinged on beauty, the handicrafters, Stickley included, were scarcely less convinced than the American middle class as a whole that the line of historical advance lay through increased mechanization. President Warren of the Boston crafts society warned that it was "not only futile but wrong, to attempt to carry on a crusade against those great systems [of production] which have made the best that there is in the modern world." Oscar Triggs of the Chicago-based Morris

Society, a far more aggressive social critic than Warren, still came back to the need for machinery—"more and ever more of it." Only Horace Traubel caught Morris's blend of the radical and the reactionary, urging that when civilization went back for something it had lost, it was not an act of retreat but "another sort of advance."[35]

In the end, the intellectual energies of the arts and crafts movement exhausted themselves in debates not over work but over aesthetics, petering out in a pointless argument about the merits of lopsided pottery and shaky hand-crafted tables. It was somehow a fitting symbol of the missed connections that at the utopian colony founded at Ruskin, Tennessee, in the 1890s— where Francis Wayland was preaching Ruskin "turned into the language of the common people"—the working day was precisely marked out by the shrieks of one of the steam whistles Ruskin had so furiously hated.[36]

If the machine was inviolable, there remained the possibility that the factory worker might become more happily adjusted to its rhythms. To work at small, routine tasks might not dwarf the mind if it were somehow stocked with bigger ideas and more stimulating visions. This was the conclusion Jane Addams ultimately reached, and of all those who wrestled with the problem of industrial monotony few were more humane or more perceptive than she. Addams's career was in many ways archetypal of the new generation of progressive social reformers. She had gone to college when that was still a rarity for women and had become fired there with the vision of a life "filled with good works and honest toil," only to find herself pulled back into what seemed to her the stultifying isolation of family, manners, and culture. Finally in 1889, in search of something larger and more vital, she leased an old house amid the packed immigrant tenements and small factories and sweatshops of central Chicago and plunged into the heart of what she called the "race life." By the early twentieth century, Hull House had grown into one of Chicago's best-known institutions and Addams herself into the nation's most famous and respected social worker.[37]

Addams had read "a great deal of Ruskin" during her college years, and together with her friend and cofounder of Hull House, Ellen Gates Starr, she was one of the organizers of the Chicago

Arts and Crafts Society. But while Ellen Starr journeyed to England to learn the art of hand bookbinding from one of Morris's associates, Addams remained skeptical of the handicraft alternative. Her reservations did not stem from any simple faith in progress or the machine. Her case against the arts and crafts movement was that its ideal of individual self-sufficiency seemed to her mistaken. Like many other progressive reformers, Addams was convinced that a deeper sense of mutual dependence was needed to counteract the excessive individualism of her countrymen. She agreed with Carroll Wright that the factory system had been an advance over the isolated and confining labor of the cottage artisan. Hence the handicrafters' insistence that a single workman shape each product seemed to Addams a misguided step backward. "A man who makes, year after year, but one small wheel in a modern watch factory, may, if his education has properly prepared him, have a fuller life than did the old watchmaker who made a watch from beginning to end. It takes thirty-nine people to make a coat in a modern tailoring establishment, yet those same thirty-nine people might produce a coat in a spirit of 'team work' which would make the entire process as much more exhilarating than the work of the old solitary tailor, as playing in a baseball nine gives more pleasure to a boy than that afforded by a solitary game of hand ball on the side of the barn." Ruskin's lesson, Addams argued, needed to be socialized for an increasingly complex and interdependent society. The life of the industrial laborer was to be lifted above brutality not simply by art but by "the solace of collective art inherent in collective labor."[38]

It was only a short step from this position to the crusade to foment a democratic revolution in industry, and many of Addams's friends and admirers, John Dewey among them, eventually transferred her hopes for a socialized labor into the industrial democracy movement.[39] But Addams placed her primary faith in the mind. The fundamental grievance of the man in the factory, Addams insisted, "beyond being overworked and disinherited ... [was] that he does not know what it is all about." He had no inkling of the origin or destiny of the product he manipulated, no scientific knowledge of the processes of manufacture, no understanding of the historical development of his trade and consequently no sense of connection with the industrial community of which he was a part. "A machine really represents the 'seasoned life of man,' " she wrote; there was a history to be read in it if a worker was given its clues, and through that history a consciousness of the connection of one's work with the social whole. "If a child goes into a sewing factory with a knowledge of the work she is doing in relation to the finished product; if she is informed concerning the material she is manipulating and the processes to which it is subjected; if she understands the design she is elaborating in its historic relation to art and decoration, her daily life is lifted from drudgery to one of self-conscious activity, and her pleasure and intelligence is registered in her product." A worker could be content to labor on a part, she argued, if he knew it were the part of something larger.[40]

Addams's first attempt to translate her ideas into concrete form came with the opening of a "labor museum" at Hull House, where, through craft shops, demonstrations of primitive tools and processes, exhibitions, and occasional lectures, she hoped to lay out in simple terms the historical evolution of the basic industries her Hull House neighbors worked with. The labor museum was Addams's social vision in microcosm. Her deep concern with estrangement, her desire to fuse culture and work, her faith in education, and her integral vision of society were all reflected there. The labor museum by itself, however, was obviously no match for the dimensions of the problem, and Addams reached out for larger measures. She joined the National Society for the Promotion of Industrial Education at its organization in 1906, and through her friendship with the McCormick family in Chicago she was drawn into what was known at the turn of the century as the "industrial betterment" movement. She saw in both of them germs of an attempt to seize the factories for "the kingdom of the mind." But, bent out of that course, the upshot of neither campaign was what she had hoped it might be.

The idea of using the schools to teach the discipline, the dignity, and the skills of labor had long appealed to Northerners concerned about work. From the early years of the nineteenth century, the narrowly academic curriculum of the grammar schools had come under repeated attack for overstocking the nation with clerks, traveling salesmen, office-seekers, and ladies of fashion at the expense of conscientious workmen and capable housekeepers who were not ashamed to dirty their hands at manual labor. Industrial schools for the children of the poor had appeared before the middle of the century, and by its end courses in woodworking, sewing, and cooking had seeped into the curriculum of a good many public schools. But it was in the progressive years that the idea of moving work and courses in work into the schools mushroomed into a major campaign. Between 1906, when Massachusetts took its initial steps toward the first statewide system of industrial schools, and 1917, when Congress passed the Smith-Hughes bill granting federal aid to vocational education, no other educational topic approached it in vitality. What at the turn of the century had been an idea of a fairly restricted system of trade and technical schools to train an elite of skilled workers had blossomed by 1920 into a vision of a multitude of schools of all sorts—evening, part-time, and day schools—training workers and potential workers of all ages in everything from sewing-machine operating and mine ventilation to family hygiene and citizenship.[41]

The campaign for vocational education was an extraordinarily practical movement, and on the whole Addams was in sympathy with its practical bent. She too thought the regular school curriculum too cut off from the wellsprings of social life and too narrowly focused on the needs of a tiny college-bound elite at the expense of the great mass of children who left school at age fourteen or fifteen to pass, helplessly unprepared, into what were often the most routine and deadening jobs in the industrial economy. But as the industrial education campaign gathered force, it increasingly left behind her own vision of an education that would fuse history, science, work, and culture into the integrated social vision that would support a worker through his bit of the common task. Part of the reason lay in the central role of businessmen in the industrial education campaign. They were particularly prominent in the National Society for the Promotion of Industrial Education, the strongest pressure group in the movement, where Jane Addams rubbed shoulders with Frederick W. Taylor and Anthony Ittner of the stridently antilabor National Association of Manufacturers joined forces with John Golden of the United Textile Workers. There was something curious about the presence of so many businessmen in a movement that took the skill-destroying, diseducative effects of modern industrial work as one of its central premises. But many manufacturers—machinery builders in particular—found themselves at a bottleneck in the early twentieth century for lack of skilled machinists at the top of their factory structures.[42] And the spectacular rise of German economic competition, which seemed linked in turn, somehow, to Germany's extensive system of trade and continuation schools, loosened logic and cast its specter over businessmen and educators alike.

The result was to stress not the need for cultural breadth but the need for efficiency, for an educational system that would "make of each citizen an effective economic unit," as the industrial education society's first president put the constantly repeated argument. Moreover, when organized labor joined the industrial education campaign, hoping to use the schools to pry open the channels of mobility into skilled work, its spokesmen, too, turned the "culturizing" pretensions of professional educators into a term of derision.[43] What was needed was practical job training matched to practical needs and taught by practical workmen.

But this was no more to be done in Addams's labor museum, with its demonstrations of hand spinning and its historical exhibits, than through the antiquated school courses in general carpentry. By the second decade of the twentieth century the program of the leaders of the practical wing of the industrial education movement had gelled into a demand that the school training workshops become, in essence, miniatures of a community's industrial life. In 1916 David Snedden, Massachusetts Commissioner of Education and one of the nation's leading industrial education experts, could claim that vocational educators had already won the point that industrial education in the schools was to be through real work on real machines turning out commercially salable products through the techniques of quantity production, and that attempts to mix specific education for specific jobs with general education only made a useless "hash" of the whole. The steps ahead, he announced, would be toward still more realistic education: replacing the short and "soft" traditional school day with one matched to real industrial conditions and still further distilling the theoretical and the abstract in industrial education down to that core that workers in a given trade really needed. With the same intense practicality, Charles

Prosser, secretary of the industrial education society, elaborated long lists of the immediate skills evening vocational schools might teach employed workers to help machine operators move up to the higher-paid work of a more complex machine, dress finishers to become dress inspectors, or carpenter's helpers to become full-fledged carpenters.

In place of the haphazard way in which workers fell into their life's work and scrabbled to learn its rudiments, the vocational educators imagined a system of schools meshed neatly into the economy—guiding children into jobs matched to the needs of their communities and suited to their own vocational bents and capacities, training them to take their places as competent employees, and opening the means for small but steady advances in skill and income. The vision promised more than social efficiency in the contest for the world's markets. Out of the "better adjustment of every worker to the calling in which he can work most successfully," Prosser argued, would flow the "joy" of achievement and the "uplift" and happiness of men skilled in and fitted to their work.[44]

To refashion the schools along the lines of the factories, however, was not what Addams had had in mind. From the outset she had warned that the manufacturers might capture the vocational education movement for a trade training as narrow and as stultifying as industrial jobs themselves; and what Addams had said quietly her friend John Dewey turned into an aggressive attack on the vocationalists. In an economy in which all jobs were fragile, the only industrial education that made sense, Dewey argued, was one that stressed not specific skills but flexibility, initiative, and intelligence. But beyond that, Dewey insisted, lay the larger choice between the kind of vocational education "which will 'adapt' workers to the existing industrial regime" and one which "will first alter the existing industrial system, and ultimately transform it." By the First World War a large number of progressive educators had picked up that call and had begun to insist that educators challenge the mind-numbing jobs in modern industry until, as the National Education Association demanded in 1919, "all industry becomes educational to those who engage in it."[45]

To David Snedden, the idea of teachers and their bands of schoolchildren rebuilding the industrial plants summed up all he found impractical and mystifyingly vague in Dewey and his allies. But Addams, too, had believed it possible. Ultimately she hoped that educated workers who knew the development of their crafts would simply refuse to buy products that did not reflect "some gleam of intelligence" on the part of those who made them, and that their demand for "humanized and intelligent products" would in turn revolutionize work.[46] It was, as Snedden charged, a far vaguer program—and perhaps far more naive—than his lists of practical lessons for practical jobs. Where the vocationalists put their faith in adjustment, Addams and Dewey held to a more complex vision of an education which, by engaging workers and by opening the wellsprings of commitment, would ultimately discontent them.

By 1920, neither side had won a clear-cut victory. The Federal Board for Vocational Education under Prosser's leadership put its emphasis on narrow-gauged trade education. But most of the students enrolled in the trade and industrial education programs financed under the Smith-Hughes Act entered general education classes rather than job-focused courses, and the comprehensive high schools that appeared in the twenties were far from the practicing shops and factories the vocationalists had envisioned.[47] Nor were the progressive educators or their students more successful in bending industry to educational ends, though through the project method and social studies courses they did infuse a new realism into many school curricula. What the debate and its obscuringly murky language did show was how fragile the line was between education to help workers see the full dimensions of their work and education to adapt them, unthinkingly, to it.

The industrial betterment movement, in which Addams had placed a more qualified hope, demonstrated much the same lesson. In 1902 she had singled out for praise the National Cash Register Company of Dayton, Ohio, where factory hands, salesmen, and company officers came together once a year to listen to lectures on the state of the company and its product. It seemed to her a significant step in the direction of the ideal, educative factory, which might infuse its workers with a new consciousness of the collective dimensions of their work and a new esprit de corps. As she well knew, the innovations at Dayton went beyond annual company meetings. After a series of strikes and customer complaints of botched workmanship—precisely the sort of unrest critics of industrial monotony had predicted from an uninterested, unmotivated workforce—the company had embarked on a set of imaginative loyalty-building projects. By the turn of the century these included a plant library, a company magazine, more than a dozen workers' social clubs, shower baths, free lunches, landscaped grounds, company picnics, breaks for calisthenics, and banners for punctuality.[48] The McCormick family, on Addams's recommendation, appointed a social worker to oversee a similar program at its harvester works in 1901, and by the First World War portions of the much-advertised experiments at Dayton and Chicago had spread to many of the nation's largest manufacturing corporations.[49]

Teamwork was the dominant motif of the betterment campaign. Many of the projects that passed under the heading of betterment or industrial welfare work were long overdue improvements in safety, ventilation, lighting, or sanitary conditions, prompted by more careful cost accounting practices that had begun to reveal the employer's stake in accidents and illness. But the heart of the matter was morale. Watch a group of employees coming back from a noon-hour recreation program, "fresh, zestful, [and] singing," Ida Tarbell wrote, and you saw at once the social and economic payoff of betterment work.[50] Washrooms, factory beautification, and a company-organized social life all showed their effects in happier, more committed workers, who in turn produced more and better work. Where the scientific managers in the same decades talked of the ideal factory as a marvelously efficient machine, betterment advocates talked of the ideal factory as a family glued together by social bonds into a team spirit.

But betterment's concern with morale also reflected a conviction that the surroundings of work were more critical than the work itself. If the effect of industrial labor was often deadening, they frequently insisted, it was not repetition that made it so. Borrowing the concept of habit from late nineteenth-century psychologists, they insisted that routine emancipated the worker by wearing deep and comfortable tracks in the nervous system that set his mind free for thought. Hence, if industrial employees chafed at their tasks, effective cures concentrated not on the work but on the worker's mental state. Industrial psychologists like Hugo Münsterberg argued that the fault lay in the fact that

not all psychological dispositions were alike; some nervous systems took well to repetition while others rebelled against it.
Match psyche to work through psychological testing, however,
and "the complaint of monotony will disappear." [51] Businessmen
bought Münsterberg's *Psychology and Industrial Efficiency* "by
the carload" when it came out in 1913, but the more common
argument among betterment advocates was that workers' minds,
emancipated from their tasks, had nothing to occupy them save a
morbid, restless preoccupation with their work. Their answer to
industrial monotony, accordingly, was to give industrial workers
something to think about—an article for the factory newspaper, a
coming dramatic performance, factory-made friendships, or
simply the tastefully painted surroundings. One writer, reporting
enthusiastically that cigar makers increased their output when led
in singing, proposed that all the arts be brought into the factory
to surround the worker with a "mass of delightful sense-
impressions and pleasant associations." [52] The betterment advocates never put their program this directly, but in essence their
answer to minutely subdivided labor was sufficient distraction.

Their practical programs reflected the bent of their writings.
Of the 431 establishments covered by a United States Bureau of
Labor survey of betterment work in 1916–17, 223 provided
lunchrooms for their employees, 141 employed welfare secretaries
to organize company social activities, and virtually all had some
form of safety program; but only a handful, 11 establishments,
had tried the experiment of rotating workers engaged in the most
repetitive tasks. [53] The controlling assumption of the betterment
movement—like the gist of much of Jane Addams's thought—
was that monotony was essentially a state of mind.

Addams herself would have resisted the idea put so baldly. She
had, indeed, encouraged the efforts of Chicago clothing workers
to reverse the minute subdivision of labor in their trade in 1904,
and she had publicized their struggle as a practical form of
Ruskinism. She had objected to the elements of authoritarianism
in the industrial betterment movement and to its antiunion bias.
And she never abandoned the hope that enough children
educated in schools like Dewey's would work a profound
reformation in industry and discover ways to join the instinct of
art and variation with the economics of machine production and
the joys of teamwork.

But in focusing on the estrangement of the worker from what

his job was all about, in resting the bulk of her hopes in comradeship and understanding, Addams unconsciously reflected how much there was in her solution to industrial monotony that was personal to herself and to her generation of estranged, college-trained social investigators. She had come to Chicago after seven unhappy and lonely years to plunge thankfully into its overcrowded streets and its tight-knit ethnic communities. Like others of her generation who burrowed into the unfamiliar corners of society to find out what life was really like, she was hungry for social connectedness and acutely sensitive to the problems of alienation. Accordingly, she had begun her work with social clubs at Hull House, and they remained the most durable of its activities. Like most intellectuals, however, Addams herself found the most potent salve for isolation not simply in association but in the mental adventure of making sense of her surroundings. That adventure of comprehension was one that many industrial workers could and did share. But marks of Addams's time and a projection of her own experiences were both reflected in her assumption that a man who had been taught something of the history of mining and the chemistry of combustion would find shoveling coal much the easier for the knowledge; that the young box-maker or label-paster, about whom she thought so long, would find joy in his intrinsically vacant tasks if helped to see the whole in his minute part; that monotony, in short, could be conquered by the proper mental preparation.

Most critics of industrial monotony came to a far simpler answer: if modern industrial work was soulless, then men should do less of it. "For about nine men out of ten, the only way to lessen the drudgery of work is to give them as agreeable surroundings as the work permits, and then shorten their hours," George Lorimer of the *Saturday Evening Post* argued in 1912; "the mass of the world's workers . . . will never get relief from numbing monotony in any other way." About the same time, Herman Schneider, one of the pioneers of vocational education, came to the conclusion that to try to give industrial education courses to children employed in most machine-operating trades was simply to "overload" a badly overstrained organism. Part-time schools for factory children, he suggested, should be as little like work as possible; what such workers needed above all was a brilliant, joyful antidote to counteract the "dull monochrome" of their jobs.[54] By the progressive years, most industrial critics had concluded along with Lorimer and Schneider that the best chance for creativity was to admit that it was irretrievably gone from work and to allow it scope as a leisure-time activity.

Advocates of the shorter working day gave their imaginations free rein to anticipate the ways in which the new leisure time might be used to offset the dullness of labor. The factory operative could develop leadership and responsibility in an evening social club, exercise his thwarted mental abilities with books and lectures, or satisfy a frustrated instinct of workmanship through a hobby. He might cultivate a flower garden in a city plot, join a recreation program, picnic in a public park, dance old folk dances in a school auditorium, or play a lead in a community pageant.

Yet in the reiterated proposals to organize, supervise, and enrich the anticipated leisure, to make free time more educational and more disciplined, one catches a sense of the moralists' uneasiness with the solution to which they had been driven. John Dewey was not alone in worrying that the worker's imagination, unaided, might be "frittered away upon undisciplined dreaming and sensual fancies."[55] The same progressives who recoiled from the stultifying monotony of work were often equally dismayed by the brassy amusements of their industrial society. Amusement parks, dance halls, billiard parlors, vaudeville, and, above all, movie houses flourished in the early twentieth-century cities, in part to fill the demand for islands of pleasure as brilliant and as colorful as Schneider had proposed—and as far removed from work. In the steel town of Homestead there were six nickelodeons by 1907, and they had a strong hold on the steelworkers who stopped to watch the fifteen-minute shows after their ten- or twelve-hour workdays. Cleveland, with a population of fewer than 800,000, had a movie attendance of at least 500,000 a week by 1919, and in dozens of other cities recreation investigators in the progressive years discovered the same phenomenon.[56] To many of the moralists of the progressive years, this invasion of commercialized spectator amusements seemed scarcely less threatening to the creative expression they hoped for than the machine itself. The "leisure problem," as many of the moralists began to call it with increasing discouragement in the next decade, still seemed largely a matter for the future in 1920. But President John Finley of the University of the State of New York had already warned those who had turned their hopes from socializing industry to socializing play that "it will be a far more difficult task ... to teach men to use leisure rightly than to instruct them to labor efficiently." Given the immense vexations of the latter task, Finley's was not an encouraging judgment.[57]

Perhaps, in fact, the problems of work and leisure were too tightly linked to serve as malady and antidote. Randolph Bourne suggested something of this sort in an article "In the Mind of the Worker," published in the *Atlantic Monthly* on the eve of the First World War. Writing in the wake of the well-publicized IWW strikes in Lawrence, Massachusetts, and Paterson, New Jersey, Bourne had few reassuring thoughts for his middle-class readers. "We tend constantly to assume ... that the small business man who is struggling to make ends meet, the clerk going through a monotonous routine of other people's correspondence, the factory worker spending ten hours every day over a still more monotonous machine, the small professional man or woman, moving like a cog in a gigantic system—that all these people pursue their vocation with the same zest and enterprise as does the big business man," he wrote. But the wage-earner, in fact, harbored a "smouldering apathy toward work." "Dulled and depressed by the long day, ... his brain a-whirl with the roar of the machines, [he] must seek elation and the climax which work should have given [him], in the crude and exciting pleasures of the street and the dance and the show."

But Bourne went on to argue that the factory worker's flight from the job and his "inefficient, undependable, ... and utterly 'worthless' " performance in it were signs of hope. "Distasteful ... as it must be to our sense of propriety," the wage earner's "shirking may be the best hope that we have to-day ... that the zest of men and women for life, and that more abundantly, will incorrigibly reassert itself against overwhelming odds, and force recognition of the fact that life cannot be made permanently mechanical."[58] Bourne's "mind of the worker" contained as much self-projection as Addams's or, for that matter, Wright's or Morris's. But he put his finger on the quandary hidden behind the leisure solution to industrial monotony. If work had been stripped of its possibilities for self-expression, what was left for the creative workman besides botching his work and fleeing headlong from it?

Bourne himself still hoped for work into which men could eagerly and spontaneously pour the best of themselves. The hardest wrench of values was to admit that work under modern industrial conditions was inherently harmful, its "damage" to be undone only by leisure. It was through hoping so much for work, through maximizing its creative potential, that the progressive social investigators had discovered the realities of industrial drudgery. To abandon work for the new cause of leisure was to discard the core of their initial vision. But nothing else seemed practical. Wright's arguments seemed naive; education and betterment seemed at best palliatives. As for Morris and Ruskin, their questioning of progress seemed simply quixotic. "One might as well attempt to suspend the law of gravity," Charles Prosser argued, "as to stem the evolution of modern industry toward the large-scale production, division of labor, and specialized processes by which it makes goods of a cheaper price to supply human wants and tastes."[59] So the critics of routinized work turned at last toward leisure. In other ways and through other debates that path had been prepared for them.

Play, Repose, and Plenty 4

We have had somewhat too much of the "gospel of work." It is time to preach the gospel of relaxation.

Herbert Spencer, Farewell banquet address, New York, 9 November 1882

"The chief use of a farm," Henry Ward Beecher confided to New York City newspaper readers in the summer of 1854, "if it be well selected, and of a proper soil, is to lie down upon. Mine is an excellent farm for such uses, and I thus cultivate it every day.... Though but a week here, I have lain down more hours and in more places than that hard-working brother of mine in the whole year that he has dwelt here. Strange that such industrious lying down should come so naturally to me." [1] Praise of indolence, even when offered with such self-puzzled humor, was, indeed, strange advice for most mid-nineteenth-century, middle-class Northerners, and it was stranger yet that the advice should come from Henry Ward Beecher. Ten years earlier, in the sermons published as *Seven Lectures to Young Men*, Beecher had rung the changes on the moral preeminence of industry and set out in graphic detail the terrifying consequences of idleness. Well into the late nineteenth century, anxious parents placed the volume in the hands of their sons in hopes that Beecher's bats and vermin would frighten their potentially wayward lads into the paths of sober industry. Yet Beecher himself moved in the contrary direction. Even as the *Seven Lectures* continued to sell widely, Beecher's mood shifted away from unqualified celebration of labor toward a growing appreciation of the arts of repose and a hesitant reevaluation of the place of work itself in the business of living.

Straining in opposite directions, both book and author are important clues to the uncertain drift of work ideals in industrial America. The one pointed toward the enduring hold of the values of diligence, the other toward a long flirtation with leisure. Despite the noisy, enterprising activity of the decades after 1850, despite the simultaneously gathering cult of strenuosity embodied by Theodore Roosevelt, with his nervous grin and boundless energies, these were also the years in which middle-class Northerners learned to take holidays, to play, and, with some effort, to relax—all in growing confidence that the world could afford their vacations from labor. The shift in values went beyond matters of bicycles and baseball games, though they were among the more conspicuous clues to the larger changes afoot. Slowly and hesitantly many middle-class Northerners abandoned the idea of a world so crimped and dangerous that social and psychological health alike demanded constant doing; in its place they turned their imaginations to metaphors of surplus. The factory economy was not alone responsible, for ideas are not simply tails wagging at the rear of social forces. But as the flood of goods the factories produced flowed into middle-class households, carrying new amenities, overflowing into Victorian parlors overpacked with gewgaws, the values of thrift, diligence, and self-discipline could no more remain unaffected than could the premise of scarcity. The factories had directly consumed creativity and independence in work. Indirectly they ate away at the still older pillars of the nineteenth-century work ethic, the injunctions to useful effort and diligent self-discipline that had been at the heart of the Protestant Reformation.

Beecher's own career indicated the directions of change. Beecher had preached the *Seven Lectures* as a young Indianapolis minister, struggling to make ends meet at what he later recalled as the verge of the frontier. The memory exaggerated somewhat the primitiveness of Beecher's surroundings, but it did not exaggerate his sense of living hard by a wilderness in need of civilizing. His father, Lyman, had brought the family west from one of Boston's most influential pulpits to wage war against frontier infidelity, and the son inherited the preoccupation with evils to be overcome, perils to be routed, and heroic deeds to be performed; and he poured it all unstintingly into the *Seven Lectures* of 1844. Three years later, however, Beecher was called to Plymouth Church in Brooklyn, then a thriving and wealthy suburb for New York's commercial middle class. Ultimately the move launched Beecher into a prominence unequaled by any minister of his generation; immediately it yanked him from his crimped, frontier environment and sent him, in Constance Rourke's phrase, "swimming on the tide of a new opulence."[2]

The result was to seriously undermine the wilderness metaphor in Beecher's thinking. Where Beecher's father, an evangelical crusader of the old school, had vented his nervous energies by exercising on parallel bars and shoveling sand from one corner of his basement to another, the son soon learned the pleasures of an extended summer holiday.[3] Vacations were a new habit for the suburban middle class in the 1850s, and in regular summer newspaper columns Beecher encouraged and instructed his parishioners in their use. His ideal, equally removed from the feverish labors of the city and the hectic obligations of a resort holiday, was a month or more of quiet idleness. He spent his own six weeks in the countryside engaged in what he called "meditative and imaginative farming." The happiest moments of a vacation, Beecher counseled, were to be found flat on one's back in quiet, indolent communion with nature, "a passive recipient of all the impressions which the great out-of-doors can make upon you." "For unwearied hours one drifts about among gentle, joyous sensations or thoughts, as gossamers or downy seed float about in the air, moved only by the impulses of the coqueting wind." Time passed unheeded; study was abandoned for the drowsy reverie Beecher called "dream culture." Lyman Beecher had told his parishioners that reverie was a "delightful intoxication" that led straight to damnation, but for Henry Ward the once vivid torments of an idle mind had lost their sting. His vacations, Beecher reported happily, were a "tranquil, dreaming, gazing life."[4]

Beecher's winter sermons soon radiated the vagrant summer mood. In the highest Christian life, Beecher insisted, art and luxuries were more desirable than simplicity, rest and recreation preferable to overwork, joy and laughter more necessary than somberness. He deplored the absorption of the age in activity and toil, reckless in its disregard of leisure and grim even in its amusements. He gloried in the hope that religion was "getting rid of the old ascetic side" and becoming "more hopeful, more joyful, more loving, more genial, humane and sympathetic." This attack on Protestant asceticism went hand-in-hand with an attack on theological orthodoxy. For as he explored the idea of surrender to the restful charms of nature, Beecher simultaneously cut his ties with Calvinism, exchanging the harsh, judgmental God of his father—"the frowning God, the partial God, the Fate-God," as Beecher described the concept—for faith in a "Divine Friend," joyful, merciful, and overflowing with love. In sermons such as "The Fullness of God" or "Grace Abounding," Beecher preached a message of spiritual superabundance, of a Providence not miserly, as Calvinism had had it, but extravagant. "In every part of life God has fruit ready to drop into your lap," Beecher advised; God's "providential bounties" were "incalculable." [5] All of this represented an infusion of ideas worked out far more carefully by Horace Bushnell and ultimately rooted—like Beecher's summer immersions in nature—in the same romantic rebellion that made an iconoclast of Henry Thoreau. What was original in Beecher was not his theology but the complex of interwoven moral, religious, and economic themes. "Dream culture" meshed neatly with the concept of abounding grace and that, in turn, with the experience of affluence. Not in labor alone need a Christian attempt to draw himself closer to God. In reverie, half-asleep in the midst of plentitude, one slipped as certainly into the divine presence.

The new lessons did not succeed in pushing out the old in Beecher's public statements. His collected sermons tack back and forth between the strenuous and the passive ideals, contradictions awkwardly jostling each other. Beecher at once defended luxury as the indispensable seedbed of culture, and hailed the "kind bosom of Poverty" that nurtured manly character; he complained of the violence done to youthful brains by excessive industry and unrestrained ambition, and chided those who lazily remained at the bottom of the ladder; he praised commerce, and deplored the rush into white-collar occupations in the mistaken notion that "mere exchanging" would support the race. In his quarrel with Calvinism's wrathful God, Beecher urged a concept of God overflowing with grace; intent on rebutting the fatalistic implications of Calvinistic predestinarianism, he exhorted men to "work" with God, the "great Worker," in hammering out their own salvations. "Men that love leisure never can understand what

God means, who loves occupation. Men who put their supreme idea of life in self-indulgence, cannot understand what God means, who makes self-exertion, in Himself, in angelic powers, in all His creatures, the test of real being." Yet Beecher counseled no less earnestly that the danger of the times was overactivity: "I plead for having more leisure. I plead for having more rest." As Beecher himself once admitted, the pattern of his thought was "a kind of zig-zag."[6]

In part the baffling pattern was the product of the elitism that pervaded Beecher's thought. Those sermons explicitly directed at the young, the poor, or the working class tended also to be those in which the gospel of work was most prominent; in thinking of the prosperous, overtaxed businessmen in his congregation he often chose the counsel of leisure. The elitist strain was broadcast in his novel, *Norwood*, Beecher's single, highly successful venture into popular fiction, published in 1867.[7] Located in the rural New England of Beecher's summer vacations, burdened with an overambitious plot which, in trying to encompass the Civil War, grew thoroughly out of hand, the novel was a transparent device for Beecher to expound his favorite themes decked out in literary garb. Yankee industriousness was prominent among them. Beecher set his tale among a hard-working village collection of farmers and artisans and employed a young Southern visitor, a student of political economy, to drive home the value of Norwood's thrift and diligence. But at the center of Norwood's social and intellectual life Beecher placed a leisured aristocrat, a doctor of good lineage and a college education, an intimate of nature, a romantic in theology, a cultivator of dreams, and alone of his neighbors beyond the moral need of a steady occupation. Beecher took few pains to disguise either the flattering self-portrait or the elitist message, for elitism offered a tempting means of clinging firmly both to work ideals and to dreams of indolence, of holding in check the impetus toward leisure even as one celebrated it. In an early vacation paper, Beecher had warned: "Nobody has any business to expect satisfaction in a pure country life, for two months, unless he has a decided genius for *leisure*."[8] In the word "genius" a good deal of the pattern of Beecher's thought was laid straight.

But elitism only partially explains the contradictions within Beecher's ideas. In his massive disregard for consistency one catches an uneasy sense of treading on ambiguous moral ground. Even for the best of nineteenth-century thinkers, striking a new balance between the values of work and leisure proved a difficult task, a matter of half-steps and partial retractions. In the early 1870s, Beecher himself seemed to have tumbled headlong over the waiting moral precipice when he was accused of adultery by one of his parishioners. The charge was never proved and Beecher's reputation survived the blow, but men like Godkin were quick to suggest that the scandal in Brooklyn could not have occurred had there been "anything in the smallest degree disciplinary" in Beecher's preaching.[9] Clearly there were dangers in trading self-control for spontaneity, diligence for love, the virtues of old-fashioned labor for those of a surplus economy. But Beecher served in many ways as a scout for the main guard of Northern moralists. With a hesitancy and an elitism much like Beecher's, they too began to cast about for new values in keeping with the novel experiences of rising, factory-produced affluence.

What was at stake in the debates that followed was at once a moral code and a set of interrelated psychological, religious, and economic premises. Discipline—"the breaking-in of the powers to the service of the will," as Godkin called it in his quarrel with Beecher—was central to the complex. From the seventeenth century to the twentieth, Northern moralists possessed a vivid distrust of the forces held in check by the dams and levees of the will. Relaxation, rest, and diversion were all legitimate helps in strengthening and keeping supple the power of self-control; but abandonment of the gates to the seething flood behind them was certain disaster. Long before Freud talked of the "rowdies" who burst through the censorship of the ego into the theater of the conscious mind, nineteenth-century moralists had cataloged the upwelling temptations seeking a weak spot in the armor of self-control. "Keep the watch wound, for the dark rust assaileth!" Frances Osgood warned in one of the century's widely reprinted poems.[10] Work was the indispensable core of the moral life, for work was the anvil upon which self-discipline was forged, the ultimate barrier against the assailing forces of the psyche.

Of all the acids that ate away at work and self-discipline, moreover, affluence was among the most corroding. "The power of voluntary self-denial is not equal to the temptation of an all-surrounding abundance," Beecher's father had warned in 1829, and the conviction echoed across generations of middle-class moralists. Sapping the ego, "effeminizing" the will, seducing the conscience, crippling the desire to work, luxury destroyed morality in individuals and nations alike. By contrast, adversity made character. Andrew Carnegie was not unique in celebrating the benefits of poverty. "Man owes his growth, his energy, chiefly, to that striving of the will, the conflict with difficulty, which we call Effort," William Ellery Channing had argued in 1840. To exempt mankind from "our subjection to physical laws, our exposure to hunger and cold, and the necessity of constant conflicts with the material world ... would make a contemptible race." A half-century later, after a week's immersion in the tranquility of Chautauqua Institute, William James, too, recoiled from the prospect of a life abundantly supplied and unceasingly, tepidly good. "Sweat and effort, human nature strained to its uttermost and on the rack, yet getting through alive, and then turning its back on its success to pursue another more rare and arduous still—this is the sort of thing the presence of which inspires us." The Catholic bishop John L. Spalding reiterated the theme: "If there were no obstacles how should there be energy and courage? If Nature presented no difficulties how should man be made intelligent?" "Character cannot be created," Spalding insisted; "it must be formed in the heat of the battle." [11]

As keepers of the science of wealth, economists might have been expected to assume a more favorable attitude toward abundance; but they too harbored doubts. The paradox bore endless repetition in economics texts that in tropical lands, where nature was most generous and the terms of life were easiest, society was most torpid and most impoverished; only in those climates where heroic efforts and steady toil were demanded did rich and complex civilizations flourish. Moreover, all economists worthy of the name bottomed their science on the premise of competition for limited resources. Dire Malthusian pessimism was rare among the most widely read American writers on economic subjects, even during the presumed heyday of social Darwinism. Wisconsin's John Bascom, Yale's William Graham Sumner, and M.I.T.'s Francis A. Walker did insist it was "a hard, cold, cruel world" of "unpitying poverty" and "unceasing struggle for existence," but theirs was a minority report among American economists. The stronger nineteenth-century American tradition, typified by the cotton textile manufacturer turned economist, Edward Atkinson, kept up a steady attack on the gloomiest doctrines of Ricardo, Malthus, and Darwin.[12] Yet if most nineteenth-century economists denied that men were doomed to grinding poverty, virtually none of them dissented from Sumner's argument that there was no "boon" to nature except what men earned by "labor, toil, self-denial, and study."[13] Placing production first in their textbooks, the economists insisted on the preeminence of work and savings—the prudential, disciplined virtues that really mattered in a world governed by scarcity.

Finally religion, rooted in the same cultural experiences, ratified the assumptions of trial and discipline. From virtually every Puritan-descended pulpit in the mid-nineteenth century North one heard of the stern, sovereign, and often angry God who presided over his toiling creation. A minister had "no business telling sinners of the love of God without telling them of the wrath of God" as well, Lyman Beecher complained after listening to his son, Henry, preach in 1860.[14] Like orthodox economics, orthodox religion in the Protestant mid-nineteenth-century North was dominated by a sense of contest. Opponents and seducers lay in wait for all pilgrims following the path of righteousness. In a life made hard and disciplinary for man's own good, it was the duty of a Christian to muster his resources and bear the cross of pain, to buckle on sword and armor against the assaults of sin and the world's temptations.

All these threads converged to describe a world that was stern and demanding, where character was made by contest and the health of nations forged by diligent obedience to duty—where letting go was, as Beecher seemed to demonstrate, to slide over the lip of a moral abyss. To describe the complex so neatly is to risk exaggeration; at worst, it is to revive the caricatures of Victorianism invented in the 1920s by a generation of writers in flight from the scarcity-ruled and duty-governed world of their parents and grandparents. Dissenters from the assumptions of contest and the ascetic code were rife in the mid-nineteenth-century North, from the journeymen's shops to the counting-houses of the rich to the little band of romantics at Concord. For even the sternest heirs of Calvinism, moreover, the core of the religious experience was the moment of conversion, when grace came in an unbidden flood to inundate the soul of the believer. But for most of the North's established middle-class moralists in 1850, Beecher's summer theology of abundance, influx, and rest came as an alien vision. In a culture in which Edward Atkinson could describe leisure as "the diligent and intelligent use of time by him who earns it," in which Beecher himself in his sterner moods maintained that it was the man "dying with his harness on that the angels love to take," praise of ease cut to the core of moral orthodoxy.[15]

From the 1850s on, however, in pace with the accelerating economic changes, one can trace a steadily mounting attack on the excesses of work and a growing praise of play and recreation as antidotes to the violent, all-consuming busyness of the Americans. Ministers occupied a prominent place in this literature. The *Christian Union*, founded in 1870 partly as an outlet for Beecher's sermons, became a consistent critic of the feverish strains of the age, urging "the duty of play" on its overtaxed readers. The *Andover Review*, the leading spokesman for liberal Congregationalists, endorsed the leisure idea in the mid-1880s, and a decade later the *Independent*, the *Christian Union*'s major rival among interdenominational weeklies, abandoned its former scruples and joined the ranks of advocates of sports and summer vacations. Baptist and Methodist journals proved more resistant to the gathering praise of play and leisure, but by the mid-1890s the *Chautauquan*, organ of the Methodist-dominated Chautauqua movement, was equating intoxication with work to addiction to whiskey and was groping for "a middle ground between the idler and the man who works himself to death."[16] Old sermons on the texts of Carlyle and Franklin remained a standard feature of the religious press. From Oberlin, Charles Grandison Finney cautioned that the only lawful amusement for a true Christian was the holy ecstasy of redemptive grace. Even the urbane Episcopalian Henry C. Potter told his New York City flock that in considering the recreation question the first issue to be resolved was whether they had by their work earned the right to any play at all.[17] Yet with growing frequency ministers raised their voices against the all-consuming "run, push, drive" of American life.

The outcry from the pulpits against overwork cannot be traced simply to a loss of nerve, as the charge against nineteenth-century Protestant liberalism has often run. That unchecked industry offered a short byway to unchecked indulgence had long posed a dilemma for keepers of the work ethic. John Adams had put the paradox succinctly in a series of questions to Thomas Jefferson in 1819: "Will you tell me how to prevent riches from becoming the effects of temperance and industry? Will you tell me how to prevent riches from producing luxury? Will you tell me how to prevent luxury from producing effeminacy intoxication extravagance Vice and folly?"[18] For generations the answer had been to keep men's noses so close to the grindstone as to preclude time for the debilitating effects of riches, to induce those whom work made rich to plow their energies back into honest labor. The idle, pleasure-loving aristocrat had haunted the imaginations of men like Adams. But with the ascendance of an aggressive, commercially absorbed bourgeoisie, with the invasion of the Sabbath by newspapers and railroads, and with the growing suspicion that many "Gilded Age" Northerners had no life other than their work or souls other than the buttons they sold and manufactured, many ministers came back to reexamine Adams's riddle. In doing so they increasingly turned their attention to the first step of the conundrum, to ask if excess labor were not itself the first sign of moral debauchery. "If we are doomed to be tradesmen and nothing but tradesmen," the Unitarian Henry Bellows wrote in 1845 in a recurring complaint, "if money, and its influences and authority, are to reign for a season over our whole land, let us not mistake it for the kingdom of heaven."[19] To stem the all-absorbing disease of money-making, clergymen like Bellows were willing, often eager, to preach the pleasures of art and recreation, leisure and play.

While ministers raised the specter of moral ruin through overwork, late-nineteenth-century doctors warned equally starkly of physical collapse. Well before 1850 one can find cautions against the unhealthful feverishness of American life, its nervous climate, its lack of popular amusements, and its general scramble for wealth. Tocqueville, for one, thought the nation bred insanity. Only in the second half of the century, however, was "nervousness"—or "neurasthenia"—elevated to the status of a national disease. Coined in the 1860s, the term neurasthenia

covered a bewildering variety of neurological complaints—
headaches, melancholy, dyspepsia, insomnia, and spinal pains—
and joined them all as symptoms of a general exhaustion of the
nervous energies. The gathering neurasthenic threat was first
given general currency by the Philadelphia neurologist S. Weir
Mitchell in a widely circulated pamphlet, *Wear and Tear; or,
Hints for the Overworked*, published in 1871. Mitchell pointed to
statistics that seemed to show a dramatic rise in deaths at-
tributable to nervous causes and painted a graphic picture of the
living nervous wreckage he encountered in his own practice:
burned-out businessmen and "multitudes" of young women
ruined by "over-education," headed for "the shawl and the sofa,
neuralgia, weak backs, and hysteria." A decade later, in his
American Nervousness, George M. Beard brought the whole
abnormal frenzy of nineteenth-century civilization to bear on the
disease: its high-pressure education, overspecialized and over-
rushed labor, and its bewildering noise and tempo.[20]

A year after Beard's book appeared, Herbert Spencer, author
of the phrase "survival of the fittest" and the high priest of
economic competition, lent his enormous prestige to the charge
against overwork. At the end of a three-month American tour,
Spencer left his hosts with the warning that they were dying of
excessive toil and an inadequate "adjustment of labor and
enjoyment." That Spencer was suffering painfully from a
nervous collapse of his own that had precluded all but a cursory
look at American life did not prevent his protest against the
violent whirl of business and professional life from being picked
up by the magazines of the middle class and added to the
category of national faults. The mass-circulation women's
magazines, in particular, printed scores of columns on American
nervousness indicting overwork and overworry—the "dollar
fiends" as Mitchell called them. As late as 1904, when a
neurologist tried to inter "neurasthenia" as a hopelessly vague
clinical diagnosis, he felt impelled to apologize for threatening
one of the country's "most distinctive and precious pathological
possessions."[21]

Pride, clearly, figured as strongly as alarm in the discovery of a
national intoxication with work, and there were many who could
not resist the suggestion that the killing pace was cause for
national congratulation. Yet by the 1870s the counsel of slower
living and the need for vacations, play, and rest had penetrated

even the guidebooks for young men, where it stood awkwardly
beside maxims pirated from Franklin. Some of the counsel was
less than clear. Struggling to define the model American boy soon
after the turn of the century, one writer suggested, "The boy of
success is always busy—busy studying, busy working, busy
playing, busy resting." Yet the *Saturday Evening Post*, catering
to the young businessman on the way up, instructed its readers
far more straightforwardly that the man unable to spare a
moment for rest and enjoyment was "an awful being." *World's
Work* similarly qualified its fascination with the tempo of
industrial progress by publishing health advice for businessmen
in which rest, exercise, and vacations were prominently prescribed. Under titles such as "Why Take Life So Seriously,
Anyway?" and "Fun Is a Necessity," Orison Marden's *Success
Magazine* brashly promoted the new advice. When in 1904, in
what had been a conventional judgment a generation earlier,
financier Russell Sage denounced the "injustice" of paid vacations, the *Post* dismissed Sage simply as "an awful example of
thrift and industry gone mad." [22]

The campaign against national feverishness focused on the
burdens of middle-class living, decrying the hectic pace of brain
workers, housewives, and commercial men. Only far more slowly
and with much greater hesitancy did middle-class writers recognize the wage earner as overworked or competent to profit from
greater leisure. In the first two decades after the Civil War,
manufacturers typically defended the ten- or eleven-hour day as
an essential moral safeguard for their employees. "Nothing saves
men from debauchery and crime so much as labor," a Massachusetts boot and shoe manufacturer insisted in 1878, "and that, till
one is tired and ready to return to the domestic joys and duties of
home." Yet in the following decades there was a decline in the
frequency with which convictions of this sort were publicly
expressed. Whether the change was due to a growth of reticence
on the part of employers, or whether, as seems more likely, the
businessman's own flirtation with leisure had partially eroded
older fears of the idle moment and chipped away at the elitism
that pervaded the leisure question, in turn-of-the-century collections of business testimony on the shorter-hours question the
moral argument was clearly subordinate to the employer's
concern with his margin of profit. [23]

At the same time, a significant number of middle-class writers began openly to endorse the laboring man's demand for a shorter workday. The twelve-hour day and seven-day week in the steel industry caught the attention, and indignation, of middle-class magazines soon after the turn of the century. By 1907 Theodore Roosevelt had given his presidential blessing to the eight-hour day, and two years later the Methodist Episcopal Church (North) and the Federal Council of Churches joined in calling for a general reduction of the hours of labor "to the lowest practical point." Medical research in fatigue, popularized in the briefs Louis Brandeis and Josephine Goldmark prepared in defense of women's labor laws between 1908 and 1912, helped change many attitudes toward the length of the manual laborer's workday. To later fatigue investigators, the concept broadcast by Brandeis and Goldmark that tiredness was the consequence of a specific toxin in the blood seemed naive and simplistic. Yet the pioneer manipulators of ergographs and frog muscles helped broaden the overwork campaign and give muscular fatigue a scientific standing comparable to the brain worker's neurasthenia.[24]

The long campaign against overwork served as the intellectual side to a conspicuous expansion of free time and free-time activities. The more acute observers, attempting to calculate the extent of the transformation, took to counting vacation hotels, sports events, railway ticket sales, and movie-house attendances, and their choice of indexes was not far from the mark. Time explicitly set free from work grew apace, particularly after 1900. Summer vacations for the middle classes, still rare in the 1850s, spread rapidly after the Civil War until by 1920 a week's paid vacation had become the norm for most white-collar employees. Factory workers were as yet not expected to take vacations, but the recognition of new holidays, Labor Day in particular, and, by 1900, the Saturday half-holiday in summer were important symbols of the diminishing workweek. Figures on average working hours are treacherous abstractions that disguise enormous differences between regions and industries. Nevertheless, between 1850 and the late 1880s the "normal" workweek of factory employees dropped from about 66 hours to something closer to 60 hours; it fell again between 1900 and 1914 to about 55 hours, and declined still more rapidly during the war years to about 48 hours by 1920. The result of this 25 percent shortening of the "normal" industrial workweek was a rapid rise in explicit leisure-time activities: bicycling, picnicking, camping, vaudeville, movies, amusement parks, dance halls, and a host of new participant and spectator sports.[25]

The old, rigid rhythms of the Protestant Sabbath were no match for the influx of new amusements. In the 1870s and 1880s liberal ministers, Henry Ward Beecher among them, abandoned the old, unbendingly serious ideal of rest and worship to argue for the opening of museums, libraries, and concert halls on Sundays, but even this position was overrun by the pressures of demand for recreation on what was still the workingman's one weekly holiday. The Sabbatarians mounted a gigantic petition for a federal Sunday Rest Law in 1889, and they hotly battled the forces of Sunday amusement and play on the state level throughout the progressive years. But the federal effort failed, and by 1920 most of the Sabbath laws in the Northern states had been abandoned or undermined by custom.

The Sabbath controversy stood for far more than the legitimacy of a Sunday ballgame. Sabbatarianism had been a fighting, defining point for English Puritans, and the stiff and proper regime of serious thoughts and disciplinary self-denials had formed a central part of the experience of generations of churchgoing Northern families. Nothing more clearly symbolized the injunctions to duty and self-discipline, the obligations of careful, watchful control of self and time that were at the heart of the Protestant Reformation. By the early twentieth century, however, a sizable number of Northern Protestant moralists had begun to argue that it was not in self-discipline that a man's spiritual essence was revealed but in the free, spontaneous activity of play. The concept was a romantic idea, passed through Schiller, Froebel, and Horace Bushnell into the currents of popularized romanticism that gathered strength in industrial America, flowering in the shape of kindergarten and playground movements and, most clearly, in a vital and widely read literature in praise of play. Against the old, ascetic psychologies, against the ancient distrust of the subliminal mind, the play advocates celebrated the instincts. For a boy to play at cowboys and Indians was to let the energies of humankind flood down the well-worn grooves of instinct; for a man not to play—not "to dream dreams and see visions," to fail to escape the deadly hand of compulsion—was to starve the core of his being.

Joseph Lee, the Boston aristocrat and philanthropist who became head of the Playground Association in 1910, served as the most compelling spokesman for this transvaluation of morals from discipline to spontaneity. Play, Lee maintained, was not simply restorative for work but the paradigm of what true work should be—the unforced outflow of creative energies that would no longer, like most industrial toil, leave "some of our deepest instincts ... hanging in the air." "Play is the service of ulti-mates," Lee argued, "the word that best covers the things [man] ... was wound up to do, and in the doing of which he is most himself." For a nervous, overmaterialistic, overconstricted nation, which had taken toil to excess, to let go and play, to acknowledge the buried call of instinct, had become a more vital duty than work itself.[26]

There was no missing the gospel of play, reiterated as it was in a thousand sandlot baseball games and the frenzied enthusiasms of college football. What it actually meant, however, is not entirely clear. How much of the apparent explosion of leisure activities was a mark of increased energies spent in recreation and how much was simply due to a transfer of energies from such private, inconspicuous forms as an afternoon's gossip or fishing expedi-tion into the more public, blaring modes of urban recreation is not easy to determine. A phenomenon like Coney Island was far more striking than a county fair, but it was not necessarily a mark of dwindling industriousness. By the same token, the growth of free time is an ambiguous measure. Because shortened hours of labor were frequently accomplished by squeezing periods of relaxation and amusement out of working hours, by trading long hours of casual work for shorter, more concentrated workdays, decrease in the nominal hours of labor was no sign of a diminution of work itself. What did occur was an increasing segregation of work and play into distinct categories in place of the older interfusion of free and work time. The county fair was at once a respite from labor and a celebration of the farmer's skill, but a Sunday afternoon at the sideshows of Coney Island was crossed by no memory of the week's toil.

But that observation, too, begs essential questions, for among the middle classes a great deal of the time designated as play went into activities at least as energetic as work itself. Through the influence of the colleges, YMCAs, and athletic clubs, an unprecedented number of middle-class Northerners took time from work only to pour it into still more strenuous regimes of gymnastics, muscle-building exercises, and athletics. Some of the new sports that took hold after 1850—the vogue of croquet in the 1870s, for example—catered to a vagrant mood; but others— football, baseball, rowing, and their kin—were often elevated into exaggerated paradigms of work. If one of the results of the revolution in recreation habits was to encourage the gentle arts of a summer's outing, another was to fasten the lessons of competitive striving more firmly to the rites by which most middle-class youths passed into manhood. Action was a central preoccupation of the age, broadcast in such best-sellers as Thomas Hughes's *The Manliness of Christ*, the Merriwell series for boys, or the struggle-filled tales of Jack London. The cult of strenuosity and the recreation movement grew together, minimizing the distinctions between usefulness and sport, toil and recreation, the work ethic and the spirit of play.[27]

Nevertheless, hard by the encomiums to strenuous activity on the best-seller lists appeared a small but growing library of books that advocated not effort or self-control but their psychological opposites. In place of both work and play, they preached passivity and receptivity, the need to let go the nerves and surrender the will, to "slip over" troubles and discover "the power of repose." Ignoring the noise of the athletic field, they harked back to the "tranquil," "gazing" mood of Henry Ward Beecher.

Many of the handbooks of quiet living were guides to the conquest of religious distress. Hannah Whitall Smith's best-selling *The Christian's Secret of a Happy Life* of 1883 stood for much of the genre. Smith, who reckoned her own life in alternating phases of doubt and spiritual exaltation, addressed her advice to equally troubled readers, promising a "higher Christian life" of continual victory over the thorns of disbelief, pain, and sorrow. Her secret lay in ceasing to resist, in yielding up the self utterly to the workings of God. "Let your souls lie down upon the couch of His sweet will, as your bodies lie down in their beds at night.... Let yourself go in a perfect abandonment of ease and comfort, sure that, since He holds you up, you are perfectly safe. Your part is simply to rest. His part is to sustain you; and He cannot fail." Smith carefully tried to distinguish the cultivation of spiritual passivity from idleness. Yet the goal of the will, in her counsel, was to extinguish effort until the surrendered soul rested calm on the bosom of God, immune from the buffets of common life. Smith's advice was not unique. Twenty years later Samuel D. Gordon's *Quiet Talks on Power* attracted legions of readers with much the same counsel and a metaphor of spiritual abundance still more explicitly stated. Religious doubt, Gordon wrote, meant a clog in the pipe linking the parched and troubled soul to the overflowing reservoir of grace. "How shall we have power, abundant, life-giving, sweetening our lives?" His answer was to surrender the recalcitrant will—to *"pull out the plug."*[28] "Produce, produce," Carlyle had urged an earlier generation facing the terrors of disbelief. "Away to your Callings," the Puritan Cotton Mather had urged. But in the wake of Mather and Carlyle appeared spiritual handbooks eschewing work for the parable of the lilies of the field.

Another locus of the message of repose was New Thought, a splinter phenomenon in the churches distantly related to Christian Science, which attracted many seekers of the quiet life between the mid-1890s and the First World War. New Thought never crystallized into a lasting organizational structure, but, through a large library of books led by Ralph Waldo Trine's runaway best-seller of 1897, *In Tune with the Infinite*, and several dozen struggling journals, thousands of readers had a chance to soak up the New Thought creed that the world was made up of ideas—that thought and spirit, not things, formed the essential stuff of existence. Some New Thought writers like Frank Channing Haddock, whose *Power of Will* rivaled Trine's classic in readers, turned the principle into a lesson of success through strenuous thinking. In the same vein, Elizabeth Towne punctuated her New Thought magazine, *Nautilus*, with jibes at "weaklings" who failed to direct their thoughts strongly enough at the things expected. You "sit still and let thought-power evaporate through your skulls—and run off your tongues— instead of directing it downward through the nerves and muscles of your bodies where it will do some good.... Go in to win, and stick to it." Yet the dominant counsel of the New Thought books was to hold oneself in a state of quiet expectancy, to cultivate a "nonresistant attitude" toward life and the "inward repose" that would open the gates to the "divine inflow" of the universe. "No success ever came through forced effort," one New Thought writer advised. "It creeps in easily, gently, happily."[29]

In its stress on an indwelling, generous deity, New Thought was of a piece with the larger movement of liberal Protestantism away from concepts of divine harshness and angry judgment. But what the liberal churches hinted at, converts to New Thought took as a point of faith. There were no limits and few crosses to bear in the New Thought cosmos. "Opulence is the law of the universe," Trine wrote; there was "an abundant supply for every need if nothing is put in the way of its coming." To "enter the silence," as Horatio Dresser described it, to let oneself go in the midst of divine plenty, to "become grounded in eternal reason and calm in eternal peace" was the promise that lay closest to the heart of the New Thought appeal.[30]

As the spiritually troubled souls sought and received the counsel of repose, so did the nervous. In the early nineteenth century, work had occupied a central place in the treatment of psychic disorders. To the superintendents of the asylums built as refuges for the insane in the early nineteenth century, diseased imaginations and morbid introspection seemed tightly intertwined with madness, and through regular occupation of the hands and mind they tried to insure that the insane were never idle. For the neurasthenic, however, with his neurotic aches and nervous depletion, occupational therapy was eclipsed by the "rest cure" invented and proselytized by S. Weir Mitchell.

Mitchell stumbled on the cure in 1874 when faced with a New England woman whose exhaustion and insomnia had defied tonics, spinal supporters, spas, and repeated physicians' exhortations to keep on her feet, exercise, and remain active. In something of a quandary, Mitchell sent her to bed, and after ten days of concentrated rest, with massage and electrical stimulation to prevent the deterioration of the muscles, the patient showed a marked improvement. Mitchell soon joined rest with a regime of massive overfeeding to correct the deficiency of fat and blood cells that seemed to him at the root of the psychic symptoms. In its fully evolved form, the rest cure epitomized passivity and ingestion. The patient, typically a woman, was taken out of her previous surroundings, isolated from all potentially disturbing stimuli in the care of a professional nurse, and confined to bed and heavy feeding for six to eight weeks—forbidden at first to sit up and strongly counseled against use of either hands or mind. The cure spread widely in Europe as well as America, resulting in the construction of numerous sanitariums to house the idle recuperants and making Mitchell famous as a healer of the "dilapidated." Like the vacation habit, the rest cure was a middle-class luxury, and its vogue suggests something of the weakening of work ideals at their center. To those overburdened with compulsive usefulness Mitchell counseled that their activity was not needed, that the world could get by without their nervous attentions. He offered, temporarily at least, a total reprieve from the demands of conscience, from worry, from effort itself.[31]

Soon after 1900 Mitchell's emphasis on cell depletion and the somatic causes of nervousness began to seem old fashioned, and the interests of students of psychic disorders turned to the new phenomenon of the subconscious. Dark potentials waited there, as Freud had pointed out. Boston's pioneer psychotherapist Morton Prince unearthed some of them when he uncovered a series of angry, rebellious multiple personalities under the exterior of one of his outwardly most self-controlled patients. But William James was far closer to the mainstream of American opinion in dismissing such terrors for the more optimistic faith that the subconscious was a vast latent reservoir of psychic energy and mystical inspiration.[32] Whether the subliminal energies were to be tapped through relaxation of effort or through a redoubled will James was far from clear. With many others of his generation, he struggled to find a balance between a conviction that only the useful, strenuous life was worth living and a fear that Americans were overconstricted, too tightly clamped, and dangerously ignorant of the "gospel of relaxation." Most professional psychotherapists likewise echoed James's search for a mean between effort and relaxation with eclectic prescriptions in which rest, play, and a resurrected "work cure" were freely intermingled.

Yet the early twentieth-century venture into psychotherapy that riveted public attention was not the work of professional psychologists but the effort of a talented amateur that came much closer to the relaxational ideal. In the winter of 1906-7, Rev. Elwood Worcester opened a clinic for the treatment of nervous disorders in Boston's fashionable Emmanuel Church. Modestly begun, the clinic soon attracted an astonishing amount

of publicity. Far overshadowing in the public mind the contemporaneous lecture tours of Freud and Janet, popular accounts
of the clinic's work and eagerly sought articles by Worcester and
his associate, Samuel McComb, gave most middle-class Americans their first lessons in the new psychology.[33] Worcester's
eclecticism no doubt accounted for much of the attention he
attracted. He brought psychotherapy together with large elements
of New Thought, New Testament expertise, an interest in
Buddhism, a close acquaintance with S. Weir Mitchell, and more
than a hint of the traditions of faith healing. But the Emmanuel
cure itself was the center of attention. Worcester's technique was
to join prayer with the practice of "suggestion" that had been
pioneered by Bernheim at Nancy, France. After a preliminary
period of discussion, the patient was seated in a reclining chair
and slowly urged into a "hypnoidal" state of drowsy calm, in
which his temporarily dissociated subconscious was open to the
physician's curative counsel. The result, Worcester suggested
cautiously, verged on the mystical. Implanting ideas in the
subconscious was secondary to a merger of the indwelling spirit
and the fully relaxed mind, the tapping of "those inexhaustible
subconscious powers which have their roots in the Infinite." At
an Emmanuel clinic in Northampton, Massachusetts, Lyman
Powell instructed his patients:

> Your mind is full of turmoil and distress because you have
> not rested in the peace of Jesus. . . . It is through the sur-
> rendered will that you will find the peace of God. . . .
> Swing open wide the windows of your soul to the incoming
> of these thoughts and your anxieties will disappear.

Work generally followed in the Emmanuel prescription, but the
healing touch was through repose. Prayer and therapy rested on
the same passive configuration: downing effort and opening "the
inner consciousness to the absorption of spiritual energy."[34]
    Interest in the Emmanuel clinic fell abruptly after 1909 under
the criticism of professional psychologists. Worcester's movement was a passing fad in an age that fell in love with football
and celebrated the hyperactivity of Theodore Roosevelt. How far
beyond the religiously and emotionally distressed the gospel of
passivity extended it is impossible to say. The ideal of repose
appealed more to the sick than to the well, and more to women

(who made up the bulk of both Mitchell's and Worcester's patients) than to men. Yet the spiritual guides, the rest cure, and the Emmanuel clinic are important clues that there were more uses to the new leisure time than strenuous recreation. Going beyond criticism of overwork and beyond the gospel of play, the prophets of repose struck out boldly at activity itself.

What was equally significant in the guidebooks to rest was the recurrent metaphor of abundance. Mitchell's assumption of nervous bankruptcy continued the older, familiar vein. But elsewhere, whether the telltale phrase was the New Thought concept of "supply," Gordon's reservoir of grace, or the Emmanuel notion of a vast untapped well of subconscious energies, the economic model of the prophets of repose was premised on superfluity. The play advocates had assumed that the world could afford and would be the richer for a diminution of effort. They had challenged the preeminence of the will and the old ascetic legacies of Protestantism in the name of the free flow of instinct. The advocates of rest quietly abandoned not only the doctrine of effort but the bedrock assumption of scarcity. The relationship between their visions of psychic and spiritual super- fluity and the expansive, goods-overflowing industrial economy was complex and indirect. But far removed from the bustle of the factories, one of the lessons of the industrial revolution—that scarcity and hardship were no longer the inescapable lot of man—was absorbed and broadcast.

The most formidable obstacle to the new doctrines of play, ease, and plenty was the objection of the economists. That the spiritual cosmos was filled to overflowing was one matter; that material scarcity no longer ruled, that there were ways to wealth outside hard work and disciplined savings, was another. Generations of repetition of the doctrine of usefulness stood in the way of recasting economic ideas on any other premises. "It is the iron rule in our day to require an object and a purpose in life," Nathaniel Hawthorne had complained of the regional faith on the eve of the Civil War. "It insists on everybody's adding some- what—a mite, perhaps, but earned by incessant effort—to an accumulated pile of usefulness, of which the only use will be, to burden our posterity with even heavier thoughts and more inordinate labor than our own."[35] But protests against usefulness itself were rare in the nineteenth-century North with its press of impending tasks and beckoning crusades. Moreover, if the existence of widespread poverty was any clue, the nation was indeed poor, and desperately so. Dozens of studies made in the late nineteenth and early twentieth centuries uniformly confirmed that the wages of an ordinary factory laborer were inadequate to support a family. By sending their children to work or by taking in boarders, industrial workers struggled to make ends meet, but impoverishment caught multitudes of them nonetheless. Large-scale surveys by the United States Bureau of Labor in 1901 and the United States Immigration Commission in 1908-9 found between 20 and 30 percent of wage-earning families living on total incomes of less than $500 a year, at least $100 lower than contemporary social workers' estimates of the minimum subsistence budget for an urban family.[36]

Poverty, accordingly, was undeniable in industrial America. The economists' orthodox answer was that only redoubled work, frugal investment, and ingenious invention could slowly augment the amount available to go around. Workingmen, on the other hand, had long argued that poverty was a matter not of limited goods but of a society that failed to distribute its plenty equitably. The middle-class moralists long resisted the idea, but they were not immune to the changes around them. The impressive expansion of the industrial plant, the startling new capacities of machinery, the appearance of new comforts, and a rising middle-class standard of living ultimately eroded scarcity convictions even among economists.

Ironically, it is not in times of affluence but in times of poverty—in the response to economic depression—that the shift away from scarcity concepts can be traced most clearly. Depressions—or panics, as nineteenth-century writers knew them—scattered the nineteenth- and early twentieth-century economy like recurrent whirlwinds, making failure an omnipresent threat for small businessmen and helping to ingrain the prudential, cautious virtues in the Northern middle class. In explaining the precipitating causes of economic collapse, there was much acrimonious debate over the aggravating effects of tariff, banking, and monetary policies. Yet in the middle years of the nineteenth century, particularly among the free-trade partisans who controlled economic orthodoxy, the heart of the matter was widely seen as moral. Depressions began in a fever of reckless speculation, overextended credit, and extravagant consumption, which grew in intensity until the nation finally careered into bankruptcy. "We have been living too fast, ... eagerly trying to outdo each other in dress, furniture, style and luxury," and collapse was the inevitable consequence, a Cincinnati paper censured its readers in 1857 in phrases that could be heard at every hand in every pre-Civil War depression. Panics were matters less of finance than of financial sinning, punishments for riotous living; and the cure, as for individual impoverishment, was to cut one's expenses and go back to work.[37]

The immense property destruction of the Civil War and the rapid and alarming wartime growth of the national debt added to a sense of national poverty. In the economic slump of the late 1860s and again in the far more serious depression of 1873-78, the bankruptcy theme was tirelessly reiterated. "Shovel dirt, saw wood, do any kind of reputable work, rather than abide in idleness," Washington Gladden pleaded in 1876. "The only relief for our present distresses will come through industry and frugality; through a chastening of our ambitious notions of life, and the cultivation of simpler tastes and a more contented spirit." The explanations of economists, though more complex, were in much the same vein. Oxford's Bonamy Price, in articles that circulated widely in America, blamed the crisis on excessive investments in plant and railroad construction, through which Americans had squandered capital beyond their limited means. The cause of the trouble, Price insisted, was "one and one only: over-spending, over-consuming, destroying more wealth than is reproduced, and its necessary consequence, poverty." Others, led by Horace White, former editor of the *Chicago Tribune*, laid the trouble to a general speculative mania and an enormous accumulation of debts. In either case the remedy was the same: a return to the hardpan of work and frugality.[38]

The concentration of the nation's press in the financial centers and the economists' ties to the world of commerce accentuated their preoccupation with the cataclysmic collapse of securities from which the lesson of bankruptcy seemed so obviously to follow. Yet, if from the perspective of the banker and the merchant, speculation and reckless investment were the central precursors of a panic, the chain of events familiar to manufacturers and industrial workers was of overstocked products, stagnant markets, wage cuts, and, ultimately, factory closings and unemployment. Their experience was not of extravagance followed by impoverishment but of excess products begging for consumers—of work apparently all out of proportion with ability or willingness to spend.[39]

Orthodox economists strenuously resisted the overproduction and underconsumption arguments that flowed so naturally from the experiences of manufacturers and workingmen. The argument that supply might so outrun demand as to result in a "general glut" was regularly raised as a straw man in depression arguments; but, despite its defense by Malthus and Rodbertus, from whose reformulation the overproduction thesis passed into socialist orthodoxy, the economists of the classical tradition declared the idea a heresy. The rebuttal was first made by J. B. Say, from whom the doctrine took its name, and it was put in its classic form by John Stuart Mill in his *Principles of Political Economy* in 1848. For Mill, the idea that the aggregate supply of goods could exceed the aggregate means or desire to purchase was a logical absurdity. And, though he did admit the more crucial point that the means of purchase and potential consumers might not always match and that production itself might be "ill-assorted," he followed conventional lines in attributing depressions to overextensions of the credit system and put the immense weight of his authority against any arguments posited in terms of "overproduction." Logic seemed wholly against the argument of general excess. The United States Monetary Commission report of 1877 stated what seemed self-evident in arguing that production could not outrun the development of wants nor riches produce impoverishment. "The idea that either superabundant wealth or superabundant facilities for producing it can be the inciting cause of rapidly spreading poverty is repugnant to the common sense of mankind." It was "the idlest of fancies, and wholly unworthy of serious notice."[40]

As the depression of the 1870s wore on a number of writers nonetheless risked questioning whether industrialization had not sufficiently upset common sense that bankruptcy was no longer an adequate metaphor for economic crises. In *Popular Science Monthly* in July 1877, O. B. Bunce broached the word "overproduction" to describe the periodic binges of an economy no longer governed by personal contacts between artisans and consumers; the demand of the day, Bunce suggested, was for "regulated production" that would hold in check the new "magical facility" of machinery. By the end of the year Horace White, while denying that overproduction had brought on the depression, had turned his attention to the excess manufacturing capacity in the iron, woolen, and cotton textile industries to argue that permanent prosperity would not return until tariff reduction had opened foreign markets for the domestic surpluses. The *Atlantic Monthly* printed yet another argument in the heretical vein that claimed the root of the crisis lay in the unwillingness of the rich to consume more extensively and in their quixotic and self-destructive habit of excessive saving and investment.[41] In probably the most influential of the minority reports, David A. Wells, a free trader like White and one of the nation's leading writers on economic subjects, vacillated between blaming the current state of trade on a prodigal "waste" of capital and on the effects of production "far in excess of any legitimate wants" that, for the first time, had made labor "manifestly surplus." The weight of Wells's argument, however, was against the conventional notion of national impoverishment. "The country . . . is suffering to-day," he wrote, "strange as the proposition may at first thought seem, not because we have not, but because we have; not from scarcity, but from abundance."[42]

The heresies cautiously offered in the 1870s were repeated far more confidently a decade later. The depression of the mid-1880s was an anomaly in economic annals, an international economic slump in which no financial crisis precipitated the quiet but disastrous decline of profits and wages, and the experience did much to accelerate the transition from financial and moral to industrial explanations of depression. By 1883, coal operators, iron manufacturers, distillers, shoe manufacturers, sugar refiners, and paper millers all complained of overstocked goods. Echoing their arguments, the first report of the newly created office of federal commissioner of labor in 1886 ascribed the current crisis to "overproduction . . . or, to be more correct, bad or injudicious production," by which the commissioner, Carroll D. Wright, meant virtually the same thing. "The United States has gone on perfecting machinery, duplicating plant, crowding the market with products, until to-day, this country is in the exact position of England, with productive capacity far in excess of the demand upon it, and her industries ... stagnated, the wages of labor reduced, prices lowered, and the manufacturers and merchants trying to secure an outlet for surplus goods."[43]

A more extensive argument than Wright's was that of David A. Wells, who, returning to the issues broached in 1877, offered an impressive array of evidence of the startling growth in productive capacity since the Civil War, to which he traced the current massive dislocation of markets. Still hesitant to defy economic orthodoxy, Wells nonetheless now concluded that only the term "overproduction" adequately described the imbalance of swollen supply and limited demand. Wells did not disguise the free trade bias of his case, but even such a staunch protectionist as James G. Blaine, while preferring the term "excessive production" to "overproduction," admitted that the power to produce seemed to have a "constant tendency to outrun the power to consume." *Banker's Magazine* in an editorial in 1885 suggested that the novel lesson of the depression was that "having reached the point of producing enough to satisfy all rational wants of mankind, we must stop" and cease to work so hard.[44]

Pouring over Wells's data, one of his readers found himself appalled by the evidence of rampant technological change:

> What a deplorable and quite awful picture you suggest of the future! The wheel of progress is to be run over the whole human race and smash us all, or nearly all, to a monstrous flatness! I get up from the reading of what you have written scared, and more satisfied than ever before that the true and wise course of every man is to get somewhere a piece of land, raise and make what he can for himself, and try thus to get out of the crushing process.... Do you really think the "game pays for the candle"?[45]

Wells rejected the pessimism, arguing that the temporary evils of industrialization were "infinitesimal" compared with the benefits to follow. Like most of the economists who broached the overproduction argument, Wells thought of gluts as temporary dislocations, rejecting the fears raised by workingmen of permanent surpluses or uncontrolled labor displacement by machinery. The depression of 1893–97, moreover, was ushered in by the familiar phenomenon of boom and collapse, which helped to turn the attention of academic economists back to the credit and financial system. Measured against the sophisticated business cycle theory worked out by Thorstein Veblen, Wesley C. Mitchell, and others before the First World War and against their careful analysis of what Mitchell called the "money surface of things," excess capacity seemed as simplistic an explanation for depressions as national bankruptcy.[46]

Yet after the 1880s, Mill's rebuttal to the overproduction argument had clearly lost a good deal of its force. In phrases such as an "almost universal glut" or "a constant danger of something like 'overproduction,' " economists bent Say's law to the new realities. In 1900, in a synthesis of depression theories aimed at a popular audience, Edward Jones warned that the truism once enunciated by Mill that "if we can only produce enough, consumption will take care of itself" no longer fit the modern industrialized economy. The pressing task of modern educators, Jones announced, was to nurture new wants sufficient to match the new productive capacities. Yale's Arthur T. Hadley, who in 1885 had blamed depression distress on speculation, by 1896 concluded that modern societies stood in "perpetual danger of under-consumption." "We have for generations been cultivating motives which should make individuals reduce their consumption and increase their investment . . . and we have apparently overdone the matter."[47]

After 1900, even the compromises of the academic economists clearly lagged behind vocal segments of public opinion. The prophets of economic plenty were an odd assortment of manufacturers, imperialists, social workers, and left-wing progressives, all of whom shared the conviction that production had given way to more pressing imperatives. Champions of trusts and foreign commercial expansion were among the most vigorous exponents of the idea of excess productive capacity and of the need to control or find ways to dispose of the goods that had already saturated the American market. At the Republican convention that renominated William McKinley in 1900, Chauncey Depew of the United States Senate and the New York Central Railroad announced that "the surplus products of civilized countries in modern times are greater than civilization can consume" and thanked God that in opening the Philippine and Cuban markets the administration had averted the impending crisis.[48] Others stressed the imperative of more equitable distribution. Simon Patten, an economist with close ties to the social gospel movement, argued in a series of murky but influential books that the age of "pain" and "deficit" had given way to a "pleasure or surplus economy," if men only had the wit to see and bring their ideas into step with the "stupendous" revolution in economics. Patten's own attempts to reformulate economic theory not in terms of production and aggregate wealth but in terms of consumption patterns was more quietly reflected in the marginal utility based economics texts written after the turn of the century in which the initial section, once devoted to production and labor costs, was replaced by an analysis of demand. Social workers in their turn seized on the conclusion that poverty and pain represented the dead and enfeebled hand of the past. "There is apparently enough to suffice; the 'national dividend' is abundant and to spare," Jacob Hollander told readers of the *Atlantic Monthly* in 1912 in an article on the "abolition" of poverty. Reiterated with increasing frequency and conviction, the idea that an era of surplus had arrived, that the age-old "problem of production" had fallen before the industrial revolution, became one of the clichés of early twentieth-century thought.[49]

Finally, at the furthest extreme of the new views, men like Patten and the young Walter Lippmann announced that not only poverty but self-discipline, self-denial, obedience, chastity—all the prudential virtues of the age of scarcity—had been outmoded by the new turn of the economy. "The non-saver is now a higher type than the saver," Patten argued. "I tell my students to spend all they have and borrow more and spend that. It is foolish for persons to scrimp and save." Van Wyck Brooks, joining the prophets of economic plenty, charged that "economic self-assertion" was itself "to a large extent a vicious anachronism." Only "force of habit, the sheer impetus and ground-swell of an antiquated pioneering spirit," and a blind failure to perceive better outlets explained why men continued to pour their energies into the production of "a reckless overflow of surplus wealth."[50]

At Brooks's writing on the eve of the First World War, the suggestion that work itself might be an archaic trait remained a rare hint and a mark of youthful iconoclasm. "Those of us who live in an ease-economy are but an island in the stormy ocean,"

William James had cautioned in 1910. The war, with the conservative impact of disaster, brought back with a rush the old haunting fears of impoverishment. Bankers and schoolteachers organized a massive wartime thrift-education campaign. The *Saturday Evening Post*, which a decade earlier had warned against industry and savings "gone mad," argued in 1915 that denigration of production had reached its limit. "To meet the reasonable wants of its inhabitants the world must become richer; it must produce more.... The world is really poor."[51] Yet in the postwar depression of 1920–21, the temporarily buried argument reemerged. While the *Post* applauded the revival of the "work-and-save" doctrine after the extravagant postwar buying, while the *Review of Reviews* published the explanation of banker A. Barton Hepburn that "you cannot go on a spree without suffering in the cold gray dawn of the morning after," a businessmen's group called the National Prosperity Organization posted New York City with handbills urging the nation to "Clear the tracks for prosperity! Buy what you need now!"[52] The best cure for national impoverishment in the new industrial age, many Americans were learning, was not to tighten one's belt but to let it out a notch, not to work—work being superfluous—but to consume.

"Any honest man" can understand financial questions, "because they are also, and equally, moral questions," Rev. Leonard Bacon had proffered one of the commonplaces of his day in 1873.[53] By 1920 many writers found it considerably harder to talk about economic matters with the same moralistic assurance. Over-saving, overproduction, underconsumption, unwillingness to buy in the midst of panic—the new depression explanations trans-valuated personal virtues into public disadvantages in a process that tore the Reverend Mr. Bacon's world in twain. The metaphor of abundance as insinuated into religion and psychology in the counsel to unclamp the will, to open the gates to the life-giving rush of instincts and energies, likewise essentially shifted the grounds of ethics. To take life easier, to slacken the pace, "is contrary to the spirit of all we know of the general progress of civilization," the editors of *Scribner's Magazine* objected in the midst of the overwork outcry.[54] But the drift of the times was toward more hedonistic moral calculi more in keeping with the new possibilities of production.

In the end, the most significant shift of the industrial age was the quietest of all: the increasing frequency with which the moralists demoted work from an essential to an instrumental virtue. "The great end of life after all is *work*," an anonymous clergyman writing in the *New Englander* had clinched an argument on the amusement question in 1851. But three-quarters of a century later, readers looking for that maxim in the middle-class press would have been hard put to find it. Even in the *Nation*, where Godkin had kept up a steady drumbeat of protest against distribution-oriented economics, arguing that only constant, unslacking toil kept the wolf from the door, one could learn by 1910 that the world had room for "an indefinite number" of people "who do not shirk work but whose appetite for it is limited."[55] Life was life, it was now said, and work only the means to it.

The legacies of the Protestant Reformation still had a good deal of life to them in 1920. Of all the pillars of the work ethic, the predilection to see the moral life as a mustering of the will against the temptations within and the trials without remained the strongest, the least affected by the industrial transformation. The new "gospel of relaxation" was full of awkward and hesitant compromises. Churchmen promoted "play" that liberated energies but not "amusement" that depleted them. Advocates of shorter industrial work hours insisted that, in the end, rested workers were more productive workers, that more work followed from greater leisure. Hannah Whitall Smith spoke for most of the religious writers in admitting that she found it "very hard to explain" the "infinitely passive and yet infinitely active" state she had in mind. In the recreation movement, opposite temperaments openly competed for primacy. Many of the recreation specialists were drawn to their careers less by the desire to liberate the instincts of play than by the wish to civilize the urban recreational wilderness of street games, dance halls, and movies. Not a few retained a vivid fear of idleness and in making recreation surveys sedulously counted, and deplored, the number of children who, failing to play, were caught merely walking or conversing. All recreation writers advertised play as an intensely serious endeavor. Play was not idleness, nor leisure loafing. As for the economists' embrace of the idea of economic surplus, from the point of view of a John Maynard Keynes it was as yet an uncertain union. The concepts of a "mature economy" of limited work or of a cybernetic revolution that would do away with work entirely were fears for other generations.

Part of this apparent confusion was simply a matter of language, the inevitable consequence of trying to force new meanings into old vocabularies. Most middle-class Americans slowly found their way toward new balances of work and leisure that were more comfortable than the conservative constraints of language made them appear. Most of them, having absorbed something of the long attack on overwork and nervous self-repression, found ways to blend the new gospel of relaxation with the older, sterner concept of character, just as large numbers of them traded Lyman Beecher's angry God for Henry Ward Beecher's and Dwight L. Moody's infinitely tender one without abandoning the faith that the world had pressing work for them to do and urgent crusades to be mounted.

Nevertheless, the erosion of the familiar certainties of discipline and duty had gone far enough to pose new and nagging questions. Commenting on the current move to increase the difficulty of golf course hazards, the *Saturday Evening Post* mused that the apparent object of the masculine world "to make its work easy and its play difficult ... makes the job of the moralist a hard one." [56] To conceive of depressions—economic, spiritual, and moral—in terms of impoverishment made the counsel of renewed work and redoubled will a simple and appropriate response. To conceive of moral breakdown as rooted in overwork or economic crises in overproduction, to conceive of work as play and repose as energy, was to put middle-class Northerners onto unfamiliar ground. In its creature comforts, the new terrain was infinitely more enticing than the old. But amid the ever increasing stock of factory-made products, fashioned by a sort of toil that increasingly could be justified only by appeal to the character-building, disciplinary psychology that the profits of that toil were rapidly eroding, it was harder than before to find the accustomed moral landmarks. Slowly Henry Ward Beecher's puzzlements caught up a whole society.

Splinterings: Fables for Boys 5

Plane and Plank [illustrates] the contrast
between a young mechanic of an inquiring
mind, earnestly laboring to master his
business, and one who feels above his calling,
and overvalues his own skill, ... though the
incidents of the hero's career are quite stirring,
and some of the situations rather surprising.
> William T. Adams, *Plane and Plank; or,*
> *The Mishaps of a Mechanic* (1870)

What happens to values when the material props are cut out from
beneath them? That is to pose too grandiose a question, surely;
yet the slicing away of material context was precisely what
happened to work values in industrial America. The work ethic
had rested on a set of premises about the common, everyday
work of men that made sense, by and large, in the North of
1850. Work was an outlet for self-expression, a way to impress
something of oneself on the material world. Work was a means to
independence and self-advancement. In a society in which tasks
seemed to press from all sides, in which there was an economy to
build and the wolf to be kept from the door, even the most
onerous drudgery carried the sanctity of contributing to the
common good. But the factories undermined each of these
premises; the compulsive zeal to produce fashioned a new kind of
economy and disturbingly unfamiliar forms of work. As jobs were
divided, simplified, and routinized in the quest for efficiency, as
outlets for individuality narrowed and skills disappeared, a wedge
was driven between art and work, creativity and labor, self and
job. As the factories grew larger and more regimented, as offices
and commercial establishments grew more factorylike, and as
more and more of the workforce assumed the role of employee,
the possibilities of an ordinary worker's gaining economic independence steadily receded. Finally, as the factories periodically
glutted the markets, stopping the wheels of commerce, as it

seemed, by the sheer volume of goods they produced, some of the confidence was drained from the certainty that the unstinted energies of all the land's potential workers were sorely needed. As middle-class Northerners recognized the shifts around them—as the best of them tried, and failed, to wrest this new uncreative, quasi-free, and perhaps unneeded labor to their ideals—what happened to those ideals themselves?

The answer hallowed by common sense is that values shift, laggingly and painfully, scraping over new ground until they come to rest on a firmer footing. Elements of that process are unmistakable in industrial America. The erosion of scarcity convictions was the most evident sign of ideas pulled in the tow of material change, but there were others. From Jane Addams to the industrial democracy advocates to the employment managers who built on the betterment work begun at Dayton, Ohio, early twentieth-century moralists began increasingly to define work in collective terms, matched to the new realities of collective enterprise. As the self-sufficient worker disappeared in fact, nineteenth-century ideals of self-sufficiency slowly gave way to ideals of teamwork more suited to an industrial and bureaucratic society. By the same token, success writing grew more involuted in the face of narrower opportunities, retreating from the domain of work and habits to the less pregnable citadels of mental attitude and self-confidence. Phrases that once carried immense potency, like "free labor," simply lost their currency and disappeared.

Yet the striking phenomenon of the age was not change but persistence amid change. Or, to be precise, it was the endurance of the outer husk of the work ethic as an increasingly abstract ideal, more and more independent from work itself. No one should expect consistency from any society, but in moral matters in industrial America it is clear that the right and left hands increasingly lost converse with each other. The appeal to the dignity and nobility of work was too old, and often too useful, to give up, even as it grew more and more painful to look closely at labor itself, and even as habits and values shifted, half-acknowledged, under the familiar rhetoric. If one aspect of the impact of industrialization on work ideals was to set in motion forces of change, another was to split things apart—to separate off the old phrases and old homilies from the roiling confusion of everyday life.

Nowhere was the splintering process clearer than in the stories written for boys growing up in nineteenth- and early twentieth-century America. With the conspicuous, and overblown, exception of Horatio Alger, children's fiction has rarely found a place in history books; nor have children themselves ever had much of an entry there. The socialization process by which children are won over to the moral visions of their elders has been taken peculiarly for granted by students of the past. And yet it is by no means a simple process. Somehow values must be passed intact between generations if an ethic is to endure; somehow the constantly infiltrating young must be made allies of the old and the wise. Nineteenth- and early twentieth-century moralists were acutely aware of this, and they poured prodigious energies into the creation of schools and school systems to train the young, turned out the first widely read child-rearing handbooks for the guidance of parents, and produced an enormous outflow of magazines and fiction aimed for the first time specifically at children.

What place children's tales occupied in the welter of socializing influences that bore on children growing up in industrial America, how they compared in influence with the official homilies of schools and churches or the far more powerful pressures of peers and families, it is impossible to say. Like so many other aspects of nineteenth- and early twentieth-century culture, children's reading divided along lines of class and respectability. That which was admitted to library shelves in an age when children's librarians took their censoring responsibilities with immense seriousness was the work of writers whose values belonged to Protestant, middle-class, moralistic America. Louisa May Alcott, Jacob Abbott, and *St. Nicholas Magazine* occupied a social world clearly distinct from that of *Elsie Dinsmore*, the dime and nickel novelists, and *The Boys of New York*. Children's tales divided along lines of sex as well, though there was some half-ashamed crossing over on the part of boys and more adventurous forays on the part of girls into each other's libraries. Finally, children form a relationship with their fiction that is unfathomed and still quite mysterious. Certainly they do not read in any humdrum, literal way, but as persons engaged— extraordinarily impressionable and extraordinarily obtuse. Specific incidents gouge indelible tracks in the memory, as any adult who has gone back to his childhood books discovers, while page upon page rolls off into oblivion. The English historian of children's literature, F. J. H. Darton, reread the *Swiss Family Robinson* of his youth and came away from the reencounter amazed at his "wholly erroneous recollections" of one of his favorite boyhood stories. "I never knew ... that it was full of the most extravagantly laboured piety," he remarked. "All I remembered was that a very large snake swallowed the donkey and was killed when comatose from repletion; that the family had a house in a tree; that they tamed and rode ostriches, made lassoes, built a boat, tapped the india-rubber tree, ... and found a salt mine." For generations before that, American children reared on *Pilgrim's Progress* had likewise managed to skirt its theology, overleap its moral, and fasten upon what one of them recalled as the "gorgeous and bloody romance" of Christian's duels with Apollyon and the Giant Despair.[1] All children's stories in this sense are twice-told tales—the teller's words revised, elaborated, and severely edited in the intermediary of the child's imagination. The children's tale and the adult's tale are not the same story.

Nevertheless, if the children's tales designed for respectable, middle-class households are uncertain clues to the experiences of childhood, they form an invaluable guide to the mind of the adult moralist, particularly in an age when writing for children was not yet cut off as a distinct, subliterary profession. Harriet Beecher Stowe and William Dean Howells, Jack London, Carl Sandburg, and a host of lesser-known figures wrote for both adult and child audiences in these years. But writing for children imposed special responsibilities. Cornered by the young, particularly by boy readers bound for careers and economic responsibilities, the storytellers could not avoid themes of work and duty. They could not evade the task of setting forth the ethical formulas a child would need to carry with him into the snares and responsibilities of adult life. The career of work values, accordingly, is not all to be found in volumes of social economy. One facet of it is spread out, dusty, knee-high, on children's bookshelves.

The book world of a middle-class child growing up between 1830 and the mid-1850s was small and exceedingly earnest.[2] *Pilgrim's Progress* was a staple in respectable Protestant households. It might share company with a volume of the *Arabian Nights*, or Perrault's fairy tales, or their more horrific English counterparts, though none of these were held in good repute in the early nineteenth century. Few homes with any books at all were without some product of the burgeoning Sunday school publishing industry, either in the form of a young person's moral and spiritual guide or the tearful, joyous tale of a dying, heaven-bound child. But the dominant figures of the early nineteenth-century middle-class nursery were Maria Edgeworth and Jacob Abbott. In enormously widely selling books, they brought not tears, or fantasy, or the allegorical mysteries of Bunyan, but a solid, rock-certain world of reason, fact, discipline, and diligence. In this carefully ordered world, work was inescapable.

Few children's writers have ever approached the influence of either of these apostles of reasonable morality. Maria Edgeworth was an English writer who served as helpmeet and collaborator to her father—an inventor and educational theorist, a friend of James Watt and the elder Darwin, and a classic representative of the marriage of science and bourgeois morality that became known as utilitarianism. Maria Edgeworth's first tales, originally written for the improvement of her brothers and sisters, came to America in the late 1790s; almost a century later, American publishers were still bringing out new editions of her most famous and revealingly titled collection, *The Parent's Assistant*. Bronson Alcott, transcendentalist that he was and rebel against utilitarianism, read Edgeworth's stories to his daughters Anna and Louisa May; Edward Everett Hale at the age of sixty-five was certain he could reproduce a large amount of her "Harry and Lucy" from memory.[3] Jacob Abbott, on the other hand, was a home-grown storyteller, a Maine-born educator, Congregationalist minister, one-time tutor of mathematics and natural philosophy, and successful author who wrote the first of his Rollo books largely by accident in 1835. Like Edgeworth's stories, these New England set tales quickly found a large and loyal audience. Two dozen Rollo books came after the first, followed by a highly influential child-rearing guide and more than a hundred other children's titles before Abbott's death in 1879.[4]

What joined the two writers was a common loyalty to the moral universe of John Locke and Benjamin Franklin. The child who opened an Edgeworth or an Abbott story entered a family-centered world, presided over by preternaturally calm and rational parents. Stories were made out of the most ordinary of occurrences, spun into concise moral lessons, and interwoven with generous instruction in the practical and natural sciences. Magic, sentiment, and high adventure had no place amid this pervasive, didactic reasonableness. Edgeworth herself warned that tales like *Robinson Crusoe* cultivated a taste for adventure "absolutely incompatible" with the "sober perseverance" essential to adult life, and her stories, like Abbott's, never lost sight of that preparatory function.[5] Their tales were explicit, everyday conduct guides for a world in which both physical and moral laws reflected the governing rationality of things and the consequences of behavior were as certain as the results of scientific experiment. Diligence, perseverance, self-control, and dutifulness were not merely external injunctions in their stories; they were essentials, the code of ordered habits set by an ordered universe.

Certainly no child reading an Edgeworth or an Abbott tale could escape the intertwined lessons of work and discipline. Edgeworth's most famous stories drove the point home through the device of contrast. In "Waste Not, Want Not," she matched a young, carelessly wasteful fop against his frugal cousin to show how a saved package string returned in the teeth of need to reward the character of its owner. In "Lazy Lawrence," which came to America under the more straightforward title "Idleness and Industry," she followed the same formula, posing a poor but industrious boy against the village idler. Through perseverance, ingenuity, and exceptional dutifulness, poor Jem wins the means to pay off his mother's pressing debt; but Lawrence, destitute of self-control, desperate for relief from "the unsupportable fatigue of doing nothing," slides relentlessly into gambling, theft, and, finally, prison.[6] Stories like these were choosing tales. They set a child at the head of the network of forked roads that dominated the landscape of early nineteenth-century children's literature—work or idleness, discipline or recklessness, truth or falsehood, duty or disobedience—and impressed on him the necessity to choose aright.

Abbott, too, employed the carrot and stick of the contrast tale, but his *Rollo at Work*, which appeared in 1838, is in many ways the more revealing story. Barely a tale at all, it is a parent's guide to the teaching of diligence, written for child readers. In it, step by step, through a series of gradually more difficult tasks, through reason, patience, and, when these fail, a short stint of bread-and-water punishment, the six-year-old Rollo is weaned by his father from the child's world of play and fancy to the persevering, systematic labors of adulthood. "You see it is very necessary ... that you should have the power of confining yourself steadily and patiently to a single employment, even if it does not amuse you," Rollo's father tells him after Rollo has found an hour of sorting nails unbearably dull. The fault of boys, Abbott warned, was to expect work to be as much fun as play. On the contrary work "requires *exertion* and *self-denial*"; it was the mark of a man to know that, and to "expect that [work] will be laborious and tiresome, and ... go steadily forward notwithstanding."[7] Just as Edgeworth insisted on the divide between goodness and misbehavior, Abbott insisted on the gulf between the frivolous child and the disciplined adult. Growing up, the child reader learned, was a laborious process of self-conquest, habit grafted upon self-disciplined habit.

In the new children's magazines that began to appear in the late 1820s, lesser writers broadcast many of the same assumptions and mined the same devices. Only Samuel G. Goodrich drew the line against sentiment as rigidly as Abbott or Edgeworth or larded his endless stream of Peter Parley tales with quite so many facts. Yet, for all their susceptibility to sentiment, few secular children's writers strayed far from Goodrich's insistence that children's writing must be fashioned from everyday, tangible experiences capable of "sensible representation," or from the central moral of life as a labor of self-discipline.[8] In the domestic, didactic universe of "sensible things" the writers produced, the lessons of work were reduced to certain repeatable formulas. The contrast tale was one of these, posing the industrious against the lazy and conceited schoolboy, the mere trader against the maker of tangible things, the idle child against the busy world of nature, or the quiet and useful forget-me-not against the showy tulip. Another formula hymned the joys of usefulness in the story of a child, cocooned in a world of playthings, who is finally released into the more satisfying universe of duties and responsibilities. Still another formula was the story of experiment with idleness, in which the child reader, lured into the prospect of a week of delicious, irresponsible leisure, watches it all collapse into boredom and unmitigated disaster. One such storybook boy, granted his wish to be as idle as a butterfly, is chased by an enraged bull, gorges himself painfully on cherries, falls out of a tree, and finally comes home, sobered, to announce that "it is by industry and study alone, that men become great and esteemed."[9]

Tales like these drummed home not the heroic virtues but the sober, prudent economic ones. From the young, still-impulsive Rollo to the hired boy Jonas—a steady farmer, a skillful mechanic, and a paragon of industry—to Rollo's wise and perfectly self-controlled father, the lessons a boy must learn were set out step by step, just as a tribe of Lazy Lawrences warned of the alternatives. With incident and moral fused together in common didactic purpose, it would have been hard for a child to miss the point that systematic, self-disciplined work told—in happiness, in contribution to the common good, and in tangible reward. Nowhere were the assumptions behind the nineteenth-century work ethic set out more clearly or more persuasively.[10]

A generation after 1850, however, the openly didactic, work-tied tale seemed a relic of the past. "What have become of the 'Rollo' books of our infancy?" Henry James asked in 1875 in a searing review of Louisa May Alcott's *Eight Cousins*. "The child-world [then] was not a world of questions, but of things," not of "shrill" and precocious children but of respectful and obedient ones. The Abbott books, still in print at the turn of the century, had more life to them than James knew. But he was right in pointing to a major shift in writing for the young. Middle-class Northerners raised on Abbott and Edgeworth had begun to tell children quite different kinds of tales than had been told to them.[11]

One of the signs of the "new era" in children's literature, as its partisans hailed it, was the ascendancy of the fairy tale. Early nineteenth-century moralists had distrusted stories "calculated to entertain the imagination, rather than to improve the heart or cultivate the understanding." William S. Cardell, author of the immensely popular *Jack Halyard*, dismissed the Mother Goose rhymes and fables as "trash" not written by "sensible" people. But in the wake of Hans Christian Andersen's stories, which came to America in the late 1840s, the publication of imaginative tales, both old and new, grew rapidly. The *Youth's Companion* held out against the trend, but in the children's magazines of the second half of the century its resistance was lonely and eccentric.[12]

Joined with the triumph of the fairies was the retreat of the intrusive moralist. Twain announced baldly at the outset of *Huckleberry Finn* that anyone trying to find a moral in it would be banished; but far more conservative writers than he turned against what one reviewer called "the old-fashioned stories, with a moral or pious reflection impending at the close of every sentence." Increasingly, children began to speak up in children's tales, to tease their fanciful and indulgent storytelling papas, and to demand, and sometimes to get, stories without any moral to them.[13] Yet another sign was the appearance of a new kind of boys' tale—a nostalgia-filled story of boys still half-savage, the best part of them not yet broken to the prim, restrictive conventions of civilization. Thomas Bailey Aldrich's *The Story of a Bad Boy*, which appeared in *Our Young Folks* in 1869, was the first of the line which led through Twain to Booth Tarkington's *Penrod*. In one of these tales, Charles Dudley Warner told the young readers of *St. Nicholas*: "Of course the perfectly good boy will always prefer to work and to do 'chores' for his father and errands for his mother and sisters, rather than enjoy himself," and he would always rather split kindling than "go a-fishing." But Warner had only heard of one boy like that, and he had died of a morbid case of obedience.[14]

All of this amounted to a heady infusion of romantic ideals into the children's book world. The new children's writers turned deliberately from the understanding to cultivate the imagination; they overran Abbott's world of wise adults and "sensible" things and planted the standard of the innocent, glory-trailing child, fresh from the dews of heaven. By 1865 a reviewer in the *Atlantic Monthly* could contend: "We have ceased to think it the part of wisdom to cross the first instincts of children, and to insist upon making of them little moralists, metaphysicians, and philosophers, when great Nature determines that their first education shall be in the senses and muscles, the affections and fancies."[15]

What accounted for the sudden new turn of children's tales is hard to determine. Part of it, clearly, was due to the same slow diffusion of romantic ideals that seeped into the churches in the second half of the nineteenth century, sent Henry Ward Beecher sprawling and gazing in the midst of nature, and gave sanctity to the term "play." By the turn of the century, opponents of industrial child labor had turned to the same conventions to argue that the real harm of early factory toil was that it crippled the soul of the child at the time when it was just opening itself to love, to poetry, to "the eternal and infinite" truths.[16] But it is also unmistakably true that after 1850 many children's writers turned away from "sensible" things in recoil at the directions of economic change. The fairies were never needed more, they insisted, than in the modern, relentlessly matter-of-fact world where children "grope up and down the tunnels of brick and stone." Retreating to preserves of the imagination or to rural and child-centered oases of boyhood memory, children's writers tried to carve out a place unviolated by either industrial society or sharp-elbowed didacticians. A child's magazine should be a "pleasure-ground," the editor of the model of them all, *St. Nicholas*, proposed in 1873. "Let there be no sermonizing, ... no wearisome spinning out of facts, no rattling of the dry bones of history."[17]

In practice, the children's writers' revolt amounted to half a revolution at best. Annie Moore did send a fairy on a visit to a beehive in the first volume of *St. Nicholas* and had her emerge, her subversive innocence intact, to suggest that they try "less work and more dancing." But the tone of most American fairy tales was far more serious than this. Louisa May Alcott's fairies, for example, danced in the interstices of a life of good deeds and busy "toil." James Russell Lowell invented a bad, dream-inducing fairy called Fan-ta-si-a and a good one called El-bo-gres. Much later, in the feminine, gentle land of Oz, Dorothy learns that it would not do at all to have everything one wished for, for then "there would be no eager striving to obtain the difficult, ... and the pleasure of earning something longed for, and only to be secured by hard work and careful thought, would be utterly lost." Clearly writers did not find it hard to cap old lessons in the new and deceptively fanciful bottle of the allegorical tale.[18]

Moreover, many of the new imaginative stories went far beyond patient industry to enjoin the most arduous heroism and, ultimately, self-sacrifice. Children are "the only revelation we have, except Divine revelation itself, of that pure and natural life we dream of, and liken to heaven," one of Maria Edgeworth's bitterest critics, Julian Hawthorne, pleaded; "at the least we might refrain from moralizing." But Hawthorne's own tales were far from fanciful, amoral pleasantries. "Long ago, before the sun caught fire, before the moon froze up, and before you were born, a Queen had three children," his own most widely read fairy tale began. But she left her children, and they lived alone in their castle and castle garden, with a high hedge around it and a great forest around that, which was the domain of gravest danger—a dwarf looking for his thousand and first trespassing child who, when caught, would break the garden's spell and turn it into thorns and brambles. The children do go irresistibly beyond the guarding hedge, of course, and the mud of pride and disobedience disfigures them, and the garden turns to desert. Only trial and pilgrimage will put it right; only when the proud Hilda consents to be yoked to a plow like a horse, and only when Frank lays himself down to be consumed as a brand in a fire, are the mud spots burned away, the dwarf's spell broken, and the blasted world set right again.[19]

This was the old Christian fable of sin, expulsion, toil, and redemption; and perceptive parents no doubt perceived the familiar bedrock under Hawthorne's disguises. But what the child saw was a world of threatening evils, immense responsibilities, and awesome sacrifices. Over and again, as R. Gordon Kelly has shown, late nineteenth-century children's stories whisked parents away and thrust the child into a position of crucially responsible isolation. "Children who read these stories were invited to regard every moment of life as precarious, unpredictable, and inevitably serious."[20] The didactic tale never set the moral stakes quite this high; the world of Jacob Abbott was never quite as stern or frightening as the child's "pleasure-ground" could be.

The new children's writers, in fact, never intended to discard the moral tale or their own deeply felt role as moralists. What they objected to was the tacked-on lesson, the obtrusive sermonizer. Thus they turned from overt instruction to the more difficult task of manipulating the child's imagination. In practice this meant abandoning the ordinariness of the Rollo stories and heightening the elements of adventure, escalating the imaginative stakes until—fully ensnared but oblivious to coercion—the child was drawn into the moral lesson.

The new children's writers faced a second and still more troubling problem in connecting the child world with adult life.

The didactic writers had led the young step by step into habits of adult virtue. But the romantic storytellers were torn between the impulse to shelter children in their laughing games and green-bordered swimming holes and the responsibility to show them that they had heroic, demanding missions waiting for them far beyond those ever expected of the clay-bound Rollos. Writers for girls generally found it possible to compromise these impulses. From Louisa May Alcott's heroines to Kate Douglas Wiggin's, storybook girls learned to transmute innocence into loving, generous sympathy and to leave playthings behind for a woman's burden. But depicting a career for boys who would have to take their places somewhere in the new, shifting, and distrusted industrial economy was another matter. The factories had made anachronisms of Jonas and his village skills. But how, off the farm, did one show a boy growing into the work of manhood?

In casting off the old formulas, the new storytellers assumed an awkward pack of burdens. They wanted both to win a child's freely given imagination and to control it; they wanted both to shelter children and to thrust them out, if only for a trial moment, into adulthood; they needed to find adult roles for boys that would win a boy's imagination and not violate the writers' own nagging doubts about industrial society. It was not surprising that things often fell apart. Sometimes, as in Hawthorne's case, the moralist seemed not to know his own moralizing. More often, particularly in the world of boys' stories, the mortar between incident and moral, the foundation stones of the storyteller's art, tended to crack and give way. Boys' story writers announced their aims in conventional ways and professed their faith in the centrality of work and self-discipline. But the announced story and the one actually told were rarely quite the same; the preface and the tale itself were often disconcertingly out of joint. One of the results of an age of dislocating change was that its counsel to the young grew increasingly split and uncertain.

William T. Adams is a case in point. Though he is forgotten now, under his pen name Oliver Optic he was one of the late nineteenth century's most prolific and successful boys' authors. "There is a period in the life of every youth, just about the time that he is collecting postage-stamps, and before his legs are long enough for a bicycle, when he has the Oliver Optic fever," a critic noted the phenomenon in the 1880s. Carl Sandburg consumed every Optic book the Galesburg, Illinois, library possessed at the end of that decade; and as late as 1900 schoolboys in Stockton, California, threaded their way past such rivals as Henty and Alger to pick out Optic as their favorite author.[21]

Adams was a New England moralist in background and in convictions. He was a school principal until he turned to full-time writing in the mid-1860s and thereafter was a school committee member, a temperance lecturer, a member of the Massachusetts state legislature for a term, and a Sunday school superintendent most of his adult life. He wrote his first boys' book in 1854 for the benefit of his Sunday school class, and though the plot included excitements of a sort unknown to Rollo and his friends—a fight, a robbery, a near-drowning, and an immense amount of nautical lore—*The Boat Club* was a story within the Abbott tradition. Under the guidance of a watchful father, Optic's boys learned to mend their recklessness, control their tempers, and obey their parents—to achieve the discipline of self the nineteenth century called "character."[22]

But Optic was restless under this sort of tale of formal, parental tutelage. As *The Boat Club* expanded into a series in the late 1850s, wise and instructive fathers vanished from Optic's stories. Thereafter his heroes were orphans, widows' sons, or children of invalid or morally crippled fathers—autonomous boys all, forced to make their own way in the world. This was a potent story formula, and Optic was the first American writer to exploit it to its fullest. He took the boy reader out of the familiar props of family life, put him into his father's costume, and pushed him out to wrestle single-handedly with the adult world until, at the last moment, some convenient twist of plot stuffed the boy safely back into the bosom of home and family once more.

Over the next decade, Optic's tales exploited the moralistic possibilities of the device. In *Work and Win; or, Noddy Newman on a Cruise* of 1866, he took a vagabond orphan as his hero—a bold, daring, impulsive boy, able to handle a boat and rescue shark-beset maidens, but deadly afraid of "patient, plodding labor." Optic battered him around in adult society, cast him into a hellish, tightly disciplined ship, marooned him on a Pacific island, opened him to the softening, spiritualizing influence of an

angelic child-woman, and, in the end, made a "new man" of
Noddy—no longer an "idler and a vagabond" but "industrious,
useful, and reliable." Through his painful lesson in the habits of
"stubborn toil," he had won the grace and happiness of victory
over self.[23] It was true, Optic admitted warily in the preface each
of his stories bore, that tales of this sort contained a good number
of exciting incidents, but he hoped his readers would see that
these were only the "canvas" upon which the real story—the
reformation of the hero—had been painted.[24]

But after *Work and Win*, Optic virtually abandoned all else
but "canvas." Part of the escalation of "stirring" incidents in
Optic's tales stemmed from the new pressures of full-time
authorship and the burdens of concocting a new boys' book every
three months. A larger part derived from the sudden rise of the
dime novel and story paper industries in the middle years of the
century. Intruding rudely into the moralists' domain, they forced
"respectable" boys' writers to compete with more sensational and
adventurous plots, even as they decried the new tribe of Dead-
wood Dicks and "yellow-back trash" in general. In Optic's
stories, in any event, the theme of character reformation soon
vanished as completely as the intrusive father. Optic's boys no
longer learned lessons from the outside world. Nor did they work
off their impulsive, chivalrous habits in exchange for self-
disciplined ones. They now lived in a world of rescued maidens,
distressed ships, stolen money, and tangled inheritances, and
they played at knight errantry with abandon. In this atmosphere
of contest, rivalry between fathers and sons escalated into open
warfare. Precocious boys, in one of Optic's favorite set pieces,
lashed back at the heartless men who held their mothers'
mortgages; orphans ran from the grip of cruel guardians who
wanted nothing but work out of them. Work itself, in fact,
receded to the vanishing point. *Field and Forest; or, The
Fortunes of a Farmer* turned upon the theme of Indian fighting;
Plane and Plank; or, The Mishaps of a Mechanic was a convoluted tale of robberies and lost relatives; *Desk and Debit; or,
The Catastrophes of a Clerk* revolved around embezzlement, a
sailboat, and an abducted woman. "I do not intend to weary my
readers by giving the monotonous details of my daily experience
at the desk," the narrator of the last ingenuously confessed.[25]
Optic's heroes were no less moral paragons than before, but their

fundamental code had shifted from restraint to impulse, from work to deeds of nerve and daring.

A short story published almost simultaneously with *Work and Win* showed Optic's new formula at its purest. In one eventful week, a fourteen-year-old boy—"bold as a lion, and as generous as the softest heart could desire," but who disliked work and had never done much of it—rescues a drowning girl, faces down an overbearing mortgage holder, sails his father's fishing sloop into a cornucopian fishing hole, and pilots a fog-bound steamer through a maze of shoals to safety while the grizzled captain looks on in admiration.[26] This was the Jack in the Beanstalk story in modern guise, the tale of a lazy, dreamy boy who steals a fortune from under the nose of the giant; and it was as subversive of Jacob Abbott's moral code as a tale could be.

In short, Optic helped to usher in the full-blown boys' adventure story. And yet he never admitted what he was doing. His prefaces continued to point back to the virtues of diligence and Christian forbearance; no matter that his heroes showed little of either. Adult figures continued to point to morals of self-restraint that the stories undercut. Occasionally a critic caught the troubling doubleness of the Optic tales, and Adams himself knew his dilemma. At the outset of his writing career he had announced that he would try to combine "healthy moral lessons" with enough "exciting interest" to attract the young. He hoped he had "not mingled these elements of a good juvenile book in disproportionate quantities," but that question of balance troubled him throughout his career. "Perhaps" his heroes were too smart, he warned, their circumstances extraordinary, and some of their actions doubtful. In his revival of Samuel Goodrich's merger of travel stories and geography primer, Optic admitted he found it easier to write an exciting tale than to contrive ways to insinuate the useful information he had studiously collected.[27] But he refused to capitulate to his temptations. The Sunday school superintendent wrestled with his tales, the moralist with the writer of stirring and surprising incidents, each going their increasingly separate ways.

If Optic was a particularly striking example of the peculiarly divided counsel offered to boys growing up in post–Civil War America, of the persistence of the rhetorical shell of the work ethic in increasingly incongruous settings, he was by no means unique. A second case in point is that of Optic's younger friend and protégé, Horatio Alger. Optic was instrumental in starting Alger on his postministerial career as a boys' story writer, and Optic's conventions flowed easily from Alger's pen: the autonomous boys, the crippled fathers, the cruel and exploiting guardians, and the overbearing mortgagees. As everyone knows, Alger joined these elements with pecuniary ingredients of his own into a celebration of upward mobility. His stories insisted that even the poorest boy could rise in the world if he had energy, industry, ambition, and character. He defended the dignity of labor fervently and interminably. His very titles told the tale: *Strive and Succeed, Forging Ahead, Struggling Upward, Slow and Sure.* But, as almost everyone also knows by now, Alger was all but incapable of actually showing the steady, sober advance he talked about so much. His heroes could be picked out by their eagerness to take a job and their toil-soiled hands, but, aside from city bootblacks and newsboys, he rarely showed them working. They saved their money, but luck and patronage were the architects of their fortunes. As Russel Crouse noted years ago, after puzzling through the improbable coincidences of the typical Alger tale: "Mr. Alger could have done much better by the work-and-win theory."[28]

There was no single formula to Alger's near-endless stream of stories but at least four of them. The central one, the one he talked about so often, was the story of the poor boy who made his own way in the world by a steady growth in moral habits to reap "the legitimate consequences of industry and frugality." *Ragged Dick* (1868) and *Risen from the Ranks* (1874) came as close to that formula as Alger ever managed, and in them one finds, soberly and carefully laid bare, the bedrock of prudential virtues that underlay Alger's moral cosmos. Lessons in self-education and self-control were at the bottom of both tales. By turning their energies from a boy's extravagances to study and self-discipline, by forswearing oyster-stew banquets for their dog-eared French primers and their carefully husbanded savings books, by diligence, respectability, and thrift, Ragged Dick rises to the brink of a clerkship and Harry Walton to a country editorship.[29] But much as Alger believed this carefully fashioned tale and repeated its cautiously optimistic moral somewhere in virtually all the stories he wrote, most of them were critically different.

Several of Alger's tales, as Michael Zuckerman has pointed

out, were not stories of success at all but were stories of nurture and guardianship. Mark the matchboy was the first of Alger's weak and protection-needing orphans, and, though the sheltering theme was never again as strong as in Alger's first street-urchin stories of the late 1860s, it returns in snatches long thereafter. More common was a third kind of tale, as much a success story as Harry Walton's saga, but with only the shell of that story's moral. For in these tales Alger's heroes did not work out their careers but had them thrust upon them. Over and over again an Alger hero performed a crucial act of kindness, honesty, or heroism in reward for which fortunes fell at his feet.[30] Critics have often tried to link this imposition on providence to a lingering Calvinism in Alger, but the real affinity of these stories is to the conventions of the classic, European fairy tales. Bootblacks and farm boys took the place of Cinderellas, and the magic helpers who turn the fortunes of the hero were disguised as hermits or merchant-patrons, but the formula was the same. In the enchanted Alger cosmos, if a good boy acted at the crucial moment—if he stopped a runaway horse or returned the honest change—the magic gifts were his and the princess and her father's fortune as well.

Finally, in the 1880s, yet another formula pushed all these aside—the tale of lost and recovered fortunes. In these stories fortune was not built through work and self-denial, nor was it the reward of bravery and goodness; it was a stolen legacy, and the hero's mission was not to earn it but to find it. Almost invariably the quest began in a village where the Alger hero endured the persecution of the town's rich man and the snobbery of his prideful son. And almost as invariably it ended there as well, with the revelation that the criminal was none other than the squire himself. In the last, obligatory scene, justice set things right; the squire became the poor man, and the boy assumed his rightful place.[31]

Fortune was the central constant throughout these shifting formulas. Alger wrote for every boy who had been snubbed by his schoolmates, who felt ashamed of his patched trousers, or who chafed at the dull ordinariness of small town life. He took the theme of ambition, so distrusted by the moralists of Jacob Abbott's generation, and made a romance of it. But the boy whom Alger caught up in Aladdin-like daydreams might be pardoned if he failed to follow Alger's moral. Alger insisted on the centrality of industry, but virtually all the crucial, testing incidents he showed came to his heroes at their leisure, and in the tales of recovered fortune it was essential that the hero lose his job at the outset to free him for the quest. By the same token, the rich men whom one rarely saw, the distant strangers of the city, were inspiring examples of men who had worked their way up from poverty. But there was every chance that the rich man a boy knew well, the owner of the nearest mansion, was a thief. Alger talked of life as an endeavor; but he showed it as a magical web of coincidences and, increasingly, as a detective story. The tale of rising in the world by "the legitimate consequences of industry and frugality" eluded him, and like a modern Midas he turned his moral tales into simple pecuniary fantasies.

Alger's curiously splintered universe was not wholly the result of his literary inabilities, immense as they were. His stories splayed at the seams in part because Alger himself was only half-comfortable in the industrial economy whose possibilities he celebrated so enthusiastically. He once wrote that Abbott's Jonas "must have been a very unpleasant companion for a young boy like Rollo," and clearly Alger had absorbed too much of the self-confidence of his expansive age to enter into the spirit of old-fashioned didacticism and thoroughgoing restraint out of which Jonas had sprung.[32] But if Alger admired the fluidity of his age, he was profoundly distrustful of industrialization itself. He never showed a boy actually at work in a factory. His genteel, vaguely occupied merchant-patrons were from the outset part wish-fulfillment and part anachronisms. He set most of his tales consciously in the past, in the farm, workshop, and counting-house economy that was rapidly disappearing. And in his grasping village magnates he kept up a steady, covert attack on unrestrained capitalism. Among late nineteenth-century moral-ists, Alger's was a familiar pattern. Absorbing both the extravagant confidences of an expansive economy and its nervous fears, he wrote his tales in the teeth of these difficulties, preaching his sober, cautionary lessons and weaving the heady romances that undercut them.

Both Alger and Optic worked on the edges of middle-class respectability. Their awkward compound of moralism and sheer adventure and their middling position between the dime novels and the dignified pages of *St. Nicholas* made them all the more suspect to many conservative critics. Though in practice most public libraries kept Optic and Alger stories on their shelves, church groups, book critics, and children's librarians kept up a determined attack on both authors through the 1880s. The precociousness of their boy heroes and the absence of adult instructors was worrisome. Still worse were the patently fantastic qualities of the Alger and Optic stories, the failure of their plots to recognize the world's hard and toilsome realities. In chorus, critics warned that the new boys' stories taught false and extravagant views of life. Too much reading of them too early sapped the will and crippled the intellect; they made dreamers, not workers, out of the boys they infected and drained them of "the 'clear grit' that conquers difficulties."[33] The familiar anxieties of Victorian America—about enervation and loss of self-control, about the fragility of family life, about foolhardy contravention of the edicts of scarcity—swirled around the heads of Alger and Optic. Yet the gallons of ink poured out in criticism did not prevent boys' stories in the citadels of children's writing respectability, *Harper's Young People, Youth's Companion,* and *St. Nicholas*, from growing more and more like the Alger and Optic tales—more melodramatic and more insular, the thrust of their plots increasingly at odds with the prudential injunctions drummed home so insistently a generation before, their moral lessons, in the end, increasingly confused.

The firm and patient father who had dominated Rollo's youth was the first of the casualties. Writers like William O. Stoddard, John T. Trowbridge, and Kirk Munroe did not cast their boy heroes as completely adrift as Alger or Optic; they modified their heroes' adventures, eliminated much of Alger's crass materialism, and insisted that rewards be clearly tied to some degree of character reformation. But they could not resist the formula of the familyless, autonomous boy, and for two decades after 1880 the story of the orphan boy (or girl) cast abruptly into the world and winning selfhood and a career was a staple plot of serial story writers.[34]

Gang stories, boarding school stories, and Boy Scout stories—all in sudden celebration of group solidarity and the importance of fitting in—nearly wrested the autonomous, self-dependent boys from the stage in the first two decades of the twentieth

century. But in this eruption of Progressive group consciousness
into boys' literature, adults were scarcely more important than in
the orphan boy genre. Parents hovered on the distant peripheries
of these tales, never quite comprehending it all, their proprieties
interfering with the essentials of a boy's life. If the orphan boy
stories played on a boy's resentments at domineering and constraining parents, the school stories played on his sense of their
irrelevance, depicting an exclusively adolescent world, where a
wise and distant headmaster might offer counsel but, for a boy's
imaginative purposes, there were never any parents at all.[35]

Still more striking than the eradication of parents from boys'
stories was the triumph of the chivalrous, heroic virtues.
Children's magazine editors in the middle years of the century
tried carefully to blend examples of bravery with lessons in
self-control and still more critical lessons in contentment. J. A.
Judson's tale in 1877 of a work-weary shoemaker who tried being
king for a spell and found honest cobbling a far happier trade
played on one of the most popular of all children's story
formulas. "I do my work honestly—that is the thing; / Then
Jamie the cobbler's as good as the king!" the sobered shoemaker
pointed the moral.[36] But as the level of strenuosity rose in
children's magazines, particularly in the 1890s, this sort of story
was increasingly pushed aside by far more adventurous plot
formulas. By 1896 the editors of the *Youth's Companion* were
moved to complain of a surfeit of heroism; sagas of small boys
saving trains were "played out," they warned contributors, and
mortgage-raising heroes "must be very dextrously managed."[37]
Yet by then adventure tales had set all other stories to rout in
Harper's Young People, and a decade later the formula overran
St. Nicholas's "pleasure-ground." Boys defeated black-armored
knights and rescued girls from burning buildings; signing on as
cabin boys, they piloted ships between the jaws of icebergs; they
thwarted strikes and disarmed mutineers; over and over they won
crucial football games and made the clinching baseball play. In
one act of skillful daring, they leaped directly into manhood. As
they moved from metaphors of diligence and self-control to those
of heroism, boys' story writers did not mean to denigrate work.
A fervent faith in duty endured. But the new stories no longer
praised the character-building reward of effort; rather, they
made a romance of victory.

Finally, and most telling of all, boys' story writers found it increasingly difficult to connect their lessons in duty with the work their society offered. They celebrated the outward thrust of life, the moment of passage when a boy set aside his childish ways and took up a man's burden. But they did so through a strategy of retreat, by withdrawing, like Alger and Optic, into a safer and simpler world than any growing boy faced. Occasionally, in a story of coal mining or an engineering saga, some of the toil and realities of an industrializing society did penetrate boys' stories.[38] It was a condition of librarian approval that a boys' story writer could not resort to simple pasteboard melodrama, as Alger and Optic tended to do. Yet over and again boys' story writers retreated to anachronistic settings: a medieval tourney, the Indian-embattled West, a pioneer farm, or a fishing smack.

Intention sometimes wrestled with plot in these matters. Elijah Kellogg, as serious and didactic a moralist as wrote for boys after 1850, took up the question of careers in *The Young Ship-Builders of Elm Island* in 1870 and promised to illustrate the stage in life when a boy begins to "toil for exacting masters or the public, enter into competition with others, feel the pressure of responsibility, learn submission, and [be] tied down to rigid rules and severe tasks." But the tale Kellogg actually told was of a pioneer boatbuilder and farmer, who, staking out life on the Maine coast in the early years of the republic, had no master at all.[39] On the other hand, Rudyard Kipling knew fully what he was about when, in *Captains Courageous*, one of the most popular boys' stories of them all, he rolled his hero off the deck of a gleaming steam liner into a time-worn Gloucester fishing schooner to make a worker and a man of him. It was in isolated places like this, immune from time, that work retained its clear, moral meaning.

The tension between the impulses of aggressiveness and retreat were still more evident in the boarding school stories that pushed all else before them after 1900. The insistently athletic plots of the school stories drove home the strenuous virtues and celebrated the final heroic plunge to victory. Just as Theodore Roosevelt suggested, the school story writers took the football field as life's metaphor, and they insisted on the theme of preparation. Athletics taught "manliness," "courage," "perseverance," and "character"; they gave a boy "a good, hard grip on the world."[40] But, in fact, between the surrogate work of sports and the universe of adult vocations the storytellers offered no passage at all. Their boarding schools were insular and self-contained. In the distant future a vaguely defined professional or business career awaited the schoolboy athlete, but he was not eager for it. "I don't care about rushing things, or long for worlds to conquer," one of Albertus Dudley's heroes remarked. "All I want is to stay right here and win the Hillbury game."[41] Alger and Optic, despite their break with the didactic tradition, had never doubted that a boys' story writer must, in the end, move his heroes into adult life. But in the school stories, where graduated boys looked on wistfully like children outside a dime-store window, adulthood was a form of exile. The boarding school, like Kipling's Gloucester schooner or Alger's providential economy, was a setting for moralists half-distrustful of their industrial age—a refuge where a writer could spin out lessons of duty, endeavor, and heroism, uncomplicated by the disturbing confusions of work in the society at large.

Yet even in retreat the boys' story writers' counsel was splintered and Janus-faced. The more genteel storytellers' works did not divide on quite the same fault lines as the Alger and Optic stories, but they, too, were as often as not fractured tales, didactic point and story itself at odds. The tenuous relation between incident and moral was particularly evident in the school stories. According to the stylized formula these followed, a new boy entered boarding school isolated, friendless, and in some measure flawed. Guided by the captain of one of the school's teams and warned by the example of the school's bullies and snobs, he tackled his failings, and the result of his efforts, in the end, was sweet and exhilarating triumph. In the big game toward which the whole story pointed, the boy—no longer new or flawed—clinched the crucial victory and left the playing field a hero.[42] The first part of the formula—the story of character reformation—offered generous opportunities for instruction. Schoolboys learned to slough off lethargy and cowardice, keep their tempers, and endure their disappointments. Above all, and with terrifying coerciveness, they learned to fit in—to subordinate themselves to the conformity of the team, to escape the burdens of isolation by melting into the collective spirit of the school. The school stories tolerated neither introverts nor rebels. In the flush of athletic victory, one of Ralph Henry Barbour's figures put the realization he shared with countless other schoolboy characters: "I've learned a good bit since I came to Hillton.... I've learned that it's a mighty good thing to do as you're told, and to obey authority, and not to think that you know everything, because you don't."[43]

Nothing could be more direct or more insistent than this denial of self. Yet the storytellers, try as they would, could not sustain it. The schoolboy's final triumph was always single-handed; he left the field not as a supporting member of a well-integrated team, but conspicuously and individualistically a hero. Moreover, few boys' writers ever invested a fraction of the energy in the theme of character reformation that they gave to the detailed description of athletic prowess. The limits of their moralizing come clear when one holds them against the most successful Catholic school story writer, Father Francis Finn. For Finn never let the joys of competition overshadow the themes of discipline and penance. In his insistence on an athlete's strict training and "heroic self-restraint," in his Rooseveltian fulminations against "the effeminate tendencies of the century," Finn spoke in the authentic accents of the work ethic.[44] But his far more popular Protestant competitors did not care half so much for training as for victory, and in their short stories the theme of character reformation tended to drop out altogether. In the compressed short-story formula of Ralph Henry Barbour, the most successful of the school story writers, even effort all but vanished. Over and over an unknown boy was called to play in a crucial game; and in an easy, spectacular display of unrecognized talents, he won the contest.[45]

This unvarnished tale of wish-fulfillment was at the bottom of the longer school story, however much the overt moral contradicted it. Despite talk of toil and effort, what the school story writers actually showed was a place where ultimate victory was certain, where a lonely boy could break through his isolation in one burst of unqualified heroism. Overt celebrants of effort and solidarity who depicted life as a single-handed triumph, the boys' writers could not keep from telling two school stories, intertwined but distinct. Lessons in character and conformity were the moralist's tale; the big game was a boy's perfect fantasy.

The school story writers were not alone in their curiously divided counsel. No author was as popular with the boy patrons of the New York City libraries in 1917 as Joseph Altsheler. Barbour ran a distant second and Twain fifth to this Kentucky-raised editor of the *New York World.* Librarians were scarcely less enthusiastic about Altsheler's stories, holding them up as anti-dotes to the dime novels and the Tom Swift and Hardy Boys sagas and other syndicate-written potboilers.[46] The "Young Trailers" books, a string of tales of Indian fighting on the Kentucky frontier that Altsheler began in 1907, formed one of his most successful series, and, though formula quickly superseded invention, the title volume remains as seductive a boys' tale as any writer of his generation told. Altsheler made the story out of an amalgam of James Fenimore Cooper and Jack London, adopting from Cooper the tradition of the impossibly skillful woodsman and from London the primitivistic theme he had made famous four years earlier in *The Call of the Wild.* Altsheler's young hero, Henry Ware, was a boy out of sorts with the dull pioneering toil of clearing and farming. Schoolwork was painful and ploughing was "a trial to both the muscles and the spirit." Henry felt instead the lure of the deep, cool, and restful woods, where "everything grew by nature's aid alone, and man need not work, unless the spirit moved him to do so." The "old thought" tugged at him: "To roam as he pleased, to stop when he pleased and to sleep when he pleased!" The wilderness echoed with this call of primeval, paradisiacal freedom, and Henry, wandering farther and farther from home and settlement, finally succumbed to it. Seized by an Indian band, he cast off the last vestiges of civilization and became one with his captors, leading their "careless, easy life," all his primitive instincts gratified.[47]

But Altsheler was too much the moralist to leave Henry in this leisured, savage paradise, just as he was too much the romantic to chain him to a plough. Henry learns of a threatened Seneca attack on his father's settlement, rushes back to organize the town's defenses, and doggedly, painfully tries his hand at farming once more until the spirit snaps. But in his second rebellion against his father and his father's ways, Henry resists the desires that still draw him to the Indians and takes up the calling of a scout and hunter, a defender of the vital boundary between the civilized and the primitive. Altsheler insists on the morality of Henry's action. He gave up "the far, sweet vision of a life utterly wild and free" and turned his face toward "duty." He would not "throw aside all responsibility for others, roving the wilderness absolutely free from care. He knew that he would have work to do, he felt that he should have it, and now he saw the way to do the kind of work he loved to do.... He experienced a new thrill keener and more delightful than any that had gone before; he was doing for others and the knowledge was most pleasant."[48]

"We've been chose," one of Henry's companions echoed the old doctrine of the calling.[49] But no boy would have described Henry's new vocation as work. Living in a forest lodge by himself, hunting in the fastness of the woods, tracking Indians and defeating them single-handedly, Henry had rebelled against a boy's civilization of mothers, schools, and chores and emerged the victor. However Altsheler balanced the compromises and reiterated the rhetoric of responsibility, *The Young Trailers* was a subversive tale in a work-oriented society. It retold for middle-class schoolboys the classic dream of primitive, workless abundance and reverberated with romantic longings. But in the tradition of story writers that stretched back to William T. Adams, the teller could not fully countenance his tale. Against all the weight of evidence, Altsheler insisted it was a story of careers and responsibility.

Altsheler's tale comes close to summing up the tendencies of boys' story writing after 1850. Adult yearnings and memories of boyhood fantasies welled up into idylls of heroism, fortune, and ease. Discomfort with industrial society pushed the storytellers into anachronistic or timeless settings. Their tales were shot through with covert warfare between fathers and sons, between plodding toil and chivalrous adventure. The sober world of fact gave way to the heady realms of the imagination. In all these ways, the story writers rebelled against Jacob Abbott's world of obedience, discipline, and self-control, and in the end they shattered it beyond reconstruction. The result was to profoundly change the meaning of work that would echo in the minds of their boy readers. But writers for boys could not pass their sweet, seductive visions across the generations without qualification. Long after their stories had cast off for unfamiliar shores, they clung to older abstractions of diligence and duty, as if the familiar moral language would rectify their inability to show what work was like in their unfamiliar and unsettling age.

Do children's stories really matter? It is tempting to read into tales like these preparatory lessons in the hedonistic impulses of the 1920s or the more gradual twentieth-century displacement of work from the center of middle-class life to the status of a vaguely disagreeable necessity. Certainly, as long as children remained adept at skirting overt moralizing to fasten upon the memory-ingraining, dramatic stuff of incident, to let incidents go their independent way in a child's tale was to open up a nest of subversive possibilities. But child life may not move on the same trajectories as children's fiction. The collective impact of schools, for example, surely outweighed the imponderable influence of an Alger or an Altsheler. By 1920 schools caught up far more of the lives of far more children than ever before. And with the exception of a few nurseries of progressive ideas, schools remained scarcely less committed to obedience and discipline in 1920 than in the 1860s, when visitors to model New York City schools marveled at the lines of silent children "as regular as rows of machine-planted corn." [50] On the other hand, children have always been adept at building fantasy with the slimmest of materials. Charles Dudley Warner, looking back on his New England boyhood in the 1830s, the years of the Rollo stories, recalled that if he could have had his way "he would have discovered a cave full of diamonds, and lots of nail-kegs full of gold-pieces and Spanish dollars, with a pretty little girl living in the cave, and two beautifully caparisoned horses, upon which, taking the jewels and money, they would have ridden off together, he did not know where." Stephen Crane's Whilomville boys at the turn of the century, mouthing the speeches of buccaneers and highwaymen, were not discernably different. [51]

Nevertheless, children's tales do hold a particularly important clue to the mind of adult moralists in an age of change. Their movement from instruction to instruction-within-amusement, from stories of work to stories of play and heroic endeavor, was of a piece with the larger, steady erosion of the force of the ascetic side of the work ethic in Northern middle-class life. The story-tellers' rebellion against the disciplining ethics of a scarcity-ruled world meshed with the message of the popular theologians and the more hesitant conclusions of the economists, just as their cultivation of the child's fancy mirrored the trend in moral thinking away from the edicts of vigilant self-control. By the same token, the arc that ran from Edgeworth's cautious acknowledgment of upward mobility, to Alger's celebration of ambitious individualism, to the school story writers' ambiguous code of group solidarity reflected something of the rise, triumph, and final disarray of the idea of success in nineteenth- and twentieth-century America. Finally, the storytellers' acute discomfort with the new shape of industrial toil matched the contemporaneous drive to remove child laborers from the shops and factories, where, for children at least, the old link between work and virtue seemed finally to have snapped and work to have been stripped of its moral and educational possibilities. Between the world of children's fiction and the adult world there was a complex web of interconnections. None of these movements in adult society, however, showed quite as clearly as the contrast between Jacob Abbott and his literary descendants how far and how fast some of the moralists had moved from the older, far less complicated confidences of their parents and grandparents.

And yet the doubleness of boys' tales, their awkward compound of old values and new, is in the end as significant a phenomenon. If the actions of boy heroes changed in dramatic ways, the codes they professed, particularly the code of duty, possessed a remarkable endurance. That code, in fact, increased in intensity as the stakes in boys' stories escalated and the burdens thrust upon children multiplied. Duty in Rollo's matter-of-fact world of gardens to tend and nails to sort was a far less awesome responsibility than it was for Julian Hawthorne's children or Altsheler's Henry Ware with the fate of civilization bearing down upon their slender shoulders. Even in the school stories, where the primary work was play, the responsibilities of the big game loomed as an inescapable presence. Work ideals, in short, grew stronger as their ties to practice loosened, more momentous as they lost their workaday context. This was not sheer paradox. As the realities of work shifted in disturbing ways, part of the boys' story writers' response was to idealize the distrusted life around them, to comprehend it in the morally clear-cut surrogates of football games and frontier warfare, to raise the code of duty to an increasingly generalized abstraction. Work, Love, Woman, Duty: it was by divorcing the pure outer shell from sordid reality that nineteenth- and early twentieth-century Americans dealt with so many of the changes in economic, family, and moral life that unnerved them.

As the factories wedged into ethics, splitting off work ideals from their supporting context, those ideals did not lose their force. In fact, as the idea of the moral centrality of work grew increasingly abstract, it grew in many ways increasingly useful. It offered storytellers, in particular, a way to encompass the doubts of adulthood within the still more than half-believed moral codes of their youth without explicitly violating them. Outside the realm of boys' stories, work ideals cut loose from habit and context likewise had their uses. Even where potential resistance might have been expected, an abstract faith in work permeated debates, some of them only loosely related to work itself. Workingmen, many of whom had never converted to the inner compulsions of the work ethic, protested their condition in terms of the dignity of labor. Middle-class women restless with their lot seized upon the issue of idleness. Politicians of diametrically opposed persuasions appealed to the clichés of the work ethic and turned questions of finance and policy into simpler morality plays of industry and laziness. As in the stories told to boys, behavior and professed ideals did not always match, nor did the old phrases always fit the meanings forced into them. As an impelling ethos of a region and class or as a paradigm of the everyday work of industrial society, the mid-nineteenth-century amalgam of work ideals cracked and eroded. But the effect of tearing away the context of the work ethic was not to diminish work as an idea, but to pitch discussions of work on a new level of abstraction. In that form, even as things came apart, faith in work survived to badger the consciences and shape the thinking of Northern Americans.

Sons of Toil: Industrial Workers and Their Labor

The Sons of Toil go forth upon the earth
as demigods.
> George Coolidge, *The Joys of Toil* (1850)

The workers are the saviors of society; the
redeemers of the race.
> Eugene V. Debs,
> "Industrial Unionism" (1905)

The work ethic was in its origins a middle-class affair. Its constituent faiths reverberated most strongly among the sober, Protestant churchgoing, propertied segments of Northern society. Such men might be farmers as well as college professors, clerks as well as bankers, for the "middling classes" possessed of skill, property, and a measure of economic independence formed a broadly defined group in the nineteenth century. A Booker T. Washington or a William Jennings Bryan held to a faith in the moral centrality of work every bit as deep as that of a Theodore Roosevelt or an Andrew Carnegie. But in terms of the power to enforce, the work ethic was a businessmen's creed. In the industrial towns of the North, it was preeminently the faith of those who owned and managed the mills—of those whose comfortable houses climbed the hills above the factories and the cramped and pinched dwellings of the workers they employed.

There could be no mistaking the manufacturers' allegiance to the gospel of work. It was reiterated in voluminous testimony and driven home in the long hours and labor discipline of the factories. Even the architecture of the mill districts reflected it. In scores of nineteenth- and early twentieth-century mill towns, no feature stood out more prominently than the great, looming bell towers of the factories. Originating as simple cupolas perched on the ridgepoles of the early, barnlike textile mills, the bell towers assumed an imposing presence as the century wore on.

153

At the model plant George Pullman constructed outside Chicago in the early 1880s, the bell tower was a massive Victorian structure, its great illuminated clock face reflected by the pool in front of it. In the textile city of Manchester, New Hampshire, the mill towers, dominated by the great brick bell tower of the Amoskeag Mills, lined the Merrimack River in a regular, imposing phalanx.

Even far less pretentious bell towers than these, their lines revealing the century's shifts in aesthetic taste, showed signs of architectural imagination rarely found elsewhere in the mill districts. Such towers rose above the utilitarian clutter of the buildings around them much like church spires in a slum; nor is the parallel farfetched. Where clocks and watches remained rare, factory bells served the essential, utilitarian function of ringing the labor force out of bed, into work, and home again at the day's end. But in the more ornate bell towers there are clearly marks of faith as well as necessity. In their great clock faces and clanging bells, the towers broadcast the mechanization of work and time, the narrowing and tightening of the injunction to diligence that was at the heart of the industrial transformation of work. They loomed as monuments to a creed of regular, untiring industry to which many of their builders held themselves accountable and which all of them hoped to impress upon the older, far less systematic work rhythms that still prevailed outside the factory gates. No other symbol caught the factory masters' revolutionary faith or the obligations it entailed for the new industrial workforce quite so vividly.[1]

The men and women who worked within the factories left no such permanent or conspicuous record of their feelings about time and labor. Save for occasional testimony before government investigating committees and the responses gleaned by haphazard surveys of state bureaus of labor statistics, there is little recorded evidence of the opinions of rank-and-file workers. Even such basic behavioral data as rates of work attendance and labor turnover are scarce for most of the nineteenth century when many factories were run virtually as independent baronies by foremen uninterested in the tedium of record keeping. The shards of evidence historians work with contain incomparably more information about labor organizations than about the values and habits of ordinary laborers, even though the unions never managed to enroll more than a tenth of the manufacturing labor force at any time before the First World War. Labor history that would try to focus on the worker at his job is a more than usually hazardous enterprise.

Yet there is ample evidence that large numbers of industrial workers failed to internalize the faith of the factory masters. Long in advance of the hesitant middle-class recognition of the claims of leisure, workers dreamed of a workday short enough to push labor out of the center of their lives. By reporting irregularly for work, moving restlessly from job to job, or engaging in slowdowns and work restrictions, industrial laborers stubbornly resisted the new work discipline the factory masters tried to impose upon them. Such workers made industrialization a turbulent, bitterly contested process. And yet even active dissenters from middle-class models of diligence were not immune to the pervading belief in the values of hard work. Even as they fabricated visions of leisure or resisted the compulsions of factory toil, industrial workers kept up a steady insistence on the special dignity and worth of those who soiled their hands with honest labor. The phenomenon is particularly striking evidence of the ways in which the factories strained work values everywhere, wrenching habits and splitting ideas apart. But it also shows something of the ways in which a work-tied culture perpetuated its attenuated faiths, even among potential rebels in anomalous circumstances. If to probe the habits of industrial workers is to find abundant evidence of dissent from the work standards of the factories, to probe the rhetoric of the spokesmen they pushed forward from their ranks is to find a working-class version of the work ethic—albeit far from that of the bell towers.

How much of a man's life should work consume? No work-related question is more central than this, and none in the nineteenth and early twentieth centuries divided workers and employers more sharply. The early factory masters took over the traditional sun-to-sun workday, stretched it to between twelve and fourteen hours of labor winter and summer alike with the introduction of gas lighting in the 1830s and 1840s, and brought the full weight of generations of moralizing to bear in justification. "Labor is *not* a curse," they insisted; "it is not the hours per day that a person *works* that breaks him down, but the hours spent in dissipation." Give men "plenty to do, and a long while to do it in, and you will find them physically and morally better."[2]

But among workingmen, the drive to shorten the hours of labor was a long and fervent struggle. The campaign began early in the nineteenth century with the appearance of the first self-conscious workingmen's organizations. By the 1840s the ten-hour movement had moved into the New England textile mills, producing a massive flood of shorter-hours petitions, the largest, from Lowell in 1846, containing signatures equivalent to almost two-thirds of the city's cotton mill operatives.[3] After 1850 the shorter-hours demand—now typically put in terms of the eight-hour day—was at the forefront of every organized labor effort. The National Labor Union at its first convention in 1866 declared a federal eight-hour law "the first and grand desideratum of the hour," and, though the organization drifted shortly thereafter toward rival programs of cooperatives and currency reform, many of its member unions clung firmly to the original platform. P. J. McGuire of the Carpenters, for example, told a congressional committee in 1883 that the reduction of working hours was the "primary object" of the union he headed. The American Federation of Labor under Samuel Gompers was a still more persistent champion of the shorter workday—"eight hours to-day, fewer to-morrow," as Gompers defined the cause. The shorter workday was "the question of questions," the only one which "reaches the very root of society," Gompers declared in the 1880s, and over the next twenty years he labored tirelessly to promote strikes over the issue. Nor did the labor left disagree. For Bill Haywood of the IWW, the only fit motto for the working class was "the less work the better."[4]

"However much they may differ upon other matters, ... all men of labor ... can unite upon this," Samuel Gompers wrote in defense of the eight-hour issue in 1889.[5] If the unions, particularly the nonfactory building trades unions, led the agitation for the shorter workday, there was more than Gompers's testimony to indicate that the shorter-hours dream had a strong hold on the larger number of nonunionized workers as well. For three decades after 1869, until they turned to the neutral and duller task of compiling purely statistical data, many of the new state bureaus of labor statistics took upon themselves the task of canvassing the opinions of the workingmen they took to be their constituents. Who these often nameless workers were and how their opinions found their way into print is not clear, but, taking opinion samples as they come, none more closely approaches the rank and file of labor than these. And when they posed the working-hours question, the surveys repeatedly turned up strong, often overwhelming support for the shorter-hours demand.[6] "We go into the factory too young and work too hard afterwards," a New Jersey glass blower put the recurrent complaint in the mid-1880s. A decade and a half later, Thomas Jones, a nonunion Chicago machinist, interrupted his testimony on the un-American and anti-Christian policies of trade unions to interject that "we nonunion men are not opposed to more pay and shorter hours; not at all."[7]

Twice in the nineteenth century, moreover, the shorter-hours demand mushroomed into popular crusades unsurpassed in their intensity by any other of the era's labor issues. The first wave of enthusiasm began quietly in 1865 with the organization of the Grand Eight-Hour League of Massachusetts by a small group of Boston workingmen. Three years later workingmen's Eight-Hour Leagues had proliferated throughout the Northern states and, together with the trade unions, had succeeded in writing the eight-hour day in the statute books of seven states and forcing an eight-hour law for federal employees through Congress. Riddled with loopholes, the legislation proved a hollow victory, and workers angrily turned to more aggressive tactics. In Chicago some 6,000 to 10,000 workers walked off their jobs on 1 May 1867 in a massive demonstration to demand enforcement of the new Illinois eight-hour law, and strikes, rioting, and some machine breaking followed in its wake. A year later in the anthracite coalfields of Pennsylvania, similarly angered workers abandoned the coal pits and, marching from mine to mine, shut down virtually all operations in the state's leading coal-producing county in a bitter three-month strike. Only in the building trades did the first eight-hour campaign bear fruit, and many of those gains evaporated in the depression of the 1870s. But the experience suggested something of the emotional reserves behind the shorter-hours issue.[8]

The second eight-hour crusade of the mid-1880s was still larger and more spontaneous than the first. When in 1884 the Federation of Organized Trades and Labor Unions issued a call for a general eight-hour demonstration to take place on 1 May 1886, it was a quixotic gesture on the part of a weak and barely solvent organization. But the call fell on unexpectedly fertile ground. Over the next two years, workers flocked into the labor unions filled with hopes for a shorter working day. The Knights of Labor, the chief recipient of the influx, ballooned from 104,066 members in July 1885 to 702,924 members a year later, and the newcomers threatened to overwhelm the organization. Grand Master Workman Terence Powderly waged a vigorous fight to dampen the strike fever of the local Knights assemblies. In place of a general strike, Powderly proposed an educational campaign and a nationwide essay contest on the eight-hour question and, that failing, championed a less than realistic scheme to shorten the working day through a coooperative agreement between the Knights and a yet unformed general association of the nation's manufacturers. A month before the day set for the demonstration, P.M. Arthur of the strongly organized locomotive engineers denounced the whole affair as a demand for "two hours more loafing about the corners and two hours more for drink." Yet notwithstanding such foot-dragging at the top, 190,000 workers struck for the eight-hour day in the first week of May. In Milwaukee, according to the Wisconsin Bureau of Labor and Industrial Statistics, the shorter hours issue was "*the* topic of conversation in the shop, on the street, at the family table, at the bar, [and] in the counting room." Beginning with a monster picnic on 2 May, the crusade turned grim and bloody as police opened fire on workers intent on shutting down the city's iron and steel works. In Chicago, the center of the movement, May opened with police and worker battles, some five hundred individual strikes, and still more imposing demonstrations.[9]

Despite Samuel Gompers's best efforts over the next decade and a half, the general strike of 1886 was never repeated. Most workers who walked off their jobs in the late nineteenth and early twentieth centuries struck over wage-related issues, not working hours; and where the wage question pressed most heavily or where hours reduction meant a cut in pay, hours demands generally made little headway. Yet, larger on the average than wage strikes, shorter-hours walkouts possessed a peculiar intensity.[10] And in the massive garment workers' strikes of 1910–11, the IWW-led silk workers' walkout in Paterson, New

Jersey, in 1913, the great steel strike of 1919, and elsewhere, the shorter-hours issue smoldered under the surface of many of the era's most famous labor disputes long after the experience of 1886 had faded from memory.

Where rank-and-file workers divided from union leaders was not over the desirability of shorter working hours—whose appeal cut across lines of ideology and unionization—but over rationale. For most union spokesmen the eight-hour day was essentially a link in a complex economic equation whose upshot was wages. A large number of the late nineteenth century's most influential labor leaders—Gompers, George E. McNeill of the Knights, and Adolph Strasser of the Cigarmakers among them—learned the eight-hour creed in the 1860s from a self-educated Boston machinist, Ira Steward. In Steward's argument, wages fell to the minimum standard of living workers would tolerate, and leisure was the one effective means of raising both. Let "the ragged—the unwashed—the ignorant and ill-mannered" have time "to become ashamed of themselves," to raise their expenses and desires, and the demand for higher wages would no longer be resistible. "The *idea* of eight hours isn't eight hours," Steward insisted; "it is *less poverty*!"[11] As late as 1915, Steward's jingle

> Whether you work by the piece
> Or work by the day
> Decreasing the hours
> Increases the pay

could still be found in the pages of the *American Federationist*. And if this was by then a remnant of an increasingly old-fashioned idea, the argument that pushed Steward's aside in labor circles in the 1890s took an equally instrumental attitude toward leisure. Shorter working hours were a means of spreading the work being relentlessly whittled down by machinery, ironing out the boom and bust cycles of the economy, or employing the unemployed.[12]

One can find appeal to all of these arguments among the respondents of the state bureaus of labor statistics; but far more often than union leaders, the men whose ideas were preserved there demanded leisure not as a means but as an end in itself. "I do not believe that God ever created man in order to spend his life in work and sleep, without any time to enjoy the pleasures of the world," a New Jersey miner wrote in 1881. A Pennsylvania workingman reiterated the theme; to know "nothing but work, eat and sleep" was to strip a man of his humanity, to make him "little better than a horse." In an argument particularly appealing to the middle-class moralists, some workingmen proposed to turn the time set free from work into labors of self-education, but in the records of the bureaus of labor statistics such men are few. In 1880 the Massachusetts bureau tried to find out what textile mill operatives would do with more leisure. Most proposed to rest, read the newspaper, visit, look around 'to see what is going on," and spend time with their families.[13] For all the complex intellectual rationale behind the eight-hour campaigns, the essential appeal of the shorter day was the obvious one: the promise of relief from toil.

It is the privilege of moralists, as vigorously exercised in the mid-twentieth century as in the nineteenth, to point to decay. But the chasm between the work ideals of those who stood inside and outside the new work forms and employee relations was present virtually from the very beginning. "Toil, toil, toil, unending," the sweatshop poet Morris Rosenfeld protested in the plaint that echoed deeply through the most vocal segment of those caught in the new half-free, time-pressed labor of the factories. While the middle-class moralists, torn between the allure and the apparent dangers of leisure, wrestled with questions of pleasure and duty, industrial workers crossed far fewer inner compunctions as they struggled to pare down the looming place of labor in their lives. "Eight Hours for Work. Eight Hours for Rest. Eight Hours for What We Will." To Samuel Gompers, the persuasively symmetrical rallying cry of the eight-hour crusade was the workers' "fling-back" at the ethic of all-consuming industry.[14]

The long contest over the length of the industrial workday was the first of the workingmen's quarrels with the ethos of the bell towers. The second, far less open conflict took place over labor discipline, made tighter and more exacting as working hours shrank and employers turned to closer supervision and a faster work pace to recover their losses. How well industrial workers adjusted to the increasingly regimented labor of the factories is not easy to determine. Crisscrossed by deep lines of ethnicity, industry, and region, there was nothing uniform about the workforce in industrial America, and the evidence about their work behavior is incomplete, often inextricably mired in prejudice, and frequently contradictory.

European observers, for example, generally came away strongly impressed with the energy and discipline of American industrial workers. James Burn, an English hatter who spent an unhappy sojourn in the United States during the Civil War, returned home to pour out his complaints of the "fire-eaters" in his shop who had fallen upon their work with "ravenous appetites for labour," savagely devouring every scrap in sight. Thirty years later a delegation of French workingmen puzzled over the absence of "hurly burly" in the factories they visited. "Work in the American shops is altogether different from what it is in France," one of them remarked. "Nobody talks, nobody sings, the most rigorous silence reigns." A British trade union delegation that arrived a few years later on a more comprehensive tour was less inclined to agree. Except for the shoe factories, where by English standards the machines worked at breakneck speed, the Englishmen concluded that the Americans did not work essentially harder than the British and that the "everlasting hustle" of the American workshops was a "myth." But even the British unionists, whose report was generously self-serving, could not conceal their surprise at the absence of beer and liquor in the American shops and the general sobriety of American workers.[15]

Yet, running counter to the Europeans' repeated stress on the peculiarly industrious temper of the Americans, there is abundant evidence that adjustment to the factory regime did not come easily. At a Lowell, Massachusetts, plant in 1867, for example, the management posted a set of new work rules stipulating that the factory gates were to be kept locked during working hours and that the men were to keep their work clothes on during the day. It seems an unexceptionable requirement by most twentieth-century standards. But to the machinists, the idea that they could not come and go from their work as free men was "a system of slavery" that threatened time-honored traditions and time-honored rights. Led by the machinist who reported the incident to the Massachusetts Bureau of Statistics of Labor, the men struck, and in the compromise that resulted the gates were left unlocked.[16]

The incident at Lowell was unique neither in its circumstances nor its implications. In the movement from farm and artisan shop into the mills, old prerogatives and work habits clashed over and again with the factory masters' strange and galling standards of discipline and work pace. Workers unwilling to break their accustomed mores to the discipline of the mills—hard-drinking potters and cigar makers, "intractable" Polish and Italian peasants in the textile mills of southern New England, or Maine factory hands who threw over job and employer each summer for the freedom of their farms and fishing boats—could be found throughout the factories as the new economic order pushed aside the old.[17] It was only by draconian fining policies that punished lateness or visiting and talking on the job by fines of up to half a day's pay that many employers managed to create the silence and discipline that so caught the eye of the Europeans.[18]

For many workers in industrial America, moreover, adjustment to the employers' demand for regular, clock-disciplined work never came at all. From the highly paid, British-born mule spinners of Fall River to common, unskilled laborers, a conspicuous fraction of workers simply failed to convert to the creed of day-in and day-out labor. Irregular work patterns were most common in casually supervised piecework trades where work itself was often fitful and a day's lost pay might be partially recovered by harder work the next. But even in the highly disciplined New England textile mills, managers in the 1870s were sometimes hard-pressed to keep their machines running on the hottest days of the summer for lack of workers. As one textile manufacturer testified in 1878: "Our mill operatives are much like other people, and take their frequent holidays for pleasure and visiting."[19] Sickness, accidents, and lack of work—dominant elements in the lives of all workers in industrial America—inflated the high absence rates found in virtually all factory payroll records before the turn of the century. As time went on and industrial discipline tightened, moreover, the places where a worker could take a day off with impunity narrowed. In the anthracite coalfields where underemployment was chronic, "blue Mondays" and a thick calendar of immigrant holidays persisted well into the twentieth century; but among the hard-pressed New York City garment workers, the prohibitions against labor on the Jewish Sabbath fell increasingly into disuse. By the turn of the century, as a Massachusetts survey made clear in 1904, the factories had succeeded in exacting far more regular attendance at work than the old hand trades and village shops. Yet in small-town textile mills from Vermont to North Carolina, managers still made the best of a bad bargain and shut down on the day the circus arrived. And where management was lax or jobs easy to come by, as at a large number of manufacturing plants during the First World War, employers found themselves missing as much as a tenth or more of their workforce on a normal workday.[20] "The general indisposition" of factory hands "to work steady," as a Chicopee, Massachusetts, mill agent put the complaint in 1859, remained far from cured sixty years later.[21]

A second act of rebellion was to quit. Systematic studies of labor turnover did not begin until the second decade of the twentieth century, but what they found then was a strikingly mobile workforce, rattling from job to job at a rate astonishingly high by modern standards. According to data gathered for the years from 1905 to 1917, the majority of industrial workers changed jobs at least every three years. But mobility was not evenly spread through the workforce. In normal times, one in three factory workers moved considerably faster than the norm, staying at his job less than a year and often only days or weeks. At the Armour meat-packing plant in Chicago, for example, the average daily payroll numbered about eight thousand during 1914. But to keep that many employees, the company hired eight thousand workers during the course of the year, filling and refilling the places of transients. Larger surveys of textile mills, automobile plants, steel mills, clothing shops, and machine works showed turnover rates at least as high as the 100 percent reported at Armour. In the woolen industry between 1907 and 1910, turnover varied between 113 and 163 percent, and at casually managed plants or regions troubled by labor shortages it ran still higher. It reached 232 percent among New York City cloak, suit, and skirt shops in 1912–13, 252 percent in a sample of Detroit factories in 1916, and the bewildering rate of 370 percent at Ford in 1913. The most extensive study, undertaken by the United States Bureau of Labor Statistics and using data from 1913–14, found a "normal" turnover rate in the factories of 115 percent, and, given the depressed economic conditions in those years, that figure, if it erred at all, underestimated the normal amount of job changing.[22]

Before the turn of the century, moreover, it is likely that the pattern was much the same. One-quarter of the mill girls employed at Lowell in the mid-1840s, for example, had been at their jobs a year or less. At the Lyman Mills in Holyoke, Massachusetts, in 1860, where the labor force was composed largely of immigrant Scotch rather than Yankee women, more than half the workforce was made up of such short-term workers. Even at the model Pullman plant in 1894, a fifth of the men employed had less than a year's tenure.[23] Certainly nineteenth-century employers complained loudly of what one of them termed the "nomadic system of employing men," and, by offering bonuses for steady work or, more frequently, demanding that those who left without adequate notice forfeit one or two weeks' back wages, they made strenuous efforts to escape it. Called upon to defend wage withholding in the 1870s, a Massachusetts textile mill agent insisted that if a mill did not keep back workers' wages it would simply wake up to find all its hands gone by morning.[24]

Why did so many workers change jobs so often? Not until just before the First World War did employers begin to count the numbers who quit as distinct from those laid off or fired, and even then such categories were far from clear-cut. A worker might well prefer to quit rather than endure the unpleasantness of being fired or wait for the layoff he sensed was imminent. Some of the transients, like the hapless tailor uncovered at Ford who had taken a position as a machinist, hoping against hope to learn the trade before being found out, cannot really be said ever to have held their jobs at all.[25] Nonetheless a good deal of the turnover was clearly voluntary. The best students of the early twentieth-century workforce were convinced that quitting workers made up well over half and perhaps as many as three-quarters of all those who left their jobs. Fluctuations in the turnover rate bear out their emphasis on the high proportion of voluntary transients. Turnover was far higher in years when jobs were plentiful than in depression years, when all who had jobs worked hard and anxiously to keep them; and throughout the course of the year, turnover rose in spring and fell in winter in a cycle that apparently had far more to do with the wanderlust Terence Powderly had noted long before among railway machinists than with industrial conditions.

Attempts to probe still further into the reasons behind the high quit rates ran up against walls of reticence. Skilled workmen sometimes defended moving about as a way to learn more than one branch of their increasingly specialized trades. Yet very few of those who were willing to talk about why they had quit claimed they had a better job in hand, and, in most of the plants investigated, less than a third cited better opportunities as their grounds for leaving. The quitters were "dissatisfied," looking for something else to turn up, or "leaving town." The generally mobile workforce, in short, hid a core of compulsively restless employees, amounting to perhaps one in seven workers in the year 1913-14, according to one careful estimate. Unbroken to industrial discipline, they shuttled from job to job, oblivious to the ethos of the bell towers.[26]

Even those who turned up regularly for work and stuck by their jobs were not necessarily committed to the new work discipline. Throughout the industries workers maintained their own work norms and work customs, which effectively undercut the formal factory rules and the expectations of the factory masters. Like so many of the essentials of working-class history, most of the outlines of these shop cultures have been lost beyond recovery. But one aspect was brought into relief by the argument over output restriction set off by a bitter Chicago building trades dispute in 1900. In its wake, even union sympathizers like Clarence Darrow and Jane Addams joined the chorus of concern over deliberate production restriction. The Bureau of Labor's monumental effort to clarify the issue, however, reported that restrictive practices were far older and more widespread than all but the harshest critics had suggested. Only a few skilled workers at the height of their power—glassblowers, potters, iron molders, and puddlers and rollers in the iron and steel mills—maintained openly acknowledged limits on their day's work. But the report concluded that clandestine shop agreements to enforce production quotas were common throughout the factories among union and nonunion workers alike.

Such informal compacts were highly unstable, and they broke down repeatedly under pressure from employers or from workers themselves. Yet the mood behind the output agreements was dead serious, and at times the results could be dramatic. In 1901, in a brief flush of unionization, sheep and cattle butchers slowed down the lines of the Chicago packing plants by some 30 percent until the new regime fell apart in a disastrous strike. Where workers could not control the factory pace, they could at the least turn their resentments against the exceptionally fast worker. "The common sentiment of the workman is strong and severe against those whose output is materially above the average," the Bureau of Labor reported. Hog, rooter, boss's pet, bell-horse, swift, rusher—the factory names for the unusually diligent worker amounted to a string of epithets.[27]

Thanks to the labors of investigators at the federal arsenal at Watertown, Massachusetts, we know about one of these shop cultures in some detail, and the precipitating incident, fittingly enough, was a direct clash between a group of skilled workers and the clock. In the summer of 1911, the arsenal management was in the early stages of introducing the Taylor system into the Watertown plant. The first time studies had been made in the machine shop in June. But the commandant was anxious for results and particularly anxious to see improvements made in the foundry, where he was convinced that the molders were systematically holding output down to a fraction of what it should be. On 10 August, accordingly, a Taylor-trained time-study expert appeared in the foundry to time one of the molders at a routine task. The angry molders met that evening and resolved to quit if more time studies were made. When they were resumed the next day, the entire molding force struck. The walkout at Watertown was not the first workers' protest against scientific management. Employees at the Rock Island arsenal had succeeded in halting the introduction of Taylorism there in 1908, and both the American Federation of Labor and the International Association of Machinists were actively campaigning against Taylorism in the summer of 1911. But the Watertown strike was a local, spontaneous affair, and coming in the midst of the boom of popular enthusiasm over Taylor's work it precipitated both a great deal of embarrassing publicity and two teams of investigators, who over the next two months tried to piece together what had happened.[28]

The investigators found not only the molders but the machinists, too, in seething discontent. Many of the strikers were convinced that the time studies were a prelude to drastic rate cuts, a prospect reinforced by the fact that, in eliminating the "waste motions" from the job he observed, Taylor's man had cut the

worker's time by
subsequent introdu
foundry. Several of
read the more flam
ment," worried that
trade and the eventu
it. Others, the forem
instruction from ab
never themselves pou
simply gave back sto
ture that time studies
In the end, most stud
dispute came as the
Taylor system too al
unconsulted workers.[2

But the focus of the
their testimony return
man's stopwatch. Wh   ... procedure were involved, it is clear that what was essentially at stake for most of the
Watertown employees was the nature of work itself. Autonomy
was part of the matter. To work under continuous observation
was to keep a man "in a constant state of agitation," the molders
complained. "There are men standing over you all the time, and
of course you are almost drove to it. You have got to keep pegging
at it and working." To work under the constant eye of a boss was
nerve-racking; it was "getting down to slavery."[30] But equally
threatening was the idea that a man should account for his time
by seconds, that he should keep at his work with the unremitting
persistence of a machine. That was not the way the Watertown
employees had been accustomed to work. Machinists had had
time to talk and rest while their automatic lathes and planers
were running, and in the foundry the commandant complained
that none of the arsenal management could tell if a molder were
busy or simply keeping busy. Whatever the case in the foundry,
the piecework-paid metal polishers at the arsenal did effectively
enforce a common, mutually agreed upon work pace, checking
out a uniform amount of material and stretching the last pieces
or helping out those caught short if they finished early.

Measured against these accustomed work norms and liberties,
the second-by-second accounting of scientific management came

[rotated text in margin:] as an alien intrusion. Under the
to work there every second of
man who can do that I do
George White protested
in the same place all
Labor without ro
longer hard
Lowell ma
Time
relea

new system a man "would have
the eight hours, and if there is any
n't believe I ever saw him," machinist
; "I never saw a man who can stand right
day and work every instant for eight hours."
om for rest or talk or a moment's loafing was no
ork but—in a reiteration of the phrase used by
hinists long before—"getting down to slavery."[31]
and discipline, the lessons of the bell towers made
tlessly precise, formed the core of the matter not only at
atertown. The same quarrels ran through the shorter-hours
crusade, the absenteeism and turnover, and the output quotas as
well. Another machinist, thrown into prominence by the scientific
management controversy, tried to sum up the mood of his fellow
workers in a debate with Frederick W. Taylor in 1914: "We don't
want to work as fast as we are able to. We want to work as fast as
we think it's comfortable for us to work. We haven't come into
existence for the purpose of seeing how great a task we can
perform through a lifetime. We are trying to regulate our work so
as to make it an auxiliary to our lives."[32]

Not all industrial workers, of course, dissented so fully from
middle-class ideas of time and labor. The sociology of work ideals
cannot be simply reduced to two monolithic camps: work-
obsessed businessmen outside the factories and restless, work-
weary wage earners within them. The cotton weaver who wrote
the Massachusetts Bureau of Statistics of Labor in 1879 that it
should not forget that "hard, untiring labor is necessary for the
prosperity and well-being of our country" was by no means
unique among workingmen in his convictions. An antiunion shoe
cutter in the same year complained of the "idle, unthrifty,
beer-drinking, don't-care sort of people, who are out at the
elbows, and waiting for some sort of legislation to help them."
"In this country, as a general thing," he protested, hard work
and a will to succeed could get any self-reliant man ahead in the
world. Unionized workers, too, were not immune from the faiths
in activity and self-advancement that comprised the work ethic.
The journal of the Knights of Labor in its first years was
punctuated with the homilies long familiar to middle-class
moralists: the ennui of idleness, the creative power of labor, the
"room at the top." Offering a "Recipe for a Good Union" soon

after the turn of the century, the *Journal* of the Amalgamated Meat Cutters and Butcher Workmen turned to the pushy maxims of the *Saturday Evening Post*: "Grit. Vim. Push. Snap. Energy.... Fire all loafers, croakers and deadbeats."[33] Turnover studies revealed not only a core of drifters but a minority of extraordinarily steady employees in the factories. Everywhere, as at Watertown, individualistic, success-driven workers bucked the ethics of group solidarity and helped to sabotage the fragile output quotas. Just as workers' economic ideas and Sunday habits infected middle-class Northerners, so the work ideals of the middle-class moralists seeped into the factories. Discipline, sobriety, ambition, and diligence were not class monopolies in a land where the sense of class itself was unusually weak.

Much of the behavior that looks on the surface like rebellion, moreover, turns out on closer inspection to be considerably more complicated. Some of the restless job changing, for example, was due less to clashes over work values than to the fact that the industrial economy itself was highly unstable. Regularly counting out time in good years and bad alike, the factory bell towers belied the boom and bust cycle that afflicted virtually every industry in industrial America and caught up workers in repeated cycles of overtime work and unemployment. Such swings were most violent in the clothing trade, where the year was divided into two intensely busy seasons, interrupted by twelve to eighteen weeks of slack work or none at all. Boot- and shoemaking, glassmaking, meat-packing, canning, and foundry work followed similar seasonal cycles. Elsewhere, particularly in the steel mills and coal mines, irregular changes in demand brought volatile fluctuations in employment, aggravated in the steel industry by the steel-makers' policy of running their works at full production or not at all. Depressions repeated the famine and surfeit cycle on a larger and still more catastrophic scale. Of the 28,000 male wage earners in manufacturing and mining surveyed by the Immigration Commission in 1909, when the economy was still recovering from the financial panic two years before, almost half had been out of work two months or more during the preceding year. Even in 1892, notwithstanding the nation's general prosperity, Pennsylvania steel mills, carpet mills, rubber boot factories, window glass factories, and coal mines all shut down for a month or more.[34]

The boom and bust experience had a deep impact on the

workforce. "At one time they drive us like slaves, and at other times we have to beg for work," a Brooklyn Knights of Labor official protested in 1883 in the complaint that recurs again and again in the bureaus of labor statistics reports and in immigrant letters. Let the work be heavy, "but may it last without interruption," a Polish brickworks laborer pleaded. But the economics of cheap labor took precedence over steady employment, even though the result worked to undercut the factory goal of steady, clockwork labor—ingraining habits of irregular work on potentially steady workers and uprooting others in the constant scramble for jobs. A Pennsylvania miner, explaining the fact that he had changed his residence five times during 1885, argued that "if I had stopped at one place, I should not have worked half of my time." Employers complained repeatedly of their short-term workers. But men like this not only bore the stamp of the economy that made them but provided what the factory masters sorely needed—a reserve army of irregular, highly mobile workers able to iron out the gyrations of a still far from rationalized economy.[35]

If the industrial economy was capable of making mobile, footloose employees out of potentially steady workers, it was equally capable of making exceptionally diligent employees out of some of those who came to the factories from wholly alien work experiences. Laborers drawn directly from the peasant villages of Europe to the American mills and factories could be found everywhere in the industrial North. By the end of the first decade of the twentieth century, according to the Immigration Commission's survey, one out of every three employees in the Northern cotton textile mills, the soft coal mines, the iron and steel mills, and the meat-packing plants was a European-born worker who had come to America directly from agricultural labor.[36] Many such laborers never made the adjustment to the new and strange expectations of the factories. A sizable fraction simply left and returned home. Others, clinging to the ways they had always known—the unsteady rhythms of agricultural work and the holidays sanctified by the creeds of folk Catholicism—augmented the constant turbulence of the American factories. But with some of the migrants the experience of dislocation was just the reverse, to break down resistance to the norms of factory toil and counter some of the general restlessness of the industrial workforce with converts to the factory masters' faith.

The making of an exceptionally diligent worker out of the European peasant was a complex process, but it began with the fact that most migrants to industrial America, particularly after the passing of the great famines of the middle years of the nineteenth century, were not uprooted but ambitious, self-uprooted emigrants, drawn not from the most impoverished regions of Europe but from those in the throes of economic change. Often the emigrant had been on the move as a temporary farm laborer in Europe before friends, letters, or the example of a successful returnee, with his watch chain, confident manners, and American slang, turned his thoughts toward the United States. The immense wages possible in America and the chance to work one's way up through the ranks and statuses that seemed so fixed in Europe—the prospect of wearing a white collar and polish on one's boots "like one of the gentry," as the young Slovenian, Louis Adamic, imagined it—dominated the vision of America throughout much of peasant Europe. Children often embellished the American legend with visions of streets paved with gold, but few adult emigrants doubted that the price of their ambitions would be severe and exacting toil. "The hard work of America is no joke," an Irish emigrant wrote home about 1890, and the phrase "runs like a constant refrain" through the letters of Irish emigrants, according to a recent scholar. In the same manner, Emily Balch, traveling through Austria-Hungary in 1905, found the Slavic peasants she encountered "deeply convinced that the work [in America] was harder than at home, and that there was nothing but hunger for the man who did not work."[37]

Most emigrants, finally, brought with them not only ambition but some measure of faith in toil itself. Peasant work ideals lacked the sharp, driving edge of the American work ethic, but ideas of the health-giving and useful powers of labor were not unique to Americans. Sometimes, in fact, the convergence was very close. Trying to console his American daughter-in-law on the death of her child, a Polish Catholic farmer turned to the language of Thomas Carlyle, urging her not to grieve, "for you are sick from grief," but to "work as much as you can" so that "you will have no time to grieve." "When a man works, he is healthy," he wrote, "but when he loafs around in vain he gets weaker and weaker." Even in southern Italy, where time ran more slowly than in Galicia and the working year might be less than half as long as in America, folk songs warned "lazy" girls that they would never earn themselves a husband.[38]

The expectations, the willingness to work, and the faith in labor all ran very deep. Another Polish Catholic, determined to go to America "to earn some hundreds of rubles there within two or three years," wrote an emigration assistance league that his priest had tried to dissuade him from the journey, "show[ing] me the dangers, the terrible work there which often costs one's life, and in general the reasons why it is not worth leaving here." But, he concluded, "I was not persuaded."[39]

What happened to such migrants next depended critically on the circumstances of their encounter with the American economy. Some immigrants found "easy work" and wrote happily of the fact in letters home; others had the strain of adjustment cushioned by relatives or strong immigrant subcultures. But if an immigrant arrived without friends or industrial skills, he often went through the painful shock of unemployment followed by entrapment in a brutal round of temporary jobs. Edward Steiner, who emigrated from central Europe in the 1880s, may serve as an example for nameless others. Landing in New York City, he found his first job in the clothing industry, but the slack season soon dried up the work. He tried to eke out a living in other short-term jobs in a bakery, a feather-renovating shop, and a sausage factory, abandoned the city for harvest work, moved on to a Pittsburgh steel mill where his job ended in a layoff, worked in a coal mine until a strike halted production, tried a job in a South Bend plough factory until he became ill from the heat and the damp, moved on to a Chicago machine shop where he was fired for lecturing his fellow employees, and shuttled on through more harvest, mine, and factory work—all in the space of about two years.[40] Whether he went "on the tramp," like Steiner, or scrambled for a foothold in the casual labor market of the city, the job the immigrant had so eagerly anticipated often eluded him. And the combination of extravagant hopes and the trauma of finding and keeping a job worked together to shatter village norms of labor, to undercut the props of tradition, and to confuse what was "proper" work and what was unacceptable drudgery.

One can follow a part of this process in the letters of an immigrant boy who arrived from Poland in a Connecticut mill town in the summer of 1913. At once ambitious and deeply homesick, he missed the holidays that went by unnoticed in America, begged for news from home, and claimed he did not let an hour pass without thinking of his family and village. But the old ways of work, unmentioned in the series, were simply too far away to think of. By fall, when the factories began to close for the slack season, he wrote that he now no longer did anything but eat, sleep, and toil. "We must be very attentive in our work, every hour, because if anything is bad we are without work," he warned himself, and in the sentence one catches a sense of both the speed and the manner in which the new standards of labor might be learned and absorbed. Native-born farm boys—upward-striving, work-motivated youngsters unprepared to resist the demands of the factory—experienced the same round of shock and alienation from past habits, often with the same results. The labor economist John R. Commons noted the phenomenon early in the twentieth century: "Migration tears a man away from the traditions, the routine, the social props on which he has learned to rely.... Partly fear, partly hope, make the fresh immigrant the hardest ... worker in our industries."[41]

All these factors, then, qualified the clash of work norms in the factories. Men reared in the work ethic, migrants wrenched from the standards of the past, and workers willing to chain themselves to the long hours and discipline of the factories in exchange for its material rewards and the chance of escape all rubbed shoulders with the more restless wage earners in the mills. But they did not set the dominant temper. With time and experience many of the tradition-torn migrants assumed more independent, more assertive, and more fractious habits. Others, who began with ambitions and hopes, ultimately decided that the costs of this form of toil were too high, just as most of the middle-class sojourners who tried their hand far more briefly at factory work came to the same conclusion. Resistance to factory expectations can be found among first-generation industrial workers and the children of mill children, among the immigrant Chicago slaughterhouse workers and the native-born machinists and molders at Watertown, among highly skilled pieceworkers and the army of drifting, unskilled industrial laborers. Absenteeism, mobility, and worker slowdowns were the most obvious manifestations of values in conflict. The long tradition of surplus-based working-class economic theories was another. Most commonly of all, alienation from factory labor amounted simply to an inner turn of mind—a withdrawal of interest from work and indulgence in the dream of the day when men would no longer live to work but would make labor "auxiliary" to their lives.

Throughout the factories industrial workers chafed at their jobs and dreamed of leisure; they engaged their employers in long and bitter disputes over working conditions. But if they rallied to leaders at all, it was not to men who denigrated work but to those who insisted on its inherent value. Their mirroring of one of the central clichés of the culture they contested was not accomplished without some twinges of resentment and anxiety. William Sylvis, the iron molders' leader who dominated the labor movement in the 1860s, complained of the surfeit of appeals to the "dignity of labor" by demagogues, politicians, and "effeminate non-producers" looking for "a stepping stone to gain notoriety or promotion." Terence Powderly likewise recalled suffering through the harangues of politicians on the nobility of the men who toiled, and a half-century after Powderly's experience Eugene Debs berated labor audiences for their susceptibility to the same flattery. Let a politician offer up some praise to the "horny handed sons of toil," Debs chided, and it "fetches you every time." [42] Yet what made the hypocrites particularly galling to labor spokesmen like Sylvis, Powderly, or Debs was that for each of them the rhetoric was second nature. No theme was more enduring in the labor movement than an appeal to the dignity of labor and the worth of those who did the world's "real" work.

The tradition was manufactured in part out of pride and in part out of a sense of acute degradation. The rhetoric worked at all only by virtue of the very abstraction and conventionality of its premises. But for workers pushed to the wall by industrialization and often abused by the keepers of the work ethic, who found by some galling paradox that their dirty hands were a brand of inferiority in a society filled with obeisances to labor, praise of work offered too useful and too essential a weapon in the battle for status and self-respect to ignore. Thus, below the bell towers and with their own share of incongruity, workers turned a piece of the work ethic into an enduring labor tradition.

Skilled workers, acutely conscious of their declining status, were the first to turn to the language of the work ethic to protest their lot. Condemnation of "irrational, anti-republican and unchristian opinions in relation to the worth and respectability of *manual labor*," as a Massachusetts labor leader put the plea in the 1830s, begins well before the middle of the nineteenth century. When the bricklayers and masons organized in the mid-1860s, they promised to combat the sentiments that elevated wealth above usefulness and industry, the professional above the workingman; and their pledge, with variations, was a staple of nineteenth-century union platforms. Such protests were directed not only at the prejudices of outsiders. Is God "less because His mechanical hand formed the mountains?" Richard Trevellick, of the Ship Carpenters appealed to workingmen. "No fellow toilers; He is not less because He worked; neither are you." William Sylvis was one of the most effective orators in the dignity of labor vein, transforming protest into soaring, self-dignifying affirmation. Labor, he told audiences of workingmen, "is the foundation of the entire political, social, and commercial structure.... It is the base upon which the proudest structure of art rests—the leverage which enables man to carry out God's wise purposes—the source from which science draws the elements of its power and greatness, ... the attribute of all that is noble and grand in civilization." As for those who labored, they were "the bone and muscle of the nation, the very pillars of our temple of liberty."[43]

This style was spread and institutionalized in the Knights of Labor in the 1880s. Terence Powderly, the Knights' Grand Master Workman from 1879 to 1893, was in many ways a man out of step with his times and the organization he led. He was a temperance man in an age of hard-drinking laborers, an exceedingly cautious leader in an era of violent strikes, a skilled railroad machinist whose career had brought him up against little of the encroaching factory order, and a divided man on the shorter-hours issue that so agitated the Knights in their most vigorous years. But Powderly brought an abundance of pride to the labor movement, a deep and encompassing sensitivity to the dignity of labor. He was particularly fond of the story of his encounter with the dandified artist James McNeill Whistler, who had looked down his monocle sneeringly at his first specimen of the "horny-handed sons of toil" and had been readily reciprocated with an insult and a perfervid lecture on the image of God in the meanest workingman. It was a story that told a good deal both about Powderly and about the Knights, who played upon the theme of pride strongly in their day in the 1880s. "We mean to uphold the dignity of labor," to "affirm the nobility" of all who work in the sweat of their brows, new members learned in the ritual of initiation:

> In the beginning God ordained that man should labor,
> not as a curse, but as a blessing; not as a punishment,
> but as a means of development, physically, mentally,
> morally, and has set thereunto his seal of approval in the rich
> increase and reward. By labor is brought forth the kindly
> fruits of the earth in rich abundance for our sustenance and
> comfort; by labor (not exhaustive) is promoted health of
> body and strength of mind; labor garners the priceless
> stores of wisdom and knowledge.... "Labor is noble and
> holy." To glorify God in its exercise, to defend it from
> degradation, to divest it of the evils to body, mind and
> estate, which ignorance and greed have imposed; to rescue
> the toiler from the grasp of the selfish is a work worthy of
> the noblest and best of our race.

Such a body had no place for drones or idlers, Powderly insisted; it was a union of "the real bone and sinew of the land."[44] No doubt many Knights refused to take such formulas seriously, ignored the ritual, and dismissed the pretensions of their title. Yet the theme of the aristocracy of toil crops up elsewhere in the 1860s and 1870s—in the National Guard of Industry, the Sons of Vulcan, the Knights of St. Crispin, or the Sovereigns of Industry. The last, a New England–centered workingmen's cooperative league, put the ideology of the struggling labor movements of the post–Civil War years most succinctly: "Labor ... creates everything and does everything, and is the protector and preserver of all."[45]

The Knights was the last major labor organization to preserve the fraternal paraphernalia of rituals, passwords, symbol-laden emblems, and resonant titles, which gave an important anchor to workers caught in the toils of status collapse in the post–Civil War years. But the dignity of labor theme survived the demise of the fraternal style and of the Knights itself in the 1890s. Shorn of some of its piety and more florid nineteenth-century phrases, the rhetoric passed into labor's left wing, where socialists like Debs turned it into an appeal to the revolutionary consciousness of the working class. "You workers are the only class essential to society," Debs tirelessly exhorted labor audiences after the turn of the century. "The workers and producers, the builders and delvers ... are the creators of society and the conservators of civilization, and when they come to realize it they will conquer in the struggle for supremacy and people the earth with a race of free men." The omnipresent socialist icon of the worker's upraised bare arm, rippling with labor-hardened muscles, wordlessly broadcast the same message. In full rhetorical flight in a Labor Day message in 1904, Debs insisted that "the Toiler is the rough-hewn bulk from which the perfect Man is being chiseled by the hand of God."[46]

This fervent praise of work meshed awkwardly at times in socialist rhetoric with equally fervent praise of leisure. The regime of the working class promised to make all men workers and at the same time, for all intents and purposes, to do away with work. Under socialism labor time would be whittled down to four months a year, Bill Haywood of the IWW promised, perhaps even to an hour's work a day in Upton Sinclair's version. When Haywood described the coming socialist factory to striking Paterson, New Jersey, silk workers in 1913, it was a vision for wage earners tired to their very bones with labor. There would be a dining room with unsurpassed food and a brilliant orchestra, Haywood assured them, a library and an art gallery, a swimming pool and a gymnasium, private marble bathrooms, and morris chairs to work in "so that when you become fatigued you may relax in comfort." "It is ridiculous for sane people to work all day and every day," Haywood wrote elsewhere. "One of the worst features about the members of the working class is that they do not think themselves happy unless they are hard at work." They had got themselves into the rut of work and did not know when "to give up the bad habit."[47]

Yet among themselves, socialists wrangled over the title of worker, accused each other of having never touched their hands to real labor, and quarreled over whether socialist speakers should appear in bourgeois suits or workingmen's overalls—all in what Daniel Bell has termed a "cult of proletarian chauvinism." Haywood himself, testifying before the Commission on Industrial Relations in 1915, burst out in self-contempt at his move into labor organizing from the genuine toil of the mines. "The real people who have to be considered are the workers," he told the commission, "the productive workers, the ones who make society, who build the railroads, who till the soil, who run the mills. I have done no work for 10 or 15 years and I am a parasite; I recognize that.... I am doing a thing I ought not to be called on to do."[48] This doubleness was not simply due to the burdens of Marxist theory. In their pride in work and visions of leisure, in their sense of the historic mission of the working class and their dreams of all but abolishing work, the socialists were very close to the center of working-class thought.

The American Federation of Labor represented a more hard-bitten style than the socialists, the Knights, or their mid-nineteenth-century predecessors. Encomiums to the dignity of labor appeared only infrequently in the *American Federationist* or the journals of the AFL's member unions, and then most frequently in the poetry columns. "All honor to the brown and skillful hand, / The swell of muscle, the nerve like steel," the *Machinists' Monthly Journal* editorialized in 1910, but more typical was the platform John F. Tobin of the Boot and Shoe Workers offered the Commission on Industrial Relations: "less work to more workers for better pay and shorter hours."[49] Samuel Gompers, the self-conscious industrial proletarian whose drinking annoyed Powderly and whose step-at-a-time practicality angered the socialists, tirelessly preached the same antiromantic doctrine. He argued insistently for the eight-hour day, not entirely as a means of reducing unemployment and raising wages, but as the legitimate right of those "who have borne the awful strains and burdens of exacting toil." Against the cult of unchecked production he argued for cultivation of consumption and, in Herbert Spencer's phrase, for the "gospel of relaxation." Not until the antiunion movement was at its height after 1900 did Gompers compromise the dream of lessened toil by taking up the argument that eight-hour workers would make up production losses by more efficient work. Even then Gompers threw his energies against scientific management's version of the work ethic, damning Taylor's system as reducing men to "mere machines."[50]

But Gompers's response to Taylor's charge of widespread worker malingering was to retreat into the rhetoric of pride. "The heart of the workingman is sound," Gompers insisted in the

American Federationist in 1911, when the scientific management controversy was at its height; "he who calls him an habitual loafer, an upholder of 'soldiering,' traduces him.... Our wage-workers despise sneaking methods, are by training and on principle averse to taking a man's money without rendering full equivalent, and would infinitely rather 'fight it out' with an unfair employer, and have done with it, than adopt the unmanly, dishonorable, puerile methods ascribed to them by ... 'Doctor Taylor.' ... It is uniformly harder to pretend to work than to really work." The argument was disingenuous, but Gompers employed it over and over again in the early twentieth century for both trade-union and nontrade-union audiences. There was not "in the whole world, civilized or uncivilized, a working people who toil so hard, who give so much of their mental and physical effort in their work, as do the American people." "When European workmen come over to this country and stand beside their American fellow workingmen it simply dazes them—the velocity of motion, the deftness, the quickness, the constant strain ... and it is some months, with the greatest endeavor, before [they] can at all come near the production of the American workingman." Other AFL chieftains involved in the fight against Taylorism seconded the theme. "The American workman, as to skill, ingenuity, and quantity of output, has no equal, let alone a peer, on the face of God's green earth," the machinists' union head argued before a congressional committee.[51] The defensive posture of the trade unions in the decade before the First World War, under siege both from the courts and from manufacturers, does not entirely explain away the reappearance of the phrases of the Knights' initiation ritual slightly disguised in the language of labor's self-appointed pragmatists.

Certainly there were impelling reasons for those who presumed to speak for workingmen to seize upon the phrases of the work ethic. Early nineteenth-century America had offered its shop workers identities of place and trade—a fraternity of craft secrets, skills, and time-hallowed symbols. In labor parades in the 1860s and 1870s, workers still bore their trade traditions proudly. In the Chicago eight-hour parade of 1867, according to a contemporary report, "the Stone Cutters Union had three trucks with operatives cutting ornamental masonry. The Iron Molders Union truck was drawn by eight noble horses, and contained men at work on the finer branches of iron molding. The Ship Carpenters and Caulkers Union had a full rigged ship and yawl boat with busy workmen thereon."[52] By the middle of the twentieth century, with the eight-hour day and five-day week finally realized, the hobbies a worker possessed and the way he spent his weekends had begun to fill some of the same self-defining purposes. But industrial America, in blasting skills and undermining traditions, left the majority of its industrial wage workers with only the simplest common denominator of labor. If the semiskilled factory hand did not claim his place as a worker, industrial society offered few other opportunities for assertion of his dignity. Protest movements are not successfully made on the theme of exploitation alone. Thus even those profoundly alienated from their work rallied to leaders who knew the rhetoric of pride, who defended the wage earner as the "bone and sinew" of the nation, his labor as a marvel of efficiency, and insisted that work itself was noble and honorable.

Seizing on the theme of work, industrial wage earners tried to turn the North's pervasive moralism to their own ends. But to join the factory masters on their own terms did not come without costs. One of them was, at times, to force the labor movement into a style of circumlocution. Denying against the preponderance of evidence that output quotas existed, AFL spokesmen took refuge in the considerably more ambiguous formula: a fair day's wage and a fair day's work. By the same token the Knights' pledge to defend a form of "labor (not exhaustive)" scarcely did explicit justice to the contests over labor discipline that swirled only half-acknowledged in the factories. Circumlocutions were common in all discussions of work in industrial America, but the evasions peculiar to labor spokesmen made it considerably easier for those outside the factories to miss what the noise and tumult was all about.

The second, more obvious cost was to entrench in the labor movement a schism between rhetoric and action, the language of work pride and practical alienation. From the restless industrial workers of the nineteenth century to the hard hats and survey respondents of the twentieth, the tension between pride in one's job and estrangement from it has a long and enduring history. But the final price was the most anomalous, to add the voices of men weary with work to the chorus of Carlylean phrases that pervaded industrial America. What such men meant, of course, was not the tightly supervised, clock-driven work toward which the factories were evolving. It had little in it of the ascetic obsessions of a man like Taylor. Perhaps it was not work at all. But even for those who chafed at labor, the appeal to the moral centrality of work was too useful to resist. Pitched in the abstract, it turned necessity into pride and servitude into honor; it offered a lever upon the moral sentiments of those whose power mattered. But in the process, a work-immersed culture exacted its due from its largest body of rebels.

Idle Womanhood: Feminist Versions of the Work Ethic

> We demand that, in that strange new world
> that is arising alike upon the man and the
> woman, where nothing is as it was, and all
> things are assuming new shapes and relations,
> that ... we also shall have our share of
> honored and socially useful human toil.
>
> Olive Schreiner, *Woman and Labor* (1911)

The factories were not the only locus of restlessness in industrial America, nor were wage earners alone in turning the abstract phrases of the work ethic into a cry of protest. In the middle-class world, restlessness began at home. The "unquiet sex," as it was known, was woman. Poet and columnist Ella Wheeler Wilcox looked up from her mail at the turn of the century to announce that the letters reflected a "volcano" of seething feminine discontent. "Beneath jeweled corsages beat restless hearts," Wilcox claimed; "from under the flower-laden brims of modish hats look unhappy eyes, gazing out into the world with longing for an indefinable something."[1] Only a peculiarly obtuse reader of events would have dared to contradict her, for by 1900 observers of middle-class women were marking signs of disquiet everywhere. The rising incidence of divorce and the falling birthrate, the eager rush of women into the colleges and the failure of many of them afterward to settle down as expected with husband and family, the mushroom growth of women's organizations, the press for equal suffrage, and the sheer volume of words devoted to "the woman question," all attested to the ferment Wilcox found aboil in her correspondence. It was a surprising occurrence and to many Northern moralists a deeply disturbing one. Few places had seemed more immune to the dislocations of an industrializing society than the solid, roomy houses that lined the tree-arched streets and fronted the boulevards of every

Northern town and city, self-consciously cut off from the toil and turbulence around them. But behind facades as solid and confident as those of the factories, middle-class households harbored their own festering germs of discontent.

Explanations of the phenomenon varied widely. Conservative observers charged up the evident uneasiness of middle-class women to a loss of moral backbone. Responsibility, altruism, and stoic endurance all seemed to have given way before a giddy, noisy, self-centeredness. Defenders of the "new woman" countered that she was not in flight from duty but in simmering revolt against oppression. Certainly equality was not woman's lot, and her list of injustices was a long one. She was a victim of legal discrimination, a half-person in the courts, and a nonentity at the ballot box; she was sexually exploited and medically misunderstood; if she worked outside the home she was paid half a man's wages, and if she toiled at housework and child-rearing she earned nothing at all; she was barred from most of a man's world and, in her own, hobbled by tightly constraining codes of convention and propriety.

But simply to catalog women's grievances could not prove satisfying. Ultimately, questions of cause and essence demanded answers. The organized women's movement siezed on suffrage as the crux of the "woman question," finding in political powerlessness the key to the ills that beset women, channeling women's discontents into the long campaign for the vote, and finally investing immense and—as it turned out—exaggerated hopes in the Nineteenth Amendment. No rival panacea matched the force of this. And yet for a large number of the era's most articulate and widely read feminists, suffrage was too narrow an answer. What was essentially wrong with woman, they claimed, could not be rectified by politics alone; it was that she had lost her productive work.

Feminist versions of the work ethic were never more than a single, though strikingly prominent, cluster of threads in the tangled debate over the status of women. But themes of work, idleness, and feminism were intricately and compellingly intertwined in the literature of middle-class womanhood. At best, it was said, woman was underemployed, her days filled up with the unproductive, inefficient make-work of an "idle busyness." At worst, she was an abject parasite, hostage to a code of ornamental idleness that left her useless and unfulfilled. In either event, woman was an anomaly in the toiling, busy world around her, consigned to leisure in an experiment with a leisure class that had been an abject failure. What she needed above all else was to go to work. Shouldering its way into work-exempt parlors, setting etiquette guides atumble, the work ethic brought its enormous reserves of power to the women's movement. But in the end it was a peculiar way of putting the case—abstract, unwittingly class-bound, and morally commonplace—as if the pressures of moral convention had pushed middle-class women to define their restlessness in a language simpler and narrower than their intents.

Two women, standing at either end of the industrial years— Harriet Beecher Stowe and Charlotte Perkins Gilman—illustrate at once the possibilities, the force, and something of the peculiarities of the argument. Harriet Beecher Stowe is remembered, as no doubt she hoped to be, as a crusader against slavery and a tilter at the lingering influence of Jonathan Edwards on New England theology.[2] But questions of womanhood were never far below the surface of any of her writings. From *Uncle Tom's Cabin* through her novels of New England life, Stowe poured out a pent-up sense of the hardness of woman's lot: the wrenching death of children, the irresponsibility of husbands, the hectoring of a harsh, male-dominated theology, the entrapment, and the quiet suffering. The bond uniting the devout, self-sacrificing Uncle Tom and Little Eva, the young, angelic heroine of Stowe's most famous novel, was not simply the affinity of believing Christians; it was the tie of submission that made slaves and women kin. Yet when, at the height of her career, Stowe turned directly to the woman question, her focus was not on hardship but on idleness, and her advice was simple almost to the point of the prosaic. The matter with woman, she argued, was that she had fallen to the cult of fashion and lost the will to labor.

Stowe had previously sketched the ideal of competence and duty she had in mind in her portrait of the Widow Scudder in *The Minister's Wooing*, a historical novel written in the wake of her antislavery successes and set in the Newport, Rhode Island, of the 1790s. Katy Scudder was a paragon of what Stowe called "faculty." She could "harness a chaise, or row a boat; she could saddle and ride any horse in the neighborhood; she could cut any garment that ever was seen or thought of, make cake, jelly, and wine, from her earliest years in most precocious style." But Katy Scudder's triumph was her kitchen, where breakfast arose "as if by magic," the floor gleamed from fresh sanding, and the pewter never showed signs of tarnish. "To her who has faculty, nothing shall be impossible," Stowe wrote:

> She shall scrub floors, wash, wring, bake, brew, and yet her hands shall be small and white; she shall have no perceptible income, yet always be handsomely dressed; she shall have not a servant in her house, with a dairy to manage, hired man to feed, a boarder or two to care for, unheard-of pickling and preserving to do,—and yet you commonly see her every afternoon sitting at her shady parlor-window behind the lilacs, cool and easy, hemming muslin cap-strings, or reading the last new book.[3]

When in 1864, moved by weariness with war thoughts and the chance to transmute the experiences of house-building into income-producing articles, Stowe began a column on domestic manners in the *Atlantic Monthly*, she used her forum to broadcast that ideal of the woman of "faculty." Against the tug of fashion, she pleaded for women who did their own housework; against the inroads of selfish indulgence, she praised those women of "strong minds and ever-active industry" who followed their labors as an act of self-discipline and "deep interior sacrifice." The theme of decay pervaded Stowe's views of womanhood. From the old, country-bred New Englanders to the new urban upstarts, from Katy Scudder to the present belles of Newport, skilled in waltzing, French grammar, and the mysteries of puffs and ribbonry yet utterly ignorant of domestic lore, women had fallen from nobler days. "My mother was less than her mother," one of Stowe's characters announced sadly, "and I am less than my mother." Still worse was the coming race of women, reared to be "pets of society" and "*lazzaroni* of the parlor and boudoir"—fragile and incompetent women, ravaged by ennui, shattered in nerves, and helpless before the servants in their kitchens who did the work they no longer knew how to do. Selfishness and antidomesticity were at the bottom of woman's malaise. "Some task, some burden, some cross, each one must carry; and there must be something done in every true and worthy life, not as amusement, but as duty,—not as play but as earnest work." "We have not yet realized fully the true dignity of labor," she pleaded, or "the surpassing dignity of domestic labor."[4]

In this conception of the woman question, Stowe drew heavily on the ideas of her elder sister, Catharine Beecher, who spent a lifetime campaigning for the dignity of household labor and whose themes and phrases flowed through Stowe's columns with the freedom of sisterly plagiarism. Beyond Catharine Beecher, moreover, lay a strong New England tradition. In the 1830s, when the sheltered, servanted middle-class woman had begun to appear in numbers as a token of her husband's affluence and as an antitype to his frenetic industry, William A. Alcott's *The Young Wife* had urged upon women the moral and economic advantages of doing their own work and dispensing with domestic servants. The most prominent of the daughters of New England—Lydia Maria Child, Louisa May Alcott, Elizabeth Stuart Phelps, and Julia Ward Howe—were likewise vocal critics of the idle woman. We are not put on this earth merely to be happy or cultured, Phelps told *Harper's Monthly* readers in 1868. "We are put here mainly to be disciplined and to be of use."[5]

By the middle years of the nineteenth century, however, this tradition was under siege from newer ideals of pure grace and ornament. The model of the leisured woman, unsullied by toil, drew strength from several sources: the seductive example of the European manor house and the Southern plantation, the demands of men for a domestic oasis from busyness, and the longing of women to shift their burden of domestic toil onto someone else's shoulders. The dream of leisure, still taboo for men, insinuated itself into nineteenth-century, middle-class Northern culture as a code for women, and the ensuing debate caught all women's writers in the cross-currents of ideals. The new ideal found outlets from the elaborate fashion plates of *Godey's Lady's Book*, to guides to the convoluted etiquette of leisured living, to essayist Mary Abigail Dodge's still more forthright insistence that housekeeping with servants was "the only way of life tolerable to an adult Christian." It was man's lot to work, branded on him as he left the gates of Eden, Dodge argued in explicit rebuttal to Stowe; women stood outside that curse, "divinely designed" for a "state of repose, ease, leisure."[6] Stowe, on the other hand, spoke for an older tradition. Standing at the same crossroads in ideals, she threw in her lot with the past, with ideals of duty and competence.

There were more unsettling conclusions waiting in the counsel of work for women, however, and in *My Wife and I*, a didactic novel of manners written for her brother's *Christian Union* in 1870 and 1871, Stowe came close to embracing some of them. She had warmed up for the task with a novelette, *Pink and White Tyranny*, a parable on the themes of selfishness and sacrifice, in which Stowe mismatched an old-fashioned, hard-working Yankee with a charming, self-centered, socially ambitious, and utterly unprincipled parasite, described the wreck which followed, and insisted that divorce was unthinkable. But in the more ambitious tale that immediately followed, Stowe argued that one of the ways out of such domestic tragedies was to break down the conventions that forced single women, often desperately, toward marriage. The heroines of her tale were three "new women," one of them a New England farm girl, the other two daughters of a newly rich New York City merchant, and all of them deeply discontented with the narrow boundaries of women's "sphere." Nursed on the heroics of Carlyle and dreams of duty, they found themselves trapped in "objectless, rootless, floating" lives— hemmed in by a daughter's obligations, burdened with idleness or tied to housekeeping when their natures cried out for more vital work—and yet with no possibility of relief except through marriage. "A woman's lot! and what is that, pray?" Stowe protested through one of her heroines, but "desperate dullness, and restraint, and utter paralysis, ... to sit with folded hands and see life drifting by—to be a mere nullity." To break free from home, to take up a career, to earn one's place in the professions society unjustly reserved for men, to vote (at least for a separate women's parliament) were all preferable, Stowe insisted, to this aimless deadening vacuity. Having gone so far toward militant feminism, Stowe in the end worked herself back to safer ground. She sent two of her heroines off to Paris to study medicine at the novel's end, but their choice of celibacy and a career, much as she defended them, was clearly second best. The work she gave to the most sympathetically portrayed of her three restless women was the work of an old-fashioned, loving marriage, filled with domestic chores and family duties. The newest woman at her best was a woman of domestic "faculty."[7]

Clearly the themes of idleness and domestic work were at the forefront of Stowe's thoughts on womanhood, and yet in her case the counsel of labor had perplexing anomalies. While insisting on the dignity of household labor, Stowe was herself a chaotic and unwilling housekeeper, who found domestic labors, even with servants, oppressive. She worked under "serious natural disadvantages" in matters of order and system, as she confessed to her husband, and her first fourteen years of marriage were marked by frequent breakdowns and occasionally by flight from the family state for recuperation.[8] Nor did Harriet's mother, of whom she cherished vividly idealized childhood memories, exactly fit the model of "faculty." A charming woman of gentle and aesthetic temperament, her chief delight was not the kitchen but fancywork: drawing, fine needlework, and elaborately decorated furniture. Aunt Esther Beecher, who served as the model for Stowe's *Atlantic Monthly* pieces, was indeed an embodiment of the order, precision, and self-sacrifice she celebrated there. Catharine Beecher, however, remembered her aunt as an overly compulsive woman, bewildered by her responsibilities, and did not recall her household administration gladly.[9] Perhaps because she felt she had had her say years before, the biography Stowe helped her son put together is markedly silent about this "stocking-darning saint" who served the Beecher family so devotedly. But certainly Stowe knew well the phenomenon of the compulsive New England woman. Even as she pleaded for the dignity of work, she peopled her novels with examples of work gone to extremes—cross, austere, overclamped women, blind to beauty, obtuse to the promptings of the heart. From Miss Ophelia of *Uncle Tom's Cabin* to Miss Asphyxia of *Oldtown Folks*, they were nothing but "working machine[s], always wound up and going."[10]

In the best and most deeply felt of her novels, in fact, it is not work that saves but love, and the women of "faculty" are second best to their daughters. No figure more clearly compelled Stowe's imagination than Little Eva, the half child, half angel whose spontaneous, instinctual love heals the bitter wounds of adulthood. As Katy Scudder's daughter Mary in *The Minister's Wooing* or as Mara in *The Pearl of Orr's Island*, Stowe came back to the figure and the message it contained over and again. To become as little girls, to see with the directness of a child, to recover from overintellectualized, overmannered, and over-worked life the spontaneity of children was, in the end, Stowe's way out of the crosses of woman's lot. Whatever the outer shell of her concept of womanhood, this was its inner heart. Love and compulsive industry, Eva and Stowe's toiling, always precise Aunt Esther, were not complements but polar opposites.

None of this suggests that Harriet Beecher Stowe's belief in the dignity of labor, and of domestic labor in particular, was insincere. She preached it too often and too earnestly for that. But in the gap between experience and advice, in her free copying from her sister Catharine, and in the distance between her artistically barren domestic stories and those novels into which she poured her imagination freely, it is difficult to put away the suspicion that Stowe's overt counsel to women was less than an adequate summation of her sense of women's needs. Perhaps there was something of an act of expiation in her praise of the "faculty" that eluded her and the work she found so painful. Perhaps there was evasion, too, in her flight into a masculine persona for *My Wife and I* and her *Atlantic Monthly* pieces. But there is also a hint of writing by formula, as if, when face to face with the woman question, her rich, complex, and sentimental imagination were seeking refuge in safe, familiar conventions of work and idleness.

Charlotte Perkins Gilman was, at first glance, a far different sort of woman from her distant cousin, Stowe. Where Stowe insisted that the kitchen was the cornerstone of the home, Gilman wanted to banish it entirely. Where Stowe put her deepest hopes in sentiment, Gilman preached an almost asceptic faith in science. Stowe was a professed moderate among feminists; Gilman prided herself on radicalism. And yet what joined them was a repeated insistence on work, a common stress on the economic heart of the woman question, and, in the end, a sense of meanings ampler than the tight and straitened language into which they chose to force them.

Between the 1890s and the First World War, Gilman was one of the most widely known and prolific writers on the woman question, turning out a prodigious flow of books, verse, lectures, and articles; but almost all of her later writings were in some way elaborations on her first book, *Women and Economics*, which appeared in 1898. It began with the point fundamental to

Gilman's thinking, that woman was man's economic dependent; alone of all nature's creatures, the human female depended utterly on her mate for subsistence, and the results had been crippling. Confined to the home while men wrestled with the hard, character-building world, cut off from anything in the least invigorating, earning nothing on her own, woman had lost the skill and courage that rightfully belonged to her and had been left with the traits of vassalage: weakness, delicacy, and a clinging dependence on men. The consequences, Gilman argued, had been disastrous not only for women but for the evolution of the species, as each woman passed on her crippled nature to her still more handicapped offspring. Gilman was not, like Stowe, preoccupied with idleness. Women drudged unceasingly, she insisted, but their housekeeping, child-rearing tasks were toil of the most primitive kind—unspecialized, cut off from contact with others, not true work at all. Above all, by housework a woman earned nothing, saw no tangible economic reward, gained no independence. Gilman's solution was clear from her premises: women, single and married alike, needed to go to work, not at home, but outside it. To allow married women to take up paying work, Gilman proposed to drastically reorganize the traditional household, abolishing domestic cooking, housework, and much of domestic child-rearing, abandoning the old house structure for blocks of kitchenless apartments efficiently serviced by professional catering, cleaning, and nursery services.[11]

Gilman's plan for domestic reform was not difficult to comprehend, but she was harder pressed to make clear to others all she had in mind by the term "work." Housekeeping was not "work," in Gilman's terms, and those who did it were not productive citizens. Gilman debated the point with the suffrage movement's most effective orator, Anna Howard Shaw, before an audience of New York City working-class women in 1909 and lost the contest ignominiously. Gilman argued that women who stayed at home were nonproductive, first because they received no pay and second because most of what they did was useless, inefficient, and, in the economic sense, "parasitical." Shaw countered that married women worked and that their labors were the mainstay of both home and husband. Asked to decide the contest, the vast majority of listeners found Shaw's argument the more convincing.[12]

The crux of Gilman's difficulty in communication was that she had contrived a peculiar definition of work that did not match the assumptions of her New York audience. For Gilman, work was not simply the expenditure of energy. Work was an act of social interchange, "not an individual process but a collective one." "No expression of energy of sufficiently high grade to be called 'work' is done to gratify oneself" or one's immediate relations, she argued in her most extreme attempts to make the issue clear. "Work is a social service ... not a process of taking care of oneself, but a process of taking care of one another." Economic independence, by the same token, was not simply a matter of income-producing labor. Nor did it mean autonomy. It meant, rather, to have a place in the collective effort of "social economics." By these standards, women's domestic labors, however essential or demanding, were not "work," nor could any kind of mutual contract between husband and wife alter her state of dependence. It was not a woman's tasks themselves that were at fault. "Even cleaning, rightly understood and practised," she wrote, "is a useful, and therefore honorable, profession." The fault with woman's labor was that she toiled apart from the world, at the service of so few people, without the cooperative interchange essential to genuine work.[13]

Gilman's accomplishment, though it was rarely recognized as such, was to construct an elaborate sociological metaphor around the term "work." Possibly she herself did not realize exactly what she had done. In the autobiography she wrote in her sixties, attempting to explain the attacks of mental fatigue that had repeatedly crippled her ability to work or think, Gilman described herself as a lonely young girl, given to regimes of self-discipline and self-improvement, who, soon after marriage, had suffered a severe nervous breakdown that only separation alleviated. Her own explanation of the psychic malaise was a combination of her youthful "over-training," which had secretly exhausted her mental energies, and "mismarriage." Yet clearly as important a factor was an acute sense of suffocation. Reared by a strong-willed mother determined that a daughter should remain in her mother's "sphere" until marriage, who censored Charlotte's letters and invitations until she was twenty-one, Gilman embarked on her stoic training in self-discipline in part as a desperate attempt to carve out an identity of her own. Quietly she cultivated immensely heroic visions. In one of the pieces of advice that she fixed on her mirror, she told herself that if she lived "(as live I do), for others—if all my desires for self-improvement are solely with a view to the elevation of the race—if my mission is to lead a self-sacrificing life" she must "crush all personal sorrow and drop the whole ground of self-interest forever."[14]

At twenty-one she was finally free to pursue that mission. At twenty-four she was disastrously married. Love was not a question in her sudden breakdown, for she remained close to her first husband even after their divorce. At issue seems to have been an intense fear of entrapment. The poetry she wrote in the decade after separation reverberated with themes of stifled heroism: a lighthouse-keeper driven mad by his confinement, a baby stunted by its mother's suffocating love, and, most frequently, the theme of the painfully constricting life of housekeeping. The same motifs reappeared much later in Gilman's short fiction. Her heroines suffered under the hot embraces of eager suitors and turned with relief to resolute, yet gentle and undemanding lovers. Artistic natures were cramped under the confines of custom. To be a woman, she wrote, was "to live over again in her own person ... restriction, repression, denial; the smothering 'no' which crush[es] down all her human desires to create, to discover, to learn, to express, to advance." The self-denying altruism of marriage, she discovered, was a torment. But where Stowe appealed to the wellsprings of sentiment, Gilman's first book of verse pleaded for far less emotional, less intense, less confining human relationships.[15]

A number of influences helped Gilman move from verse to coherent social philosophy: Darwin, Herbert Spencer, Lester Ward, and, above all, Edward Bellamy, whose cause she embraced wholeheartedly in 1890 and whose influence repeatedly emerges in Gilman's writings. But Gilman was not fond of Bellamy's bureaucratic centralism. In the end, oddly enough for a socialist, her model of social organization most closely resembled Adam Smith's vision of capitalism, where gainful work was practical altruism, where businesslike cooperation made for perfect mutuality. Thus, woman's need for paying work meant far more than a job in Gilman's writing; it became a shorthand for a universe of free, unstifled, mutually helpful relationships, where one could serve without crushing the self. To move from the kitchen into a career was to enter "a world of men and women humanly related, ... working together, as they were meant to do, for the common good of all." [16]

In *Human Work*, the book on which she worked the longest and of which she was most proud, Gilman made clear how fully she had charged the term "work" with meanings unconnected with the everyday toil of society. But of all her major books, *Human Work* had the fewest readers, and frequently Gilman found it easier simply to urge women to move into paying jobs, reorganizing the home to meet the new circumstances, and trust that her audience would comprehend the larger meaning of her slogans. But, as her New York experience showed, Gilman risked a good deal in attempting to pour all she had in mind into the metaphor of work, even into her favorite phrase, "human work." The advantage of casting her vision of a broader yet less intense network of social relations in terms of woman's need for labor, was that the formula—the human need for work—was so familiar.

Not all feminists found themselves drawn as compellingly as Stowe or Gilman to issues of work and idleness, and it is not hard to find those who, like Anna Howard Shaw, stubbornly resisted the temptation to cast the woman question as a problem of labor. Yet part of the attraction of the argument that women were cut off from work was its ability, like the case for suffrage, to absorb so many other grievances. Were not women's high-strung nerves, neurasthenic tics, and debilitated bodies the predictable results of idleness? Was not woman's debased status before the law made understandable by the fact that she was not a full, productive member of society? After generations of isolation in the home had stripped women of the traits essential to compete successfully with men, was it surprising that they were paid less than a man's wages? Suffrage, too, could be construed as a labor problem. One of the frequently employed suffragist arguments after the turn of the century contended that since women's traditional work had fled from the home to the school and factory it was imperative that women continue to supervise their age-old tasks through the ballot. To vote was to work in a broader home, to engage in the job of "municipal housekeeping."

Work was equally intertwined with quieter but no less vital

issues of domestic politics. Until just before the First World War, long-standing customs of reticence and modesty inhibited all but a handful of women from publicly raising the matter of sexual relations within marriage. But there were a good number of indirect indications of discontent with the burdens of incessant maternity and the demands of sex. Through the literature of the victimized woman—the ruined working girl, the wronged wife, or the unwilling prostitute—runs a flood of antimasculine resentment. Harriet Beecher Stowe risked her reputation to indict her childhood hero, Byron, for incest—a propriety-defying, self-sacrificing gesture in the name of beleaguered womanhood, akin to the energies later generations of women poured into anti-prostitution and social purity campaigns.[17] But the sense of idle purposelessness compounded the question of sex. An advocate of women's work, writing in the *North American Review* in 1904, admitted the fear that economic competition with men might "unsex" women, raising a "hoyden" race of "Amazonian viragos." Yet the alternative, to strip from woman all her functions save reproduction, was still worse—to drift into "the langorous incapacities of Oriental dreams, where sex overshadows all mental and moral values." "Shall we float blindly down the current of unearned luxury and busy idleness, as our Asiatic and European sisters have done, until we find ourselves, like them, valued principally for our bodies?" another advocate of woman's work queried.[18] Idleness made women victim not only to sexual demands but to desire itself; in Gilman's deliberately ambiguous phrase, the leisured woman was "oversexed."

Just as themes of sexual exploitation and idleness interfused, so were issues of family authority compounded by the matter of a woman's unpaid household labors. Throughout the period, debates swirled around questions of property and inheritance rights, marriage allowances, the power a wife deserved in budgeting and spending, the share due her from her husband's wages. For a generation of feminists, Gilman's call for "economic independence" became an encompassing way of summing up grievances of both sex and power, a shorthand for tensions of rights and liberties buried inside the marriage relation.

Perhaps the most encompassing of all grievances for middle-class women was a feeling of constrictedness within the accustomed "sphere" of respectable womanhood. "Oh, to be a wild

Kossack!" Emily Greene Balch wrote in one of her Bryn Mawr notebooks after reading Gogol's *Taras Bulba*. "Fight hard and drink hard and ride hard.... Our clothes grow strait. Oh, for a horse between the knees, my blood boils, I want to fight, strain, wrestle, strike.... To be brave and have it all known, to surpass and be proud, oh the splendour of it! This is a nice sensible book review isn't it?" Irony brought Emily Balch back to a more sober equilibrium, but the desire to play a man's part, if only in the imagination, to plunge into a masculine world of action and contest, to put into practice dreams nurtured on Carlyle and Byron, to smash the conventions of proper womanhood reverberate in the memoirs of the period's restless women. Maud Nathan, trying to describe the feeling of a daughter of wealth in the New York City of the 1880s, copied the poem of a girlhood friend into her autobiography:

> To sit behind the gilded lattice pane,
> With perfumed toys idly play,
> Whilst watching with a beating heart and kindling eye
> The stream of life that passeth by.

Lydia Commander, writing twenty years after Nathan's memories, claimed that the "price of motherhood" was a kind of mental chloroforming. Even *Harper's Bazar* described the average house as a "prison and a burden and a tyrant" that fettered a woman's thoughts and consumed her vitality. "The modern woman," the editors urged, "ought deliberately and resolutely to refuse to be housed." For these women, the deepest grievance of their class and sex was suffocation in feminine respectability.[19]

Athleticism, higher education, the suffrage movement, and sexual assertiveness all offered possible avenues of escape; but for many women the clearest alternative to the constrictions of domesticity was a paying job. Louisa May Alcott was one of those who took that step, writing triumphantly in her diary of the money her pen was earning. Rheta Childe Dorr's memoirs of her midwestern girlhood dwelt in the same spirit on the act of disobedience through which she gained her first job. Even Susan B. Anthony, though she was vague as to details, claimed once to have fought for a chance to work as a cotton mill operative in her father's factory. Particularly for women of the middle class, toil was rebellion, To escape feminine suffocation, to have a purpose in life, to play a heroic part in the world, frequently came to be to engage, like men, in work.[20]

But once, somewhere in the past, women had had real work to do. Feminist versions of the work ethic not only stretched out to encompass a host of women's grievances within the terms "work" and "idleness"; but many of them also incorporated a deep sense of loss and violation. It was not simply that woman was condemned to inutility; men had invaded her household, broken her tools, and stolen her labor from her. The most commonly blamed villain was industrialization. Harriet Beecher Stowe stood at the head of a long tradition in her veneration of the women of the "pre-railroad" age—skilled, industrious, and a vital factor in economic life. Once the home had been "a complete economic unit," Scott and Nellie Nearing wrote in 1912, "self-sustaining, impregnable, the pride and mainstay of Western civilization." The sociologist Mary Roberts Coolidge, writing in the same year, described "our manufacturing grandmothers" as engaged in "an immense and stimulating field of action"; they were skilled producers, equals of their husbands, masters of "a miniature factory." Many of those who wrote of woman's subsequent fall from industry into idleness laid the blame, like Stowe, on the seductive effects of aristocratic standards of value. But Coolidge's answer was that woman's plight was that of other hand laborers under the factory regime, her job taken away by the mills, leaving her with only a monotonous, petty fragment of her former work.[21]

The theme was already established by the mid-nineteenth century. In 1869, Mrs. C. F. Peirce wrote in alarm that "the mighty mechanical powers are rolling, rolling [women's work] away from under us. In great part it is already gone, and sewing-machines, washing-machines, machines for every smallest office, are taking from us the little that is left of the old manual labor by which we once fed and clothed the world." Virginia Penny, in a book published the same year, called for a confiscatory tax on all men who, working at traditionally feminine trades, had elbowed women out of the work that rightfully belonged to them. After the turn of the century, the argument that women had been stripped of their work by industrialization became virtually

ubiquitous. Housekeeping, it was said, was a "vanishing industry," the home a "deserted workshop," and women "robbed"
of their age-old tasks by machinery. In 1913 an English feminist,
writing in the *Century* on the disappearance of household industries, felt impelled to apologize for an argument "so old and
so trite!"[22]

The second, more complex version of the tale located the theft
of women's work deep in antiquity. The father of a distinctive
woman's anthropology, though few Americans read him save at
second hand, was the Swiss jurist Johann Jakob Bachofen, who,
in 1861 in *Das Mutterrecht,* opened a long anthropological
assault on the historical primacy of the patriarchal family and
male-dominated society. Patriarchal society, Bachofen argued,
was the last stage of an evolution that had taken society from a
primitive, unorganized horde through a matriarchate of women
until, weakened by internecine struggles, the "gynocratic" regime
had finally been toppled by men. Bachofen's theories were based
on imaginative and, to most observers, idiosyncratic readings of
myth and religious symbolism, but his idea of an age of "mother-
right" gained force from the discovery of matrilineal kinship
patterns by the first anthropological fieldworkers. At the end of
the nineteenth century, Bachofen's vocabulary was current
enough for the self-taught American sociologist Lester Ward to
appropriate it for a still more sweeping theory of female primacy,
which Gilman called "the greatest single contribution to the
world's thought" since Darwin. Ward's account, still more clearly
than Bachofen's, was a tragedy. Nature had begun as feminine,
spinning off a puny, helpless strain of males as a biological
afterthought. In human society, too, "maternity was everything."
But in the end man had turned on woman, pulled down the
age-old "gynaecocracy," and enslaved his creator.[23]

Bachofen was primarily concerned with questions of power and
religion, and Ward with biology and eugenics, but other theories
of the matriarchate focused on labor. In 1894, the ethnologist
Otis T. Mason published a careful study of primitive societies
that described work as women's unique business. Primitive man
had wandered, fought, and hunted, he argued, but it was woman
who had worked, invented the arts of agriculture and the crafts,
created stable communities, and held primitive society together.
Mason's viewpoint was progressivistic; if modern women were

exempt from work it was because they had earned their place by ages of toil. Yet, if one took instinct theory seriously, Mason's evidence seemed to lead to other conclusions. In a series of influential articles on sex and industry, sociologist W. I. Thomas maintained that when restless, "katabolic" man, his hunting fields exhausted, had turned upon woman, mastered her, and usurped her tasks, she had lost touch with her inner "anabolic" nature. "To work is a distinctive mark of femininity," Lydia Commander insisted, drawing out the same moral from Ward's and Mason's evidence. With man, labor was an acquired habit; with woman it was the "inherent tendency" of her nature. But by cunning and brute strength, man had taken it all from her.[24]

How far these anthropological speculations penetrated the thought of well-read women is not easy to determine, but they had a strong appeal to many women intellectuals. Not only Gilman and Commander embraced them but Elizabeth Cady Stanton and even, much more tentatively, the conservative editors of *Harper's Bazar*. By 1911, the suffragist Anna Garlin Spencer could repeat the story of the primitive working woman whose tools had been stolen from her by man with the air of telling a long-familiar tale.[25] Certainly the story contained the potent stuff of myth, with its themes of feminine superiority and masculine betrayal, its explicit plot of captivity and entrapment, and its overtones of violation. Like the history of the stripping away of the work of the colonial household by the industrial revolution, it reverberated with a sense of lost purpose and lost power. Man had leaped into woman's place, casting her rudely aside, walling her off from her inner nature. The tale was yet another example of how encompassing the theme of work could be.

Not all feminist versions of the work ethic were alike in the meanings they gave to work or to women. Joined as they were by a preoccupation with inutility, on these questions they broke into distinct camps. The oldest and safest version—a staple of feminist writing from Mary Wollstonecraft through the caustic acid of Thorstein Veblen—was to attack the thoroughly idle woman of wealth, her days consumed in aimless rounds of social engagements, dress, and gossip.

By the middle years of the nineteenth century, however, moderate feminists like Stowe had begun to turn the same language to the daughters of the middle class, caught between adolescence and marriage in the convention that no daughter whose father was capable of supporting her should go to work outside the home. There were multitudes of such women, it appeared, living the aimless lives that oppressed Stowe's heroines, growing up to be incompetent housewives and utterly helpless mothers should the all-too-common fact of widowhood overtake them. Domestic training for girls was an obvious, vital necessity. But feminists of all sorts were increasingly willing to urge that girls of every economic status should likewise be trained in some sort of income-drawing career—to rub off their self-centeredness, to fill up the vacant years before marriage, and, most important, to make a woman less vulnerable to the economic catastrophes that potentially awaited her.

The proposition that married women should work for pay, on the other hand, was a far more radical suggestion and breasted much stronger prejudices. In the 1850s, a few feminists had broached the idea of combining paid work and marriage, and at the Woman's Congress of 1873 Antoinette Brown Blackwell had delivered an impressive call for the opening of part-time work for married women, save those with small children. But it was Edward Bellamy's *Looking Backward* at the end of the 1880s—a book of extraordinary impact on late nineteenth-century feminists—that seems to have made current the idea that all women needed and owed it to society to work outside the home.[26] By the early twentieth century, among "advanced" writers on the woman question, the matter was no longer in doubt and the language of feminism had grown at once more militant and encompassingly abstract. *"We take all labor for our province!"* not as a gift but as "WOMAN'S RIGHT," the South African novelist Olive Schreiner wrote in the demand that became the touchstone of radical feminist thought in the progressive years and split the women's movement in two in the 1920s over the issue of women's protective labor laws. Were women to be barred from unsafe work, or were they, taking it up, to make it safe for all workers? "Before women can improve on men's ways," Elsie Clews Parsons anticipated the answer of radical feminists in 1914, "those ways, one and all, must be open to women."[27]

In writers like Schreiner, moreover, the abstract fused with a sense of intense urgency. In a language quickly copied by

American writers, she insisted on the momentousness of the choice ahead: a race of "laboring and virile" women, equals of their ancient ancestors, or, more likely, a race of pure "sex parasites," their last shreds of work stripped away from them, useless except as "mere instrument[s] of sexual indulgence." After 1900, the rhetoric of protest and apocalypse—"woman" and "labor," "work" and "parasitism"—showed a tendency to swallow up all lesser distinctions.

Many of the women who read pieces of Schreiner's *Woman and Labor* in the women's magazines or who pushed it onto the best-seller list in 1911 found her language of "sex parasitism" absurd and deeply disturbing. One such woman angrily wrote the editors of *Harper's Bazar* that the trouble with women was that they were overburdened with work and had not learned how to be "parasitical enough."[28] Yet even conservatives on the woman question, women who insisted that a woman's place was at home and that the home was something more than an abandoned factory, found themselves drawn to define their case in the language of a paying job. The *Ladies' Home Journal*, uncomfortable "in these screeching days of sex-equality," ridiculed the idea of working wives; but in its place the *Journal* stories in the progressive years held up a model of the middle-class woman as a business partner in her husband's success, doing her share by maintaining an efficiently managed home. To oversee a well-run house, the magazine editorialized, was a "science," "a business as big as the affairs of men." Other writers broadcast the same theme. The housewife was engaged in the work of "household management"; she was supervisor of the "home department," director of a "social laboratory." Even marriage could be put into the language of work; it was a matter of persistence, industry, and patience—woman's "specific share of the world's work." Womanhood itself, Ida Tarbell wrote, was a "business."[29]

Not only did this vocabulary represent a remarkable infusion of business language into the sphere once held apart for love and sentiment; increasingly women's writers began to describe the shortcomings of the home in terms of its failure to imitate more fully the systematic methods of the factories. In the middle years of the nineteenth century, typical discussions of the "servant problem" made their appeal to the heart, urging that Christian forbearance, a place at the table, and patient training would cure the strains of domestic employment. By the 1890s, the more frequent advice was to make domestic service more like the industries with which it competed, with fixed hours, carefully stipulated duties, overtime pay, and, if possible, a total elimination of the custom of living under the employer's roof.[30] A generation later, moderate women's forums like the *Ladies' Home Journal* were willing to argue that wives, too, deserved regular, businesslike budgets if they were to fulfill their jobs as the home's purchasing agents.[31]

Nowhere was the message of housekeeping as a business enterprise advanced more strongly than in the home economics movement after the turn of the century. As they pushed their field toward the status of a full-fledged science, home economics instructors urged women to think of their work in terms of practical finance and sentiment-free engineering. Where late nineteenth-century housekeeping manuals interlarded instruction in manners and cooking with obligatory poetry, the housekeeping texts of the early twentieth century instructed women in the need for habits of budgeting and accurate record keeping, the merits of motion-elimination studies, the usefulness of careful schedules of the day's work, and the immense advantages of electricity. The vision of the gleaming, mechanized kitchen, so tantalizingly in the air in 1920, was a vision of the heart of the home made over into a woman's factory.[32]

This rhetorical convergence toward business phraseology did not eliminate the deep and emotionally charged cleavages between those who urged single women into temporary careers and those who demanded paying work for all women, those who argued that housekeeping was not real work and those who insisted it was woman's fundamental job. But even cautious writers on the woman question found themselves drawn to the sweep of the abstract and the morally charged language of work. "Woman" needed work, not make-work or simply duties of the heart, but a real and economically vital job.

Were women really underemployed in industrial America? Among restless, middle-class women there could be no doubt about the force of the conviction or its usefulness in summing up the welter of grievances that bore on them: the sense of powerlessness and entrapment, claustrophobia and lost purpose. But to move from the rhetoric of feminism to the sociology of women's work is to stumble over a new set of anomalies.

There was indeed a class of genuinely leisured women, conspicuous in their exemption from virtually all domestic and non-domestic toil and often mildly contemptuous of the moiling lot of their husbands. But the number of genuinely leisured women was far smaller than might have been surmised from the literature of feminism, where their frightening example loomed so large. All observers agreed that to gain partial exemption from domestic work was impossible without servants and that for genuine leisure a multiple-servant household (cook and "second girl" at the minimum) was indispensable. It is impossible to know exactly how many such households there were, but the *Outlook* writer who in 1910 voiced the opinion common in the middle-class press that the "majority of housewives" suffered under the difficulties of incompetent servants was manifestly wide of the mark.[33] If one simply divides the census count of all domestic servants by the nation's total households, the ratio stands at one servant to every eight households in 1870, drops to one per ten or eleven households between 1880 and 1900, and drops again sharply to one per eighteen households by 1920. Even these figures are inflated by the inclusion of servants working outside private homes in hotels, restaurants, and boarding houses, and they say nothing about multiple-servant households. But if a Massachusetts poll of 1898 was representative of the nation as a whole, fewer than 5 percent of all families in 1870 and fewer than 2 percent of all families in 1920 employed sufficient servants to harbor a thoroughly ornamental woman.[34] Childless women with a single, exceptionally competent servant and daughters of the moderately well-to-do added something to the total. But clearly it was not "woman" but a tiny sliver of womanhood, its work shifted upon the shoulders of other women, who suffered from thoroughgoing idleness.

Below the conspicuously idle was a second group, perhaps twice as large as the first, employing a single servant and partially relieved from household work to an extent dependent on the competence and permanency of their combined cook and house-maid. But the great majority of married women "did their own work" for their families and, in a large number of working-class households, for one or more paying boarders as well. And for most of them, even in 1920, the revolution in household conveniences had barely begun. When feminists wrote of the household as a "denuded workshop," they had in mind the disappearance of the spinning wheel and the soap vat and the drawing-off of domestic industries from baking to dressmaking into the mills and commercial shops. Some of the changes show up clearly in the studies of working-class family budgets made between the early 1890s and the end of the First World War. In 1890, most working-class women still did all the family baking at home and made most of the women's and children's clothing, to say nothing of washing, ironing, cooking, cleaning, stove-stoking, water-hauling, and children-minding. A decade and a half later, bakery bread had supplanted home baking in most New York City working-class households, ready-made clothing had significantly reduced the amount of home sewing, gas burners had replaced the sweltering coal stove for summer cooking, and family budgets showed a sprinkling of factory-prepared foods and a sparing use of commercial laundries. But in middle-sized cities like Syracuse and Fall River, home bread making and dressmaking were still the rule in working-class households; laundering for working-class women remained everywhere primarily a matter of hand tubs, washboards, and muscles; and even in 1918 in Philadelphia fresh vegetables still far overshadowed the consumption of canned goods.[35]

Laborsaving appliances were yet further from the reach of most families. As late as 1920, only a third of the nation's homes were wired for electricity, and fewer than a third of those possessed a washing machine or a vacuum cleaner. Electric irons no longer needing to be heated on top of the stove had entered the mail-order catalogs only eight years earlier; iceless, electric-powered refrigerators were virtually unknown.[36] For a normally skilled and normally thorough woman, the efficiency-minded home economist Christine Frederick claimed in 1920, housekeeping exclusive of child-rearing duties was at minimum a nine-hour-a-day job.[37] Domestic labor was indeed unspecialized, socially inefficient work, as Charlotte Perkins Gilman charged. But clearly most housekeeping women were scarcely pressed to invent tasks to keep themselves busy.

Finally there were those women whose work was part of the money economy. They were clustered, by and large, in as demanding and poorly paid trades as industrial America offered. In 1870, 90 percent of women wage earners worked in four occupations: as domestic servants, farm workers, factory hands, and seamstresses. The rapid opening of clerical work to women after the turn of the century shifted the balance toward white-collar trades; but even in 1920, 60 percent of all gainfully employed women still worked in manual occupations, the overwhelming number of them in the same trades that had loomed so large fifty years earlier. Wage earners were a distinct minority among women. The census counted 15 percent of all women over sixteen gainfully employed in 1870 and 24 percent in 1920, though both figures were undoubtedly underestimates, particularly of the most hard-pressed of women workers, married women forced to eke out the family income by work taken in at home. Experience with wage earning, however, was much more common in women's lives than such figures suggest. The great majority of gainfully employed women were single girls, working in the interval between coming of useful age and marriage, when social pressure sent them home once more. And such working daughters were by no means rare. In 1900, a third of all women beween the ages of sixteen and twenty were engaged in paid work; in 1920, almost half—42 percent—of all eighteen- and nineteen-year-old women were at work for pay.[38]

If work made character, if emancipation was a paying job, here was the advance guard of feminism. Certainly it was logical to expect that middle-class feminists who wrote of woman's need for work should have admired these working women, particularly those in the factory trades who had broken out of the constraints of domesticity into paying work as hard as any man's. Here and there one does find explicit romanticization of the working girl and more than a trace of envy. By doing "hard things, under trying conditions, and under the supervision of men upon whom the conventional tears, temper, and coquetry have no effect," working women had sloughed off the emotionalism that crippled their wealthier sisters and joined "a strong and selected class," Mary Roberts Coolidge wrote. Henrietta Rodman of the Feminist Alliance pushed the point still further: "Our sisters of the poorer class have the most fundamental right for which we are struggling—the right for economic independence, the right to continue their chosen work after marriage."[39]

But those middle-class career women who looked most closely at women industrial workers often came away from the encounter with a disturbed, half-betrayed sense of recoil. One of the rare accounts of the meeting of a middle-class woman and the factory girl was published anonymously in 1905 as *The Long Day: The Story of a New York Working Girl as Told by Herself.* It purported to be the autobiography of a schoolteacher, reared in a Presbyterian family in western Pennsylvania who had been forced, penniless and alone, to New York City to earn her living in its factories and sweatshops. Working her way out of abject poverty, she had risen through the secretarial ranks to an editorial position in a religious publishing house. The melo-dramatic tale did not ring exactly true, and there was much in the account that was deliberately obscure and a good deal that was manifestly improbable. But through some means, perhaps as an investigative sojourner, the author, Dorothy Richardson, had acquired a knowledge of women's trades that was graphic, detailed, and shot through with the pain of the raw worker.

It was her co-laborers, more than her work, that in the end preoccupied Richardson, and the picture she offered reflected the full shock of class encounter. She described her first factory as looking "for all the world like a gaunt, ugly, unkempt hag, frowning between bleared old eyes that seemed to coax—nay, rather to coerce me into entering her awful house. The instant impression was one of repulsion, and the impulse was to run away. But there was fascination, too, in the hag-like visage of those grim brick walls, checkered with innumerable dirty windows and trussed up, like a paralytic old crone, with rusty fire-escapes. It was the fascination of the mysterious and of the evil." Whatever her background, Richardson knew full well the art of a controlling metaphor. For she described her pilgrimage through the laundries, sweatshops, and factories of the city in the same terms, as that of a shocked innocent, moving wide-eyed through an underworld of vice and ignorance. The culture into which she had been thrown, she reported, was made up of frowzy and stained attempts at fashion, of minds crammed with cheap romantic literature and obscenity, of slacked work, quarrelsome tempers, and loose morals, of "fat, heavy, dough-colored," and "stupid" faces and the slouching gait of congenital degeneracy. Richardson did describe a brief, idyllic interlude in an artificial flower factory, where the work was skillfully done and the paper roses and the gentle manners of the Jewish working girls seemed matched in charm and dignity. But what she claimed to have found in the main was not the "proud, independent, self-reliant, efficient" working girl of the romanticizers, but women with neither interest nor skill in their work, victims of their jobs and of their poverty.[40]

Other wanderers across class lines into the world of women's labor brought back less strident reports but did not disguise the strain of the experience. Bessie Van Vorst was a "gentlewoman," novelist, and moderate progressive, who with her sister-in-law briefly joined the ranks of wage-earning women, toiled in factories in Pittsburgh, Chicago, and western New York, and described her experiences in *Everybody's Magazine* in 1902 and 1903. Among the very poor and among married wage earners Van Vorst felt a sorority built of hardship. But like Richardson, she was not prepared for the extravagances in dress and romantic imagination of the unmarried working girls. They seemed to her self-centered egoists, not antitypes but mirror images of their idle, pleasure-seeking sisters. Van Vorst did not despair of such girls, suggesting that their aesthetic instincts might be profitably directed into industrial artwork, but it had been an ambivalent meeting.[41]

Six years later *Everybody's Magazine* published a second series on women's work, the outgrowth of the factory experiences of a journalist, prominent feminist, and active advocate of women's work, Rheta Childe Dorr. Dorr, who had dismissed Van Vorst's articles as "valueless," emerged from her experience as an industrial wage earner too consumed with anger and sympathy to write the articles she had envisioned. *Everybody's* put her reports in the hands of William Hard who, over Dorr's strenuous objections, turned out a story of women's triumphant invasion of industry. Her own experiences had been not with the character-building worth of work, which Hard trumpeted, but with women's degradation; and as she admitted much later, she had been acutely disappointed in her expectations of the working girl. Like Van Vorst she experienced moments of intense feelings of comradeship. But in place of selfless stoicism she had been shocked by strikers' riots and scenes of hair-pulling. Instead of independence, she had found meek girls docilely handing over their wages to their fathers. Most disturbing of all, factory girls, with their romantic visions and their hearts set on marriage, seemed as anxious to get out of work as she herself, deserting a wealthy husband, had been desperate to get into it. It seemed to Dorr that she had found not heroism but "children to be led to freedom."[42]

Class bias—sometimes venomous, more often accountable to the myopia of narrowly constrained experience—pervaded middle-class culture, and it should come as no surprise that women were not exempt. As isolated as any members of Northern society, middle-class women were particularly unprepared for the encounter across the divide of class—for the contrast between their own conscientious work commitments and the resentments and indifference, the sometimes desperate strategies of escapism, by which working-class women tried to wall off self from job. By the same token, as inhabitants of a tightly self-contained social world, it was not surprising that middle-class feminists—educated, servant-employing women for the most part—should so readily confound the experiences of their class with those of "woman." Where even the cook in one's kitchen remained so clearly a stranger, it was all the easier to construe an oppressive sense of personal inutility as the parasitism of the sex. If the result was to urge work where toil was fully the norm, middle-class women were no more prone to confuse private experience and social fact than were their husbands, trumpeting the chances to rise to the top against an equal preponderance of evidence.

But perhaps, even as a counsel for themselves, work—pure and simple—was not exactly what those middle-class women who wrote of women's need for labor had in mind. Clearly the hunger ran deeply for something more demanding and useful than ornamental daughterhood, something far broader and less constrained than unmitigated tending of home and children, and something more independent than submissive wifehood. When they turned these discontents into concrete visions, most feminists imagined women emancipated from the home into the professions and white-collar occupations—what Gilman tended to call "human work" and Schreiner the "mental" employments. The period's scores of guides for career-seeking women were shot through with this assumption. But feminists often found it hard to resist celebrating the gross statistical rise in women's gainful employment as a clear-cut sign of progress or, like Schreiner, writing simply and sweepingly of "work."

In part the tactic was a reaction to decades of insistence that anything laborious was outside a gentlewoman's "sphere." "Women were not intended to work,—not because work is ignoble, but because it is as disastrous to the beauty of a woman as is friction to the bloom and softness of a flower," Harriet Beecher Stowe quoted a male editorialist in the 1860s. "She is to be kept from the workshop world, where innocence is snatched with rude hands, and softness is blistered into unsightliness." Two generations later a writer in the *Century* put the same case more poignantly. "Somewhere in the stress and strain of endeavor and advance there must be stopping-places where one may rest and dream a little," he pleaded; there must be "centers ... of some sort where one may momentarily drop out from the moving column, and, free of the noise and dust, feel one's soul."[43] It was woman's task to provide these touches of beauty and oases of calm for men harried by their work, ambitions, and insecurity. But for middle-class women who found their role as islands apart from the main channels of life stunting and acutely claustrophobic, it was natural to rise up against all the occupational taboos that so visibly hemmed in respectable womanhood.

In another part the tactic stemmed from the difficulty of finding words that adequately described the life that generated so many discontents. Certainly middle-class women faced a paradoxical set of expectations. They were to work but—like Katy Scudder reading calmly behind the lilacs—not seem to work. They were to do or oversee a tedium of details, but not let their thoughts slip away from the ideal things that were uniquely women's. They were to be close and careful budgeters with none of the materialism that afflicted males. They were to run a household, yet return themselves in the census as unemployed. Even women with servants, by most accounts, were far from economically useless. But engaged in labors without the status of work, they were the more tempted to call the whole idleness and demand a "real" job.

If contorted expectations and resentment played their parts, however, the most important factor in shaping feminist versions of the work ethic was simply the push and pressure of a work-tied

culture that still made labor (for men) a moral absolute. For
many daughters of the middle class, growing up within earshot of
the heroics of their brothers' libraries, absorbing from the new
women's colleges an intense sense of mission, the result was a
sense of loss and emptiness. "You see hard workingmen lifting
great burdens; you hear the driving and jostling of huge carts,"
Jane Addams wrote, "and your heart sinks with a sudden sense of
futility."[44] Not that driving carts was what Addams wanted to do
any more than the bread making she tried briefly under the force
of Tolstoy's example of self-sacrificing common labor, or any
more than that Stowe found personal dignity in housework. But
the work ethic left its impress of guilt, just as it left its impress on
feminist solutions. To turn women's restlessness into a demand
for work was to tap an immense reservoir of moral feeling,
perhaps the largest that lay open to nineteenth- and twentieth-
century feminists. Ultimately the argument turned even conservatives out of the language of sentiment and into the language
of jobs and labor. But the result was also to simplify the welter of
women's grievances and dilute the issues at stake—to help make
constriction synonymous with idleness, purpose with labor, freedom with the duties of a paying job. Though it was neither quite
true nor quite adequate, the story of woman, her spinning wheel
in splinters, sealed off from useful endeavors made a potent
moral tale. But it also suggests how readily the rhetoric of the
work ethic, muddying distinctions and obscuring meanings,
could become a tyrannizing commonplace.

The Political Uses of Work Rhetoric

This we commanded you, that if any would
not work, neither should he eat.

2 Thessalonians 3:10

Once upon a time, everyone worked and everyone was happy. Even shrewd Discount and clever Donothing labored with a will, exchanging what they made with their neighbors on a simple labor-for-labor measure. No land was richer or more contented. But then Discount put his mind to things and invented interest, mortgages, securities, and currency contraction and soon lived off the toil of the land as a banker. Donothing, in his turn, appointed himself tax collector and began to fatten idly on the tributes of officeholding. All the others worked twice as hard as before, but still they found themselves growing steadily poorer, the fruits of their labor drained away while Discount and Donothing rolled in unearned wealth. Finally Plowem, Makem, Reapem, and their neighbors discovered the roots of their plight, enacted the program of the National (Greenback-Labor) Party, and drove the idle drones from the hive. With the land blooming once more, Discount and Donothing turned back penitently to the honest occupation of farming and changed their names to Useful and Dosomething.

Such was the fable that Colonel S. F. Norton told in *Ten Men of Money Island*, an enormously popular contribution to the money and banking controversies of the 1880s and, if its publishers are to be believed, one of the forgotten bestsellers of the late nineteenth century.[1] Only the foolhardy would bracket Norton's tale of the rise of idleness with the classical elegies of man's fall into work from an innocent leisure. Yet if sheer repetition is one of the marks of successful mythmaking, the fable of the drones who slipped into the busy, contented hive and found a way to live off the fruits of someone else's labor deserves to rank as one of industrial America's most vital legends. In the world of politics, Norton's tale—with variations—possessed myriad uses.

The myth began with a sense of moral loss, passed down intact, despite the trumpetings of progress, from the earliest Puritan moralizers. From Thorstein Veblen's lament of the burial of the instinct of workmanship under layers of waste, pecuniary emulation, and contempt for labor, to Harriet Beecher Stowe's canonization of the departed race of women of "faculty," to Frederick W. Taylor's indictment of rampant industrial "soldiering," or the anxious editorial complaint of the rush from manual work into white-collar gentility, a sense of lost virtue was inextricably entangled with discussions of work. Somewhere in the past, perhaps only a generation or so removed, men and women had worked hard and without complaint, had reaped what they earned, and had been happy.

But for its cutting edge the myth demanded a villain. From beggar to millionaire, this figure was capable of a bewildering variety of outward guises; yet his essential characteristics were unmistakable. He was a mixture of indolence and shrewdness, sloth and ambition, too lazy to earn his living by his own toil yet ever eager for the chance to appropriate the labors of someone else. In the hive of industry he was corrupter, thief, and parasite—in short, the perfect drone. Who the idle parasites really were and where their unearned incomes came from were matters that divided Northerners into bitterly contending political camps. But on the question of treatment, no authority approached the force of Saint Paul. The Populist platform of 1892 reaffirmed his injunction, "if any will not work, neither shall he eat." So did the socialist John Spargo; so did the nation's foremost proponent of laissez-faire, William Graham Sumner. Nor was this union of opposites against the slothful at all unusual, for in its broad outlines Norton's fable carried an appeal that had little respect for conventional ideological barriers. Advocates of competitive capitalism and the socialist commonwealth, money cranks and genteel ladies bountiful joined in declaring their allegiance to a commonwealth of labor and raised their voices against the lazy and parasitic. Together they helped make idleness one of the most popular weapons in the arsenal of rhetorical invectives. More important, they helped to transform not only the overriding social question of the age—the coexistence of enormous wealth and abject poverty—but a host of lesser political issues as well into the morally charged language of work and idleness.

If this habit of thinking simplified most of what it touched, if its premises were vague enough to turn the rhetoric of radicalism and conservatism at times and in places into near mirror images of one another, it offered in return the sense of moral urgency and the drama of clear-cut choices that is the essential stuff of social movements. In a perplexed and often fearful nation, it offered a shortcut to thinking. Nowhere did the work ethic, ripped loose from context, find a more comfortable home than in the world of politics.

One of the examples of the interfusion of political ideology and the rhetoric of work was to be found among the North's political radicals. They seem at first glance a splintered lot, moving serially across the political stage: greenbackers and antibank men preoccupied with questions of money and interest; converts of Henry George's *Progress and Poverty*, ready to drive all landlords out of business with a single confiscatory tax on rents; Populists; and Marxian socialists. The deep tactical and ideological differences between them often gave the left the appearance of a sectarian battlefield. But the long history of mutual recrimination obscures the extent to which the third-party radical movements on the left were joined in assumptions and personnel.

The continuity is clearest in the case of those radicals for whom money questions loomed the largest. Veteran antibank and anti-interest campaigners such as Norton or the Populist presidential candidate James B. Weaver moved easily from the greenback parties of the 1870s and 1880s into the Populist campaigns of the 1890s, carrying principles and platforms with them.[2] Socialists and single taxers, adhering to more elaborate systems of belief and, in the Marxist case, to a thicket of unfamiliar terminology, were considerably less flexible. The Socialist Labor Party denounced both Populism and the single tax movement as refuges for economic ignoramuses and stalking-horses for bour-

[margin handwritten note: Radical continuity]

geois opportunists; Henry George, in return, threw the socialists out of his United Labor Party and dismissed Marx as "the prince of muddleheads."[3] Feuding of this sort, nonetheless, did not prevent frequent interchange of men and doctrines. The guiding spirit of the Socialist Labor Party, Daniel De Leon, served his apprenticeship in the single tax movement, while the Socialist Party not only took an ex-Populist, Debs, as its perennial standard-bearer but absorbed a heavy influx of rank-and-file Populists, particularly in the Middle West and Southwest.

What essentially made such exchanges possible was a vivid sense of exploitation. That was the touchstone of all the movements on the left. What made a man a radical was the sense of living in a society pushed to "the verge of moral, political, and material ruin," as the Populists put it in 1892—the sense of inhabiting a nightmarish world where the rich grew ever richer by riding on the backs of the middling and the poor. In comparison with this, work values had a distinctly secondary place. And yet without the legacies of the work ethic the radical style would not have been the same. Issues of work and idleness did not make the American radical movement, but they infused, energized, and, in the end, left their distinctive stamp on virtually all the cries of economic protest to be heard in industrializing America.

One of the most obvious signs was the potency of the phrase "labor creates all wealth." As a slogan it cut across sectarian lines on the left, gave radicals of all stripes a common ground, and covered over fundamental differences of economic analysis. Except in the hands of the more theoretically inclined Marxian socialists, the phrase did not stand for a labor theory of value, as is often assumed. Radicals of all sorts confused the issue by citing Ricardo and Adam Smith when it suited their purposes. But most were essentially indifferent to the classical economists' concern with the source of prices, and many of those who did address the issue, including Henry George and the leading greenback prophets, Edward Kellogg and Alexander Campbell, flatly rejected the labor theory of value as economists understand the term— that is, the belief that prices are essentially set by labor costs.[4] For most radical spokesmen the central issue was not the source of prices but the source of wealth, and the force of the slogan derived far less from economics than from its stubborn moral affirmation of the indispensability of those who toiled and

produced. Labor was the bedrock of society, the original source
of all things useful. "Is not labor the producer of all wealth?"
Henry George asked; "is it not labor that feeds all, clothes all,
shelters all, and pays for all?" Greenbacker Edward Kellogg
developed the theme more expansively: "Labor has effected every
improvement in our country; it has built our cities; cleared,
fenced, and improved our farms; constructed our ships, railroads, and canals. . . . Let men neither sow nor reap, let manufacturing cease, commerce be suspended, and what would be the
condition of our country?" Eugene Debs, who asked the same
question, a repeated theme of radical oratory, gave the answer:
"The warehouses would stand empty, factories would be silent,
ships and docks would rot, cities would tumble down, and
universal ruin would prevail." If oratory of this sort left the
definition of labor vague and disconcertingly expansive, if it
disguised more economic issues than it revealed, its strength lay
in its enlistment in the radical cause of that commonplace of
nineteenth-century morality—that only workers counted.[5]

The impress of the work ethic was equally visible in the
demand that almost invariably followed—that those who worked
had a right to the full fruits of their labors. The contention
possessed the tremendous force of simple logic for most of those
on the left. Only when set against William Morris's leisure-filled
fantasy of freely given goods did the American radicals' concern
with the mechanisms of calculation—their schemes of labor-time
payments and labor-for-labor exchanges (the roots of which
Marx once credited to Benjamin Franklin)—reveal its peculiarly individualistic cast. Nonetheless, communistic ideas of
economic justice made far less headway in America than those
that promised to link a man's reward directly with his work. "We
want a system in which the worker shall get what he produces and
the capitalist shall produce what he gets," Eugene Debs put the
well-worn demand, as familiar to Georgites and Populists as to
socialists.[6] Between the several competing phrases—the "full
fruits" of a man's labor, its "whole product," or its "full social
value"—lay as many theoretical quarrels as were papered over by
the term "labor." But it was part of what bound the disparate
radical movements together that the first approximation of all of
them was that a man's rewards ought to match the labor he
expended.

It is the way of protest movements to take a society's professed values and push them to the limits where commonplaces turn suddenly subversive. Yet invectives, too, have their uses and their subtle contagions. If one of the consequences of immersion in a society conspicuously dedicated to the value of work was to heighten the force of the term "labor" and of work-tied ideas of justice, another was to interfuse themes of exploitation and idleness. "Who's born for sloth?" labor leader and greenback convert William Sylvis asked. "I answer, the capitalist—the idle, luxurious, extortionate capitalist."[7] The idleness charge was gratuitous and, in a land where even extortionate capitalists seem to have worked peculiarly hard at their callings, it was perhaps altogether wrong. But from Sylvis through Norton's knavish do-nothings and long beyond, the compound themes echoed through radical rhetoric.

The linkage was particularly close in the case of Henry George. His *Progress and Poverty*, which quickly became nineteenth-century American radicalism's single most potent gatherer of converts, was forged out of a number of factors: the land disputes that agitated George's California in the 1860s and 1870s; George's own occasionally desperate financial struggles as a restless, underemployed printer; and the autodidact's confidence with which he took on the classical economists from Adam Smith to Mill and reduced them all, as it seemed, to logical tatters. But intertwined with these was a preoccupation with time and idleness. At the depths of his worst string of ill fortune in the mid-1860s George had launched a diary—an experiment, he wrote, "to aid me in acquiring habits of regularity, punctuality and purpose." In it he had bitterly confessed his laziness, his waste of time, his failure to seize his opportunities, and his feeble self-control. The diary entries disappeared as George's fortunes improved, but the preoccupation with idleness remained, and the moral energies he had once turned inward to the idle self found a new target in the empty, unproductive lands engrossed all through the heart of California by railroad corporations and land speculators. *Progress and Poverty*, which he completed in 1879, amounted to an elaborate attempt to put the full burden of modern poverty upon such landowners by showing that in the economic nature of things they inevitably seized the lion's share of the wealth that manufacturers, merchants, and workers jointly

toiled to make. But for George, as for many of his firmest
converts, that economic demonstration was impossible to disen-
tangle from a simpler, morally charged recoil at the vacant lots and
land tracts that stood out so insolently in every bustling city,
accumulating value without social return. Rent was at once the
extortionate and the idle factor in George's arguments, producing nothing, doing nothing. The landlord was "absolutely useless," a "mere appropriator." "This, and this alone, I contend
for," he could ultimately reduce his case to its simplest moral
core: "that he who makes should have; that he who saves should
enjoy."[8]

Something of the same process of thought undoubtedly occurred among many of those hard-pressed, overextended farmers
and businessmen who forged the old animosity toward bankers
and moneylenders into a similarly encompassing economic indictment shortly after the Civil War. "Money creates no wealth,"
Alexander Campbell, one of the prominent early figures in the
greenback movement, put the rationale of money radicalism most
succinctly; "it only gathers up and appropriates to its owner
things already produced." The full weight of economic blame
that George had laid upon rent, greenbackers and many Populists turned upon interest. In their minds it was fully as idle and still
more grasping. Without a source of doctrine comparable to
Progress and Poverty, the anti-interest forces repeatedly split over
competing remedies. Yet however much their measures might
differ—some championing cheap government-issued loans,
others the abolition of government bonds, the repeal of debt
collection laws, the unlimited coinage of silver, or paper currency
inflation—all of them were shaped to the figure of the bloated
moneylender turning mere paper into an unearned fortune—
avoiding "the universal doom of work" (as Populist Ignatius
Donnelly protested) "by living on the crystallized and compounded labors of others."[9]

But it was in the rhetoric of persuasion that the themes of
exploitation and idleness slid together most easily. In much of
radical propaganda they were virtually interchangeable. Producers and nonproducers, the robbers and the robbed, shirkers and
workers, the idle, parasitic rich and the laboring poor—in the
dualistic divisions that split the radical universe, the charges were
almost invariably on the same side. "The garments of the 'lilies'
of the land, 'who toil not, neither do they spin,' are died [sic] in the

innocent blood of labor," one greenback writer maintained in a more than usually desperate search for the just metaphor. The omnipresent radical cartoon image put the indictment more simply and more powerfully in the figure of the richly clad banker, landlord, or capitalist, a diamond stickpin shining gaudily on his breast and almost always obese. "He consumes, you produce," Debs once explained the capitalist's paunch. "That is why he runs largely to stomach and you to hands." If the bloated belly of the cartoon villain stood for gorged wealth, it was also the clear mark of a man who did no work.[10]

It was not merely the force of convention that compelled radical publicists repeatedly back to the idleness charge. Unlike the depredations of simple highwaymen, the exploitation of the rich was hidden under layers of economic complexity. The genius of a George, an Edward Kellogg, or a Marx was to penetrate that arcane world and discover at last the mechanism of expropriation. But the very ingenuity required to solve the economic riddle made their achievement all the harder to compress into the vocabulary of stump oratory. What was most obvious about the very rich were their delicate hands, their yachts and horses, and their ample, brocaded bellies. It was their idleness, in the end, that made their acts of robbery certain.

Not all radicals felt comfortable amid this pervasive, simplified moralism. Socialists, in particular, often felt the strain acutely. Socialism in America was no exception to the fusion of economic and moralistic preoccupations so central to nineteenth- and early twentieth-century radicalism. This was clearest in what might be called "vernacular" socialism, which filtered Marx through the older, morally immediate categories of robbery and laziness. The tradition began at the outset with Laurence Gronlund's *The Cooperative Commonwealth* of 1884, the first popular exposition of Marxian thought in America. Offering German socialism "digested" by an "Anglo-Saxon mind," Gronlund defined surplus value as the "fleecings" of labor, capital as "*accumulated fleecings*," and the capitalist as a man with an income gained "*without any work* on his part." If this was not Marx, it was an immensely potent socialism nonetheless—probably by sheer numbers of converts the dominant socialism in early twentieth-century America. Its distinguishing mark was an ethical simplicity that set it off clearly from purer socialist wranglings. The Socialist Labor Party's Daniel De Leon, master of both Marxian dogmatics and the vernacular style, gave a brilliant illustration of the latter in his widely circulated "What Means This Strike?" Speaking to striking textile workers at New Bedford in 1898, De Leon assumed the role of a stock investor, skipping down to Florida, cooling off in the Adirondacks, running the gauntlet of gambling dens and lazing in fashionable European resorts, doing nothing useful and all the while collecting his inexorably mounting dividends. If workingmen made up their minds to keep all they produced, De Leon told the cheering crowd, "THE CAPITAL-IST WILL HAVE TO GO TO WORK."[11]

To socialists other than Gronlund and De Leon, however, the vernacular style was often a distinct embarrassment. The deepest resistance came from those intent on preserving the scientific standing of the movement. With a vivid Marxian distrust of "utopianism," they resisted any moralistic innovations on the socialist vocabulary. The result was that while De Leon's Socialist Labor Party platform indicted the system under which "labor is robbed of the wealth it alone produces," leaders of the Socialist Party of the early twentieth century effectively excluded from their platforms the bald statement that labor creates all wealth or more than a hint of the manner in which wealth would be distributed in the coming socialist commonwealth. John Spargo, one of the party's leading theoreticians, insisted that the slogan "all wealth is produced by labor and, therefore, ought to belong to the laborers" was a simplistic distortion of Marxian economics that contained the seeds of a "demagogic" glorification of manual labor. Spargo likewise objected that the demand, "to each the full value of the product of his toil," was no less unscientific and reactionary. It belonged to the past when a single man had made a product from beginning to end, he argued, not to industrial economies where each man's labor merged indistinguishably from others' "in the stream of collective effort." Spargo's contentions were to a great degree shared by Morris Hillquit, the dominant figure in the party's large Eastern wing. Modern socialists, he wrote in 1909, had given up the idea, which had fascinated earlier socialist generations, of labor certificates or labor-time checks that would credit each worker with his precise contribution of toil; they were beginning to recognize that the idea of to each according to his labor was no longer sound socialist doctrine. In a socialist commonwealth that took care of its weak and its infirm, Hillquit maintained, need should rule, not labor.[12]

Yet while reservations such as Hillquit's and Spargo's helped shape the party platforms, they did little to stifle the tradition of vernacular socialism among the rank and file. Debs, never comfortable with Marxian abstractions, always preferred ethical specifics. "You don't need the capitalist," he told enthusiastic audiences. "He does nothing and gets everything, and you do everything and get nothing." The capitalists "fleece and pluck; you furnish the wool and the feathers." The *Appeal to Reason* offered much the same fare to its army of a half million readers. The essential idea of surplus value was that "all profit is robbery." Dividends were "the modern name for loot," capital was "the canned muscles of other men."[13] In the same way, the idea of labor-time checks survived despite the criticism of more scientific socialists. Advocates of the idea acknowledged the computational difficulties involved in labor-for-labor payments and offered a variety of schemes to adjust differences in individual skill and disagreeability of tasks, some of them, particularly De Leon's suggestion that jobs be graded according to the rate of induced tissue decay, oddly reminiscent of Taylorism.[14] But the difficulties, formidable as they were, were more than recompensed by the inevitable corollary of the labor-check scheme, that those who did not labor at all would be prevented from living at the expense of the rest. "The idler under Socialism will starve if he does no work," millionaire socialist Gaylord Wilshire asserted confidently. Another socialist writer put the matter still more simply: "No product, no income."[15]

Norton's fable had said as much with equal intensity. Landlord, banker, tax collector, capitalist—they were all idle. Simplifying, turning the stubborn issue of wealth and poverty into the more dramatic stuff of workers and idle parasites, harnessing the moral energies of the work ethic to the cause of radical change, Norton's categories were not easily resisted.

"Curiously enough," John Spargo wrote in totting up his objections to the phrase "to each according to his toil," "the principle of remuneration which is most commonly set forth in the popular propaganda literature of Socialism is . . . that of pure Individualism."[16] There was a good deal of truth in Spargo's suggestion. To move from the literature of radicalism to the writings of its opponents is a kind of looking-glass experience in which the familiar symbols reappear, now turned to different ends. The drones are excoriated and the workers praised, the clever guises of idleness relentlessly exposed, and hope held out for the day in which all will work and the do-nothings will be driven from the land.

One particularly conspicuous example of the way these categories could serve equally well as a conservative creed was E. L. Godkin's *Nation*. Joseph Pulitzer, asked why he did not follow Godkin's journalistic example, was said to have replied that he wanted the ear of the nation, not that of a select committee. Godkin was content with the select committee, a modestly sized audience of well-educated, well-placed Northern readers. He offered them laissez-faire economics, a ready wit and a penchant for irony, and a running, urgently serious attack on all the radicalisms of the day: currency inflation, paper money, free silver, Georgism, Populism, and socialism. There was no justice in any of them, Godkin warned, only a clever scheme "for getting hold of other people's money without working for it."[17]

As Godkin described it, laziness, in fact, was the wellspring of radicalism. Beginning in visions of something for nothing, the inevitable upshot of every radical cause was some device that would enable the idle and incompetent to live at the expense of the frugal and the industrious. At bottom they were all "communistic"—all plans to allow the nation's drones and deadbeats to escape the consequences of their laziness. For a moment in the 1870s, Godkin wondered if the factory were not responsible for the communistic contagion. Unlike agriculture or outdoor manual labor, which "keeps down mental activity and strengthens the love of routine," he wrote, "working under cover, at trades that call for dexterity rather than strength, seems to give the brain a morbid energy which finds relief in imaginary rearrangements of society."[18] But the mania was clearly too widely diffused to make this more than a passing explanation. The *Nation* crusaded against state regulation of railroad rates on the grounds that the idea was "rank communism" and flagrant "spoliation"; it assailed Senator Henry W. Blair's proposals for a federally financed campaign to eradicate illiteracy as giving the South school funds it was too shiftless to raise for itself; it opposed the income tax as an assault on savings and industry.

Mother of all delusions was the protective tariff; like the rest, it was a "socialistic" contrivance that enabled a few to get rich without working. "If we threw our argument into the [Henry George] form," Godkin wrote in 1887, "we should say that God meant human society to be organized always, and on the whole, in the interest of the industrious, prudent, self-denying, ingenious, shrewd and honest people; and will on no account permit it to be controlled by the lazy, stupid, and shiftless." It was not a parody but a replication of George's creed, only that the villains and the sufferers had been silently interchanged.[19]

Except for the brilliance of Godkin's style, there was nothing unique in his enlistment of the work ethic in conservative causes. The mode of argument particularly appealed to those inclined toward laissez-faire and the ideology of free trade, but to indict social discontent as a mark of shiftlessness and radicalism in particular as inspired by dreams of simple expropriation were copybook maxims among a wide spectrum of politically orthodox Northerners. Kansas journalist William A. White, for example, lampooned Populism as a plan to "put the lazy, greasy fizzle who can't pay his debts on the altar, and bow down and worship him." Railroad president George F. Baer charged that "in nine cases out of ten it is the lazy, mischievous, and vain who eternally rant about an equality which should make the industrious support the idle, the honest divide with the dishonest, the upright and pure-minded associate with the base, vile, and obscene." Theodore Roosevelt, in what was probably the most widely read indictment of socialism of his day, claimed that socialism was "merely another way of saying that the thriftless and the vicious ... should be entitled to take out the earnings of the intelligent, the fore-sighted, and the industrious." From shiftlessness flowed indifference to property rights, after which the string of conservative shibboleths followed one by one: socialism would confiscate wives and property alike, dissolve families, and eliminate ambition, until civilization finally sank into a torpid, deadening uniformity.[20]

The same charges were readily extended to other groups and other causes. Nativists denounced the immigrant as Europe's tired, stolidly ambitionless failure who had no place in busy America. Opponents of labor unions castigated strikes as "organized idleness," instigated by "vampires that live and fatten on ... honest labor." Even more sober discussions of the labor question were dominated by the figure of the "walking delegate," the trade union organizer who, it was charged, insisted that the lazy and the industrious be paid alike, held down output, and, when feeling surly, threw his cowering workmen off the job without himself soiling his hands at honest toil.[21] Thomas Nast, fertile inventor of symbols, filled the pages of *Harper's Weekly* with the figure of a low-browed, dissolute, ne'er-do-well Irishman abetted in his follies by a black-garbed skeleton decked out with a union delegate's sash labeled "Communist." They were "bummers" and "dead heads" who preyed on honest toilers, the drones of the looking-glass world of conservatism.[22]

At times the convergence of radical and conservative rhetoric went still further. The favorite radical slogan, to each according to his contribution, was equally a conventional part of the conservative's moral arsenal. Lincoln's statements were the most famous in this vein, and his claim that government should work "to secure to each laborer the whole product of his labor" echoed for generations through the radical press. Lyman Abbott of the *Outlook*, Henry Ward Beecher's heir and later Theodore Roosevelt's staunch supporter, took as his own the still more forthright motto: "To each worker his produce, his entire produce, nothing but his produce."[23] Men like Abbott approached the slogan "labor creates all wealth" more gingerly. Many politically orthodox Northerners followed Francis A. Walker or W. H. Mallock in celebrating entrepreneurial ability, not labor, as the essential mainspring of progress. Yet American Telephone and Telegraph president Theodore N. Vail had no objections to the phrase "all wealth is created by constructive and productive work" or to the idea that "labor should manage industry and get all the profits," as long as the terms were understood to include all labor, not merely manual labor. Josephine Shaw Lowell, aristocrat and charity worker, wrote still more confidently that the labor theory of wealth was "simply a truism." "The few people that don't belong to the laboring classes don't amount to anything."[24]

Despite such convergences, the rhetoric of conservatism was not simply radical moralism stood, as it were, on its head. The fundamental difference was the conservative's insistence on an identity between labor and property. None of the radical camps unequivocally threw all men of property out of the ranks of labor, and land and money radicals frequently extended the status of workingman to the "active" capitalist or entrepreneur in order to single out more clearly the idle landlord or money-changer. In the radical universe, however, more than usual wealth was normally a sign of ingenious robbery. But the labor theory of wealth held other possible conclusions, ratified by as unimpeachable an authority as John Locke. Since only work made wealth, then to the conservative mind property was simply prima facie evidence of a man who labored. The old argument was not simply a means of allowing the man of wealth to share in the moral sanctity of labor without undergoing a potentially embarrassing inspection of his habits, though it did conveniently serve that purpose. It was as important that the formula effectively dismissed all inherent conflicts between economic classes. As in Thomas Nast's famous drawing, laborer and capitalist were joined as Siamese twins. They belonged alike to the genus *industriens*—the one representing present toil, the other "stored" or "condensed" labor.[25]

But if property presupposed industriousness, the corollary followed almost unavoidably that poverty was proof of idle viciousness. Throughout the industrial years, spokesmen for orthodox morality tirelessly reiterated the presumptive connection between economic and moral failure. Henry Ward Beecher ranked poverty not among the misfortunes but among the sins, with a faith in individual effort that kept discussions of immiserization revolving long afterward around the cardinal points of drink and laziness. In the most notorious statement of them all, Yale's William Graham Sumner claimed that "a drunkard in the gutter is just where he ought to be. Nature is working away at him to get him out of the way, just as she sets up her processes of dissolution to remove whatever is a failure in its line."[26] Yet many conservatives who readily made the connection between poverty and moral bankruptcy were unwilling to follow Sumner to his laissez-faire conclusion. In their eyes, immiserization was a pressing matter for public attention, not because they thought poverty was rooted in social conditions but because it seemed to have urgent social consequences. For as most conservative moralists saw them, the poor were not merely sufferers from their own incapacities. In their idleness, they were at once a moral contagion and a severe economic burden. Wheedling, begging, consuming far more than they produced and living conscienceless on the toil of others, they seemed to many middle-class Northerners simple parasites of the economic underworld. In the logic that made failure, idleness, and beggary akin, it could hardly be otherwise.

Such attitudes did not wholly dominate the orthodox view of the poor. If those who attended most closely to the problems of late nineteenth-century poverty were deeply impressed with the immorality of idleness, they were also heirs to the traditional, gentler lessons of Christian charity, and their attempts to reconcile the two moral strains involved no little intellectual struggle. One example, particularly revealing in the simplicity with which it posed the issue, was a didactic novel published in 1877 by J. G. Holland, editor of *Scribner's Monthly* and one of the nation's most prominent secular moralists. Holland's story, *Nicholas Minturn*, revolves around an idle young man of wealth who improbably decides to dedicate himself to the upraising of the poor. His more worldly-wise friends counsel that the most urgent need of the poor, if not the whipping post, is sufficient hunger or pain to set them to work. Nicholas rejects their callous advice and takes up his task only to fall prey to a trio of beggars who skillfully manipulate his naive generosity. Outraged and sobered, Nicholas sets the police on the impostors and, reinforced by the arm of the law, dragoons them into employment and sobriety. The beggars in gratitude take up public preaching of the gospel of work, and when Nicholas's romantic desires reach their inexorable fulfillment the poor of New York hire a boat to serenade the wedding.[27]

Such a novel was clearly an exercise in somewhat desperate and thereby all the more revealing fantasy. Holland prefaced his tale with a text from Carlyle: "He that will not work according to his faculty, let him perish according to his necessity; there is no law juster than that." But Holland's fantasies of social harmony went well beyond the needs of justice. The gist of his message was the righteous anger of love, and the burden he placed upon those who would take up charitable work was, somehow, to keep that antithesis in balance.

Holland's interest in the poor seems not to have persisted much beyond *Nicholas Minturn*. But he wrote with an editor's knowledge of the debates of the day; and, if he transmuted ideas into the all too simplistic symbols of a mediocre novelist, he had absorbed many of the influences that dominated social work for the next generation. The vehicles for what was called the "new charity" were the charity organization societies, established in most Northern cities soon after 1877 in reaction to the haphazard relief practices of that depression decade.[28] Their hallmark was an attitude toward poverty not unlike Holland's: a divided, complex, and, at its core, radically ambivalent mixture of sentimentalism and callousness. The sympathetic side of the charity organization societies was institutionalized in a corps of "friendly visitors," largely recruited from the ranks of well-to-do women. The societies' expectations of a visitor were boundless enough to have frustrated even the most hardy or talented volunteer. She was to personalize charity, thereby discouraging the assumption that poor relief was a right owed the needy by the state. She was to break down the barriers of social class and open the poor to the influences of purity and refinement. But, above all, she was to be a friend, offering "the touch of soul to soul, the flow of hope to the heart exhausted of hope, of courage to the heart depleted of courage." She was to supply that thing most needed, the New York Charity Organization Society instructed its visitors: "sympathy, encouragement, and hopefulness."[29]

Yet true friendship should do nothing to injure the character of the befriended; and it was in enforcing this maxim that the harsher side of the divided mind of the new charity took priority. Identifying character with willingness to work, and more than half convinced that the cause of poverty lay in the fault of the impoverished, charity organization societies struggled desperately to avoid measures that might permanently cripple the desire to labor. Visitors were advised to try to find or, if necessary, make work for the poor and to raise their wants and ambitions until the pinch of dissatisfaction became acute enough to goad them into labor. But the particular fear of the new charity was the "pauperization" of the poor—the utter destruction of the will to work by misguided, dependence-ingraining assistance. Poverty, then as now, is a matter of money, but "pauperization" concerned character, and it was by far the deeper fear of the charity-organization workers. Soup lines, general relief, a thoughtless nickel passed into a beggar's pocket—the traditional responses to poverty were all worse than useless, for the surest consequence of each was to sap the desire to labor and thereby perpetuate the root cause of impoverishment. "We are still dominated by this shadow of the past," Helen Campbell argued in the 1880s, "and call it charity to give a man food which he has not earned, thus destroying his moral sense if he is good, and precipitating him still farther on a downward course, if he is bad."[30]

Here, in short, was the work ethic turned into a horror of chronic dependency. Faced with ne'er-do-wells and drunkards, charity-organization leaders advised against hindering the punishments attached by God to willful idleness; faced with the wives and families of such men, they cautioned that the only permanent remedy was to refuse all help until the husband reformed or the wife rose up and banished him. "Anything," Josephine Shaw Lowell wrote, was better than "teaching the dreadful lesson that it is easy to get a day's living without working for it."[31]

Soon after the turn of the century, professional social work passed into the hands of a younger, significantly less moralistic generation. They were somewhat embarrassed by the word "charity," which they allowed to lapse from use, and they were far more impressed than the charity workers of the 1880s and 1890s by environmental forces. By 1909, Edward Devine, Mrs. Lowell's successor at the New York Charity Organization Society, could announce that "personal depravity is as foreign to any theory of the hardships of our modern poor as witchcraft or demoniacal possession.... These hardships are economic, social, transitional, measurable, manageable."[32]

But outside the professional welfare agencies, the moralistic view of poverty remained, most clearly in discussions of the two most visible species of the poor: the beggar and the tramp. Neither was without his admirers. The mendicant *lazzaroni*, particularly when encountered abroad, often seemed picturesque figures, and there were many who, like William Dean Howells, were troubled but cheerful givers. "Tramping" remained a respectable term for a country hike well into the 1880s, and the outdoor propensities of the tramp allowed him to share in some of the better connotations of his title. But the appearance of large numbers of vagrants in the depression of the 1870s brought a vigorous assertion of harsher viewpoints, together with a rash of severe antivagrancy laws. The dean of the Yale Law School told a national gathering of charity workers in 1877 that the tramp was a "lazy, shiftless, sauntering or swaggering, ill-conditioned, irreclaimable, incorrigible, cowardly, utterly depraved savage." J. G.

Holland, his *Nicholas Minturn* only recently completed, charged that by refusing to work the tramp had forfeited all rights and was "no more to be consulted, in his wishes or his will, in the settlement of the question as to what was to be done with him than if he were a bullock in a corral." Even after the conditions that drove the urban poor into mendicancy had been widely advertised and after firsthand explorations had taught tramp observers to recognize the casual laborer—the hobo—within the ranks of trampdom, the moralistic response predominated.[33]

In some part the public fascination with the beggar and the tramp stemmed from the fact that there was a good deal of visible mendicancy in turn-of-the-century America, easily enough to be alarming. No one made a reliable count of street corner beggars, though their presence intrudes itself repeatedly into urban-set fiction as an inescapable part of city life. As for tramps, estimates extrapolated from police records and railroad accident rates varied from 46,000 in 1893 to half a million in 1908, or somewhere between one and six out of every thousand Americans.[34] And yet the attention given, particularly in the case of the tramp, clearly exceeded any reasonable estimate of his numbers. Editors not only readily published scores of remedies for the tramp menace, but eagerly sought out firsthand reports of life in the tramp underworld. Josiah Flynt Willard, himself afflicted with wanderlust and engaged in a losing battle with drink, was the most famous of those who spread out for middle-class readers the secrets of a "blowed-in-the-glass-stiff." In his wake came others, who ventured into the hobo "jungles" by the railroad tracks, struck up a correspondence with an exceptionally literate vagrant, sought him out in jails and lodging houses, or spent their own sojourn in "beggardom" and told of what they had seen.[35]

Like Flynt, virtually all of them passed quickly over the casual laborers, though their statistics clearly showed that such men dominated the tramp population. What captured their attention was the idea of a fraternity of men flagrantly and thoroughly idle. It was this shameless rebellion against all work that fascinated as well as alarmed turn-of-the-century moralists, and in the end it made the tramp the conservative's closest counterpart to the radical's bloated millionaires. Both were figures cut out of the pasteboard but compelling stuff of melodrama. They were the clear-cut villains on a stage of toilers and savers, focal points for furtive envy and moral outrage. But both inventions were as useful in other ways. Just as the millionaire simplified economics, so the tramp cut through the tangled issue of poverty to its moral heart. He was the quintessence of economic failure, a man who hated work—a product not of social forces (save misguided generosity) but of compulsive laziness.

Yet however much the tramp might fascinate, there were few suggestions that he be left in peace. By the turn of the century there was a common, if not always heeded, body of rules for dealing with the mendicant: suppression of handouts, sweeping arrests of all vagrants and beggars, and work tests to single out the genuine shirker from the simply unemployed. Beyond these measures, many social workers, inspired by European examples, began to dream of colonies for the willful poor, where their idleness could be contained and the painful lessons of labor learned. The idea took specific form in a widely circulated and detailed farm colony proposal written by Edmond Kelly in 1908. Kelly had joined the Socialist Party the year before, but his plan was introduced into the New York legislature in 1909 with the endorsement of prominent conservatives and most of the state's organized social workers. Kelly went to great pains to insist that the idlers be treated with some respect, minimizing the institutional aspects of the farm through unobtrusive supervision and dignified uniforms. But laziness was not consistent with rights save the right to labor. Through a complicated scheme of indeterminate sentences, Kelly proposed that none of the colonists be allowed to leave until he had proved himself capable of self-support.[36]

Kelly's tramp colony, although approved in modified form by the legislature, was never constructed. But the widely recurrent idea held a significance even in its practical failure. Like the socialists' unrealized labor-time checks, it summed up a vision of a Pauline utopia, where none would be burdened with the support of idleness because none would be allowed to be idle.

The most effective fables take care not to sketch their characters in too great detail lest their idiosyncrasies overshadow the moral. Surely one of the central reasons for the persistence of the myth of the drones who lived off the toilers, for its ability to cross between political camps and its enduring rhetorical effectiveness, was the vagueness and almost indefinite expandability of its categories. As to what defined a worker there were many competing answers. A few writers, inspired by the example of Tolstoy's shoemaking labors, drew the line at those engaged in the work of their hands. Mainstream socialists, on the other hand, expanded the definition of the working class to include intellectuals, reversed the long-standing radical prejudice against lawyers, and went so far as to divide bitterly over the status and political potential of labor-employing farmers and small businessmen. Farmers, in their turn, had no doubts about their claims as workers and frequently assumed the term "producer" as exclusively their own; but both debtors, who were said to make industry flourish by linking personal skill to borrowed capital, and manufacturers also laid claim to the status of "producers." Still other writers, embracing commercial as well as manufacturing interests, drew the line between work and idleness as that between "active" businessmen and mere investors and silent partners.

In this expansion of categories, the right of the businessman to a place in the ranks of the working classes was so frequently claimed that it was not surprising that some writers, like Alexander Campbell or William Jennings Bryan, would complete the symmetry and claim that the "real capitalists" and businessmen of the nation were its workingmen.[37] But the example was not frequently imitated, less because the idea seemed preposterous than because few Northerners of any status were willing to relinquish their claims as workers. Businessmen like Henry Lee Higginson wrote of "toiling terribly" at their labors. "Brain workers" defended themselves as engaged in tasks far more laborious than any pick-and-shovel labor. Speculator-turned-muckraker Thomas W. Lawson divided the factors of production into "body labor," "mind labor," "machinery labor," and "capital labor," and while the terminology was clearly eccentric, it suggested something of the magnetic force of the term "labor."[38]

Manual laborers occasionally protested against this style of assertion. Type founder Edward King told a congressional committee in 1883 that many of those who claimed to be workingmen were so only in a "Pickwickian" sense of the term. But when the workers were enumerated, even radical spokesmen so begged essential questions as to allow grounds for all, or nearly all, the Pickwickian claimants. In Alexander Campbell's definition "all who, by the labor of the head or hand, restore to society an equivalent for what they receive from it" were workers. Eugene Debs, equally sweepingly, defined the working class as comprising all those who "increase the knowledge and add to the wealth of society." J. P. Morgan, instructing the Commission on Industrial Relations on terminology in 1915, put the matter most simply: "the most of us work in this country."[39]

The term idler was equally indistinct, equally inflatable, and politically still more potent. The most common targets were at the extremes—the tramp and the millionaire—but the potential recipients of the charge of laziness were virtually limitless. During World War I selective service officials, in an official declaration of sorts, wrote off gamblers, race track habitués, and clairvoyants as idlers, and dismissed waiters, domestic servants, ushers, passenger-elevator operators, and baseball players as persons engaged in "non-useful" occupations.[40] But the list could be easily expanded. Not only radicals and paupers, immigrants and union organizers, bankers and bondholders, but college students, middlemen, ward politicians, dandies, war pensioners, and society women all drew the ire of the defenders of industriousness.

At times the charge of idleness was put to the service of private, occasionally eccentric campaigns. On the eve of the American entry into the war, a small group of efficiency engineers, disciples of Frederick W. Taylor, wrote President Wilson to suggest their willingness to take "the control of the huge and delicate apparatus of industry out of the hands of idlers and wastrels"—by which they meant businessmen—"and deliver it over to those who understand its operations."[41] But the rhetoric of work and idleness, service and simple parasitism, had far broader political uses as well. From Grover Cleveland through Woodrow Wilson, Democratic politicians consistently denounced Republican high tariff policies as destructive to self-reliance by coddling the protected manufacturers. In the 1890s, farm representatives mounted a concerted effort to eliminate short sales in agricultural products under the slogan of driving the "gamblers" out of the commodities market; critics of stock market abuses insisted that Wall Street was the greatest "gambling hell" of all. The unsuccessful efforts to introduce social insurance on European models during the progressive years stumbled on a number of objections, but not the least was the fear that industry and frugality would be crippled by the proposals.[42]

The work ethic was by no means the only moral force loose in the world of politics. Its limits were clearest in the tariff debates, where the Democratic protests against unearned special favors ran up against the Republican argument that, in the cutthroat world market, the tariff was the cornerstone of everyone's prosperity. But often partisans of both sides of a political debate found it expedient to denounce the other side in the elastic terms of work and laziness. The monetary controversies of the post-Civil War years were a particularly striking example, as defenders of the gold standard and paper money advocates inveighed against each other for scheming to get something for nothing and opening the door wide to gamblers and speculators. Later, in the bitter debates over graduated income and inheritance taxes, opponents criticized the measures as simple "war" upon industry and frugal living, while advocates argued that no man legitimately earned the income of a millionaire and that if the government did not intervene his heirs would at best become idle wastrels.[43] Infinitely flexible, work rhetoric sometimes threatened to turn politics into a hall of mirrors.

And yet there was nothing puzzling about the device itself. Where work had served so long as a moral imperative, it is not surprising that the charge of laziness should have touched so vital a nerve. It offered an invitingly broad and tempting bridge between the moral energies of a democratic society and the abstruse realms of law and economics. It pervaded politics not only because it simplified but because it turned questions of policy into the more vital language of myth and moral drama. Perhaps it is fair to say that, though it was by no means new, it was the distinctive propaganda of industrial America. But like most propaganda it was more than a glittering cover to the causes it adorned. Nothing more clearly helped those Americans who lived through the wrenching unfamiliarities of industrialization preserve their ties to the work faith of an earlier age than this constant, public warning against the wiles of idleness. The habit served as a sheet anchor for a society in which work and work ideas were both in the midst of dramatic transformation.

But in its focus not on work but on laziness, the practice also allowed its users to evade the most unsettling issues afoot. It offered a way of thinking about work at once intense and vague about what working was or what it should be. To turn work rhetoric in the negative was to blunt the nagging issues of independence, creativity, and necessity that the older phrases raised so insistently and inconveniently. It was to reshape the rhetoric of work into both a handier and a safer weapon, all the more suited to men troubled about labor. In the end, no other legacy of the work ethic survived as well as the outcry against idleness or outlasted the custom of calling someone else a do-nothing.

Epilogue: Charles W.
Eliot and the Quest
for Joyful Labor

There can be no public happiness without . . .
satisfaction from the daily work of the masses
of mankind.

> Charles W. Eliot,
> "Content in Work" (1904)

By the second decade of the twentieth century, another fable
haunted the minds of a number of Americans. As they watched
the relentless advance of factories and automatic machinery
sweep away so much of the familiar and alter the social landscape in unexpected and disturbing ways, the story they turned to
was that of Frankenstein and his rebellious creation. Where most
of man's tools had remained inert in his hands, machinery
seemed somehow to have slipped from control. In making work
easier, mechanization had made work far less easy to endure; in
becoming man's indispensable servant, the machine had become
a capricious master. "Machinery is aggressive," Emerson had
written long before. "All tools are in one sense edge-tools, and
dangerous."[1]

And yet to tell the tale in that way is to breathe a life and an
autonomy into steam and steel which they never possessed.
Industrialization is essentially a story of values, not inventions.
And if it is an ironic tale, it is not because the mechanical
servants ran amok but because in it one can watch an ethos
consume itself. Certainly in that sense there were ironies aplenty.
The result of an extraordinary and extraordinarily democratic
flowering of invention, reaching down to the workbenches of
innumerable ordinary mechanics, was, in the end, to excise
creativity from much of common work. The achievement of two
generations of boundlessly individualistic and ambitious entrepreneurs was to eclipse the old, individualistic workshop economy

with a new, faceless world of system, large-scale enterprise, and intricate bureaucracies. The upshot of the ascetic energies poured so earnestly into the factories to wall off the discipline of work from the haphazardness of life was ultimately to turn the essential allegiance of most Americans away from their jobs and into the more satisfying, work-free business of leisure. In the service of the work ethic, in short, Northerners built a world in which its values were no longer at home.

We are accustomed to think of such reflections as a recent discovery. We offer them as perspicacious; we condemn them as sign of a contemporary loss of nerve. But the furor over work is old; the issues that at times are still able to badger the modern conscience were raised long ago. Nor was it solely the nation's iconoclasts and rebels—its Thoreaus, its Randolph Bournes, or its Bill Haywoods—who forced the debate. The industrial transformation of work pressed inescapably on virtually every moralist. If during the years in which the modern American economy took shape, most of them could not resist praising what had been accomplished—if most of them readily saw the hand of God and Progress in the nation's extraordinary catapult into the status of the world's preeminent workshop—few of the keepers of the nation's moral conscience could successfully down all their doubts about the world they and their countrymen were so busy making. Such doubts were readily deflected to easier targets. Immigrants and anarchists, slaveholders and plutocrats absorbed a good many of the nervous tics spawned by an industrializing society. But they did not absorb all the North's moral energies, as the long and earnest hunt for industrial remedies attests. As economic life shifted, many of those who held most dearly to the old work codes had worried directly about the fate of their values in the new and strange world of factories and factorylike labor.

Of these, few worried as long, as hard, or as revealingly as Charles William Eliot. Eliot was a member of well-to-do Boston society by birth, a chemist by training, and a part of Harvard both by occupation and by family inheritance. At the age of thirty-one, temporarily adrift from teaching, he had been offered the superintendency of the Merrimack Mills in Lowell. He turned the position down for a professorship, however, and four years later assumed the presidency of Harvard, where he proceeded to transform the school into one of the first of the modern American universities. By the turn of the century, Eliot had emerged not only as the nation's most widely known college president but as something of a national oracle on educational and moral matters, his opinions—on religion, on government, on literature, and on family life—eagerly reprinted in the magazines of the middle class. In a nation of moralists, Eliot belonged to a handful of the most prominent.[2]

Eliot stumbled on the labor issue, however, almost wholly by chance. As an ardent libertarian, whose primary curricular reform had been to replace the old compulsory course of college study by a system of electives, Eliot had never been comfortable with the labor union ethos of collective solidarity. In 1896, he had described the "scab" laborer, brave enough to go his own way, as a "creditable type of nineteenth century hero." The remark passed off virtually unnoticed. But when Eliot repeated the idea in some impromptu remarks in 1902 in the midst of an aggressive employers' antiunion drive, Boston's workingmen responded with a barrage of angry criticism. For a student of labor relations, it was an unpropitious beginning. But in the aftermath Eliot set out to study the causes of labor discontent in earnest, corresponding widely with industrial managers, accumulating boxes full of pamphlets and clippings, and writing, in all, some forty lectures and articles on the labor question before his death in 1926.[3]

Antiunionism remained a prominent part of Eliot's message. He willingly lent his name to the open-shop drive of manufacturers' organizations and stubbornly repeated his objections to the boycott and union label, the uniform wage, the exclusion of nonunion workers from employment, and, above all, workers' agreements to limit the pace of their labor. All such practices seemed to Eliot to fly in the face of duty and liberty alike, and he brought the argument not only to businessmen's forums but, on one widely publicized occasion, before an audience of workingmen who heard him out in resolute silence.

But Eliot's primary concern was not with labor unionism but with work and with the conditions both of mind and circumstance that made work a rewarding, energizing, "joyful" activity. As quick as he was to condemn labor union practices, Eliot was equally ready to blame employers for the fact that so much of modern labor fell below that standard and that so many laborers, accordingly, looked on work simply "as something to be avoided to the utmost." He did not think the problem of contented work an intractable one. Throughout the business and professional occupations, Eliot argued, one could find eager and willing workers, employed under conditions that allowed them to reap a profound satisfaction from their jobs. His own career confirmed the point, but such careers were all too rare. The pressing task was to make those same conditions of employment democratic, to extend them beyond a fortunate elite into the work of the nation's great mass of ordinary workers. No other industrial issue was as pressing as this, Eliot insisted, and none more vital to the public welfare. For the alternative—for the nation to decide to seek its happiness not in its work but in its pleasures alone—was to give up all chance for happiness whatsoever. "Joy in work," he pleaded, "should be the all-pervading subject of industrial discussion." In Eliot's hands, as in those of so many of his predecessors, the work ethic, colliding with the factories, turned into a case for industrial reform.[4]

Eliot's search for means to inject the rewards of work he knew from experience into the heart of industrial labor surely proved a far longer journey than he had anticipated. For two decades he turned the subject over again and again. Work that was worthy of the name, he argued, should provide possibilities for advancement, incentives for pride and ambition, and an element of risk and danger. It should involve variety and freedom, "the free play of the powers of observing, thinking, and judging during labor, . . . and the artistic motive and method." It should have room for cooperation and grounds for loyalty. In trying to reduce these principles to specifics, Eliot gathered up one by one virtually all the ideas then in the air for the reformation of industrial work. Beginning with a plea for steady employment and job security, Eliot added pensions for disabilities and old age, arbitration of industrial disputes, factory betterment efforts, industrial education, an employee voice in shop discipline and the settlement of grievances, some form of incentives "beyond wages," whether in the form of piecework, Taylor's premium system or profit sharing, rotation of employees between the most monotonous jobs, and mechanization of those that remained intractably dull. For a moment he endorsed the breakup of the large-scale factory altogether into smaller, electrically powered, rural plants. None of these alone seemed adequate for the scope of the problem. Even taken all together, Eliot's ever-longer lists of recommendations reflected an unsatisfied sense of urgency. He was certain only that "on the right solution of this problem depends the whole future of the industrial democracy."[5]

Finally, in 1913 Eliot found a more lasting answer in profit sharing. A visit to a small Massachusetts profit-sharing firm generated a voluminous correspondence and an unhesitant endorsement of the idea. Two years later, inspired by the worker-management councils of the Philadelphia Rapid Transit Company, one of the early experiments in "industrial democracy," Eliot joined his call for profit sharing with an endorsement of "cooperative management." The combination, Eliot argued, "goes to the root" of the industrial issue. It presented the workingman with "exactly the same motive for strenuous, zealous, loyal labor, day in and day out . . . that the owner or the manager feels." It touched "the fundamental thing, . . . the state of mind, the spirit and temper, in which laborers do their daily work." Through the rise and fall of the subsequent industrial democracy crusade, Eliot held tenaciously to that faith, pouring the convictions of the work ethic and the immense moral confidence of his time and class into the cause of industrial reform.[6]

But if Eliot was a particularly striking example of the way the debate over the industrial transformation of work wrenched open even the cloisters of Cambridge and of the critical energies that debate could enlist as men like Eliot tried to preserve what they most valued of the old in the face of the new, his example showed something of the distinctive limits of that debate as well. There were, for example, points on which Eliot found it very difficult to make up his mind. Industrial monotony was one of these. Eliot alternately condemned the "incessant, monotonous repetition" of factory labor and insisted that the issue had been exaggerated by professional labor agitators. "Nothing can be more discouraging to an intelligent or ambitious workman than to be kept day after day and year after year doing in an automatic way the same piece of work," he maintained; and yet he found it hard to imagine any job that would not be interesting to a dedicated and imaginative worker.[7] Eliot wavered in much the same way on the question of factory discipline, on the one hand urging industrial managers to devise methods of supervision tight enough to search out every tendency toward "shiftless, sluggish, uninterested" labor, as a duty not only to their stockholders but to their employees as well, and on the other hand criticizing scientific management as incompatible with liberty.[8]

In the end, both questions came back to Eliot's larger indecision over the essential source of discontented labor. Even as he urged reform on industrial managers, Eliot refused to discard the conviction that the key to happiness in work lay less in the job than in the state of mind of the worker. It was his refusal to resolve that question that gave all of Eliot's labor writings the form of a twofold list of obligations. If management's duty was to correct the conditions of employment, labor's was to recognize that only unstinted, loyal work made a sure foundation for joy and happiness, to reject "absolutely" the idea "that leisure rather than steady work should be the main object of life."[9] In short, Eliot would not cut apart his double message that though industrial work cried out to be made worthy of the energies of men, the mass of men had never learned to be worthy of their work. But it was certainly a more dichotomous formula than Eliot knew, half of it—the painstakingly developed half—couched in the language of moral and industrial specifics, the other in the simpler, more voluble language of moralistic abstractions.

Eliot's ideas on leisure reflected something of the same tension between fact and convention. Although on occasion he suggested that the best to be done with the dullest of industrial society's jobs was to reduce the hours of employment, Eliot was for the most part profoundly unsympathetic to the shorter-hours drive that agitated the industrial plants of his day. "The notion that if one could only cut down or stop work one would be happy, is fit only for a lazy savage," he insisted. What made a people civilized was their capacity for hard, steady work, "day after day, and year after year." He preached the same message as readily to his faculty as to workingmen, reminding them that "the common amusements of society have no charm for scholars" and that an evening at the theater was simply wasted. In his own person Eliot exemplified the tremendous energies middle-class Americans could still invest in their vocations, regularly working twelve-hour days during the school term. And yet somehow he saw no contradiction between this stress on tirelessly steady work and his regular summer vacations at Mt. Desert Island, without which, he once acknowledged, he would "hardly have more time for reflection and real living than an operative in a cotton-mill."[10] Clearly, ideas of work and leisure swirled no less uneasily in Eliot than in most of the moralists of his day. In defense of Eliot's consistency, scudding before the Maine winds in the intimate grasp of nature was for him undoubtedly a patently different sort of pleasure than an evening of artificial theatricals, and as a worker in ideas perhaps many of them came to him there. But the story suggests again the pull of moral abstractions even in the face of fact and habit.

The tension rested in the fact that for Eliot work values served not one function but three. At bottom they formed a personal code, a fraction of whose product lies stuffed in some four hundred boxes in his university's archives, inert but impressive evidence of the energies the work ethic impelled. Second, they formed the cutting edge of a long and earnest quarrel with the industrial transformation of work. But if the work ethic propelled men like Eliot into the center of the factory controversy, it likewise formed a refuge, a set of moral certainties to fall back on and repeat the more strongly because, in the end, so much about them was so uncertain. As his experiment with a useful life which was not all work went unacknowledged, as his lists of industrial specifics jostled with simpler moralistic exhortations, Eliot showed the temptations of the reassurative uses of work ideals. For all his driving energies and his reformer's zeal, it was there that Eliot felt most at home.

To Samuel Gompers, Eliot lived in a world he did not in the least understand. It was the angry charge of an aggrieved man, and it was not on the whole true, or at least not any more true of Eliot than of most of his countrymen, groping their way through the unfamiliar. But there was a stubborn old-fashionedness about Eliot by the turn of the century. He was an individualist at a time when the currents of social thought were turning to collective ideas of social welfare. On the woman question, Eliot was an unreconstructed conservative, insisting to the end *contra* the economic feminists that the focus of a woman's life and education should be motherhood. Even in his own university, Eliot was something of a stranger. His study recommendations of ten hours of daily work, one hour of social duties, and the

keeping of the weekly Sabbath were as manifestly out of touch
with the student mores of his day as his campaign against the
collegiate frenzy for football. Two weeks after Boston labor
unionists had sat quietly through Eliot's address on the labor
issue, another speaker mentioned Eliot's "doctrine of joy in
labor" and drew forth a long chorus of derisive laughter. Even his
immense popularity as a moralist stemmed in large part from the
reassurance of hearing once more the lessons of an all but
departed age.

But Eliot's search for measures of industrial reform had led
him into the thick of contemporary debate. And both that debate
and the energies that Eliot at seventy threw into it are reminders of
how rapidly, how thoroughly, and how unnervingly men had
transformed the nature of work. Harnessing their faith in
constant, useful doing to the engine of profit and the new possibilities of invention, they had built an awesome industrial
workshop. But in the process they had produced a kind of work
that even for the most ascetically tempered Northerners butted up
against deeply planted values and stubborn prejudices. The result
was a series of anxious efforts to haul work and values back into
accord. From the cooperators' attack on hireling wage labor, to
the progressive moralists' campaign against factory monotony, to
the restless discontent of industrial workers, Northerners had
tilted against the industrial regime, where time and discipline
were screwed to an unfamiliar pitch, skills split, and autonomy
undermined. In powerlessness and timidity most of the reform
efforts failed, and with this failure much of the presumptive tie
between common work and morality came apart. By 1917, amid
the mounting doubts and questionings, it proved for many
moralists a distinct relief to go to war and let patriotism, for a
spell, answer the vexed problem of what it was that made most
men's labor anything more than an inescapable burden. But as
work and work ideals were wrenched apart, the old presumption
of the essential value of work endured. In Eliot's lay sermons, in
the tagged-on morals of countless boys' tales, or in the symbols of
the political cartoonist, the familiar equation remained.

"There are many ways to accommodate change," John William
Ward has written. "A favorite one is man's happy ability to keep
talking one way while acting another."[11] It is an unimpeachable
historical observation and more than a reflection on human

foolishness. The grooves of thought and language are deep ones, particularly at the level of morals, and even in the midst of change conscious values are not easily wrenched from the familiar ruts. Work and idleness, ethical poles apart, with leisure occupying a gray and aristocratically tainted position somewhere in between—even now the essential linguistic structure for thinking out loud about work shows little sign of the storm and stress of the attitudinal changes that have roiled beneath it. But it is also true that change intensifies fixities as men struggle to reaffirm the threatened. Not only inertia is at work in such instances, but the mutation of doubt into conventions of faith— the more versatile, the more reassuring, and in some ways the more potent in their ideal remove from the confusions of everyday life. American history has had its ample share of examples. From the rhetoric of republican simplicity and frugality by which the Jacksonians salved their practical experiment in restless speculation, to the doctrineless religious revival of the faith-shaken Eisenhower years, to the hollow versatility of the term "peace" in a war-torn nation, stress has repeatedly hardened anxiety into ideals, generated words to cling to even as one strode off into the forbidden and the unknown.

Work was no exception. As its economic underpinnings shifted and raised the ideals at stake, one of the results was to imbue the terms work and laziness with an immense, nervous power. The rhetoric of the work ethic saturated politics, spilled over into feminism, and set an enduring labor union style. It lent its moral authority to a host of causes, not the least of which was industrialization itself. But the other side of the phenomenon was the tendency of even the most careful discussions of work, as in Eliot's case, to veer off into the abstract. What was it that made work the aim of life? As industrialization gutted the old answers, leaving only the rationale of discipline, and in its ever greater flow of consumer goods undermining even that, it became increasingly harder to say. Even to define work itself was no longer an easy matter. U.S. Steel's chairman Elbert H. Gary wrestled inconclusively with the point in 1918: "It is hard work to work hard whatever one does, and to the extent that one does work hard he, of course, is doing hard work. That is perfectly evident."[12] But the circumlocutions suggest that it was scarcely as evident, even to Gary, as he would have liked. Gary's belabored pronouncement was only one of many hints that the rhetorical shell of the work ethic disguised an increasingly tenuous substance. As the old work ideals were wrenched from context, morals slid with increasing ease into the reassuring language of moralism.

What, indeed, was work? In the mid-1870s, casting about for a cartoon device to represent the honest workingman, Thomas Nast seized upon the figure of a square-jawed, paper-capped blacksmith. He marched through the pages of *Harper's Weekly* and, in imitation, through dozens of other news sheets as well, beset by death-wielding "communists" and bloated profiteers, as a symbol of what made work for Nast's readers so potent a value. His firmly set jaw revealed the character-building discipline of work, the muscles of his bare arm its usefulness, the tools he held in his hand its skill, and his blacksmith's apron—in a device that went back to Longfellow—its sturdy independence. Nast's figure brought together the best that nineteenth- and early twentieth-century Northerners had hoped of work. He was a figure untouched by the industrial invasion, and in the 1870s he held an element both of longing and of credibility. But a half-century later the paper-capped blacksmith, still a stock symbol of the editorial cartoonist, was simply an unexamined anachronism.

The fate of the work ethic itself was neither quite as neat nor quite as poignant as the tale of Nast's blacksmith. Work ideals would still move men long after that paper-hatted symbol finally disappeared, and a piece of those ideals, reified in factorylike jobs throughout the economy, would order still more of them about. But it would be hard to say that most of modern work matched the moral hopes, rooted in an earlier day, that were still unexaminedly expected of it. Horace Traubel's charge—and Eliot's—to question economic life "to the wall" until all work is "the sort of work some man may love" still dogs the present as an unanswered challenge.

Notes

Introduction

1. Thomas Carlyle, *Past and Present* (1843; New York: Charles Scribner's Sons, 1918), p. 183; Walter Houghton, *The Victorian Frame of Mind, 1830-1870* (New Haven: Yale University Press, 1957), pp. 253, 254; Ednah D. Cheney, ed., *Louisa May Alcott: Her Life, Letters, and Journals* (Boston: Roberts Brothers, 1889), p. 128.

2. William R. Stewart, *The Philanthropic Work of Josephine Shaw Lowell* (New York: Macmillan, 1911), p. 156.

Chapter One

1. Henry D. Thoreau, *Reform Papers*, ed. Wendell Glick (Princeton: Princeton University Press, 1973), p. 156.

2. Sebastian de Grazia, *Of Time Work, and Leisure* (New York: Twentieth Century Fund, 1962), chap. 1; Clinio L. Duetti, "Work Noble and Ignoble: An Introduction to the History of the Modern Idea of Work" (Ph.D. diss., University of Wisconsin, 1954), pp. 22-24. Cf. Hannah Arendt, *The Human Condition* (Chicago: University of Chicago Press, 1958), p. 80.

3. Hesiod, *Works and Days*, trans. Richmond A. Lattimore (Ann Arbor: University of Michigan Press, 1959), p. 32; Vergil, *Georgics*, quoted in Daniel Bell, "Work and Its Discontents: The Cult of Efficiency in America," in his *The End of Ideology* (Glencoe, Ill.: Free Press, 1960), p. 227.

4. David B. Quinn, ed., *The Roanoke Voyages, 1584-1590*, 2 vols. (London: Hakluyt Society, 1955), 1:108; *Travels and Works of Captain John Smith*, ed. Edward Arber, new ed., 2 vols. (Edinburgh: John Grant, 1910), 1:727.

5. *The Complete Essays of Montaigne*, trans. Donald M. Frame (Stanford: Stanford University Press, 1958), pp. 153-54; Leo Marx, *The Machine in the Garden: Technology and the Pastoral Ideal in America* (New York: Oxford University Press, 1964), p. 49; Charles L. Sanford, *The Quest for Paradise: Europe and the American Moral Imagination* (Urbana: University of Illinois Press, 1961), pp. 83-84. See also Howard M. Jones, *O Strange New World. American Culture: The Formative Years* (New York: Viking Press, 1964), chaps. 1-2; Loren

Baritz, "The Idea of the West," *American Historical Review* 66 (1961): 618–40; Louis B. Wright, *The Colonial Search for a Southern Eden* (University: University of Alabama Press, 1953); Hugh Honour, *The New Golden Land: European Images of America from the Discoveries to the Present Time* (New York: Pantheon, 1975), chap. 1.

6. Peter N. Carroll, *Puritanism and the Wilderness: The Intellectual Significance of the New England Frontier, 1629–1700* (New York: Columbia University Press, 1969), p. 68; David Bertelson, *The Lazy South* (New York: Oxford University Press, 1967), pp. 39, 45. The theme is extended in Marx, *Machine in the Garden*, chap. 2, and in George H. Williams, *Wilderness and Paradise in Christian Thought* (New York: Harper and Brothers, 1962), chaps. 3–4.

7. Alexis de Tocqueville, *Democracy in America*, ed. Phillips Bradley, 2 vols. (New York: Alfred A. Knopf, 1945), 2:152; Francis J. Grund, *The Americans in Their Moral, Social, and Political Relations*, 2 vols. (London: Longman, Rees, Orme, Brown, Green and Longman, 1837), 2:1–2, 5. See also Marvin Fisher, *Workshops in the Wilderness: The European Response to American Industrialization, 1830–1860* (New York: Oxford University Press, 1967), pp. 64–75; Marvin Meyers, *The Jacksonian Persuasion* (Stanford: Stanford University Press, 1957), chap. 6.

8. Basil Hall, *Travels in North America* (1829), quoted in Edward Pessen, *Jacksonian America: Society, Personality, and Politics* (Homewood, Ill.: Dorsey Press, 1969), p. 13; Eric Foner, *Free Soil, Free Labor, Free Men: The Ideology of the Republican Party before the Civil War* (New York: Oxford University Press, 1970), p. 12.

9. "Industrialism," *Independent* 60 (1906): 528.

10. Edward Everett, *Orations and Speeches on Various Occasions*, 4 vols. (Boston: Little, Brown, 1850–68), 1:283, 285; Henry Ward Beecher, "Laboring Together with God," *Christian Union* 12 (1875): 388.

11. Elizabeth Stuart Phelps, *The Gates Ajar* (1868; reprint ed., Cambridge: Harvard University Press, 1964), pp. 107, 109; *The Poetical Works of Lucy Larcom* (Boston: Houghton Mifflin, n.d.), p. 313; T. DeWitt Talmage, *Trumpet-Blasts; or, Mountain-Top Views of Life* (Chicago: North American Publishing Co., 1892), p. 500.

12. Perry Miller, *The New England Mind: The Seventeenth Century* (Cambridge: Harvard University Press, 1954), p. 44.

13. Albert B. Hart and Herbert R. Ferleger, eds., *Theodore Roosevelt Cyclopedia* (New York: Roosevelt Memorial Association, 1941), p. 587.

14. William Penn, *No Cross No Crown* (1669), quoted in Frederick B. Tolles, *Meeting House and Counting House: The Quaker Merchants of Colonial Philadelphia, 1682–1783* (Chapel Hill: University of North Carolina Press, 1948), p. 53; R. H. Tawney, *Religion and the Rise of Capitalism* (New York: Harcourt, Brace and World, 1926), p. 115.

15. Max Weber, *The Protestant Ethic and the Spirit of Capitalism*, trans. Talcott Parsons (New York: Charles Scribner's Sons, 1958), p. 154. In the long and tangled debate over the Weber thesis, Weber's emphasis on the causal force of religion is repeatedly the nub of the issue. Christopher Hill, Charles H. George, and others have long contended that the stress upon work and diligence so evident in seventeenth-century Puritan circles was not essentially a product of Puritan theology but was grafted later onto the reformed doctrines by the "industrious sort of people" whom the preachers attracted. Clearly interest and theology built upon each other in the making of the Protestant ethic. But it was the religious sanction that turned systematic industry into a moral imperative, gave it a transcendent framework, and made it so easily portable to America. On the force of the idea itself, see Christopher Hill, *Society and Puritanism in Pre-Revolutionary England* (London: Secker and Warburg, 1964), chaps. 4-5; Michael Walzer, *The Revolution of the Saints: A Study in the Origins of Radical Politics* (Cambridge: Harvard University Press, 1965), chap. 6.

16. Louis B. Wright, *The Cultural Life of the American Colonies, 1607-1763* (New York: Harper and Brothers, 1957), p. 25; Cotton Mather, *A Christian at His Calling* (1701), quoted in Marie L. Ahearn, "The Rhetoric of Work and Vocation in Some Popular Northern Writings before 1860" (Ph.D. diss., Brown University, 1965), pp. 22-23. See also Tolles, *Meeting House and Counting House*, chap. 3; Stephen Foster, *Their Solitary Way: The Puritan Social Ethic in the First Century of Settlement in New England* (New Haven: Yale University Press, 1971), chaps. 4-5.

17. Sarah Hale, *Sketches of American Character* (1838), quoted in William R. Taylor, *Cavalier and Yankee: The Old South and American National Character* (New York: George Braziller, 1961), p. 136. On work rhetoric in the Revolutionary era, see Edmund S. Morgan, "The Puritan Ethic and the American Revolution," *William and Mary Quarterly*, 3d ser., 24 (1967): 3-43; J. E. Crowley, *This Sheba, Self: The Conceptualization of Economic Life in Eighteenth-Century America* (Baltimore: Johns Hopkins University Press, 1974).

18. *The Works of William E. Channing, D. D.*, 12th complete ed., 6 vols. (Boston: Crosby, Nichols, 1853), 5:158; Jonathan B. Harrison, *Certain Dangerous Tendencies in American Life* (Boston: Houghton, Osgood, 1880), pp. 253, 82. Harrison's essays were first published in the *Atlantic Monthly*, 1878-79. See also Timothy S. Arthur, "Retiring from Business," in his *Making a Sensation, and Other Tales* (Philadelphia: Godey and McMichael, 1843); Samuel T. Spear, "Retired Gentlemen," *Independent* 20 (30 April 1868): 1.

19. Lucy Larcom, "Among Lowell Mill-Girls: A Reminiscence," *Atlantic Monthly* 48 (1881): 596.

20. Henry Ward Beecher, *Seven Lectures to Young Men* (Indianapolis:

Thomas B. Cutler, 1844), pp. 20–21; William Ferrero, "Work and Morality," *Forum* 22 (1896): 363; Henry C. Potter, *Sermons of the City* (New York: E. P. Dutton, 1881), p. 275. Cf. Walter E. Houghton, *The Victorian Frame of Mind, 1830–1870* (New Haven: Yale University Press, 1957), pp. 242–62.

21. Calvin Colton, "Labor and Capital," in *The Junius Tracts, No. 7: Labor and Capital* (New York: Greeley and McElrath, 1844), p. 15.

22. Matthew H. Smith, *Bulls and Bears of New York* (1873; reprint ed., Freeport, N.Y.: Books for Libraries Press, 1972), p. 541; Beecher, *Seven Lectures*, p. 12.

23. Thomas Carlyle, *Past and Present* (1843; New York: Charles Scribner's Sons, 1918), p. 236; *The Complete Works of Ralph Waldo Emerson*, centenary ed., 12 vols. (Boston: Houghton Mifflin, n.d.), 11:297; *The Poetical Works of Augustine Duganne* (Philadelphia: Parry and McMillan, 1855), pp. 111–12. On the background of the poem, see Ahearn, "Rhetoric of Work and Vocation," chap. 3.

24. Hamilton W. Mabie, *Essays on Work and Culture* (New York: Dodd, Mead, 1901), pp. 116, 22. See also Edward E. Hale, *How They Lived in Hampton: A Study of Practical Christianity Applied in the Manufacture of Woollens* (Boston: J. Stillman Smith, 1888), pp. 232–49.

25. William C. Gannett, "Blessed Be Drudgery," in *The Faith That Makes Faithful*, ed. W. C. Gannett and Jenkin L. Jones (1887; new ed., Boston: Stratford, 1918).

26. William D. Howells, *The Minister's Charge; or, The Apprenticeship of Lemuel Barker* (Boston: Ticknor, 1887); and idem, *A Traveler from Altruria* (New York: Harper and Brothers, 1894), p. 50.

27. D. C. Coleman, "Labour in the English Economy of the Seventeenth Century," *Economic History Review*, 2d ser., 8 (1956): 280 n.

28. Bruce Laurie, " 'Nothing on Compulsion': Life Styles of Philadelphia Artisans, 1820–1850," *Labor History* 15 (1974): 337–66; Paul Faler, "Cultural Aspects of the Industrial Revolution: Lynn, Massachusetts, Shoemakers and Industrial Morality, 1826–1860," *Labor History* 15 (1974): 367–94; Herbert G. Gutman, *Work, Culture, and Society in Industrializing America: Essays in American Working-Class and Social History* (New York: Alfred A. Knopf, 1976), chap. 1; E. P. Thompson, "Time, Work-Discipline, and Industrial Capitalism," *Past and Present*, no. 38 (1967), pp. 56–97.

29. *The Diary of Philip Hone, 1828–1851*, ed. Allan Nevins, new and enlarged ed. (New York: Dodd, Mead, 1936); Douglas T. Miller, *Jacksonian Aristocracy: Class and Democracy in New York, 1830–1860* (New York: Oxford University Press, 1967), chap. 7.

30. Cf. Henry F. May, *The End of American Innocence: A Study of the First Years of Our Own Time, 1912–1917* (New York: Alfred A. Knopf, 1959), chaps. 4–6; Daniel W. Howe, "American Victorianism as a Culture," *American Quarterly* 27 (1975): 507–32.

31. Wilbur Tillett, "The White Man of the New South," *Century* 33 (1887): 769; Peter Guilday, ed., *The National Pastorals of the American Hierarchy (1792-1919)* (Westminster, Md.: Newman Press, 1954), pp. 253-56, 262; James Cardinal Gibbons, "Some Defects in Our Political and Social Institutions," *North American Review* 145 (1887): 345-54.

32. Roger Williams, *The Bloudy Tenent of Persecution* (1644), quoted in Christopher Hill, *The World Turned Upside Down: Radical Ideas during the English Revolution* (New York: Viking Press, 1972), p. 262.

33. Marvin D. Schwartz, *Collectors' Guide to Antique American Clocks* (Garden City: Doubleday, 1975); Albert S. Bolles, *Industrial History of the United States*, 3d ed. (Norwich, Conn.: Henry Bill, 1881), pp. 226-30. Cf. Thompson, "Time, Work-Discipline, and Industrial Capitalism," pp. 63-70.

34. Laurie, " 'Nothing on Compulsion,' " p. 343. See also Louis C. Hunter, "Studies in the Economic History of the Ohio Valley," *Smith College Studies in History* 19 (1933-34): 5-49; Arthur H. Cole, "The Tempo of Mercantile Life in Colonial America," *Business History Review* 33 (1959): 277-99.

35. George R. Taylor, *The Transportation Revolution, 1815-1860* (New York: Rinehart, 1951).

36. U.S. Secretary of the Treasury, *Documents Relative to the Manufactures in the United States*, 2 vols., 22d Cong., 1st sess., 1833, Exec. Doc. 308, I, 432-69; Edwin T. Freedley, *Philadelphia and Its Manufactures in 1857* (Philadelphia: Edward Young, 1858), passim.

37. Caroline F. Ware, *The Early New England Cotton Manufacture: A Study in Industrial Beginnings* (Boston: Houghton Mifflin, 1931); Hannah Josephson, *The Golden Threads: New England's Mill Girls and Magnates* (New York: Duell, Sloan and Pearce, 1949); Felicia J. Deyrup, *Arms Makers of the Connecticut Valley: A Regional Study of the Economic Development of the Small Arms Industry, 1798-1870*, Smith College Studies in History, vol. 33 (Northampton, Mass., 1948); Nathan Rosenberg, ed., *The American System of Manufactures: The Report of the Committee on the Machinery of the United States 1855, and the Special Reports of George Wallis and Joseph Whitworth 1854* (Edinburgh: University of Edinburgh Press, 1969); Peter Temin, *Iron and Steel in Nineteenth-Century America: An Economic Inquiry* (Cambridge: M.I.T. Press, 1964), chap. 5.

38. Walt Whitman, *Leaves of Grass and Selected Prose*, ed. John Kouwenhoven (New York; Modern Library, 1950), p. 174; Taylor, *Transportation Revolution*, p. 209. For a popular description of the state of the crafts, see Edward Hazen, *Popular Technology; or, Professions and Trades* (New York: Harper and Brothers, 1841).

39. *The Complete Poetical Works of James Russell Lowell*, ed. Horace Scudder (Boston: Houghton Mifflin, 1911), p. 51.

40. Norman Ware, *The Industrial Worker, 1840-1860: The Reaction of American Industrial Society to the Advance of the Industrial*

Revolution (Boston: Houghton Mifflin, 1924); Hugo A. Meier, "Technology and Democracy, 1800-1860," *Mississippi Valley Historical Review* 43 (1957): 618-40; Marx, *Machine in the Garden*, chap. 4.

41. Herbert G. Gutman, "Social and Economic Structure and Depression: American Labor in 1873 and 1874" (Ph.D. diss., University of Wisconsin, 1959), pt. 2; idem, "The Worker's Search for Power: Labor in the Gilded Age," in H. Wayne Morgan, ed., *The Gilded Age: A Reappraisal* (New York: Syracuse University Press, 1963); David A. Wells, *Recent Economic Changes* (New York: D. Appleton, 1890), p. 398.

42. Blanche E. Hazard, *The Organization of the Boot and Shoe Industry in Massachusetts before 1875* (Cambridge: Harvard University Press, 1921); David N. Johnson, *Sketches of Lynn; or, The Changes of Fifty Years* (Lynn, Mass.: Thomas P. Nichols, 1880), pp. 332-56; T. A. D., "Modern Shoemaking," *Atlantic Monthly* 40 (1877): 669-74; Terence V. Powderly, *Thirty Years of Labor, 1859-1889* (Columbus: Excelsior Publishing House, 1889), p. 21.

43. George E. Barnett, *Chapters on Machinery and Labor* (Cambridge: Harvard University Press, 1926), chaps. 3-4; Warren C. Scoville, *Revolution in Glassmaking: Entrepreneurship and Technological Change in the American Industry, 1880-1920* (Cambridge: Harvard University Press, 1948).

44. Gutman, *Work, Culture, and Society*, pp. 237-40.

45. Gutman, "Social and Economic Structure," p. 234; Robert Ozanne, *A Century of Labor-Management Relations at McCormick and International Harvester* (Madison: University of Wisconsin Press, 1967), p. 3; Daniel Nelson, *Managers and Workers: Origins of the New Factory System in the United States, 1880-1920* (Madison: University of Wisconsin Press, 1975), pp. 6-9.

46. U.S. Bureau of the Census, *Abstract of the Fourteenth Census, 1920* (Washington, D.C., 1923), pp. 998-99.

47. John Buttrick, "The Inside Contract System," *Journal of Economic History* 12 (1952): 214; Leland Jenks, "Early Phases of the Management Movement," *Administrative Science Quarterly* 5 (1960): 421-47; Nelson, *Managers and Workers*.

48. Egal Feldman, *Fit for Men: A Study of New York's Clothing Trade* (Washington, D.C.: Public Affairs Press, 1960), p. 110; John F. Fraser, *America at Work* (London: Cassell, 1903), pp. 155, 157; Horace L. Arnold and Fay L. Faurote, *Ford Methods and Ford Shops* (New York: Engineering Magazine, 1919), pp. 106-9; R. R. Lutz, *Wage Earning and Education*, vol. 24 of the *Cleveland Education Survey*, 25 vols. (Cleveland: Cleveland Foundation, 1915-17), p. 97.

49. U.S. Senate, Committee on Education and Labor, *Report upon the Relations between Labor and Capital*, 4 vols. (Washington, D.C.,

1885), 1:757; Ozanne, *Century of Labor-Management Relations*, pp. 20–28.

50. These percentages are based on the population and manufactures statistics gathered in the eighth and fourteenth censuses. The region covered comprises the New England, Middle Atlantic, and East North Central census districts.

51. William G. Moody, *Land and Labor in the United States* (New York: Charles Scribner's Sons, 1883), p. 74; Hiram M. Drache, *The Day of the Bonanza: A History of Bonanza Farming in the Red River Valley of the North* (Fargo: North Dakota Institute for Regional Studies, 1964), p. 111. See also Lawanda Cox, "The American Agricultural Wage Earner, 1865-1900: The Emergence of a Modern Labor Problem," *Agricultural History* 22 (1948): 95–114.

52. W. E. Fohl, "Division of Labor in Bituminous Coal Mining," *Engineering Magazine* 40 (1910): 175–80; Joseph Husband, *A Year in a Coal-Mine* (Boston: Houghton Mifflin, 1911), pp. 17–19; J. William Schulze, *The American Office: Its Organization, Management and Records* (New York: Key Publishing Co., 1913); William H. Leffingwell, *Scientific Office Management: A Report on the Results of the Applications of the Taylor System of Scientific Management to Offices* (Chicago: A. W. Shaw, 1917); Ralph M. Hower, *History of Macy's of New York, 1858-1919: Chapters in the Evolution of the Department Store* (Cambridge: Harvard University Press, 1946).

53. U.S. Commissioner of Labor, *Thirteenth Annual Report, 1898: Hand and Machine Labor*, 2 vols. (Washington, D.C., 1899); Edward Frickey, *Production in the United States, 1860-1914* (Cambridge: Harvard University Press, 1947), p. 54; Solomon Fabricant, *The Output of Manufacturing Industries, 1899-1937* (New York: National Bureau of Economic Research, 1940), p. 44; Edmund E. Day and Woodlief Thomas, *The Growth of Manufactures, 1899 to 1923*, Census Monograph no. 8 (Washington, D.C.: U.S. Bureau of the Census, 1928), p. 34; Ross M. Robertson, *History of the American Economy*, 3d ed. (New York: Harcourt Brace Jovanovitch, 1973), p. 321.

54. Ray Ginger, *Age of Excess: The United States from 1877 to 1914* (New York: Macmillan, 1965), pp. 53–55.

CHAPTER TWO

1. Eric Foner, *Free Soil, Free Labor, Free Men: The Ideology of the Republican Party before the Civil War* (New York: Oxford University Press, 1970), p. 62.

2. *Nation* 1 (1865): 67.

3. *Equity* 2 (May 1875): 16, quoted in Irwin Yellowitz, ed., *The Position of the Worker in American Society, 1865-1896* (Englewood

Cliffs, N.J.: Prentice-Hall, 1969), p. 104; John R. Commons, et al., eds., *A Documentary History of American Industrial Society*, 10 vols. (Cleveland: Arthur H. Clark, 1910-11), 7:220; Wendell Phillips, *Speeches, Lectures, and Letters: Second Series* (Boston: Lee and Shepard, 1905), p. 152; E. L. Godkin, "The Labor Crisis," *North American Review* 105 (1867): 213.

4. David Montgomery, *Beyond Equality: Labor and the Radical Republicans, 1862-1872* (New York: Alfred A. Knopf, 1967), p. 26.

5. Samuel Eliot, "Relief of Labor," *Journal of Social Science* 4 (1871): 139; Godkin, "Labor Crisis," p. 211; Godkin, "The Labor Crisis," *Nation* 4 (1867): 335.

6. Frederick L. Olmsted, *A Journey in the Seaboard Slave States* (New York: Dix and Edwards, 1856), pp. 386-88; Francis A. Walker, *The Wages Question* (1876; New York: Henry Holt, 1891), pp. 76-77.

7. Washington Gladden, "Is It Peace or War?" *Century* 32 (1886): 566.

8. *The Collected Works of Abraham Lincoln*, ed. Roy P. Basler, 8 vols. (New Brunswick, N.J.: Rutgers University Press, 1953-55), 3:462, 478-79. See also Richard Hofstadter, "Abraham Lincoln and the Self-Made Myth," in his *The American Political Tradition and the Men Who Made It* (New York: Alfred A. Knopf, 1948).

9. George F. Parsons, "The Labor Question," *Atlantic Monthly* 58 (1886): 106; "John D. Rockefeller on Opportunity in America," *Cosmopolitan* 43 (1907): 372.

10. David A. Wells, "How Shall the Nation Regain Prosperity?" *North American Review* 125 (1877): 130; Richard T. Ely, *Social Aspects of Christianity and Other Essays* (New York: Thomas Y. Crowell, 1889), p. 97.

11. Frances W. Gregory and Irene D. Neu, "The American Industrial Elite in the 1870's: Their Social Origins," in *Men in Business: Essays in the History of Entrepreneurship*, ed. William Miller (Cambridge: Harvard University Press, 1952); William Miller, "American Historians and the Business Elite," *Journal of Economic History* 9 (1949): 184-208. This is even more true if wealth, rather than occupational prominence, is taken as the measure of success. See Edward Pessen, *Riches, Class, and Power before the Civil War* (Lexington, Mass.: D. C. Heath, 1973).

12. In making these calculations from the ninth census of 1870, I have followed David Montgomery's procedure in *Beyond Equality*, pp. 448-51, with two important modifications. Montgomery assumed that all workers engaged in the manufacturing and mechanical trades except "manufacturers" and jewelers were wage earners. This seems to me to beg the central question, and I have preferred to use the number of "hands employed" returned in the census of manufactures instead. Second, I have dealt with those occupations outside manufacturing where

employees and essentially self-employed persons might be mixed in significant proportions (barbers, launderers and laundresses, draymen, and teachers, for example) by throwing the whole class into an indeterminate category rather than to hazard a guess. The tendency of both these assumptions, however, is to set the minimum number of wage earners too low. The actual proportion of wage earners in the labor force, as a result, should be assumed to be somewhat closer to the upper figures given than to the lower.

No gross limits such as these can substitute for knowing how many wage earners successfully crossed the line into self-employment. But though social mobility studies have flourished in the decade since the appearance of Stephan Thernstrom's path-breaking *Poverty and Progress: Social Mobility in a Nineteenth Century City* (Cambridge: Harvard University Press, 1964), most have given up the self-employment question in favor of more readily measured—and smaller—indexes of success. For a thoughtful discussion, see Clyde Griffen, "Occupational Mobility in Nineteenth Century America: Problems and Possibilities," *Journal of Social History* 5 (1972): 310–30.

13. Nathaniel C. Fowler, Jr., *The Boy: How to Help Him Succeed. A Symposium of Successful Experiences* (1902; New York: Moffat, Yard, 1912), p. 181. See also Wilbur F. Crafts, *Successful Men of Today and What They Say of Success* (New York: Funk and Wagnalls, 1883); *The Problem of Success for Young Men and How to Solve It: An Educational Symposium by Successful Men and Leaders of Thought* ... (New York: W. R. Hearst, 1903); Irvin G. Wyllie, *The Self-Made Man in America: The Myth of Rags to Riches* (New Brunswick, N.J.: Rutgers University Press, 1954).

14. William Mathews, *Getting on in the World* (1872; Chicago: Scott, Foresman, n.d.), p. 99.

15. Orison S. Marden, *Pushing to the Front* (New York: Thomas Y. Crowell, 1894); *Success* 13 (1910): 662; *Success* 9 (1906): 612. For Marden's background see Margaret Connolly, *The Life Story of Orison Swett Marden* (New York: Thomas Y. Crowell, 1925); Richard M. Huber, *The American Idea of Success* (New York: McGraw-Hill, 1971), chap. 10.

16. John G. Cawelti, *Apostles of the Self-Made Man: Changing Concepts of Success in America* (Chicago: University of Chicago Press, 1965), chap. 6. Marden, *The Young Man Entering Business* (New York: Thomas Y. Crowell, 1903), pp. 110–16; Miller, *Men in Business*, p. 299; B. C. Forbes, "How I Pick a $25,000 a Year Man," *American Magazine* 82 (Sept. 1916): 18.

17. Horatio Alger, Jr.: *Brave and Bold; or, The Fortunes of a Factory Boy* (1874); *Tom Thatcher's Fortune* (1888), a variation on the same plot; and *Mark Manning's Mission: The Story of a Shoe Factory Boy*

(1905). Alger's hero inherits the factory in the second tale but promptly sells it to become a commission merchant. For a further discussion of work in children's tales, see chapter 5.

18. John Mitchell, *Organized Labor* (Philadelphia: American Book and Bible House, 1903), p. ix. For an indication of the reaction, see Jane Addams, *Newer Ideals of Peace* (New York: Macmillan, 1907), p. 146.

19. Terence V. Powderly, *The Path I Trod* (New York: Columbia University Press, 1940), p. 269; James C. Sylvis, *The Life, Speeches, Labors and Essays of William H. Sylvis* (Philadelphia: Claxton, Remsen, and Haffelfinger), p. 118. See also Norman Ware, *The Industrial Worker, 1840-1860* (Boston: Houghton Mifflin, 1924), chap. 13; John R. Commons and Associates, *History of Labour in the United States*, 4 vols. (New York: Macmillan, 1918-35), esp. 2:430-38; Gerald N. Grob, *Workers and Utopia: A Study of Ideological Conflict in the American Labor Movement, 1865-1900* (Evanston, Ill.: Northwestern University Press, 1961), pp. 19-21, 44-48.

20. Commons, *Documentary History*, 9:151-52.

21. *Workingmen's Advocate*, 26 Aug. 1866, quoted in Yellowitz, *Position of the Worker*, p. 101.

22. Rollo Ogden, ed., *Life and Letters of Edwin Lawrence Godkin*, 2 vols. (New York: Macmillan, 1907), 1:11. Cf. Alan P. Grimes, *The Political Liberalism of the New York "Nation," 1865-1932* (Chapel Hill: University of North Carolina Press, 1953), chap. 2.

23. *Nation* 5 (1867): 162.

24. Godkin: "The Labor Crisis," *North American Review* 105 (1867): 206; "The Coming of the Barbarian," *Nation* 9 (1869): 45; "Cooperation," *North American Review* 106 (1868): 158.

25. Godkin: "The Future of Capital," *Nation* 12 (1871): 429; "Cooperation," p. 162; "The Eight-Hour Muddle," *Nation* 4 (1867): 374; *Nation* 11 (1870): 271. In the same vein, see Horace Greeley, *Essays Designed to Elucidate the Science of Political Economy* (Philadelphia: Porter and Coates, 1869), chap. 20; Joseph Cook, *Socialism, with Preludes on Current Events* (Boston: Houghton Mifflin, 1880), pp. 83, 107-18, 130-44; D. M. Means, "Economic Aspects of Coöperation," *Nation* 43 (1886): 537-38.

26. R. Heber Newton, *Social Studies* (New York: G. P. Putnam's Sons, 1887), p. 94; Commons, *History of Labour*, 2:53, 433. For other surveys, see Massachusetts Bureau of Statistics of Labor (MBLS), *Seventeenth Annual Report* (Boston, 1886), pp. 192-229; *History of Coöperation in the United States*, Johns Hopkins University Studies in Historical and Political Science, vol. 6 (Baltimore, 1888).

27. *North American Review* 115 (1872): 212.

28. Godkin, "Coöperation and Character," *Nation* 43 (1886): 305; Henry D. Lloyd, *Labor Copartnership* (New York: Harper and Brothers,

1898); Francis G. Peabody, "Industrial Co-operation in England," *Forum* 8 (1889): 274.

29. Sedley Taylor, *Profit-Sharing between Capital and Labour* (London: Kegan Paul, Trench, 1884).

30. The officers of the profit sharing association were Nicholas P. Gilman, a Unitarian clergyman who served as the organization's moving spirit, Carroll D. Wright of the United States Bureau of Labor, the economist Francis A. Walker, and N. O. Nelson, a St. Louis plumbing goods manufacturer.

31. Nicholas P. Gilman, "Industrial Partnership," *Arena* 1 (1890): 269–82; Carroll D. Wright, "Industrial Necessities," *Forum* 2 (1886): 315; MBLS, *Seventeenth Annual Report*, pp. 234, 231. For reiteration of the theme see Edward E. Hale, *How They Lived in Hampton: A Study of Practical Christianity Applied in the Manufacture of Woollens* (Boston: J. Stillman Smith, 1888); Washington Gladden, *Tools and the Man: Property and Industry under the Christian Law* (Boston: Houghton Mifflin, 1893), chap. 8; and William E. Barns's symposium on the issue, *The Labor Problem: Plain Questions and Practical Answers* (New York: Harper and Brothers, 1886).

32. Nicholas P. Gilman: *Methods of Industrial Peace* (Boston: Houghton Mifflin, 1904), p. 9; *Socialism and the American Spirit* (Boston: Houghton Mifflin, 1893), pp. 284, 292. For Nelson's career and ideas see "My Business Life," *World's Work* 19 (1909–10): 12387–93, 12504–11.

33. American Society of Mechanical Engineers (ASME), *Transactions* 8 (1886–87): 630–32; F. J. Kingsbury, "Profit Sharing as a Method of Remunerating Labor," *Journal of Social Science* 23 (1887): 25–36; Arthur W. Burritt et al., *Profit Sharing* (New York: Harper and Brothers, 1918). For the hardening attitude of organized labor, see Martin A. Foran, *The Other Side* (Washington: Gray and Clarkson, 1886), a profit-sharing novel by the former president of the coopers' union; Barns, *Labor Problem*, chap. 5; R. L. Bridgman, "Labor's Solution," *Outlook* 75 (1903): 179–80; National Civic Federation, Welfare Department, *Profit Sharing by American Employers* (New York: National Civic Federation, 1916), pp. 233–54.

34. Nicholas P. Gilman, *Profit Sharing between Employer and Employee* (Boston: Houghton Mifflin, 1889), pp. 364–66, 382–89; Paul Monroe, "Profit Sharing in the United States," *American Journal of Sociology* 1 (1896): 685–709; Boris Emmet, "Extent of Profit-Sharing in the United States," *Journal of Political Economy* 25 (1917): 1019–33; W. Jett Lauck, *Political and Industrial Democracy, 1776–1926* (New York: Funk and Wagnalls, 1926), pp. 144–45.

35. N. O. Nelson, "Profit Sharing," *Independent* 71 (1911): 858.

36. National Industrial Conference Board, *Employee Stock Purchase*

Plans in the United States (New York: National Industrial Conference Board, 1928), p. 35.

37. National Civic Federation, *Profit Sharing*, p. 220; George W. Perkins, "Practical Profit-Sharing and Its Moral," *World's Work* 22 (1911): 14625; Perkins, "Let Workers Share in Profits," *American Employer* 2 (1913): 151; Walter Wellman, "The Steel Corporation Points the Way," *American Monthly Review of Reviews* 27 (1903): 328; Andrew Carnegie, *Problems of To-day: Wealth, Labor, Socialism* (1908; Garden City, N.Y.: Doubleday, Page, 1913), pp. 75, 64.

38. John A. Garraty, *Right-Hand Man: The Life of George W. Perkins* (New York: Harper and Brothers, 1960), pp. 109-14; John A. Fitch, *The Steel Workers* (New York: Russell Sage Foundation, 1911), pp. 207-14; Robert Ozanne, *A Century of Labor-Management Relations at McCormick and International Harvester* (Madison: University of Wisconsin Press, 1967), pp. 86-95; *American Federationist* 16 (1909): 47.

39. ASME, *Transactions* 8 (1886-87): 653-59; Henry Roland, "Six Examples of Successful Shop Management," *Engineering Magazine* 12 (1897): 996-97; Mark Perlman, *The Machinists: A New Study in American Trade Unionism* (Cambridge: Harvard University Press, 1961), pp. 28-32; National Industrial Conference Board, *Systems of Wage Payment* (New York: National Industrial Conference Board, 1930), p. 9.

40. For example, J. Slater Lewis, "Works Management for the Maximum of Production," *Engineering Magazine* 18 (1899): 202; William B. Weeden, *The Social Law of Labor* (Boston: Roberts Brothers, 1882), p. 295.

41. Frederick W. Taylor: *Shop Management* (New York: Harper and Brothers, 1912), p. 33; "A Piece-Rate System: Being a Step toward Partial Solution of the Labor Problem," ASME, *Transactions* 16 (1895): 856-83. For fuller studies of Taylor's life, environment, and influence, see Frank B. Copley, *Frederick W. Taylor: Father of Scientific Management*, 2 vols. (New York: Harper and Brothers, 1923); Monte A. Calvert, *The Mechanical Engineer in America, 1830-1910: Professional Cultures in Conflict* (Baltimore: Johns Hopkins University Press, 1967); and Samuel Haber, *Efficiency and Uplift: Scientific Management in the Progressive Era, 1890-1920* (Chicago: University of Chicago Press, 1964).

42. Robert F. Hoxie, *Scientific Management and Labor* (New York: D. Appleton, 1915), p. 140. For Taylor's description of the technique of time study, see Copley, *Taylor*, 1:225-28.

43. Clarence B. Thompson, ed., *Scientific Management* (Cambridge: Harvard University Press, 1914), pp. 264, 134; Haber, *Efficiency and Uplift*, p. 24.

44. Thompson, *Scientific Management*, p. 266; John P. Frey, "Scientific Management and Labor," *American Federationist* 23 (1916): 360.

45. Copley, *Taylor*, 2:423; Charles B. Going, "The Efficiency of Labor," *American Review of Reviews* 46 (1912): 333, 335. See also U.S. Commission on Industrial Relations, *Final Report and Testimony*, 11 vols. (Washington, D.C., 1916), 1:1003–4; Ida M. Tarbell, *New Ideals in Business* (New York: Macmillan, 1916), chap. 8; Frederick W. Taylor, "Testimony before the Special House Committee," in his *Scientific Management* (New York: Harper and Row, 1947), pp. 155–56, 243–46; and, for this position at the extreme, William C. Redfield, "The Moral Value of Scientific Management," *Atlantic Monthly* 110 (1912): 411–17.

46. Lyman Abbott: *Reminiscences* (Boston: Houghton Mifflin, 1915), pp. 410–11; "Industrial Democracy," *Forum* 9 (1890): 658–69; *The Industrial Problem* (Philadelphia: George W. Jacobs, 1905), chap. 3. Milton Derber, *The American Idea of Industrial Democracy, 1865–1965* (Urbana: University of Illinois Press, 1970).

47. Glenn Frank, *The Politics of Industry: A Foot-Note to the Social Unrest* (New York: Century, 1919), pp. 17, 20. The pages of the *Survey* during 1918–19 provide the best indication of the reconstruction fever. See also Harry F. Ward, *The New Social Order* (New York: Macmillan, 1919); John A. Ryan, *Social Reconstruction* (New York: Macmillan, 1920); Frederick A. Cleveland and Joseph Schafer, eds., *Democracy in Reconstruction* (Boston: Houghton Mifflin, 1919); Edwin Wildman, ed., *Reconstructing America: Our Next Big Job* (Boston: Page, 1919).

48. *A Compilation of the Messages and Papers of the Presidents*, 20 vols. (New York: Bureau of National Literature, n.d.), 17:8713–14; Lauck, *Political and Industrial Democracy*, chap. 2; James Gilbert, *Designing the Industrial State: The Intellectual Pursuit of Collectivism in America, 1880–1940* (Chicago: Quadrangle, 1972), chap. 4; David Brody, *Steelworkers in America: The Nonunion Era* (Cambridge: Harvard University Press, 1960), pp. 220–23.

49. National Industrial Conference Board, *The Growth of Works Councils in the United States*, Special Report no. 32 (New York, 1925), p. 5; William L. Stoddard, *The Shop Committee* (New York: Macmillan, 1919), p. 22.

50. Lauck, *Political and Industrial Democracy*; Glenn E. Plumb and William G. Roylance, *Industrial Democracy: A Plan for Its Achievement* (New York: B. W. Huebsch, 1923); John Leitch, *Man to Man: The Story of Industrial Democracy* (New York: B. C. Forbes, 1919); Paul W. Litchfield, *The Industrial Republic* (Boston: Houghton Mifflin, 1920); John R. Commons, et al., *Industrial Government* (New York: Macmillan, 1921); Ray S. Baker, *The New Industrial Unrest* (Garden City: Doubleday, Page, 1920). For one of the most consistent of these

experiments, see Kim McQuaid, "Industry and the Co-operative Commonwealth: William P. Hapgood and the Columbia Conserve Company, 1917-1943," *Labor History* 17 (1976): 510-29.

51. Samuel Crowther, "The Fetish of Industrial Democracy," *World's Work* 39 (1919): 23.

52. John A. Ryan, *Social Doctrine in Action: A Personal History* (New York: Harper and Brothers, 1941), p. 119.

53. *Century* 101 (1921): 410-11.

54. Earl J. Miller, *Workmen's Representation in Industrial Government* (Urbana: University of Illinois, 1924), pp. 110-11; David Brody, "The Rise and Decline of Welfare Capitalism," in *Change and Continuity in Twentieth-Century America: The 1920's*, ed. John Braeman et al. (Columbus: Ohio State University Press, 1968), pp. 162-65; Samuel Gompers, *Labor and the Employer* (New York: E. P. Dutton, 1920), p. 291.

55. "The Fate of the Salaried Man," *Independent* 55 (1903): 2002-4; Henry A. Stimson, "The Small Business as a School of Manhood," *Atlantic Monthly* 93 (1904): 337-40; Leon E. Truesdell, *Farm Population of the United States*, Census Monograph no. 6 (Washington, D.C.: U.S. Bureau of the Census, 1926), p. 128; John D. Black and R. H. Allen, "The Growth of Farm Tenancy in the United States," *Quarterly Journal of Economics* 51 (1937): 393-425.

CHAPTER THREE

1. Nathan Rosenberg, ed., *The American System of Manufactures: The Report of the Committee on the Machinery of the United States 1855, and the Special Reports of George Wallis and Joseph Whitworth 1854* (Edinburgh: Edinburgh University Press, 1969); Henry Roland, "The Revolution in Machine-Shop Practice," *Engineering Magazine* 18 (1899): 177-200.

2. Josephine Goldmark, *Fatigue and Efficiency*, 3d ed. (New York: Russell Sage Foundation, 1913), pp. 61, 65-66; John A. Fitch, *The Steel Workers* (New York: Russell Sage Foundation, 1911). See also Paul H. Douglas, *American Apprenticeship and Industrial Education* (New York: Columbia University, 1921), chap. 5.

3. *The Works of William E. Channing, D.D.*, 12th complete ed., 6 vols. (Boston: Crosby, Nichols, 1853), 5:160; Ralph W. Emerson, *English Traits* (1856), in *The Complete Works of Ralph Waldo Emerson*, centenary ed., 12 vols. (Boston: Houghton Mifflin, n.d.), 5:166-67; Herman Melville, "The Tartarus of Maids," *Harper's New Monthly Magazine* 10 (1855): 673-78; U.S. Senate, Committee on Education and Labor, *Report upon the Relations between Labor and Capital*, 4 vols. (Washington, D.C., 1885), 2:549.

4. The text of Potter's speech was a point of some contention in the ensuing debate. The most widely circulated version was published in the

New York Times, 6 May 1897, p. 6. Among criticisms of the address, see *New York Times*, 6 May 1897, p. 6; *Chicago Tribune*, 9 May 1897, p. B2; *Independent* 49 (1897): 13. Potter replied to his critics in "Man and the Machine," *North American Review* 165 (1897): 385–92.

5. William D. Howells, "A Sennight of the Centennial," *Atlantic Monthly* 38 (1876): 96, quoted in Alan Trachtenberg, ed., *Democratic Vistas, 1860–1880* (New York: George Braziller, 1970).

6. Morton Cronin, "Currier and Ives: A Content Analysis," *American Quarterly* 4 (1952): 317–30; Walter F. Taylor, *The Economic Novel in America* (Chapel Hill: University of North Carolina Press, 1942), p. 325; *Harper's New Monthly Magazine* 83 (1891): 965.

7. Edward E. Hale, *How They Lived in Hampton: A Study of Practical Christianity Applied in the Manufacture of Woollens* (Boston: J. Stillman Smith, 1888), pp. 244–45.

8. Walter Crane, *An Artist's Reminiscences* (New York: Macmillan, 1907), pp. 379–80. Cf. B. O. Flower, "Plutocracy's Bastiles," *Arena* 10 (1894): 601–21.

9. Josiah Strong, *Our Country: Its Possible Future and Its Present Crisis* (New York: American Home Missionary Society, 1885), pp. 143–44.

10. *New York Times*, 6 May 1897, p. 6.

11. Washington Gladden, *Working People and Their Employers* (Boston: Lockwood, Brooks, 1876), pp. 14–15; Edward Atkinson, "Commercial Development," in *The First Century of the Republic: A Review of American Progress* (New York: Harper and Brothers, 1876), pp. 207–9; Starr H. Nichols, "Men and Machinery," *North American Review* 166 (1898): 611.

12. James Leiby, *Carroll Wright and Labor Reform: The Origin of Labor Statistics* (Cambridge: Harvard University Press, 1960).

13. Carroll D. Wright: "The Factory System as an Element in Civilization," *Journal of Social Science* 16 (1882): 110, 122; s.v. "Factory," *American Supplement to the Encyclopaedia Britannica* (*Ninth Edition*) (Philadelphia: Hubbard Brothers, 1891), 2:828–29. Wright's full investigation was published as "Report on the Factory System of the United States," U.S. Census Office, *Tenth Census, 1880: Manufactures* (Washington, D.C., 1883), pp. 527–610. The argument, virtually word for word, can be found again in Wright's *Some Ethical Phases of the Labor Question* (Boston: American Unitarian Association, 1902), chap. 3.

14. Wright, "The Relation of Economic Conditions to the Causes of Crime," *Annals of the American Academy of Political and Social Science* 3 (1893): 115.

15. Wright, "Does the Factory Increase Immorality?" *Forum* 13 (1892): 347.

16. Wright: "The Ethical Influence of Inventions," *Social Economist*

1 (1891): 273, 269; "Factory System as an Element in Civilization," p. 125.

17. Nichols, "Men and Machinery," p. 609; George L. Bolen, *Getting a Living: The Problem of Wealth and Poverty—of Profits, Wages and Trade Unionism* (New York: Macmillan, 1903), p. 374n; Frank B. Copley, *Frederick W. Taylor: Father of Scientific Management*, 2 vols. (New York: Harper and Brothers, 1923), 1:325-28. See also Alexander E. Outerbridge, Jr., "Educational Influence of Machinery," *Engineering Magazine* 9 (1895): 225-31; T. N. Carver, "Machinery and the Laborers," *Quarterly Journal of Economics* 22 (1908): 210-32.

18. Wright, "Ethical Influence of Inventions," p. 340.

19. Walter A. Wyckoff, *The Workers: An Experiment in Reality*, 2 vols. (New York: Charles Scribner's Sons, 1897-98); Richard T. Ely, *Ground under Our Feet: An Autobiography* (New York: Macmillan, 1938), p. 188; Lillian Pettengill, *Toilers of the Home: The Record of a College Woman's Experience as a Domestic Servant* (New York: Doubleday, Page, 1903); Charles R. Walker, *Steel: The Diary of a Furnace Worker* (Boston: Atlantic Monthly Press, 1922).

See also Annie M. MacLean, "Two Weeks in Department Stores," *American Journal of Sociology* 4 (1899): 721-41; Amy E. Tanner, "Glimpses at the Mind of a Waitress," *American Journal of Sociology* 13 (1907): 48-55; Maud Younger, "The Diary of an Amateur Waitress," *McClure's Magazine* 28 (1907): 543-52, 665-77; Jessie Davis, pseud., "My Vacation in a Woolen Mill," *Survey* 40 (1918): 538-41; Frances Donovan, *The Woman Who Waits* (Boston: Richard G. Badger, 1920); *Four Years in the Underbrush: Adventures as a Working Woman in New York* (New York: Charles Scribner's Sons, 1921); Cornelia S. Parker, *Working with the Working Woman* (New York: Harper and Brothers, 1922); Allen F. Davis, *Spearheads for Reform: The Social Settlements and the Progressive Movement, 1890-1914* (New York: Oxford University Press, 1967); Christopher Lasch, *The New Radicalism in America, 1889-1963: The Intellectual as a Social Type* (New York: Alfred A. Knopf, 1965).

20. Wyckoff, *The Workers, East*, p. 66.

21. Ibid., p. 71.

22. John Dewey, "Play," in *A Cyclopedia of Education*, ed. Paul Monroe, 6 vols. (New York: Macmillan, 1911-13), 5:726.

23. Frank T. Carlton, *Education and Industrial Evolution* (New York: Macmillan, 1908), p. 66; H. F. L. Orcutt, "Machine-Shop Management in Europe and America," *Engineering Magazine* 17 (1899): 397; Neil M. Clark, *Common Sense in Labor Management* (New York: Harper and Brothers, 1919), chap. 7; "Making Work Pleasant," *Saturday Evening Post* 185 (25 November 1912): 24.

24. *The Works of John Ruskin*, ed. E. T. Cook and Alexander

Wedderburn, 39 vols. (London: George Allen, 1903–12), 10:180–269. For Ruskin's life, environment, and influence on America, see John D. Rosenburg, *The Darkening Glass: A Portrait of Ruskin's Genius* (New York: Columbia University Press, 1961); Herbert L. Sussman, *Victorians and the Machine: The Literary Response to Technology* (Cambridge: Harvard University Press, 1968); Roger B. Stein, *Ruskin and Aesthetic Thought in America, 1840–1900* (Cambridge: Harvard University Press, 1967).

25. Margaret Spence, "The Guild of St. George: Ruskin's Attempt to Translate His Ideas into Practice," *Bulletin of the John Rylands Library* 40 (1957): 147–201; Titus M. Coan, "Ruskin's 'Fors Clavigera,' " *Appleton's Journal*, n.s., 5 (1878): 58–75; H. E. Scudder, "St. George's Company," *Atlantic Monthly* 42 (1878): 39–51.

26. E. P. Thompson, *William Morris: Romantic to Revolutionary* (London: Lawrence and Wishart, 1955). Morris's socialistic phase began in 1883 when he joined the Social-Democratic Federation, and it reached its high-water mark in 1890.

27. "Art and Its Producers" (1888), in *The Collected Works of William Morris*, ed. May Morris, 24 vols. (London: Longmans, Green, 1910–15) 22:352; "Art, Wealth, and Riches" (1883), ibid., 23:157.

28. "A Factory as It Might Be," "How We Live and How We Might Live" (1885), "Useful Work *versus* Useless Toil" (1884), in G. D. H. Cole, ed., *William Morris* (London: Nonesuch Press, 1946).

29. "The Prospects of Architecture in Civilization" (1881), in Morris, *Collected Works*, 22:150; "Art and Its Producers," ibid., p. 353.

30. Max West, "The Revival of Handicrafts in America," U.S. Bureau of Labor, *Bulletin*, no. 55 (1904), pp. 1573–1622; Robert J. Clark, ed., *The Arts and Crafts Movement in America, 1876–1916* (Princeton: Princeton University Press, 1972).

31. Allen H. Eaton, *Handicrafts of New England* (New York: Harper and Brothers, 1949), p. 283; H. Langford Warren, "Our Work and Prospects," *Handicraft* 2 (1903): 186. See also Frederic A. Whiting, "What the Arts and Crafts Movement Has Accomplished," *Handicraft* 3 (1910): 94.

32. Freeman Champney, *Art and Glory: The Story of Elbert Hubbard* (New York: Crown Publishers, 1968); Robert W. Winter, "American Sheaves from 'C.R.A.' and Janet Ashbee," *Journal of the Society of Architectural Historians* 30 (1971): 320. The Hubbard quotations are from *A Message to Garcia and Thirteen Other Things* (East Aurora, N.Y.: Roycrofters, 1901), i; Champney, *Art and Glory*, p. 169; *The Philosophy of Elbert Hubbard* (East Aurora, N.Y.: Roycrofters, 1916), pp. 23–24.

33. Jane Addams, "A Function of the Social Settlement," *Annals of the American Academy of Political and Social Science* 13 (1899): 43;

Edward P. Pressey and Carl P. Rollins, *Arts and Crafts and the Individual* (Montague, Mass.: New Clairvaux Press, 1904); Horace Traubel, "Degeneracy and the Artsman," *Artsman* 2 (1905): 297, and "Keeping in the Historic Line," *Artsman* 1 (1904): 248. See also the socialist *Comrade*, edited by John Spargo and others, 1901-5.

34. Vida D. Scudder, *A Listener in Babel* (Boston: Houghton Mifflin, 1903), p. 318.

35. Warren, "Our Work and Prospects," p. 187; Oscar L. Triggs, "The New Industrialism," *Craftsman* 3 (1902): 105; Traubel, "Degeneracy and the Artsman," p. 289.

36. Charles H. Kegel, "Ruskin's St. George in America," *American Quarterly* 9 (1957): 412-20; Herbert N. Casson, "The Ruskin Cooperative Colony," *Independent* 51 (1899): 193.

37. Jane Addams: "Bread Givers" (1880), Addams Papers, Swarthmore College Peace Collection; *Twenty Years at Hull-House* (1910; New York: New American Library, 1961), p. 48. A half-dozen important studies round out Addams's ideas: Christopher Lasch, *New Radicalism*, chap. 1; Jean B. Quandt, *From the Small Town to the Great Community: The Social Thought of Progressive Intellectuals* (New Brunswick: Rutgers University Press, 1970), chap. 7; John C. Farrell, *Beloved Lady: A History of Jane Addams' Ideas on Reform and Peace* (Baltimore: John Hopkins University Press, 1967); Daniel Levine, *Jane Addams and the Liberal Tradition* (Madison: State Historical Society of Wisconsin, 1971); Allen F. Davis, *American Heroine: The Life and Legend of Jane Addams* (New York: Oxford University Press, 1973). Addams's own remarkably perceptive *Twenty Years*, however, remains in many ways the best of them all.

38. Addams: *Twenty Years*, p. 48; *The Spirit of Youth and the City Streets* (1909; New York: Macmillan, 1918), pp. 126-27; *Democracy and Social Ethics* (1902; reprint ed., Cambridge: Harvard University Press, 1964), p. 219. See also "Arts and Crafts and the Settlement," *Chautauqua Assembly Herald* 27 (9 July 1902): 2-3.

39. For example, Helen Marot, *The Creative Impulse in Industry* (New York: E. P. Dutton, 1918).

40. Addams: *Democracy and Social Ethics*, p. 211; "Social Education of the Industrial Democracy," *Commons*, 30 June 1900, p. 2; *Spirit of Youth*, p. 122.

41. Berenice M. Fisher, *Industrial Education* (Madison: University of Wisconsin Press, 1967); Sol Cohen, "The Industrial Education Movement, 1906-17," *American Quarterly* 20 (1968): 95-110; Marvin Lazerson, *Origins of the Urban School: Public Education in Massachusetts, 1870-1915* (Cambridge: Harvard University Press, 1971), chaps. 3-7; Lawrence A. Cremin, *The Transformation of the School: Progressivism in American Education, 1876-1957* (New York: Alfred A. Knopf, 1961), chap. 2.

42. Douglas, *American Apprenticeship*, chap. 5.

43. Henry S. Pritchett, "The Aims of the National Society for the Promotion of Industrial Education," National Society for the Promotion of Industrial Education (NSPIE), *Bulletin*, no. 5 (1908), p. 22; American Federation of Labor, Committee on Industrial Education, *Industrial Education*, 62d Cong., 2d sess., 1912, S. Doc. 936, p. 9. For an example of the full-blown attack on the "culturists," see Andrew S. Draper, "The Adaptation of the Schools to Industry and Efficiency," National Education Association (NEA), *Journal of Proceedings and Addresses* (1908), pp. 65-78.

44. David Snedden, "Vocational Education in Massachusetts: Some Achievements and Some Prospects," *Manual Training Magazine* 18 (1916): 3-4; W. A. O'Leary and Charles A. Prosser, "Short-Unit Courses for Wage Earners in Part-Time and Evening Schools," U.S. Bureau of Labor Statistics, *Bulletin*, no. 159 (1915), pp. 5-79; Marvin Lazerson and W. Norton Grubb, eds., *American Education and Vocationalism: A Documentary History, 1870-1970* (New York: Teachers College Press, 1974), pp. 135-36.

45. NSPIE, *Bulletin*, no. 6 (1908), pp. 92-97; John Dewey, "Education vs. Trade Training," *New Republic* 3 (1915): 42; Arthur F. Payne, "The 'N.E.A.' Adopts a So-Called 'National Policy of Vocational Education,' " *Industrial-Arts Magazine* 8 (1919): 364-65.

46. David Snedden, *Vocational Education* (1920; New York: Macmillan, 1929), pp. 409-10; NSPIE, *Bulletin*, no. 1 (1906), pp. 41-43.

47. U.S. Federal Board for Vocational Education, *Fourteenth Annual Report, 1930* (Washington, D.C., 1930), p. 34.

48. Addams, *Democracy and Social Ethics*, pp. 216-18; Paul Monroe, "Possibilities of the Present Industrial System," *American Journal of Sociology* 3 (1898): 729-53.

49. Robert Ozanne, *A Century of Labor-Management Relations at McCormick and International Harvester* (Madison: University of Wisconsin Press, 1967), p. 32; Stuart D. Brandes, *American Welfare Capitalism, 1880-1940* (Chicago: University of Chicago Press, 1976).

50. Ida M. Tarbell, *New Ideals in Business* (New York: Macmillan, 1916), p. 39.

51. Hugo Münsterberg, *Psychology and Industrial Efficiency* (Boston: Houghton Mifflin, 1913), p. 205. For an example of the book's reception, see *Harper's Weekly* 57 (17 May 1913): 14.

52. John Q. Adams, "The Relation of Art to Work," *Chautauquan* 38 (1903): 51. See also "Monotonous Industrial Service," *Commons* 8 (Sept. 1903): 12-13; Tarbell, *New Ideals*, pp. 45-46.

53. "Welfare Work for Employees in Industrial Establishments in the United States," U.S. Bureau of Labor Statistics, *Bulletin*, no. 250 (1919).

54. "Making Work Pleasant," *Saturday Evening Post* 185 (25 Novem-

ber 1912): 24; Herman Schneider, *Education for Industrial Workers: A Constructive Study Applied to New York City* (Yonkers-on-Hudson: World Book Co., 1915), pp. 68–70.

55. John Dewey, "The Need of Industrial Education in an Industrial Democracy," *Manual Training and Vocational Education* 17 (1916): 412.

56. Margaret F. Byington, *Homestead: The Households of a Mill Town* (New York: Russell Sage Foundation, 1910), pp. 110–12; *Commercial Recreation*, vol. 5 of the *Cleveland Recreation Survey*, 7 vols. (Cleveland: Cleveland Foundation, 1918–20).

57. John H. Finley, "The Wisdom of Leisure," *Playground* 9 (1916): 336.

58. Randolph Bourne, "In the Mind of the Worker," *Atlantic Monthly* 113 (1914): 375–82.

59. Charles A. Prosser, "The Evolution of the Training of the Worker in Industry," NEA, *Proceedings* (1915), p. 305.

CHAPTER FOUR

1. Henry W. Beecher, *Star Papers; or, Experiences of Art and Nature* (New York: J. C. Derby, 1855), p. 268.

2. Constance M. Rourke, *Trumpets of Jubilee* (New York: Harcourt, Brace, 1927), p. 170. See also Jane S. Elsmere, *Henry Ward Beecher: The Indiana Years, 1837–1847* (Indianapolis: Indiana Historical Society, 1973); Clifford E. Clark, Jr., "The Changing Nature of Protestantism in Mid-nineteenth Century America: Henry Ward Beecher's *Seven Lectures to Young Men*," *Journal of American History* 57 (1971): 832–46; William G. McLoughlin, *The Meaning of Henry Ward Beecher: An Essay in the Shifting Values of Mid-Victorian America, 1840–1870* (New York: Alfred A. Knopf, 1970).

3. Lyman Beecher, *The Autobiography of Lyman Beecher*, ed. Barbara M. Cross, 2 vols. (Cambridge: Harvard University Press, 1961), 2:84.

4. Henry W. Beecher, *Eyes and Ears* (Boston: Ticknor and Fields, 1863), pp. 128, 43; Beecher, *Star Papers*, p. 262; Rourke, *Trumpets of Jubilee*, p. 91.

5. Beecher: *Evolution and Religion* (New York: Fords, Howard, and Hulbert, 1885), pp. 135, 140; *New Star Papers; or, Views and Experiences of Religious Subjects* (New York: Derby and Jackson, 1859), p. 127; *Sermons*, 2 vols. (New York: Harper and Brothers, 1868), 2:422, 417.

6. McLoughlin, *Meaning of Henry Ward Beecher*, pp. 110, 31; Beecher, "The Profit of Rest and Retirement," *Christian Union* 13 (1876): 249.

7. Beecher, *Norwood; or, Village Life in New England* (New York: C. Scribner, 1868).

8. Beecher, *Eyes and Ears*, p. 41. See also "Christian Liberty in the Use of the Beautiful," in *Star Papers*, pp. 293–302.

9. E. L. Godkin, "Chromo-Civilization," *Nation* 19 (1874): 202.

10. Frances S. Osgood, *Osgood's Poetical Works* (Philadelphia: John E. Potter, n.d.), p. 44.

11. Lyman Beecher, "The Gospel the Only Security for Eminent and Abiding National Prosperity," *National Preacher* 3 (1829): 147; *The Works of William E. Channing, D.D.*, 12th complete ed., 6 vols. (Boston: Crosby, Nichols, 1853), 5:157; *The Writing of William James*, ed. John J. McDermott (New York: Random House, 1967), p. 648; John L. Spalding, *Socialism and Labor, and Other Arguments Social, Political, and Patriotic* (Chicago: A. C. McClurg, 1902), pp. 183, 181.

12. Francis A. Walker, "The Causes of Poverty," *Century* 55 (1897): 215; John Bascom, "Labor and Capital" (1868), quoted in Sydney E. Mead, *The Lively Experiment: The Shaping of Christianity in America* (New York: Harper and Row, 1963), p. 161. Compare Edward Atkinson, *The Industrial Progress of the Nation: Consumption Limited, Production Unlimited* (New York: G. P. Putnam's Sons, 1890). On the anti-Malthus, anti-Ricardo tradition in America, see John R. Turner, *The Ricardian Rent Theory in Early American Economics* (New York: New York University Press, 1921).

13. *Essays of William Graham Sumner*, ed. Albert G. Keller and Maurice R. Davie, 2 vols. (New Haven: Yale University Press, 1934), 1:389.

14. Clark, "Changing Nature of Protestantism," p. 834n.

15. Edward Atkinson, "Industrial Problems in the Light of History," *Forum* 18 (1894): 52; McLoughlin, *Meaning of Henry Ward Beecher*, p. 111.

16. "Work as Dissipation," *Chautauquan* 23 (1896): 97–98.

17. Charles G. Finney, "A More Excellent Way," *Independent* 25 (1873): 229–30; Henry C. Potter, *Sermons of the City* (New York: E. P. Dutton, 1881), p. 287.

18. Lester J. Cappon, ed., *The Adams-Jefferson Letters*, 2 vols. (Chapel Hill: University of North Carolina Press, 1959), 2:187.

19. Henry W. Bellows, "Influence of the Trading Spirit upon the Social and Moral Life of America," *American Review* 1 (1845): 96. See also Neil Harris, *The Artist in American Society: The Formative Years, 1790–1860* (New York: George Braziller, 1966), chap. 12.

20. S. Weir Mitchell, *Wear and Tear; or, Hints for the Overworked* (Philadelphia: J. B. Lippincott, 1871); George M. Beard, *American Nervousness: Its Causes and Consequences* (New York: G. P. Putnam's Sons, 1881).

21. Herbert Spencer, "The Gospel of Recreation," *Popular Science Monthly* 22 (1883): 354–59; Spencer, *An Autobiography*, 2 vols. (New

York: D. Appleton and Co., 1904), vol. 2, chap. 58; Charles L. Dana, "The Partial Passing of Neurasthenia," *Boston Medical and Surgical Journal* 150 (1904): 341.

22. Nathaniel C. Fowler, Jr., *The Boy: How to Help Him Succeed* (1902; New York: Moffat, Yard, 1912), p. 79; "Wasting Time to Good Purpose," *Saturday Evening Post* 173 (21 July 1900): 12; *Success Magazine* 11 (1908): 549, 458; "Do Vacations Pay?" *Saturday Evening Post* 177 (30 July 1904): 12.

23. Massachusetts Bureau of Statistics of Labor (MBLS), *Tenth Annual Report* (Boston, 1879), p. 149. From such early collections of businessmen's testimony on the shorter-hours issue as MBLS, *Report* (Boston, 1870), pp. 223-34, or Ohio Bureau of Labor Statistics, *Second Annual Report* (Columbus, 1879), pp. 280-83, to turn-of-the-century compilations—U.S. Senate, Committee on Education and Labor, *Eight Hours for Laborers on Government Work*, 57th Cong., 1st sess., 1903, S. Doc. 141; or National Association of Manufacturers, *"The Average Manufacturer" in All the States Heard in Opposition to the Eight-Hour Bill* (New York: National Association of Manufacturers, 1902)—the declining force of the moral argument is unmistakable. For its echoes in the 1920s, see James W. Prothro, *Dollar Decade: Business Ideas in the 1920's* (Baton Rouge: Louisiana State University Press, 1954), chap. 1.

24. *The Works of Theodore Roosevelt*, memorial ed., 24 vols. (New York: Charles Scribner's Sons, 1923-26), 17:511; Harry F. Ward, *The Social Creed of the Churches* (1912; New York: Abingdon Press, 1914), pp. 6-7; Josephine Goldmark, *Fatigue and Efficiency* (New York: Russell Sage Foundation, 1912), chap. 2.

25. Foster R. Dulles, *A History of Recreation* (New York: Appleton-Century-Crofts, 1965); John R. Betts, *America's Sporting Heritage, 1850-1950* (Reading, Mass.: Addison-Wesley, 1974); Richard Harmond, "Progress and Flight: An Interpretation of the American Cycle Craze of the 1890's," *Journal of Social History* 5 (1971-72): 235-57.

26. G. T. W. Patrick, "The Psychology of Relaxation," *Popular Science Monthly* 84 (1914): 590-604; Arthur S. Pier, "Work and Play," *Atlantic Monthly* 94 (1904): 675; Joseph Lee, *Play in Education* (1915; New York: Macmillan, 1921), pp. 434, 55, 494. See also Richard C. Cabot's bestselling *What Men Live By: Work, Play, Love, and Worship* (Boston: Houghton Mifflin, 1914); and, at the root of the tradition, Horace Bushnell, *Work and Play* (London: Alexander Strahan, 1864).

27. Cf. John Higham, "The Reorientation of American Culture in the 1890's," in his *Writing American History: Essays on Modern Scholarship* (Bloomington: Indiana University Press, 1970).

28. Hannah W. Smith, *The Christian's Secret of a Happy Life* (1883; new ed., New York: Fleming H. Revell, 1888), p. 42; Samuel D. Gordon, *Quiet Talks on Power* (1903; new and rev. ed., Chicago: Fleming H.

Revell, n.d.), p. 29. For an overview of the genre, see Louis Schneider and Sanford M. Dornbusch, *Popular Religion: Inspirational Books in America* (Chicago: University of Chicago Press, 1958).

29. Frances M. Björkman, "The Literature of 'New Thoughters,' " *World's Work* 19 (1910): 12472; Joseph E. Tuttle, *Prosperity through Thought Force* (1907), quoted in Richard Weiss, *The American Myth of Success: From Horatio Alger to Norman Vincent Peale* (New York: Basic Books, 1969), p. 169.

30. Ralph W. Trine, *In Tune with the Infinite; or, Fullness of Peace, Power and Plenty* (1897; Indianapolis: Bobbs-Merrill, 1933), p. 192; Horatio Dresser, *The Power of Silence* (1895; 2d rev. ed., New York: G. P. Putnam's Sons, 1907), p. 264. On the movement as a whole, see Weiss, *American Myth of Success*; Donald Meyer, *The Positive Thinkers: A Study of the American Quest for Health, Wealth and Personal Power from Mary Baker Eddy to Norman Vincent Peale* (Garden City, N.Y.: Doubleday, 1965); and Charles T. Hallinan's revealing memoir, "My 'New-Thought' Boyhood," *Living Age* 308 (1921): 606-11.

31. S. Weir Mitchell, "The Evolution of the Rest Treatment," *Journal of Nervous and Mental Disease* 31 (1904): 368-73; Jerome M. Schneck, "William Osler, S. Weir Mitchell, and the Origin of 'The Rest Cure,' " *American Journal of Psychiatry* 119 (1963): 894-95; Mitchell, *Fat and Blood: An Essay on the Treatment of Certain Forms of Neurasthenia and Hysteria*, 4th ed. (Philadelphia: Lippincott, 1885).

32. Nathan G. Hale, Jr., *Freud and the Americans: The Beginnings of Psychoanalysis in the United States, 1876-1917* (New York: Oxford University Press, 1971), chap. 9; F. H. Matthews, "The Americanization of Sigmund Freud: Adaptations of Psychoanalysis before 1917," *Journal of American Studies* 1 (1967): 39-62.

33. The *Reader's Guide to Periodical Literature* shows an enormous increase in articles devoted to suggestion, mental healing, nervousness, worry, and the subconscious in 1907-9. In all, the Emmanuel movement directly inspired some fifty articles before 1910 and was indirectly responsible for perhaps two dozen more. By contrast, for the years 1910-15 the *Reader's Guide* lists fifteen articles related either to Freud or psychoanalysis. On the Emmanuel movement, see Raymond J. Cunningham, "Ministry of Healing: The Origins of the Psychotherapeutic Role of the American Churches" (Ph.D. diss., Johns Hopkins University, 1965), chaps. 4-5.

34. Elwood Worcester, Samuel McComb, and Isador H. Coriat, *Religion and Medicine: The Moral Control of Nervous Disorders* (New York: Moffat, Yard, 1908), pp. 134, 309; Lyman P. Powell, *The Emmanuel Movement in a New England Town* (New York: G. P. Putnam's Sons, 1909), p. 172.

35. Nathaniel Hawthorne, *The Marble Faun* (1860), quoted in Howard

M. Jones, *O Strange New World. American Culture: The Formative Years* (New York: Viking Press, 1964), pp. 220-21.

36. W. Jett Lauck and Edgar Sydenstricker, *Conditions of Labor in American Industries: A Summarization of the Results of Recent Investigations* (New York: Funk and Wagnalls, 1917), p. 249; Robert H. Bremner, *From the Depths: The Discovery of Poverty in the United States* (New York: New York University Press, 1956), p. 153. See also Herbert G. Gutman, "Social and Economic Structure and Depression: American Labor in 1873 and 1874" (Ph.D. diss., University of Wisconsin, 1959), pp. 281-93; John A. Fitch, *The Causes of Industrial Unrest* (New York: Harper and Brothers, 1924), pp. 40-47.

37. Eric Foner, *Free Soil, Free Labor, Free Men: The Ideology of the Republican Party before the Civil War* (New York: Oxford University Press, 1970), p. 24. For general explorations of the response to nineteenth-century depressions, see Samuel Rezneck, *Business Depressions and Financial Panics: Essays in American Business and Economic History* (New York: Greenwood Press, 1968); Paul Barnett, *Business-Cycle Theory in the United States, 1860-1900* (Chicago: University of Chicago Press, 1941).

38. Washington Gladden, *Working People and Their Employers* (Boston: Lockwood, Brooks, 1876), pp. 62-63, 71; Bonamy Price, "One Per Cent.," *Contemporary Review* 29 (1877): 787; Horace White, "The Financial Crisis in America," *Fortnightly Review* 25 (1876): 810-29; White, "Commercial Crises," in *Cyclopaedia of Political Science, Political Economy, and of the Political History of the United States*, ed. John J. Lalor, 3 vols. (Chicago: Rand, McNally, 1882), 1:523-30. Cf. E. L. Godkin, "The Moral Side of Panics," *Nation* 17 (1873): 238-39.

39. See, for example, the opinions of businessmen and wage earners collected in Ohio Bureau of Labor Statistics, *Ninth Annual Report* (Columbus, 1886), pp. 140-48, 191-93; Irwin Yellowitz, *Industrialization and the American Labor Movement, 1850-1900* (Port Washington, N.Y.: Kennikat Press, 1977), chap. 4.

40. John Stuart Mill, *Principles of Political Economy*, 2 vols. (Boston: Charles C. Little and James Brown, 1848), bk. 3, chap. 14; U.S. Monetary Commission, *Report and Accompanying Documents*, 2 vols., 44th Cong., 2d sess., 1877-79, S. Rept. 703, 1:117-18.

41. O. B. Bunce, "Over-Consumption or Over-Production?" *Popular Science Monthly* 11 (1877): 306-16; Horace White, "The Tariff Question and Its Relations to the Present Commercial Crisis," *Journal of Social Science* 9 (1878): 117-31; Uriel H. Crocker, "Saving versus Spending," *Atlantic Monthly* 42 (1878): 691-96.

42. David A. Wells, "How Shall the Nation Regain Prosperity?" *North American Review* 125 (1877): 125, 126, 115.

43. U.S. Commissioner of Labor, *First Annual Report: Industrial*

Depressions (Washington, D. C., 1886), pp. 89, 255.

44. David A. Wells, *Recent Economic Changes* (New York: D. Appleton, 1890); James G. Blaine, *Twenty Years of Congress*, 2 vols. (Norwich, Conn.: Henry Bill, 1884), 1:213-14; "War and Good Times," *Banker's Magazine* 39 (1885): 802.

45. Wells, *Recent Economic Changes*, p. 325.

46. Thorstein Veblen, *The Theory of Business Enterprise* (New York: Charles Scribner's Sons, 1904), chap. 7; Wesley C. Mitchell, *Business Cycles* (Berkeley: University of California Press, 1913).

47. F. W. Taussig, *Principles of Economics*, 2 vols. (New York: Macmillan, 1911), 2:51; Edward D. Jones, *Economic Crises* (New York: Macmillan, 1900), pp. 67, 74; Arthur T. Hadley, "Stock Speculation and Commercial Crises," *Independent* 37 (1885): 3-4; Hadley, *Economics* (1896; New York: G. P. Putnam's Sons, 1899), pp. 148, 147.

48. *Official Proceedings of the Twelfth Republican National Convention, 1900* (Philadelphia, 1900), p. 137; Thomas J. McCormick, *China Market: America's Quest for Informal Empire, 1893-1901* (Chicago: Quadrangle, 1967), chap. 1.

49. Simon N. Patten, *The New Basis of Civilization* (New York: Macmillan, 1907); Daniel M. Fox, *The Discovery of Abundance: Simon N. Patten and the Transformation of Social Theory* (Ithaca: Cornell University Press, 1967); Jacob H. Hollander, "The Abolition of Poverty," *Atlantic Monthly* 110 (1912): 494.

50. Patten, *New Basis*, chap. 7; Walter Lippmann, *Drift and Mastery: An Attempt to Diagnose the Current Unrest* (New York: Mitchell Kennerley, 1914), chap. 13; "Extravagance as a Virtue," *Current Opinion* 54 (1913): 51; Van Wyck Brooks, *America's Coming-of-Age* (1915; Garden City, N.Y.: Doubleday, 1958), p. 17.

51. *Writings of William James*, p. 667; Donald McConnell, *Economic Virtues in the United States* (1930; reprint ed., New York: Arno Press, 1973), chap. 8; "Production and Distribution," *Saturday Evening Post* 188 (25 Sept. 1915): 20.

52. Floyd W. Parsons, "What's the World Coming To?" *Saturday Evening Post* 193 (19 Feb. 1921): 21 ff.; "The Business Outlook for 1921," *American Review of Reviews* 63 (1921): 45; "The Menace of Thrift," *Nation* 112 (1921): 256.

53. Irwin Unger, *The Greenback Era: A Social and Political History of American Finance, 1865-1879* (Princeton: Princeton University Press, 1964), p. 121.

54. "Work and Life," *Scribner's Magazine* 19 (1896): 253.

55. "Amusements," *New Englander* 9 (1851): 358; Fabian Franklin, "Business and Pleasure," *Nation* 90 (1910): 624.

56. "Hard Play and Easy Work," *Saturday Evening Post* 181 (29 May 1909): 18.

CHAPTER FIVE

1. F. J. H. Darton, *Children's Books in England: Five Centuries of Social Life* (Cambridge: Cambridge University Press, 1932), p. 118; Edmund Pearson, *Dime Novels* (Boston: Little, Brown, 1929), p. 252. See also Margaret E. Sangster, *From My Youth Up: Personal Reminiscences*, 2d ed. (New York: Fleming H. Revell, n.d.), pp. 75–79; Moncure D. Conway, "Books That Have Helped Me," *Forum* 4 (1888): 536.

2. Caroline M. Hewins, *A Mid-Century Child and Her Books* (New York: Macmillan, 1926); John C. Crandall, Jr., "Images and Ideals for Young Americans: A Study of American Juvenile Literature, 1825–1860" (Ph.D. diss., University of Rochester, 1957); Anne S. MacLeod, *A Moral Tale: Children's Fiction and American Culture, 1820–1860* (Hamden, Conn.: Archon Books, 1975).

3. P. H. Newby, *Maria Edgeworth* (Denver: Alan Swallow, 1950); Edward E. Hale, "Books That Have Helped Me," *Forum* 3 (1887): 31; Charles Strickland, "A Transcendentalist Father: The Child-Rearing Practices of Bronson Alcott," *Perspectives in American History* 3 (1969): 57–58.

4. John B. Boles, "Jacob Abbott and the Rollo Books: New England Culture for Children," *Journal of Popular Culture* 6 (1973): 507–28; Lyman Abbott, "Snap-Shots of My Contemporaries: My Father—The Friend of Children," *Outlook* 129 (1921): 55–58; Carl J. Weber, *A Bibliography of Jacob Abbott* (Waterville, Me.: Colby College Press, 1948).

5. Maria Edgeworth and Richard L. Edgeworth, *Practical Education* (1798; New York: Harper and Brothers, 1835), p. 251.

6. Maria Edgeworth, *The Parent's Assistant; or, Stories for Children* (1796; London: Macmillan, 1907).

7. Jacob Abbott, *Rollo at Work; or, The Way to Be Industrious* (1838; New York: Thomas Y. Crowell, n.d.), pp. 52, 125–26.

8. Samuel G. Goodrich, *Recollections of a Lifetime*, 2 vols. (New York: Auburn, Miller, Orton, 1857), 2:308–11.

9. "I'd Be a Butterfly," *Parley's Magazine* 1 (1833): 91.

10. The didacticism of juvenile fiction was equally shared by the most widely used early nineteenth-century school readers; see Ruth M. Elson, *Guardians of Tradition: American Schoolbooks of the Nineteenth Century* (Lincoln: University of Nebraska Press, 1964).

11. *Nation* 21 (1875): 251; MacLeod, *A Moral Tale*, chap. 5.

12. Darton, *Children's Books*, p. 96; William S. Cardell, *Jack Halyard, the Sailor Boy; or, The Virtuous Family*, 4th ed. (New York: Wilder and Campbell, 1825), pp. 17–18; Crandall, "Images and Ideals," pp. 402–5.

13. *Overland Monthly* 6 (Feb. 1871): 199, quoted in Richard L.

Darling, *The Rise of Children's Book Reviewing in America, 1865-1881* (New York: R. R. Bowker, 1968), p. 8. For an example of the indulgent storytelling style, see William D. Howells, *Christmas Every Day and Other Stories Told for Children* (New York: Harper and Brothers, 1893).

14. Charles D. Warner, "Being a Boy," *St. Nicholas* 1 (1874): 165; Anne Trensky, "The Bad Boy in Nineteenth-Century American Fiction," *Georgia Review* 27 (1973): 503-17.

15. Samuel Osgood, "Books for Our Children," *Atlantic Monthly* 16 (1865): 725.

16. Robert Hunter, "The Children Who Toil," *World's Work* 11 (1905): 6993.

17. *Library Journal* 8 (1883): 134; Mary Mapes Dodge, "Children's Magazines," *Scribner's Monthly* 6 (1873): 353. Cf. Peter Coveney's study of the uses of the romantic child in English literature: *The Image of Childhood*, rev. ed. (Harmondsworth: Penguin Books, 1967).

18. Annie Moore, "A Visit to a Bee-Hive," *St. Nicholas* 1 (1873): 34-37; Louisa May Alcott, *Flower Fables* (Boston: G. W. Briggs, 1855); James R. Lowell, "Uncle Cobus's Story," *Our Young Folks* 3 (1867): 411-18; L. Frank Baum, *Glinda of Oz* (1920), quoted in Fred Erisman, "L. Frank Baum and the Progressive Dilemma," *American Quarterly* 20 (1968): 619.

19. Julian Hawthorne: "Literature for Children," *North American Review* 138 (1884): 386, 396; "Rumpty-Dudget's Tower," *St. Nicholas* 6 (1879): 198-202, 269-73, 333-35. A similar example, by the most prominent American admirer of Hans Christian Andersen, is Horace E. Scudder's "Unlucky Fritz" in his *Dream Children* (Cambridge, Mass.: Sever and Francis, 1864).

20. R. Gordon Kelly, *Mother Was a Lady: Self and Society in Selected American Children's Periodicals, 1865-1890* (Westport, Conn.: Greenwood, 1974), p. 43.

21. Esther J. Carrier, *Fiction in Public Libraries, 1876-1900* (New York: Scarecrow Press, 1965), p. 348; Carl Sandburg, *Always the Young Strangers* (New York: Harcourt, Brace, 1953), p. 305; *Library Journal* 25 (1900): 171.

22. William T. Adams [Oliver Optic], *The Boat Club; or, The Bunkers of Rippleton* (1854; New York: Hurst, n.d.). On the origins of the story, see *Oliver Optic's Magazine* 17 (1875): 477-78.

23. Adams, *Work and Win; or, Noddy Newman on a Cruise* (Boston: Lee and Shepard, 1866), pp. 64, 287, 268-70. Adams's "Boat-Club" and "Woodville" series of the 1850s and early 1860s follow much the same formula.

24. Adams, *In School and Out; or, The Conquest of Richard Grant* (1863; New York: Hurst, n.d.), pp. 5-6.

25. *Our Boys and Girls* 8 (1870): 675. The three books were published serially in *Our Boys and Girls* in 1870.

26. Adams, "The Cruise of the Leopold; or, The Fortunes of a Good-for-Nothing," *Our Young Folks* 1 (1865): 631-37, 695-703, 757-61.

27. Adams: *Boat Club*, p. 5; *Seek and Find; or, The Adventures of a Smart Boy* (Boston: Lee and Shepard, 1868), p. 5; *Out West; or, Roughing It on the Great Lakes* (1877; Boston: Lee and Shepard, n.d.), pp. 5-6; *Shamrock and Thistle; or, Young America in Ireland and Scotland* (1867; Boston: Lee and Shepard, n.d.), p. 6.

28. Russel Crouse, Introduction to Horatio Alger, Jr., *Struggling Upward and Other Works* (New York: Crown Publishers, 1945), p. vi. For the current state of Alger criticism, see John G. Cawelti, *Apostles of the Self-Made Man: Changing Concepts of Success in America* (Chicago: University of Chicago Press, 1965), chap. 4; Michael Zuckerman, "The Nursery Tales of Horatio Alger," *American Quarterly* 24 (1972): 191-209. The old myth of Alger's secret bohemianism, though it continues to be promulgated by the modern paperback edition of *Ragged Dick*, has long since been exploded as a fabrication.

29. Alger, *Risen from the Ranks: or, Harry Walton's Success* (1874; New York: Media Press, 1972), p. 197. In his preface to that tale, Alger wrote: "In describing Harry's rise from the ranks, I have studiously avoided the extraordinary incidents and pieces of good luck which the story writer has always at command, being desirous of presenting my hero's career as one which may be imitated by the thousands of boys similarly placed, who, like him, are anxious to rise from the ranks." In *Ragged Dick*, he tacked a heroic rescue on the end of his otherwise sober counsel.

30. Alger, "How Johnny Bought a Sewing-Machine," *Our Young Folks* 2 (1866): 482-87 strips this formula to its simplest elements. *Try and Trust; or, The Story of a Bound Boy* (1873) is typical of Alger's elaboration of the type.

31. *Brave and Bold; or, The Story of a Factory Boy* (1874) and *Tom Thatcher's Fortune* (1888) are pure examples of the lost inheritance formula. Alger's "Way to Success" series of the 1880s was largely made up of stories of this sort.

32. Alger, "Writing Stories for Boys," *The Writer* 9 (1896): 37.

33. Mary A. West, *Childhood: Its Care and Culture* (Chicago: Woman's Temperance Publishing Association, 1887), p. 588. See also Carrier, *Fiction in Public Libraries*, pp. 120, 267-70, 346-53; Darling, *Rise of Children's Book Reviewing*, pp. 33-38; Franklin K. Mathiews, "Blowing Out the Boy's Brains," *Outlook* 108 (1914): 652-54.

34. For example: William O. Stoddard, "Crowded out o' Crofield; or, The Boy Who Made His Own Way," *St. Nicholas* 17 (Jan.-Oct. 1890);

John T. Trowbridge, "Phil and His Friends," *Youth's Companion* 56 (4 Jan.-22 March 1883); Kirk Munroe, "Derrick Sterling: A Story of the Mines," *Harper's Young People* 8-9 (19 July-28 Nov. 1887).

35. For example: Ralph H. Barbour, "The Triple Play," *St. Nicholas* 37 (1910): 963-68; Arthur S. Pier, *Boys of St. Timothy's* (New York: Charles Scribner's Sons, 1904), pp. 3-82; Albertus T. Dudley, *The Great Year* (Boston: Lothrop, Lee and Shepard, 1907), pp. 233-97.

36. J. A. Judson, "Nimble Jim and the Magic Melon," *St. Nicholas* 5 (1877): 34-41.

37. Editors of Youth's Companion, "Editorial Talks with Contributors," *The Writer* 9 (1896): 144.

38. For example: Munroe, "Derrick Sterling"; Edward W. Thomson, *The Young Boss* (New York: Thomas Y. Crowell, 1896); Alexander R. Bond, "With Men Who Do Things," *St. Nicholas* 40-41 (March 1913-Oct. 1914).

39. Elijah Kellogg, *The Young Ship-Builders of Elm Island* (1870; Boston: Lothrop, Lee and Shepard, n.d.), p. 4.

40. Ralph H. Barbour, *For the Honor of the School* (1900; New York: D. Appleton, 1907), p. 210.

41. Dudley, *The Great Year*, p. 152.

42. Cf. Walter Evans, "The All-American Boys: A Study of Boys' Sports Fiction," *Journal of Popular Culture* 6 (1972): 104-21.

43. Barbour, *Honor of the School*, p. 252.

44. Francis J. Finn, *That Football Game and What Came of It* (1897; New York: Benziger Brothers, n.d.).

45. Barbour, *The Arrival of Jimpson, and Other Stories for Boys about Boys* (New York: D. Appleton, 1904).

46. Arthur M. Jordan, *Children's Interests in Reading*, rev. ed. (Chapel Hill: University of North Carolina Press, 1926), table 4; *School and Society* 11 (1920): 323-24. Altsheler had a prominent place in the *Children's Catalog* (Minneapolis: H. W. Wilson, 1909; New York: H. W. Wilson, 1918), the most influential arbiter of a book's respectability after the turn of the century.

47. Joseph A. Altsheler, *The Young Trailers: A Story of Early Kentucky* (1907; New York: D. Appleton-Century, 1934), pp. 175, 48, 214.

48. Ibid., pp. 330, 323.

49. Altsheler, *The Free Rangers: A Story of Early Days along the Mississippi* (1909; New York: Appleton-Century-Crofts, n.d.), p. 365.

50. David B. Tyack, *The One Best System: A History of American Urban Education* (Cambridge: Harvard University Press, 1974), p. 54.

51. Warner, "Being a Boy," p. 165; Stephen Crane, *Whilomville Stories* (New York: Harper and Brothers, 1900).

CHAPTER SIX

1. The architectural evidence for this point still stands in many an old mill district, not yet victim to the wrecking ball and bulldozer. For examples of early factory design, see Bryant F. Tolles, Jr., "Textile Mill Architecture in East Central New England: An Analysis of Pre-Civil War Design," *Essex Institute Historical Collections* 107 (1971): 223–53; Martha and Murray Zimiles, *Early American Mills* (New York: Clarkson N. Potter, 1973).

2. Massachusetts Bureau of Statistics of Labor (MBLS), *Tenth Annual Report* (Boston, 1879), p. 149; MBLS, *Report* (Boston, 1870), p. 221; Ohio Bureau of Labor Statistics, *Second Annual Report* (Columbus, 1879), p. 281.

3. Norman Ware, *The Industrial Worker, 1840–1860* (Boston: Houghton Mifflin, 1924), chaps. 8, 10.

4. Marion C. Cahill, *Shorter Hours: A Study of the Movement since the Civil War* (New York: Columbia University Press, 1932), p. 35; U.S. Senate, Committee on Education and Labor, *Report upon the Relations between Labor and Capital*, 4 vols. (Washington, D.C., 1885), 1:315, 299, 294; *Twentieth Century Illustrated History of Rhode Island and the Rhode Island Central Trades and Labor Union* (Providence: Rhode Island Central Trades and Labor Union, 1901), p. 143; William D. Haywood and Frank Bohn, *Industrial Socialism* (Chicago: Charles H. Kerr, 1911), p. 62.

5. Gerald N. Grob, *Workers and Utopia: A Study of Ideological Conflict in the American Labor Movement, 1865–1900* (Evanston, Ill.: Northwestern University Press, 1961), p. 149.

6. MBLS, *Report* (Boston, 1870), pp. 287–98; New Jersey Bureau of Statistics of Labor and Industries (NJBLS), *Seventh Annual Report* (Trenton, 1885), pp. 237–56; Pennsylvania, *Annual Report of the Secretary of Internal Affairs, Part III: Industrial Statistics* (hereafter *Pennsylvania Industrial Statistics*), 15 (Harrisburg, 1888): 16H–28H; Michigan Bureau of Labor and Industrial Statistics (MichBLS), *Fourteenth Annual Report* (Lansing, 1897), pp. 195–96.

7. NJBLS, *Seventh Annual Report*, p. 239; U.S. Industrial Commission, *Reports*, 19 vols. (Washington, D.C., 1900–1902), 8:196.

8. David Montgomery, *Beyond Equality: Labor and the Radical Republicans, 1862–1872* (New York: Alfred A. Knopf, 1967), chaps. 6–8; Robert Ozanne, *A Century of Labor-Management Relations at McCormick and International Harvester* (Madison: University of Wisconsin Press, 1967), pp. 6–7; Clifton K. Yearley, *Enterprise and Anthracite: Economics and Democracy in Schuylkill County, 1820–1875* (Baltimore: Johns Hopkins University Press, 1961), p. 182.

9. John R. Commons and Associates, *History of Labour in the United*

States, 4 vols. (New York: Macmillan, 1918-35), 2:375-86; Donald L. Kemmerer and Edward D. Wickersham, "Reasons for the Growth of the Knights of Labor in 1885-1886," *Industrial and Labor Relations Review* 3 (1950): 213-20; Terence V. Powderly, *Thirty Years of Labor, 1859 to 1889* (Columbus, Ohio: Excelsior Publishing House, 1889), pp. 471-525; Henry David, *The History of the Haymarket Affair* (New York: Farrar and Rinehart, 1936), chaps. 7-8; Wisconsin Bureau of Labor and Industrial Statistics, *Second Biennial Report* (Madison, 1886), pp. 314-71.

10. U.S. Commissioner of Labor, *Twenty-first Annual Report, 1906: Strikes and Lockouts* (Washington, D.C., 1907).

11. Ira Steward, "A Reduction of Hours an Increase of Wages" (1865), in *A Documentary History of American Industrial Society*, ed. John R. Commons et al., 10 vols. (Cleveland: Arthur H. Clark, 1910-11), 9:290; Montgomery, *Beyond Equality*, pp. 252-53.

12. Sidney Fine, "The Eight-Hour Day Movement in the United States, 1888-1891," *Mississippi Valley Historical Review* 40 (1953): 441-62.

13. NJBLS, *Fourth Annual Report* (Somerville, 1881), p. 90; *Pennsylvania Industrial Statistics*, 17 (Harrisburg, 1890): 32E; MBLS, *Twelfth Annual Report* (Boston, 1881), pp. 450-53.

14. Philip S. Foner, *American Labor Songs of the Nineteenth Century* (Urbana: University of Illinois Press, 1975), p. 288; Samuel Gompers, *Seventy Years of Life and Labor*, 2 vols. (New York: E. P. Dutton, 1925), 1:54.

15. James D. Burn, *Three Years among the Working-Classes in the United States during the War* (London: Smith, Elder, 1865), pp. 11, 185; E. Levasseur, *The American Workman*, trans. Thomas S. Adams, ed. Theodore Marburg (Baltimore: Johns Hopkins University Press, 1900), pp. 84, 173-74; Mosely Industrial Commission to the United States of America, *Reports of the Delegates* (London, 1903).

16. MBLS, *Report* (Boston, 1871), pp. 590-91.

17. Frank Thistlethwaite, "The Atlantic Migration of the Pottery Industry," *Economic History Review*, 2d ser., 11 (1958): 274; NJBLS, *Sixth Annual Report* (Trenton, 1883), pp. 121, 128; U.S. Immigration Commission, *Reports*, 41 vols. (Washington, D. C., 1911), 10:179; Thomas R. Navin, *The Whitin Machine Works since 1831: A Textile Machinery Company in an Industrial Village* (Cambridge: Harvard University Press, 1950), p. 164. On the broader clash between old and new work values, see E. P. Thompson, "Time, Work-Discipline, and Industrial Capitalism," *Past and Present*, no. 38 (1967), pp. 56-97; Herbert G. Gutman, *Work, Culture, and Society in Industrializing America: Essays in American Working-Class and Social History* (New York: Alfred A.

Knopf, 1976), chap. 1; and my more skeptical reflections, Daniel T. Rodgers, "Tradition, Modernity, and the American Industrial Worker," *Journal of Interdisciplinary History* 7 (1977): 655-81.

18. For example, Illinois Bureau of Labor Statistics, *Fourth Biennial Report* (Springfield, 1886), pp. 501-26.

19. MBLS, *Fourth Annual Report* (Boston, 1873), pp. 495-96; MBLS, *Tenth Annual Report*, p. 159.

20. U.S. Commissioner of Labor, *Eleventh Special Report: Regulation and Restriction of Output* (Washington, D.C., 1904), pp. 509-17; Moses Rischin, *The Promised City: New York's Jews, 1870-1914* (Cambridge: Harvard University Press, 1962), p. 146; *Massachusetts Labor Bulletin*, no. 32 (1904): 210-15; T. W. Uttley, *Cotton Spinning and Manufacturing in the United States of America* (Manchester: University of Manchester, 1905), p. 22; North Carolina Bureau of Labor and Printing, *Seventeenth Annual Report* (Raleigh, 1904), p. 138; Paul H. Douglas, "Absenteeism in Labor," *Political Science Quarterly* 34 (1919): 591-608; Emil Frankel, "Labor Absenteeism," *Journal of Political Economy* 29 (1921): 487-99.

21. Vera Shlakman, *Economic History of a Factory Town: A Study of Chicopee, Massachusetts*, Smith College Studies in History, vol. 20 (Northampton, 1935), p. 148.

22. U.S. Commission on Industrial Relations, *Final Report and Testimony*, 11 vols. (Washington, D.C., 1916), 4:3507, 3510; U.S. Tariff Board, *Wool and Manufactures of Wool*, 4 vols., 62d Cong., 2d sess., 1912, H. Doc. 342, 4:983; Sumner H. Slichter, *The Turnover of Factory Labor* (New York: D. Appleton, 1919), pp. 16-27, 34-35, 44-45; Paul F. Brissenden and Emil Frankel, *Labor Turnover in Industry: A Statistical Analysis* (New York: Macmillan, 1922), pp. 50-51, 118-19. I have recalculated Brissenden and Frankel's aggregate figures throughout to eliminate the nonfactory trades from their sample.

23. Henry A. Miles, *Lowell, As It Was and As It Is*, 2d ed. (Lowell, Mass.: Nathaniel L. Dayton, 1846), pp. 162-94; Ray Ginger, "Labor in a Massachusetts Cotton Mill, 1853-60," *Business History Review* 28 (1954): 85; Stanley Buder, *Pullman: An Experiment in Industrial Order and Community Planning, 1880-1930* (New York: Oxford University Press, 1967), p. 248, n. 2. An informal poll of workingmen by the MichBLS, *Third Annual Report* (Lansing, 1886), p. 142, found that 41 percent of the 408 men replying had changed jobs within the preceding year.

24. *Pennsylvania Industrial Statistics* 15: 31E; MBLS, *Third Annual Report* (Boston, 1872), p. 376.

25. Allan Nevins, *Ford: The Times, the Man, the Company* (New York: Charles Scribner's Sons, 1954), p. 530.

26. Slichter, *Turnover*, pp. 163-85; Brissenden, *Labor Turnover*, pp. 94-96; Tamara K. Hareven, "The Laborers of Manchester, New Hampshire, 1912-1922: The Role of Family and Ethnicity in Adjustment to Industrial Life," *Labor History* 16 (1975): 253-54. The estimate of the number of "floaters" is derived from W. S. Woytinsky, *Three Aspects of Labor Dynamics* (Washington, D.C.: Social Science Research Council, 1942), p. 27, adjusted to eliminate nonfactory workers from his base data.

27. U.S. Commissioner of Labor, *Eleventh Special Report*, pp. 18, 715, and passim; Henry White, "A Labor Leader's Own Story," *World's Work* 22 (1911): 14852-53; David Montgomery, "Workers' Control of Machine Production in the Nineteenth Century," *Labor History* 17 (1976): 485-509.

28. Milton J. Nadworny, *Scientific Management and the Unions, 1900-1932* (Cambridge: Harvard University Press, 1955); Hugh G. J. Aitken, *Taylorism at Watertown Arsenal: Scientific Management in Action, 1908-1915* (Cambridge: Harvard University Press, 1960). The detailed record is in U.S. House of Representatives, *Hearings before the Special Committee to Investigate the Taylor and Other Systems of Shop Management*, 3 vols. (Washington, D.C., 1912).

29. See in particular Miner Chipman, *Efficiency, Scientific Management, and Organized Labor* (New York: Efficiency Society, 1916).

30. U.S. House of Representatives, *Taylor and Other Systems of Shop Management*, 3:1934, 1902; 1:177.

31. Ibid., 1:453.

32. John R. Commons, ed., *Trade Unionism and Labor Problems: Second Series* (Boston: Ginn, 1921), pp. 148-49.

33. MBLS, *Tenth Annual Report*, p. 127; *Journal of United Labor* 1 (1880-81): 78, 89, 105; *Journal of United Labor* 2 (1881): 121-22; Amalgamated Meat Cutters and Butcher Workmen of North America, *Official Journal* 2 (Jan. 1903): 12.

34. W. Jett Lauck and Edgar Sydenstricker, *Conditions of Labor in American Industries: A Summarization of the Results of Recent Investigations* (New York: Funk and Wagnalls, 1917), p. 77; U.S. Industrial Commission, *Reports*, 15:395.

35. Cahill, *Shorter Hours*, p. 42; William I. Thomas and Florian Znaniecki, *The Polish Peasant in Europe and America*, 5 vols. (Chicago and Boston: University of Chicago Press and Richard G. Badger, 1918-20), 2:306; *Pennsylvania Industrial Statistics*, 13 (Harrisburg, 1886): 165.

36. U.S. Immigration Commission, *Reports*, 1:297-313.

37. Louis Adamic, *Laughing in the Jungle: The Autobiography of an Immigrant in America* (New York: Harper and Brothers, 1932), p. 5;

Arnold Schrier, *Ireland and the American Emigration, 1850-1900* (Minneapolis: University of Minnesota Press, 1958), pp. 28, 20; Emily G. Balch, *Our Slavic Fellow Citizens* (New York: Russell Sage Foundation, 1910), p. 80.

38. Thomas, *Polish Peasant*, 1:388-89; *Journal of Social Science* 44 (1906): 12; Phyllis H. Williams, *South Italian Folkways in Europe and America* (New Haven: Yale University Press, 1938), p. 20.

39. Thomas, *Polish Peasant*, 5:22.

40. Edward A. Steiner, *From Alien to Citizen: The Story of My Life in America* (New York: Fleming H. Revell, 1914), pp. 53-208. For similar examples, see Eli Ginzberg and Hyman Berman, *The American Worker in the Twentieth Century: A History through Autobiographies* (New York: Free Press, 1963), pp. 75-79; Charlotte Erickson, *Invisible Immigrants: The Adaptation of English and Scottish Immigrants in Nineteenth-Century America* (Coral Gables, Fla.: University of Miami Press, 1972), pp. 247-54; Alexander Irvine, *From the Bottom Up* (New York: Doubleday, Page, 1910), chap. 6.

41. Thomas, *Polish Peasant*, 2:234; John R. Commons, *Races and Immigrants in America* (New York: Macmillan, 1907), pp. 126-27.

42. James C. Sylvis, *The Life, Speeches, Labors and Essays of William H. Sylvis* (Philadelphia: Claxton, Remsen, and Haffelfinger, 1872), pp. 413-14; Terence V. Powderly, *The Path I Trod* (New York: Columbia University Press, 1940), p. 67; *Writings and Speeches of Eugene V. Debs*, ed. Arthur M. Schlesinger, Jr. (New York: Hermitage Press, 1948), p. 215.

43. Arthur M. Schlesinger, Jr., *The Age of Jackson* (Boston: Little, Brown, 1945), p. 133; Bricklayers and Masons' International Union of America, *Constitution and Rules of Order* (Cohoes, N.Y., 1892), p. 4; *National Labor Tribune* (18 March 1882), quoted in Gutman, *Work, Culture, and Society*, p. 98; Sylvis, *Life*, pp. 111-12, 414; Bernard Mandel, *Labor: Free and Slave. Workingmen and the Anti-Slavery Movement in the United States* (New York: Associated Authors, 1955), p. 181.

44. Powderly: *Path I Trod*, pp. 194-97, 50-51; "Strikes and Arbitration," *North American Review* 142 (1886): 502.

45. Edwin M. Chamberlin, *The Sovereigns of Industry* (Boston: Lee and Shepard, 1875), p. 159.

46. Debs, *Writings*, pp. 235, 343, 164.

47. Haywood, *Industrial Socialism*, pp. 63, 62, 23; Upton Sinclair, *The Jungle* (1906; New York: New American Library, 1960), p. 331; Joyce L. Kornbluh, ed., *Rebel Voices: An I.W.W. Anthology* (Ann Arbor: University of Michigan Press, 1964), p. 197.

48. Daniel Bell, *Marxian Socialism in the United States* (1952;

Princeton: Princeton University Press, 1967), pp. 82-86; U.S. Commission on Industrial Relations, *Final Report*, 11:10582.

49. "The Immorality of Idleness," *Machinists' Monthly Journal* 22 (1910): 1109; U.S. Commission on Industrial Relations, *Final Report* 1:812.

50. Samuel Gompers: "The Eight-Hour Work Day," *American Federationist* 4 (1897): 2; "The Eight-Hour Day on Government Work," *American Federationist* 17 (1910): 1057-68; "Machinery to Perfect the Living Machine," *American Federationist* 18 (1911): 116-17. Cf. Jean T. McKelvey, *AFL Attitudes toward Production, 1900-1932* (Ithaca: Cornell University, 1952).

51. Gompers, "The Miracles of 'Efficiency,' " *American Federationist* 18 (1911): 276; Gompers, "Address before the National Civic Federation," *American Federationist* 10 (1903): 1297; U.S. Industrial Commission, *Report* 7:646; U.S. House of Representatives, Committee on Labor, *Investigation of Taylor System of Shop Management: Hearings on House Resolution 90*, 62d Cong., 1st sess., 1911, p. 37.

52. Cahill, *Shorter Hours*, p. 141.

CHAPTER SEVEN

1. Ella Wheeler Wilcox, "The Restlessness of Modern Woman," *Cosmopolitan* 31 (1901): 315.

2. On Stowe's thought and writings, see Charles H. Foster, *The Rungless Ladder: Harriet Beecher Stowe and New England Puritanism* (Durham: Duke University Press, 1954); Alice C. Crozier, *The Novels of Harriet Beecher Stowe* (New York: Oxford University Press, 1969); Gail Parker, ed., *The Oven Birds: American Women on Womanhood, 1820-1920* (Garden City, N.Y.: Doubleday, 1972).

3. Stowe, *The Minister's Wooing* (1859), in *Writings of Harriet Beecher Stowe*, 16 vols. (Boston: Houghton Mifflin, 1896-1900), 5:2-3, 12-13.

4. Stowe's column ran in the *Atlantic Monthly* under the titles "House and Home Papers" and "The Chimney-Corner" from January 1864 to September 1866. *Writings*, 8:265, 419, 98, 288, 295, 307-8, 244.

5. William A. Alcott, *The Young Wife; or, Duties of Woman in the Marriage Relation* (1837; reprint ed., New York: Arno Press, 1972), chaps. 19-20; Elizabeth S. Phelps, "Why Shall They Do It?" *Harper's New Monthly Magazine* 36 (1868): 219. See also Lydia Maria Child, *The American Frugal Housewife*, 33d ed. (New York: Samuel S. and William Wood, 1855); Louisa May Alcott, *Work: A Story of Experience* (Boston: Roberts Brothers, 1873); Julia Ward Howe, Introduction to Annie Nathan Meyer, ed., *Woman's Work in America* (New York: Henry Holt, 1891).

6. Mary A. Dodge [Gail Hamilton], *Woman's Worth and Worthlessness* (New York: Harper and Brothers, 1872), pp. 54, 94.

7. Stowe, *My Wife and I; or, Harry Henderson's History* (1871), in *Writings*, 12: 335, 105, 108.

8. Annie Fields, ed., *Life and Letters of Harriet Beecher Stowe* (Boston: Houghton Mifflin, 1897), p. 113; Charles E. Stowe, *Life of Harriet Beecher Stowe, Compiled from Her Letters and Journals* (1889; reprint ed., Detroit: Gale Research, 1967), pp. 90–98.

9. Catharine E. Beecher, *Educational Reminiscences and Suggestions* (New York: J. B. Ford, 1874), pp. 16–23.

10. Stowe, *Oldtown Folks* (1869), in *Writings*, 9:112.

11. Charlotte P. Gilman, *Women and Economics: A Study of the Economic Relation between Men and Women as a Factor in Social Evolution* (1898; reprint ed., New York: Harper and Row, 1966).

12. "Women Debate Wife's Economic Relation," *New York Evening Call*, 8 Jan. 1909.

13. Gilman: "What Work Is," *Cosmopolitan* 27 (1899): 678-82; *Women and Economics*, p. 246; *Human Work* (New York: McClure, Phillips, 1904).

14. Gilman, *The Living of Charlotte Perkins Gilman: An Autobiography* (1935; reprint ed., New York: Arno Press, 1972), p. 80.

15. Gilman: *In This Our World* (Boston: Small, Maynard, 1899); *Women and Economics*, p. 70. Gilman's chief outlet for fictionalizing was the *Forerunner*, a monthly magazine she wrote single-handedly from 1909 to 1916. For a particularly revealing sketch of marriage, see "Her Housekeeper," *Forerunner* 1 (Jan. 1910): 2-8.

16. Gilman, *Women and Economics*, p. 313.

17. Harriet Beecher Stowe, "The True Story of Lady Byron's Life," *Atlantic Monthly* 24 (1869): 295-313. Although women's publicly expressed attitudes toward sex changed rapidly in the years just before 1920, the overwhelming majority of vocal advocates of sexual freedom in the late nineteenth and early twentieth centuries were men, not women. See Sidney Ditzion, *Marriage, Morals and Sex in America: A History of Ideas* (New York: Bookman Associates, 1953).

18. Elizabeth Carpenter, "More Truth about Woman in Industry," *North American Review* 179 (1904): 224, 222; Mrs. C. F. Peirce, "Co-operative Housekeeping," *Atlantic Monthly* 22 (1868): 521.

19. Mercedes M. Randall, *Improper Bostonian: Emily Greene Balch* (New York: Twayne, 1964), p. 69; Maud Nathan, *Once upon a Time and Today* (New York: G. P. Putnam's Sons, 1933), p. 95; Lydia Kingsmill Commander, *The American Idea: Does the National Tendency toward a Small Family Point to Race Suicide or Race Development?* (New York: A. S. Barnes, 1907), chap. 7; *Harper's Bazar* 45 (1911): 57. See also Jane Addams, *Twenty Years at Hull-House* (1910; New York: New American

Library, 1961), chaps. 3–4, 6; Inez Haynes Irwin, "These Modern Women: The Making of a Militant," *Nation* 123 (1926): 553–55; Christopher Lasch, *The New Radicalism in America, 1889–1963: The Intellectual as a Social Type* (New York: Alfred A. Knopf, 1965), chap. 2.

20. Ednah D. Cheney, *Louisa May Alcott: Her Life, Letters, and Journals* (Boston: Roberts Brothers, 1889); Rheta Childe Dorr, *A Woman of Fifty* (New York: Funk and Wagnalls, 1924), p. 21; *Report of the International Council of Women, Assembled by the National Woman Suffrage Association, 1888* (Washington, D.C.: National Woman Suffrage Association, 1888), p. 162.

21. Scott Nearing and Nellie M. S. Nearing, *Woman and Social Progress: A Discussion of the Biologic, Domestic, Industrial, and Social Possibilities of American Women* (New York: Macmillan, 1912), p. 37; Mary Roberts Coolidge, *Why Women Are So* (New York: Henry Holt, 1912), pp. 106, 69. Cf. Caroline E. MacGill, "The Myth of the Colonial Housewife," *Independent* 69 (1910): 1318–22.

22. Mrs. C. F. Peirce, "Co-operative Housekeeping," *Atlantic Monthly* 23 (1869): 299; Virginia Penny, *Think and Act: A Series of Articles Pertaining to Men and Women, Work and Wages* (Philadelphia: Claxton, Remsen, and Haffelfinger, 1869), p. 154; Edna Kenton, "The Militant Women—and Women," *Century* 87 (1913): 16.

23. Johann J. Bachofen, *Myth, Religion, and Mother Right: Selected Writings of J. J. Bachofen*, trans. Ralph Mannheim (Princeton: Bollinger Foundation, 1967); Lester F. Ward, "Our Better Halves," *Forum* 6 (1888): 266–75; Ward, *Pure Sociology: A Treatise on the Origin and Spontaneous Development of Society* (New York: Macmillan, 1903), chap. 14; George E. Howard, *A History of Matrimonial Institutions*, 3 vols. (Chicago: University of Chicago Press, 1904), vol. 1, chaps. 1–3; Gilman, *Living of Charlotte Perkins Gilman*, p. 187.

24. Otis T. Mason, *Woman's Share in Primitive Culture* (New York: Appleton, 1894); William I. Thomas, *Sex and Society: Studies in the Social Psychology of Sex* (Chicago: University of Chicago Press, 1907); Thomas, "Woman and the Occupations," *American Magazine* 68 (1909): 463–70; Lydia Kingsmill Commander, "The Self-Supporting Woman and the Family," *American Journal of Sociology* 14 (1909): 752–57.

25. Anna Garlin Spencer, "The Primitive Working-Woman," *Forum* 46 (1911): 546–58. See also Gilman, *Women and Economics*, chap. 7; Elizabeth Cady Stanton, "The Matriarchate, or Mother-Age," *Transactions of the National Council of Women of the United States, 1891* (Philadelphia: J. B. Lippincott, 1891), pp. 218–27; *Harper's Bazar* 45 (1911): 57; Nearing, *Woman and Social Progress*, chap. 2.

26. Caroline H. Dall, *The College, the Market, and the Court; or,*

Woman's Relation to Education, Labor, and Law (1867; reprint ed., New York: Arno Press, 1972), pp. 208–9; Antoinette Brown Blackwell, "The Relation of Woman's Work in the Household to the Work Outside," *Papers and Letters Presented at the First Woman's Congress of the Association for the Advancement of Woman, 1873* (New York, 1874), pp. 178–84. On Bellamy's influence on the women's movement, see Mari Jo Buhle, "Feminism and Socialism in the United States, 1820–1920" (Ph.D. diss., University of Wisconsin, 1974), chap. 3.

27. Olive Schreiner, *Woman and Labor* (New York: Frederick A. Stokes, 1911), pp. 172, 65; Elsie Clews Parsons, "Feminism and Conventionality," *Annals of the American Academy of Political and Social Science* 56 (1914): 47. On the women's labor laws debate, see J. Stanley Lemons, *The Woman Citizen: Social Feminism in the 1920s* (Urbana: University of Illinois Press, 1973), chap. 7; Harriot Stanton Blatch and Alma Lutz, *Challenging Years: The Memoirs of Harriot Stanton Blatch* (New York: G. P. Putnam's Sons, 1940), pt. 5.

28. "Miss Schreiner's Papers on Women," *Harper's Bazar* 36 (1902): 296. See also Simon N. Patten, "Some New Adjustments for Women," *Independent* 61 (1906): 674–81.

29. *Ladies' Home Journal* 31 (May 1914): 5; *Ladies' Home Journal* 33 (Sept. 1916): 34; Anna A. Rogers, "Why American Marriages Fail," *Atlantic Monthly* 100 (1907): 290; Ida M. Tarbell, *The Business of Being a Woman* (New York: Macmillan, 1912).

30. For example: Mrs. Amelia E. Barr, "The Servant-Girl's Point of View," *North American Review* 154 (1892): 729–32; Jane Addams, "A Belated Industry," *American Journal of Sociology* 1 (1896): 536–50; Lucy Maynard Salmon, *Domestic Service* (1897; New York: Macmillan, 1901).

31. *Ladies' Home Journal* 33 (Dec. 1916): 36.

32. Compare, for example, Mrs. John A. Logan, *The Home Manual* (Philadelphia: J. W. Keeler, 1889), with Christine T. Herrick, *A-B-C of Housekeeping* (New York: Harper and Brothers, 1915) or Christine Frederick's Taylor-inspired *The New Housekeeping: Efficiency Studies in Home Management* (Garden City, N.Y.: Doubleday, Page, 1914), originally published in *Ladies' Home Journal* 29 (Sept.-Dec. 1912).

33. Juliet Robb, "Our House in Order," *Outlook* 95 (1910): 356.

34. Janet M. Hooks, "Women's Occupations through Seven Decades," U.S. Department of Labor, Woman's Bureau, *Bulletin*, no. 218 (Washington, D.C., 1947), p. 139; *Massachusetts Labor Bulletin*, no. 8 (Oct. 1898): 2–3.

35. Robert W. Smuts, *Women and Work in America* (New York: Columbia University Press, 1959), pp. 12–13; Robert C. Chapin, *The Standard of Living among Workingmen's Families in New York City* (New York: Russell Sage Foundation, 1909); Louise B. More, *Wage-*

Earners' Budgets: A Study of Standards and Cost of Living in New York City (New York: Henry Holt, 1907); U.S. Bureau of Labor, *Report on Condition of Woman and Child Wage-Earners in the United States,* 19 vols., 61st Cong., 2d sess., 1910-12, S. Doc. 645, vol. 16, chap. 3; Bureau of Municipal Research of Philadelphia, *Workingmen's Standard of Living in Philadelphia* (New York: Macmillan, 1919), chap. 4.

36. U.S. Bureau of the Census, *Historical Statistics of the United States, Colonial Times to 1957* (Washington, D.C., 1960), p. 510; J. Frederic Dewhurst and Associates, *America's Needs and Resources: A New Survey* (New York: Twentieth Century Fund, 1955), appendix 8-1; Siegfried Giedion, *Mechanization Takes Command: A Contribution to Anonymous History* (1948; New York: W. W. Norton, 1969), pp. 42, 512-627; Ruth S. Cowan, "The 'Industrial Revolution' in the Home: Household Technology and Social Change in the 20th Century," *Technology and Culture* 17 (1976): 4-8.

37. Christine Frederick, *Household Engineering: Scientific Management in the Home* (Chicago: American School of Home Economics, 1920), pp. 69-72. For earlier descriptions of a housewife's work, see Abby M. Diaz, *A Domestic Problem: Work and Culture in the Household* (Boston: J. Osgood, 1875), and idem, *Bybury to Beacon Street* (Boston: D. Lothrop, 1887), particularly chaps. 10-11.

38. U.S. Bureau of the Census, *16th Census of the United States, 1940, Population: Comparative Occupational Statistics for the United States, 1870-1940* (Washington, D.C., 1943), pp. 92, 122-28; Robert W. Smuts, "The Female Labor Force: A Case Study in the Interpretation of Historical Statistics," *Journal of the American Statistical Association* 55 (1960): 71-79; U.S. Bureau of the Census, *Statistics of Women at Work, Based on Unpublished Information Derived from the Schedules of the 12th Census, 1900* (Washington, D.C., 1907), p. 134; U.S. Bureau of the Census, *Abstract of the 14th Census, 1920* (Washington, D.C., 1923), p. 534.

39. Coolidge, *Why Women Are So,* pp. 366, 325; June Sochen, ed., *The New Feminism in Twentieth-Century America* (Lexington, Mass.: D. C. Heath, 1971), pp. 49-50. See also Mary Gay Humphreys, "The New York Working-Girl," *Scribner's Magazine* 20 (1896): 502-13; Vida D. Scudder, *A Listener in Babel: Being a Series of Imaginary Conversations Held at the Close of the Last Century* (New York: Houghton Mifflin, 1903).

40. [Dorothy Richardson], *The Long Day: The Story of a New York Working Girl as Told by Herself* (New York: Century, 1905), pp. 59-60 and passim. Frances Donovan, *The Woman Who Waits* (Boston: Richard G. Badger, 1920), the record of the experiences of a school-teacher as a Chicago waitress, followed much the same vein in its preoccupation with sex.

41. Mrs. John Van Vorst and Marie Van Vorst, *The Woman Who Toils: Being the Experiences of Two Ladies as Factory Girls* (New York: Doubleday, Page, 1903), first published in *Everybody's Magazine* 7–8 (Sept. 1902–Jan. 1903); Mrs. John Van Vorst, "The Woman of the People," *Harper's Monthly Magazine* 106 (1903): 871–75.

42. Dorr, *Woman of Fifty*, chaps. 6–7, 10–12. Dorr's memoirs are considerably franker than her public statements about her experiences: "The Women Strikers of Troy," *Charities* 15 (1905): 233–36; "Christmas from behind the Counter," *Independent* 63 (1907): 1340–47.

43. Stowe, *Writings*, 8:303–4; "Women of Leisure," *Century* 60 (1900): 632.

44. Addams, *Twenty Years*, p. 92.

CHAPTER EIGHT

1. The first chapters of *Ten Men of Money Island* were originally published in 1879 in response to a hard money tract, David A. Wells's *Robinson Crusoe's Money* (1876), from which Norton derived part of the structure of his tale. It was published in full as a pamphlet in 1884 and as a serial in the *New York World* in 1891. By 1895 its publishers claimed translation into six languages and sales of half a million copies. "Publisher's Note," S. F. Norton, *Ten Men of Money Island; or, The Primer of Finance*, rev. ed. (Chicago: Schulte, 1895). Norton was a veteran of the antibanking crusades, editor of the Chicago *Sentinel*, and an unsuccessful candidate for the Populist presidential nomination in 1896.

2. Chester M. Destler, *American Radicalism, 1865–1901: Essays and Documents* (New London: Connecticut College, 1946), chap. 1; Kirk H. Porter and Donald B. Johnson, *National Party Platforms, 1840–1956* (Urbana: University of Illinois Press, 1956).

3. Charles A. Barker, *Henry George* (New York: Oxford University Press, 1955), p. 564. For Marx's equally low opinion of Henry George, see Daniel Bell, *Marxian Socialism in the United States* (Princeton: Princeton University Press, 1967), p. 28.

4. *The Complete Works of Henry George*, 10 vols. (New York: Doubleday, Page, 1904), vol. 6, chaps. 10–14; Edward Kellogg, *A New Monetary System* (New York: Rudd and Carleton, 1861), pp. 41–42; Alexander Campbell, *The True American System of Finance* (Chicago, 1864), p. 4.

5. George, *Complete Works*, 8:272; Kellogg, *New Monetary System*, p. 19; Eugene V. Debs, "Labor Strikes and Their Lessons," in *Striking for Life: Labor's Side of the Labor Question*, ed. John Swinton (1894; reprint ed., Westport, Conn.: Greenwood Press, 1970), p. 316.

6. John R. Aiken, "Benjamin Franklin, Karl Marx, and the Labor Theory of Value," *Pennsylvania Magazine of History and Biography* 90 (1966): 378–84; *Writings and Speeches of Eugene V. Debs*, ed.

Arthur M. Schlesinger, Jr. (New York: Hermitage Press, 1948), p. 233.

7. James C. Sylvis, *The Life, Speeches, Labors, and Essays of William H. Sylvis* (Philadelphia: Remsen, Claxton, and Haffelfinger, 1872), p. 158.

8. Henry George, Jr., *The Life of Henry George, Complete Works of Henry George*, 9:146-53, 156-58; *Journal of Social Science* 27 (1890): 83; U.S. Senate, Committee on Education and Labor, *Report upon the Relations between Labor and Capital*, 4 vols. (Washington, D.C., 1885), 1:504; George, *Complete Works*, 2:86.

9. Campbell, *American System of Finance*, p. 11; Ignatius Donnelly, *The Golden Bottle* (1892; reprint ed., New York: Johnson Reprint Co., 1968), p. 157.

10. W. H. Gibbs, *No Interest for Money, Except to the Government* (Lyons, Iowa: n.p., 1879), p. 55; Debs, *Writings and Speeches*, p. 232.

11. Laurence Gronlund, *The Cooperative Commonwealth* (1884; reprint ed., Cambridge: Harvard University Press, 1965), pp. 6-7, 20, 23; Daniel De Leon, *What Means This Strike?* (1898; New York: New York Labor News Co., 1958), pp. 7-8, 13.

12. John Spargo, *Applied Socialism* (New York: B. W. Huebsch, 1912), pp. 184, 181; Spargo, *Socialism: A Summary and Interpretation of Socialist Principles*, rev. ed. (New York: Macmillan, 1909), pp. 221-30; Morris Hillquit, *Socialism in Theory and Practice* (New York: Macmillan, 1909), pp. 114-18; Hillquit, "The Socialist 'Plan' of Wealth Distribution," *Putnam's Monthly and the Reader* 4 (1908): 54-57; Ira Kipnis, *The American Socialist Movement, 1897-1912* (1952; reprint ed., New York: Greenwood Press, 1968), pp. 204-5. Spargo knew the vernacular style well enough to use it in his enormously condescending simplification of socialism for working-class readers, *The Common Sense of Socialism* (Chicago: Charles H. Kerr, 1908).

13. Debs, *Writings and Speeches*, pp. 201, 252; *Appeal to Reason*, 28 Aug. 1909, p. 2, 17 April 1909, p. 1, 27 May 1909, p. 1.

14. Gronlund, *Cooperative Commonwealth*, pp. 120-26; Allan L. Benson, *Socialism Made Plain* (Milwaukee: Milwaukee Social-Democratic Publishing Co., 1904), chaps. 5-6; *Wayland's Monthly* 56 (Dec. 1904): 9, 14-16, 31-32; H. P. Moyer, *ABC of Socialism*, Wilshire Leaflet no. 6 (New York: Wilshire's Magazine, n.d.); Daniel De Leon, *Fifteen Questions* (1914; New York: New York Labor News Co., 1957), pp. 14-21.

Marx, who suggested the idea of labor-time checks in volumes 2 and 3 of *Capital*, was far from sure that they were suited to the fully developed socialist state. See M. M. Bober, "Marx and Economic Calculation," *American Economic Review* 36 (1948): 348-54.

15. Gaylord Wilshire, *Socialism: The Mallock-Wilshire Argument* (New York: Wilshire Book Co., n.d.), p. 29; Fred D. Warren, *Freeman*

or Slave: A Book of Suppressed Information (Girard, Kans.: Appeal to Reason Press, n.d.), p. 62.

16. Spargo, *Applied Socialism*, p. 180.

17. William M. Armstrong, *E. L. Godkin and American Foreign Policy, 1865-1900* (New York: Bookman Associates, 1957), p. 12; Godkin, "Plenty of Money for the People," *Nation* 60 (1895): 474.

18. Godkin, "The Sources of Communism," *Nation* 26 (1878): 318.

19. Godkin, "The Granger Collapse," *Nation* 22 (1876): 58; *Nation* 17 (1873): 36; E. P. Clark, "A Bill to Promote Mendicancy," *Nation* 42 (1886): 142-43; Godkin, "Economic Fiction," *Nation* 60 (1895): 214-15; Godkin, "Protection and Socialism," *Nation* 58 (1894): 189-90; Godkin, "Socialistic Platitudes," *Nation* 44 (1887): 505.

20. William A. White, "What's the Matter with Kansas?" (1896), quoted in George B. Tindall, ed., *A Populist Reader* (New York: Harper and Row, 1966), p. 198; George F. Baer, "Work Is Worship" (1902), *Addresses and Writings* (Lancaster, Pa.: n.p., 1916), p. 249; Theodore Roosevelt, "Socialism: Where We Cannot Work with Socialists," *Outlook* 91 (1909): 623.

21. W. H. Mallock, "Trade Unionism and Utopia," *Forum* 11 (1891): 211; Edward M. Steel, "Mother Jones in the Fairmont Field, 1902," *Journal of American History* 57 (1970): 300; Maxwell H. Bloomfield, *Alarms and Diversions: The American Mind through American Magazines, 1900-1914* (The Hague: Mouton, 1967), pp. 79-84.

22. Morton Keller, *The Art and Politics of Thomas Nast* (New York: Oxford University Press, 1968).

23. *The Collected Works of Abraham Lincoln*, ed. Roy P. Basler, 8 vols. (New Brunswick, N.J.: Rutgers University Press, 1953-55), 1:412; Lyman Abbott, "Industrial Democracy," *Forum* 9 (1890): 663.

24. Theodore N. Vail, *Views on Public Questions* (n.p.: n.p., 1917), pp. 281, 280; William R. Stewart, *The Philanthropic Work of Josephine Shaw Lowell* (New York: Macmillan, 1911), pp. 342, 371.

25. For example, Pierre Lorillard, "Labor and Condensed Labor," *North American Review* 143 (1886): 536-38. Working from Nast's cartoon, Finley Peter Dunne satirized the idea mischievously in "The Labor Troubles," *Dissertations by Mr. Dooley* (New York: Harper and Brothers, 1906).

26. Henry Ward Beecher, "Economy in Small Things," quoted in Henry F. May, *Protestant Churches and Industrial America* (New York: Harper and Row, 1949), p. 69; *Essays of William Graham Sumner*, ed. Albert G. Keller and Maurice R. Davie, 2 vols. (New Haven: Yale University Press, 1934), 1:481.

27. Josiah G. Holland, *Nicholas Minturn* (New York: Scribner, Armstrong, 1877).

28. On the background of the charity organization movement and

early social work, see Robert H. Bremner, *From the Depths: The Discovery of Poverty in the United States* (New York: New York University Press, 1956); Marvin E. Gettleman, "Charity and Social Classes in the United States, 1874-1900," *American Journal of Economics and Sociology* 22 (1963): 313-29, 417-26; Roy Lubove, *The Professional Altruist: The Emergence of Social Work as a Career, 1880-1930* (Cambridge: Harvard University Press, 1965); Hace S. Tishler, *Self-Reliance and Social Security, 1870-1917* (Port Washington, N.Y.: Kennikat Press, 1971), chap. 2.

29. Oscar C. McCulloch, "The Personal Element in Charity," National Conference of Charities and Corrections (NCCC), *Proceedings* (1885), p. 340; Charity Organization Society of the City of New York, *Handbook for Friendly Visitors among the Poor* (New York: G. P. Putnam's Sons, 1883), p. 1.

30. Helen Campbell, "Certain Convictions as to Poverty," *Arena* 1 (1889): 108.

31. Mary E. Richmond, *Friendly Visiting among the Poor: A Handbook for Charity Workers* (1899; New York: Macmillan, 1918), pp. 50-57; Stewart, *Philanthropic Work of Josephine Shaw Lowell*, p. 145.

32. Edward T. Devine, *Misery and Its Causes* (1909; reprint ed., New York: Arno Press, 1971), p. 11.

33. NCCC, *Proceedings* (1877), p. 112; "Once More the Tramp," *Scribner's Monthly* 15 (1878): 883. For the persistence of the attitude, see James Forbes, "Suppression of Mendicancy in Greater New York," *Charities* 9 (1902): 478-80; NCCC, *Proceedings* (1903), pp. 379-86, 401-4, 416-17; and Orlando Lewis's highly influential "The American Tramp," *Atlantic Monthly* 101 (1908): 744-53.

34. J. J. McCook, "A Tramp Census and Its Revelations," *Forum* 15 (1893): 760; Edmond Kelly, *The Elimination of the Tramp* (New York: G. P. Putnam's Sons, 1908), p. 1.

35. Josiah Flynt Willard [Josiah Flynt], *Tramping with Tramps: Studies and Sketches of Vagabond Life* (New York: Century, 1900); Willard, *My Life* (New York: Outing Publishing Co., 1908); McCook, "Tramp Census"; McCook, "Leaves from the Diary of a Tramp," *Independent*, vol. 53-54 (21 Nov. 1901-26 June 1902); Charles E. Adams, "The Real Hobo: What He Is and How He Lives," *Forum* 33 (1902): 438-39; Theodore Waters, "Six Weeks in Beggardom," *Everybody's Magazine* 11 (1904): 789-97; 12 (1905): 69-78; James Forbes, "The Tramp; or, Caste in the Jungle," *Outlook* 98 (1911): 869-75; Alice W. Solenberger, *One Thousand Homeless Men* (New York: Russell Sage Foundation, 1911).

36. Kelly, *Elimination of the Tramp*; Paul T. Ringenbach, *Tramps and Reformers, 1873-1916: The Discovery of Unemployment in New York* (Westport, Conn.: Greenwood Press, 1973), pp. 125-28; James Gilbert,

Designing the Industrial State: The Intellectual Pursuit of Collectivism in America, 1880-1940 (Chicago: Quadrangle, 1972), chap. 5.

37. Alexander Campbell, *Address to the Voters of the Seventh Congressional District of Illinois*, 2d ed. (Chicago: n.p., 1878), p. 27; *Speeches of William Jennings Bryan*, 2 vols. (New York: Funk and Wagnalls, 1909), 1:240-41.

38. Gabriel Kolko, "Brahmins and Business, 1870-1914: A Hypothesis on the Social Basis of Success in American History," in *The Critical Spirit: Essays in Honor of Herbert Marcuse*, ed. Kurt H. Wolff and Barrington Moore (Boston: Beacon Press, 1967), p. 354; Thomas Lawson, "The Remedy," *Everybody's Magazine* 27 (1912): 602.

39. U.S. Senate, *Labor and Capital*, 2:886; Walter T. K. Nugent, *Money and American Society, 1865-1880* (New York: Free Press, 1968), p. 30; Debs, *Writings and Speeches*, p. 111; U.S. Commission on Industrial Relations, *Final Report and Testimony*, 11 vols. (Washington, D.C., 1916), 9:8097.

40. Frederic L. Paxson, *America at War, 1917-1918* (Boston: Houghton Mifflin, 1939), pp. 249-50.

41. Edwin T. Layton, Jr., *The Revolt of the Engineers: Social Responsibility and the American Engineering Profession* (Cleveland: Press of Case Western Reserve University, 1971), p. 146.

42. *A Compilation of the Messages and Papers of the Presidents*, 20 vols. (New York: Bureau of National Literature, n.d.), 12:6073; Woodrow Wilson, *The New Freedom* (New York: Doubleday, Page, 1913), p. 158; U.S. House of Representatives, Committee on Agriculture, *Fictitious Dealing in Agricultural Products* (Washington, D.C., 1892); Tishler, *Self-Reliance and Social Security*; Roy Lubove, *The Struggle for Social Security, 1900-1935* (Cambridge: Harvard University Press, 1968).

43. Irwin Unger, *The Greenback Era: A Social and Political History of American Finance, 1865-1879* (Princeton: Princeton University Press, 1964); Elmer Ellis, "Public Opinion and the Income Tax, 1860-1900," *Mississippi Valley Historical Review* 27 (1940): 225-42; "An Appeal to Our Millionaires," *North American Review* 182 (1906): 801-23; Richard T. Ely, "The Inheritance of Property," *North American Review* 153 (1891): 54-66.

EPILOGUE

1. *The Complete Works of Ralph Waldo Emerson*, centenary ed., 12 vols. (Boston: Houghton Mifflin, n.d.), 7:164.

2. Henry James, *Charles W. Eliot*, 2 vols. (Boston: Houghton Mifflin, 1930); Hugh Hawkins, *Between Harvard and America: The Educational Leadership of Charles W. Eliot* (New York: Oxford University Press, 1972).

3. Charles W. Eliot: *American Contributions to Civilization, and Other Essays and Addresses* (New York: Century, 1897), pp. 12–13; "Remarks before the [Boston] Economic Club, Nov. 10, 1902," Charles W. Eliot Papers, Harvard University Archives.

4. Eliot: *The Fortunate or Happy Conditions for a Life of Labor* (n.p.: Electrical Manufacturers' Club, 1913), p. 11; "Content in Work," *World's Work* 8 (1904): 4959.

5. Eliot: "Industrial Conditions of Public Happiness," Address at Harvard University, 2 May 1904, Eliot Papers; "Content in Work," p. 4959. See also his "Labour Unions: Their Good Features and Their Evil Ones," *Cassier's Magazine* 23 (1903): 434–40; "Address before the Boston Central Labor Union, Feb. 7, 1904," Eliot Papers; "Employers' Policies in the Industrial Strife," *Harper's Monthly Magazine* 110 (1905): 528–33; "Industrial Ethics," *Religious Education* 4 (1909): 138–45; *The Future of Trades-Unionism and Capitalism in a Democracy* (New York: G. P. Putnam's Sons, 1910).

6. Eliot: "Injurious Policies of Labor Unions," *World's Work* 28 (1914): 580; "Successful Profit-Sharing," *System* 24 (1913): 140. See also U.S. Commission on Industrial Relations, *Final Report and Testimony*, 11 vols. (Washington, D.C., 1916), 8:7985; "The Road to Industrial Peace" (1917), in Eliot, *A Late Harvest* (Boston: Atlantic Monthly Press, 1924); "Testimony before the Committee on Social Welfare, March 14, 1919," Eliot Papers; "Prophecies of Industrial Peace," *New York Times*, 28 March 1925.

7. Eliot: *Fortunate Conditions*, pp. 7, 15–18; "Industrial Ethics," p. 141; "Content in Work," pp. 4960–61.

8. Eliot: *Future of Trades-Unionism*, p. 110; "Will-Power, the Tap-Root of Efficiency," *Independent* 80 (1914): 327.

9. Eliot, "Testimony before the Committee on Social Welfare."

10. Eliot, "Injurious Policies of Labor Unions," p. 585; Eliot, "What Uplifts a Race and What Holds It Down," Address at Tuskegee Institute, 4 April 1906, Eliot Papers; James, *Eliot*, 2:16, 39.

11. John W. Ward, *Red, White, and Blue: Men, Books, and Ideas in American Culture* (New York: Oxford University Press, 1969), p. 258.

12. Quoted in James W. Prothro, *Dollar Decade: Business Ideas in the 1920's* (Baton Rouge: Louisiana State University Press, 1954), p. 68.

Index